GREAT LEADERS, GREAT TYRANTS?

GREAT LEADERS, GREAT TYRANTS?

Contemporary Views of World Rulers Who Made History

Edited by Arnold Blumberg

GREENWOOD PRESS
Westport, Connecticut • London

Library of Congress Cataloging-in-Publication Data

Great leaders, great tyrants? : contemporary views of world rulers who made history / edited by Arnold Blumberg.
p. cm.
Includes bibliographical references and index.
ISBN 0-313-28751-1
1. Kings and rulers—Biography. 2. Heads of state—Biography.
I. Blumberg, Arnold.
D107.G6789 1995
920.02—dc20 94-16066

British Library Cataloguing in Publication Data is available.

Library of Congress Catalog Card Number: 94-1

ISBN: 0-313-28751-1

First published in 1995

Greenwood Press, 88 Post Road West, Westport,
An imprint of Greenwood Publishing Group, Inc.

Printed in the United States of America

The paper used in this book complies with the Permanent Paper Standard issued by the National Information Standards Organization (Z39.48-1984).

10 9 8 7 6 5 4 3 2 1

Love work; hate lordship; and seek no intimacy with the ruling power.

Pirkei Aboth, Mishna I:10
J. H. Hertz Translation

Be ye guarded in your relations with the ruling power; for they who exercise it draw no man near to them, except for their own interests; appearing as friends when it is to their own advantage, they stand not by a man in his hour of need.

Pirkei Aboth, II, 3

Pray for the welfare of the Government, since but for the fear thereof, men would swallow each other alive.

Pirkei Aboth, III, 2

Contents

Preface

One of the most serious questions troubling students of history is the degree to which tyranny must inevitably be an aspect of government. Is it possible for a ruler to be creative and effective without abusing the civil rights of citizens?

The pro/con format of each of the fifty-two biographical profiles contained in this book gives the reader an opportunity to debate this question. All the men and women profiled here were selected because, on balance, they left a legacy of ideas, attitudes, or physical accomplishments that benefited society. They often achieved their goals, however, by tyrannical methods and by ignoring the rights of ordinary folk. Some of these leaders were primarily creative and some were primarily tyrannical. It is up to the reader to make his or her own assessments, and it is probable that no two readers will draw the same conclusions. We hope, however, that all our readers will address the essential questions that induced us to assemble these essays. Can a leader be effective without being tyrannical? At what point does tyranny destroy itself?

Each biography begins with the full name of the leader, the offices held, and the dates of the leader's lifetime. A general introduction places the leader in historical context. A biographical sketch outlines the important facts about the leader's life. The author then poses two essays, in debate format, that contrast the creative and tyrannical roles of the subject. Suggestions for additional reading follow, including at least one classic biography of the subject and other published works regarded as valuable for examining the leader's life and work.

In selecting the leaders to profile, we have deliberately excluded those tyrannical leaders who, like Adolf Hitler or Benito Mussolini, destroyed their own creativity through the excesses of their tyranny. Joseph Stalin, on the other hand, has been included because his contributions to history are still much in evidence, even though the Soviet Union has ceased to exist.

No attempt has been made to impose uniform spelling upon scholars transliterating non-Western alphabets. For the convenience of our readers, however, all names, places, or terms that display disparate spellings are cross-referenced in the index, so that it will be apparent that different spellings are in use for the same name. Because B.C., A.D., B.C.E., and C.E. relate to religious concepts, each author has chosen the terms he or she prefers when referring to events prior to Year 1 in the Gregorian calendar.

Finally, because the authors of the individual profiles did not review all of the introductions to the biographical profiles that were written by the editor, the responsibility for the contents of that part of the work is borne by the editor.

Acknowledgments

The biographical entries within these pages were written by thirty-six contributors, each of whom is an experienced scholar who has taught and pursued research concerning the great leader who is the subject of the entry. I am grateful to each of them for conforming their material to a uniform format and length, so that interested readers can derive maximum benefit from reading this work.

I appreciate the efforts of others who have made contributions that eased our progress. Dr. Barbara Rader, Senior Editor at Greenwood Press, has become a valued colleague and friend as she shared her ideas with me.

At Towson State University, I have incurred debts of gratitude to all who eased my burden by preparing teaching schedules that allowed research and writing without slighting the rights of students. Principal among these is Professor Douglas Martin, Chairman of the History Department, and Dr. Annette Chappell, Dean of the College of Liberal Arts. Other valued associates made useful suggestions concerning the names of "Creative Tyrants" or scholars competent to write their biographies. These include Professor Emeritus Mary Catherine Kahl and my encyclopedically well-informed Latin Americanist colleague Professor Ronn Pineo. I note with deep sorrow the tragic and premature death of Dr. William Sladek on November 4, 1993. From the beginning of this project, he had given me valued advice on the means of enriching our work

At the university's Cook Library, I am particularly grateful to Susan Mower, Reference Librarian, who was always ready to supply correct citation information from her computerized catalog. Patty Warden, formerly in charge of the Micromedia Section, understood the necessity of maintaining a working environment in which scholars could be productive.

Mrs. Emily Daugherty, the indefatigable secretary of the History Department, was always ready to type a hasty draft when needed or to summon an ancient essay from the depths of her computer printer. She did all of this with matchless good humor, never once intimidating a diffident historian.

My wife, Thelma Alpert Blumberg, has followed with involved fascination the gradual assembly of our fifty-two creative tyrants. Her arguments for or against the inclusion of a member of that select circle made a major contribution to this work.

Ultimately, however, the responsibility for including or excluding a specific "creative tyrant" within these pages is shared by the management of Greenwood Press and myself. We sometimes disagreed. I confide our judgment to the charity of our readers.

Akhenaten

c. 1396–1360 B.C.E.

King of Egypt, 1377–1360 B.C.E.

Called "the heretic king" by some and "the failed Messiah" by others, Akhenaten is one of the most controversial figures in ancient history. One of the earliest supporters of monotheism, he attempted to impose on traditionally polytheistic Egypt a universalist, abstract faith, with a poetic vision of a single God who created all nations. His defenders consider him centuries ahead of his time, religiously and politically; a tragic figure whose art, edicts, and name would be erased from monuments and memory, but whose religious vision would survive to influence Judeo-Christian thought and expression. His critics see him as a physically and mentally dysfunctional tyrant bent on destroying traditional Egyptian society in order to establish himself as an absolute divine-right monarch; a poetic misfit who left no religious or artistic legacy other than a warped iconoclasm.

BIOGRAPHICAL BACKGROUND

Although historians and Egyptologists know more about the king, or pharaoh, who called himself Akhenaten, or "servant of the sun disc," than any other individual in ancient Egypt, he remains an elusive figure. Born around 1400 Before the Common Era (B.C.E.), during the 18th Dynasty of the New Kingdom, or third great period of ancient Egyptian history, he became heir to the throne only because his older brother died.

His father, King Amenophis III, had broken tradition by marrying a commoner, Queen Tie, and may have made his son co-regent in 1377 B.C.E. to strengthen Akhenaten's (then named Amenophis IV) claim to royal succession. Father and son served as co-regents for eleven years, during which time they lived in separate palaces in the royal city of Thebes, the main political and religious center of the New Kingdom, located on the east bank of the Nile River, three hundred miles south of the Mediterranean delta.

During the co-regency Akhenaten also married a commoner, the beautiful Nefrititi, who, like her mother-in-law, Queen Tie, seems to have been a powerful figure. Nefrititi shared her husband's belief in the primacy of the god Aten, the sun disc, over all other gods in the Egyptian pantheon, including Ptah, Nut, Seth, Osiris and Amon, the favored gods in Thebes.

Wall paintings and carvings excavated from this period show Akhenaten, Nefrititi, and their six daughters in many domestic and natural settings. Unlike classical Egyptian art, which depicted the royal family, and especially the king, in heroic, stylized postures, artists of this period were encouraged to show the royal family realistically. In these paintings Akhenaten appears to have a malformed head and body. Shown with distended skull, slanted eyes, elongated ears, thin lips, and pronounced jaw, his head was connected by a thin neck to a body more feminine than masculine, with broad hips and thighs, large breasts, and spindly legs. Some historians think he may have suffered from a malfunctioning pituitary gland, which can produce a condition, similar to Akhenaten's, called Frohlich's Syndrome.

In year five (1372 B.C.E.) of his co-regency he gave up the name Amenophis IV, took the name Akhenaten, and began building a new royal city along the Nile north of Thebes. Located near the hills of Amarna, the city was called Akhetaten, or "horizon of the sun disc," reflecting a major break with Egyptian religious and cultural traditions.

After his father, Amenophis III, died in 1366 B.C.E., Akhetaten pronounced Aten the one and only true God, creator of all living things. He dismissed the powerful priesthood; shut down the temples in Thebes, Memphis, and other cities that were dedicated to other gods; and ordered hatchetmen to deface or destroy all references to other gods on temple walls, statues, and stelae.

By year 14 (1363 B.C.E.) of his reign Akhenaten had completed his iconoclastic destruction of Egyptian polytheism, ordering in its place a monotheism symbolized by a solar disc whose rays extended earthward, ending in hands that touched the nostrils of the king and queen. Akhenaten declared himself the only son of Aten-Re, a synthesis of the sun's physical disc and Re, the traditional sun god. In building the new royal city dedicated to Aten-Re, the king desired to make it the center of a new, universal religion.

Also in year 14, Akhenaten, seeking a male heir, married his daughter, Meritaten, and gave her precedence over Nefrititi. This incestuous relationship was not unusual for Egyptian and other ancient royalty anxious to enhance the legitimacy of their offspring while keeping others from having access to royal blood.

No child resulted from this arrangement, but Meritaten also married a young man named Smenkhkare in year 15, who was made co-regent with Akhenaten. Smenkhkare and his younger brother, Tutenkhaten, may have been from another branch of the royal family or may have been Akhenatenen's stepbrothers. When Akhetaten died at age thirty-six in year 17 (1360 B.C.E.), probably from natural causes, Smenkhkare had already died, leaving the ten-year-old Tutenkhaten as the most eligible successor to the throne. Young King "Tut" changed his name to Tutenkhamon, indicating his rejection of the primacy of Aten, and, with his advisers, returned to Thebes to begin the restoration of Egyptian polytheism.

AKHENATEN AS A GREAT LEADER

Some historians have depicted Akhenaten as an idealist and major reformer, a visionary poet and ruler who was inspired by the new and radical idea of a solitary God, Aten-Re, a universal deity who created and embraced all humankind. According to this view, Akhenaten, by promoting monotheism, was bringing a new spirit to religion, ending the secrecy, elitism, and parochialism of traditional polytheism, as well as inspiring Judaism's ethical monotheism and Christianity's universalist monotheism of a much later time.

Akhenaten also has been seen as a visionary in international affairs, who expanded on his father's enlightened foreign policy, which relied more on peaceful diplomacy than military expeditions. In contrast to 18th Dynasty warrior pharaohs, like Thutmose III and Amenophis II, and their aggressive military expansion north into Palestine-Syria and south into Nubia and Kush (modern Sudan), Akhenaten used strategic matrimonial alliances, subsidies, bribes, and loosely defined spheres of influence to maintain a balance of power with the Hittites, Mittani, and Kassite Babylonians. When necessary, he did not hesitate to use force against rebels, as in Nubia, where Egypt got its gold and where the Nile has a major source.

Akhenaten also may have sought to bring about a political revolution. By moving from Thebes to Akhetaten and by shutting down the temples to other gods, he was challenging the authority of the powerful Amon priesthood and the old family elites. By replacing them with younger men from less powerful families, he aimed to regain for the monarchy some religious and political authority that had been enjoyed by the 4th Dynasty Old Kingdom divine-right kings but that had been eroded during the ensuing centuries of the Middle Kingdom and the Hyksos (foreign) usurpation.

According to his admirers, Akhenaten also broke sharply with traditional forms of Egyptian art. By having artists and sculptors show his physical deformities and depict the royal family in ordinary domestic settings, Akhenaten was challenging classical forms that had dominated royal art for more than a thousand years. This more naturalistic and realistic "Amarna style" (after the Amarna hills east of Akhetaten) would influence Egyptian art, architecture, poetry, and language long after Akhenaten's death.

AKHENATEN THE TYRANT

Most recent historians of ancient Egypt agree with Akhenaten's contemporaries that he was far from an enlightened reformer or poetic visionary. Some see him as a political opportunist who cynically promoted Aten-Re as the only God in order to break the political power of the Amon-Re priesthood. His 18th Dynasty predecessors, who regained control of Egypt from the Hyksos invaders, included Thutmose III (1504–1451 B.C.E.) and Amenophis II (1453–1426 B.C.E.), who had militarily expanded the Egyptian empire north to the Euphrates River and south to Nubia in central Sudan. During this "Golden Age," Egyptian kings, and the aristocratic families that served them, also enjoyed economic wealth and prosperity greater than at any other time in ancient Egypt's history. Nevertheless, the 18th Dynasty kings were not divine-right monarchs, having to share sacerdotal, or religious, authority with an entrenched Theban priesthood favoring the god Amon, "the Hidden One." By crushing the Amon cult and establishing a radically new religion centered on the king as the son of the one true God, Aten-Re, Akhenaten, according to this view, was attempting to reconstruct Egypt's absolute, divine-right monarchy.

Other historians see Akhenaten as a "mad king," a physical monstrosity and mental defective, whose radical monotheism was part of a megalomania produced by gradual mental deterioration resulting from his pituitary malfunction. According to this view, Akhenaten's father, Amenophis III, having no other male heir, but seeing his son's worsening mental state, may have kept him under control during the long co-regency. It was during this brief period, from 1365 to 1362 B.C.E., after his father and before Smenkhkare was made co-regent, that Akhenaten took radical action, shutting down temples and defacing monuments dedicated to other gods, dismissing priests and promoting radical monotheism.

Finally, there are critics who see Akhenaten as neither a political opportunist nor a madman, but as a religious fanatic determined to impose his vision of religious truth without concern for coercive monotheism's disruptive impact on Egyptian society and culture. Having inherited a kingdom that was politically and economically stable, Akhenaten, according to this view, could devote his time and energy to personal interests, which included poetry, the visual and architectural arts, family life, and his relationship with God. Building on his father's interest in the sun disc as a physical manifestation of the deity, he combined it with the ancient sun god, Re, producing Aten-Re, a solitary Creator God, more emotionally and aesthetically satisfying for Akhenaten than the myriad gods of the traditional Egyptian pantheon.

Some of Akhenaten's supporters see his Creator God as the inspiration for Jewish and Christian monotheism, pointing to the similarity of phrases and images in his "Hymn to Aten" and King David's Psalm 104. But critics point out that Akhenaten's "Hymn" was typical of poetry dedicated to many Egyptian gods and was composed seven hundred years before the Old Testament. More important, his Creator God provided no moral dimension or code of human behavior, and no explanation of divine purpose or the nature of life and death, except what His son, the Egyptian king, would decree. Akhenaten's critics see his monotheism as religiously sterile, limiting God's role to creating life, with the king as universal lawgiver—in other words, the spiritual vision of a totalitarian megalomaniac.

The three critical views of Akhenaten—as opportunist, mental defective, and religious fanatic—are not mutually exclusive. His zealous imposition of monotheism on a civilization that had always been tolerant of many gods can be the product of all three interpretations. At any rate his revolutionary (or reactionary) idea of absolute divine-right monarchy died with him. The worship of Aten-Re did not reach beyond the royal family and some sycophantic courtiers. Recent archaeological excavation at Akhetaten has revealed that workmen building the new royal city left behind personal amulets to Amon, Ptah, and other traditional deities.

The new royal city was never completed. After Akhenaten's death, his successors, the young Tutenkhamon (1360–1350 B.C.E.), the old courtier Ay (1350–1347 B.C.E.), who may have been Nefrititi's father, and the commoner general Horemheb (1347–1318 B.C.E.), abandoned Akhetaten, gradually destroying everything Akhenaten had built there, using the stones to reconstruct temples and monuments to the ancient gods.

Horemheb was the last of the 18th Dynasty kings. His Edict of Restoration was a powerful denunciation of Akhenaten's reign, accusing him of heresy, anarchy, and corruption. Horemheb ordered Akhenaten's monuments destroyed and his name erased from all edifices and from the official list of Egyptian kings. For the next thousand years Egypt returned to its traditional ways, with change coming very slowly, like the Nile whose predictable flooding gave it sustenance.

Although a few historians see Akhenaten as a "good ruler," a visionary ahead of his time, or a "failed Messiah," most accept ancient Egypt's verdict that he was "the criminal of Akhetaten," who would stop at nothing to create a world subservient to his will.

SUGGESTIONS FOR ADDITIONAL READING

Aldred, Cyril. *Akhenaten: King of Egypt.* London: Thames and Hudson, 1988.

Breasted, James H. *The Dawn of Conscience.* New York: Charles Scribner's Sons, 1933.

David, Rosalie. *Cult of the Sun: Myth and Magic in Ancient Egypt.* London: J. M. Dent & Sons, Ltd., 1980.

Frankfort, H. *Ancient Egyptian Religion: An Interpretation.* New York: Columbia University Press, 1948.

Giles, F. J. *Ikhanaton: Legend and History*. Rutherford, N.J.: Fairleigh Dickinson University Press, 1972.

Newby, P. H. *Warrior Pharaohs: The Rise and Fall of the Egyptian Empire*. London: Faber and Faber, 1980.

Redford, Donald B. *Akhenaten: The Heretic King*. Princeton: Princeton University Press, 1984.

Wilson, John H. *The Culture of Ancient Egypt*. Chicago: University of Chicago Press, 1951.

Sheldon Avery

Atatürk (Mustapha Kemal Pasha) 1881–1938

President of Turkey, 1923–1938

Few men have changed their country and their society as completely as did Mustapha Kemal Atatürk. What is more, he managed to revolutionize Turkish society in only nineteen years. Of course, in the matter of how much he deserved to be called a "tyrant," opinion will depend on the viewer's perspective. In the growing Moslem fundamentalist camp today, his entire career and most of his works would be regarded as a betrayal of a holy cause. Secularized, westernized nationalists would defend even his often brutal authoritarianism as necessary and just. Certainly, it was Atatürk who deserves credit for transforming the Western image of his nation from "the terrible Turk" to the "Noble Ally" who stood fast with the United States in the Korean War and formed the eastern anchor of NATO. History plays funny tricks on dead heroes. Whether Atatürk remains the Father of his Country depends on the direction that Turkey takes in the future.

BIOGRAPHICAL BACKGROUND

Atatürk was born on March 12, 1881, in Salonika, now in Greece but then in the Macedonian province of the Ottoman Empire. As was Turkish custom, he was given only one name at birth: Mustapha. A schoolmaster later bestowed upon him the term "Kemal," meaning "perfection," in recognition of his abilities. In 1934, as president, he insisted that Turks must create surnames for themselves as part of his westernizing reform program; the National Assembly accordingly declared him to be "Atatürk," that is, "Father of the Turks."

Moslem by birth and Turkish by language, Mustapha, like many Ottomans, was of mixed genetic heritage, a product of the Balkan melting pot. His mother, Zübeyde, was fair and blue-eyed, perhaps partly of Slavic or Albanian ancestry. From her came the boy's fair complexion and domineering personality. His father, Ali Riza, was an impoverished minor government official and businessman who died when Mustapha was only seven years old. From him the boy gained two outstanding characteristics: a distaste for formal religion—in contrast to his mother's piety—and the desire to become a soldier.

The army was one institution in which a poor young man might enjoy social mobility. Commissioned an officer in 1902, Kemal (as he was then known) soon showed his talent for leadership. Along the way, he also became involved in radical politics, not unusual among young officers whose education brought them into contact with liberal ideas emanating from Western Europe. He entered into a vague association with the "Young Turks," men who hoped to reform and thereby save their country from the imperialistic ambitions of the very Europe they admired. To accomplish this, they overthrew the reactionary Sultan Abdul Hamid II in 1908–1909. Kemal, however, was not friendly enough with the Young Turk leadership to benefit much from their revolution. His rise to prominence coincided, rather, with World War I, when the Young Turks and their new, puppet sultan allied themselves with Germany. Kemal commanded major elements of the Turkish Army in the 1915 Gallipoli campaign, frustrating Britain's attempt to seize the Turkish Straits. That made him a national hero, and he was promoted to general—thus also gaining the title of "pasha," a term for high-ranking Turkish officials. He continued to fight with distinction until the Ottomans were forced to surrender in 1918.

Britain and the other Allied powers proceeded to tear the Ottoman Empire apart, taking away all of its non-Turkish-speaking provinces, forcing the sultan to be their vassal; they even gave a large area around Smyrna (now Izmir) to Greece, an old and hated enemy of the Turks, in May 1919. This caused an explosion of Turkish nationalist feeling. Mustapha Kemal Pasha immediately put himself at the head of a new, patriotic movement, becoming president of its congress in that same year, in defiance of both Allies and sultan. Resurrecting the Turkish Army, playing on disunity and war-weariness among the Allies, he led his forces against the British-sponsored Greek invaders. In his effort to defeat the Greeks, he even allied himself with Communist Russia in a common anti-Allied front, despite his policy of suppressing communism at home. Victorious in the defensive Battle of Sakarya (west of Ankara) in 1921, he crushed the Greek Army on the nearby battlefield of Dumlupinar in 1922.

In 1923, Kemal concluded the Treaty of Lausanne with the Allies and the Greeks. He recognized Turkey's loss of her Arab lands but retained Kurdistan and Armenia. The Allies in return recognized Kemal's Turkey as the fully independent successor of the Ottoman Empire. The sultanate was abolished, and Kemal was declared president of the new Turkish Republic in 1923. He then embarked upon a policy of peace with neighboring countries and a program of westernizing reform at home.

In his personal life, Kemal had always been given to excessive smoking, womanizing, and especially drinking. He married a woman named Latife in 1923, but she objected to his personal habits and they were divorced in 1925. Overwork and abuse of his health led to cirrhosis of the liver and death in Istanbul on November 10, 1938.

ATATÜRK AS A GREAT LEADER

Although a career soldier and a great general, Kemal became a man of peace after 1923, promoting good relations, even with Greece. With one minor exception, and that one settled peacefully, he did not attempt to regain Turkish territories lost either before World War I or by the Treaty of Lausanne—not even his native Salonika, lost in the Balkan Wars of 1912–1913. In part, his pacific policy flowed from one of the major elements in his reform program, Turkish nationalism. He defined nationhood in the Western way, that is, by language and political-cultural heritage; thus he abandoned the concept of earlier reformers who had hoped to unite Ottoman Turks with all other Turks, even those living far outside the old empire, or who had hoped to unite all Moslems, Turkish or not. He could therefore give up the Arab provinces without regret.

Also Western was his secularism, stemming from his youthful rejection of orthodox Islam. Here again he was more radical than most Turkish reformers. He saw old-fashioned Islam as holding back progress, so he abolished not only the sultanate (a political office akin to emperor) but also the Islamic religious office known as the caliphate; until 1922, the two offices had been held by the same man—the Ottoman sultan-caliph. He abolished the religious organizations of the Dervishes, the religious courts, and even the Islamic schools. One of Kemal's best-remembered reforms was the 1925 outlawing of the fez. Originally a Greek item of headware, the fez had become identified with Islam because it lacked a brim, thus enabling the pious to remain covered even while touching their foreheads to the ground during prayer. Kemal insisted that it must be replaced by brimmed Western hats, symbols of secularism and modern civilization. What in the West has been called anticlericalism was central to all his thought.

Although he had his own People's Republican Party, Kemal at one time promoted a two-party system that would allow for a "loyal opposition." Although he tended to treat women as sexual playthings, he promoted what a later generation would call "women's liberation"; women were encouraged to cast off the veil and in 1934 were given the right to vote and run for office. He promoted economic progress through state investment and intervention as best he could, despite the Great Depression of the 1930s. Even Turkey's writing system changed under his guidance: Western (Latin) letters were substituted for Arabic script. (Turkish is an Altaic language, not Semitic like Arabic, so the Arabic writing system had never been well suited to its needs.)

All these reforms were summed up as the "Six Arrows": Nationalism, Secularism, Republicanism, Populism, Statism, and Revolutionism. "Populism" meant that the ordinary people would be secure in their individual and equal rights regardless of religion or ethnicity; "Revolutionism" (or "Reformism") meant that the revolutionary spirit of 1919–1922 would continue to nurture reform, hastening it and keeping it pure.

Of course, Atatürk could not have accomplished any of this without help. There was already an existing reform movement for him to lead. In the early days of struggle against the Allies, the sultan, and the Greeks, he depended very much on a powerful general, Kiazim Karabekir Pasha. The women's rights movement drew strength from a prominent female literary figure, Halide Edib. Ismet Inönü Pasha was another important general—and also the chief negotiator at Lausanne, a longtime Kemalist prime minister, and finally Atatürk's successor as president. Yet throughout, it was Atatürk's genius, leadership, and willpower that made victory and reform accomplished facts.

Atatürk's movement was not unique, nor even the first of its kind. The process by which an Asian country could modernize itself by borrowing the Western concept of nationalism, along with the West's technology—and thereby fight off Western imperialism—can also be seen in late nineteenth-century Japan, as well as in the Young Turks' program itself. Yet Atatürk not only shaped and guided the Turkish version of this process, but inspired others outside of Turkey to do the same sort of thing. Egypt's leader Gamal Abdel Nasser in the 1950s and 1960s was one of his disciples.

Atatürk's memory has been preserved not only in his massive tomb in Ankara—the city he made his country's capital—but also in the traditions of the Turkish Army and of his political instrument, the People's Republican Party.

ATATÜRK THE TYRANT

It is not difficult to identify the unappealing aspects of Atatürk's life and career. Apart from his drinking and carousing, which he always kept apart from his public life, there were many things about him that some of his countrymen, and some foreign observers, found less than admirable. He played down—even kept hidden—his unorthodox religious views during the war against Greece, so long as he needed the ordinary Moslem Turkish peasant in his army; only with victory did he reveal his extreme secularism, thereby opening himself up to the charge of hypocrisy. He married Latife, a highly liberated and westernized Turkish woman, not only because he loved her but because he wanted her to be an example to the women of his country—and a lesson to its men; yet when she refused to tolerate his personal life, he divorced her according to the traditional Moslem law, a law he was soon to overthrow in favor of Western-style concepts of divorce.

He talked about bringing democracy to Turkey; yet the first time an opposition party arose, in 1924, he accepted its existence only grudgingly and soon forced its dissolution. The second time an opposition party appeared, in 1930, it was at his own insistence—it was his own experiment in democracy—but this party, too, soon collapsed when he turned against it. Nor was he above such undemocratic acts as the suppression of hostile newspapers.

He set out to build a country based on the principle of nationalism and thus was willing to give up the Arab provinces of the old empire—which the Allies held anyway—but he would not give up on the non-Turkish areas of Armenia and Kurdistan, which his forces could control. The Christian Armenians had suffered devastating persecution in the 1890s and during World War I and had been promised independence by the Allies, only to find themselves suppressed again by Kemalist Turkey. The Kurds, although Moslem, were speakers of a non-Turkish language; they had also been promised autonomy by the Allies, but Kemalist Turkey would not allow it. A Kurdish rebellion in 1925 was put down with terrible ferocity.

In some ways the worst evidence of Atatürk's tyrannical tendencies was his persecution of former comrades, such as Kiazim Karabekir Pasha, during the 1920s. Many of them had tried to slow the pace of reform, or modify it, for the sake of internal peace and democratic procedure; as a result, some of them were threatened, exiled, jailed, or even hanged, victims of show trials carried out with scant protection for the accused. Some of these people had flirted with illegal forms of opposition, it is true, and their persecution came in troubled times—in the wake of the Kurdish rebellion and of an assassination attempt upon the president; yet many of the accused were innocent of genuine crimes, guilty only of opposing their leader's will.

Much can be said in mitigation of Atatürk's behavior, of course. How many politicians put all their cards on the table while struggling to save their countries from invasion? How many politicians' use of alcohol, their sex lives—or divorces—are free from all taint? Could Kemal have survived politically if he had proposed giving away Armenia or Kurdistan? Free Armenia would probably then have claimed large territories containing Moslem majorities, and might even have attempted to unite with other Armenians under Communist Russian control—and Turkey depended on its Russian alliance, at least until 1923. Even in the case of the show trials, Kemal allowed many acquittals, including that of Kiazim Karabekir, thereby saving himself from being classed with tyrants such as Hitler or Stalin—whose enemies received no mercy at all.

At the heart of Atatürk's dictatorial ways, moreover, was his understandable and even well-founded fear of religious reaction. The Kurdish rebellion had been an ethnic matter to some extent, but it had also been led by

Islamic fundamentalists protesting the government's sudden and drastic secularist reforms. Even the anti-fez law had led to riots, hence to repression. The suppression of opposition parties was also linked to religion. The fact is that the Kemalist reform movement was based on a minority of westernized Turkish city-dwellers, whereas the mass of the peasantry had remained true to traditional Islam. Genuine democracy, therefore, might very well have led to ballot-box victories for fundamentalism, and to the undoing of all of Atatürk's reforms.

At least Atatürk was honest enough to admit that he often acted dictatorially. He said—and it was quite true—that Turkey was, after all, not yet a modern land; it would therefore have been unrealistic to expect liberalism, democracy, tolerance, and the two-party system to function properly right away. Western peoples might feel queasy about laws governing headgear, the closing of religious schools, hasty and unfair trials, and the like; yet Western peoples have had hundreds of years to achieve the degree of secularism, economic progress, nation-building, and toleration of dissent that they now enjoy—and much of that achievement has been quite recent. Kemalist Turkey had to achieve it all in a very short time if she were not to slip back into the past. At least that was Atatürk's thinking; in any case, his tyranny was not simply a matter of his own lust for power, let alone a matter of personal economic gain.

If Atatürk had lived to see the rise of fundamentalist Islam in the late twentieth century—in Iran, for example, and even in his own country—he would doubtless have been horrified; but he would also have felt that his harsh methods had been justified. In Atatürk's career, one confronts again the old question of ends justifying means. Western peoples—and Turkish liberals—might approve of most of his ends, yet still wonder about some of his means.

SUGGESTIONS FOR ADDITIONAL READING

Fromkin, David. *A Peace to End All Peace.* New York: Avon, 1989.

Kinross, Lord. *Atatürk.* New York: William Morrow, 1965.

Landau, Jacob M., ed. *Atatürk and the Modernization of Turkey.* Boulder, Colo.: Westview Press, 1984.

Shaw, Stanford J., and Ezel Kural Shaw. *History of the Ottoman Empire and Modern Turkey. Vol. 2, Reform, Revolution, and Republic: the Rise of Modern Turkey, 1808–1975.* Cambridge, Mass.: Cambridge University Press, 1977.

Tachau, Frank. *Kemal Atatürk.* New York: Chelsea House, 1987.

Volkan, Vamik D., and Norman Itzkowitz. *The Immortal Atatürk: a Psychobiography.* Chicago: University of Chicago Press, 1984.

Karl G. Larew

Prince Otto Eduard Leopold von Bismarck-Schönhausen

1815–1898

Minister-President of the Prussian Council of State, 1862–1890
Head of the Council of the North German Confederation, 1866–1871
Chancellor of Germany, 1871–1890

Otto von Bismarck founded the German Empire, with Prussia as its nucleus. He has been the subject of protracted critical discussion since his death. Some have sought to link Bismarck's character, as a statesman, to the twentieth-century excesses of the German state he founded. More particularly, the doctrine of *raison d'état*, or *Realpolitik*, has often been posited as the motivating force behind Bismarck's nation-building efforts. Those terms imply the fulfillment of the goals of the State, without regard to moral considerations. Was the Bismarckian State forged out of "blood and iron," without consideration for ethical constraints?

The debate still rages as to whether Bismarck was fundamentally a German nationalist or an old-fashioned Prussian monarchist who succeeded in subordinating all Germany to his king.

BIOGRAPHICAL BACKGROUND

Bismarck was born at the family estate of Schönhausen in Brandenburg, Prussia. His father was Ferdinand von Bismarck-Schönhausen, a Junker-aristocrat. His mother, Wilhelmine Mencken, was of upper middle-class origin, and it was through her strong influence that Bismarck discovered the solid virtues of Prussia's commercial classes, even as his father gave him a landowner's perspective on the duties of a Junker to king, church, and social class. From 1832 to 1835 he attended the universities of Göttingen and Berlin to prepare for a career in the law. In 1838–1839 he had a very brief tour in the army, which he despised, though he retained his reserve officer's commission throughout his life.

He managed to escape the stultifying legal career that had been mapped out for him, only because sudden financial difficulties for his family required him to take over the management of his father's Pomeranian estate.

By the time of his father's death in 1847, the young heir had succeeded in restoring the family's fortunes to sound condition. He then returned to Schönhausen, the principal family seat near Hamburg, in time to serve as deputy representative for his district at the *Vereinigter Landtag*, the first Prussian parliamentary assembly, born out of the convulsive revolutions of 1848.

Since the senior representative for the district was sick, Bismarck was given an early opportunity to speak in the assembly. Though in his early youth he had briefly toyed with radical politics, in his *Landtag* speeches he voiced the conservative, monarchical, and Christian values typical of the noble Prussian landed class to which he belonged. His evident loyalty gained him an entrée at the court of King Frederick William IV.

During the Revolution of 1848–1849, Bismarck advised his sovereign to repress the liberals, rather than yield to demands for restraint on royal authority. His advice was not heeded, however, and Bismarck became identified with the forces of unreconstructed conservatism and was not elected to the Frankfurt assembly. His elective service ultimately began only after a constitution and an elected parliament had been imposed upon the Prussian king. But this experience had taught Bismarck an important political lesson: henceforth, his opponents would be kept in the dark regarding his true political ideas and intentions; even the monarch, his master, would not know the complexities of Bismarck's designs until their outcome was virtually assured.

Bismarck sharpened his diplomatic skills while serving as Prussian envoy to the German Federal Diet in Frankfurt, as Prussian ambassador to the Russian court at St. Petersburg, and as Prussian ambassador in Paris. His credibility in the eyes of his king rested on the latter's assumption that Bismarck had never deviated from inflexible political conservatism. For his part, Bismarck insisted that the sovereign trust and afford his minister the widest latitude in dealing, first, with other German states while he was at Frankfurt and, later, with representatives of the European Great Powers. Indeed, as Bismarck would not brook parliamentary opposition, so he would threaten his royal master with resignation whenever the latter challenged his political judgment.

Not only the Prussian king but also Bismarck's opponents failed to recognize that Bismarck's youthful conservatism had been alloyed in the world of diplomatic experience to a pragmatic flexibility that stood in stark contrast to the rigidity of his early, parochial conservatism. He hid from a succession of royal masters his developing conviction that the age of absolutism was beyond resurrection, that national states such as Prussia, which had been transformed by liberal revolutions, would require constitutional and parliamentary government supported by the citizenry. He also failed to reveal his growing conviction (which conflicted with his deeply ingrained Prussian patriotism) that Prussia by herself could no longer play the role of great power. Bismarck realized that, for the sake of Prussia as well as the other German states, he had to develop policies that would serve to unite them all under the leadership of Prussia and its king. Above all, he recognized that such unification could only be achieved in derogation of traditional Austrian hegemonic aspirations, and therefore required a fundamental change in Prussia's conventional reliance upon a close Austro-Prussian diplomatic relationship.

Bismarck was called to the leadership of the Prussian cabinet in response to the deep constitutional crisis of 1848, which pitted the king's resolve to control the budget of the armed forces against the parliament's liberal majority, which wished to maintain control over military appropriations. Bismarck's own domestic policy, however, concerned itself more with conserving sufficient power in the hands of the king (and in his own hands) to bring about the gradual unification of the German states—a goal he instinctively sensed held far greater patriotic and political appeal for the German masses than any constitutional niceties. Thus, Bismarck justified his subjecting domestic concerns to the primacy of foreign policy throughout his long career.

From 1862, when Bismarck was called upon to head the cabinet, to 1871, when he succeeded in creating the empire, he pursued a well-hidden foreign policy agenda designed to reduce to helplessness the forces opposed to Prussia. His long-term goal was to displace Austria as the leader of the German states. He anticipated that it would be necessary to defeat France in order to do so.

The first step in his diplomatic agenda was taken when, in 1862–1863, he completely reformed the Prussian Army, sending the legislature home when they opposed his military budget, in contravention of the constitution. Next, through the secret Alvensleben Convention of 1863, he assured the Russians that Prussia would cooperate fully in suppressing Polish revolutionary strivings for independence. He thus assured himself that Russia would not force a two-front war on Prussia while she was fighting a western foe. His next step in asserting the primacy of Prussia among the German states was accomplished during and after the German-Danish War of 1864, over the Schleswig-Holstein question. Here, Bismarck managed to secure the support of Austria for the separation of those territories from Denmark, while simultaneously avoiding becoming dependent on the French Empire. In a triumph of Machiavellianism, Bismarck persuaded the French to obtain an Italian alliance with Prussia against Austria, without promising the French anything substantive in return for the favor.

Having achieved his objective of separating Schleswig-Holstein from Denmark in a short but decisive war in which Prussia was assisted by thirty-seven German states, Bismarck proceeded to the next step, that of using the Austro-Prussian condominium in occupied Schleswig-Holstein as a pretext for war with Austria. Again, after a short but decisive conflict between

Prussia and Italy on one side, and Austria and most of the German states on the other, Bismarck was able to conclude the Seven Weeks War of 1866 by dissolving the German Confederation, expelling Austria from German affairs, and forcing those North German states that Prussia did not annex outright, to accept Prussian domination in a new North German Confederation. He also moved to sign secret treaties of alliance with the four South German states which did not belong to the new confederation. While pretending to be amenable to French expansion into Belgium or Luxembourg, in compensation for Prussia's enormous expansion, Bismarck succeeded in blocking all French moves in that direction.

In 1870, France fell into the trap of contesting the claims of Leopold of Hohenzollern-Sigmaringen to the throne of Spain, though there was no reason to fear that Hohenzollern kings at Berlin and Madrid would act together against France. The French ministers, however, allowed themselves to be led to war by a puerile hunger for prestige, by sensationalist newspapers, and by the bellicose cries of the fickle Paris mob. When King William sent the famous Ems Dispatch to Bismarck, describing his repulse of the French demands concerning the Spanish throne, Bismarck was able by careful editing to make the document seem like a cause for war for anyone who read about it in either the German or the French press. To Bismarck's delight, the French declared war first, making themselves the aggressors. The ensuing Franco-Prussian War of 1870–1871, and France's defeat, led to the creation of the German Empire, German annexation of Alsace-Lorraine, and the French payment of an indemnity equivalent to a billion dollars in gold.

As Bismarck conceived it, his task was to solidify the newly created European balance of power, to position the German Empire as a fulcrum, and to encourage all states to accept the new status quo. To accomplish this, he assured the other powers that Germany was a "satiated power," with no threatening ambitions. The British navy might continue to dominate the seas, Russia and Austria might both fulfill their ambitions in the Balkans, and even the irreconcilable French enemy might build a huge colonial empire, without German objection. In an age when great powers measured themselves by the extent of their colonial possessions, Bismarck restrained the German Empire's entry into the race for colonies. He supported the spread of German commerce into Africa and Asia, but resisted massive land seizure. Indeed, one of Bismarck's last gestures in 1890 was a treaty with Britain surrendering spice-rich Zanzibar, an island off the East African coast, for the small North Sea island of Heligoland.

The accession of William II to the throne in 1888 signaled the end of Bismarck's career. The actual disagreement that led the emperor to accept Bismarck's resignation, in 1890, is of no significance. The fact is that there was no room on the same stage for two such colossal egoists as Bismarck and William II. Bismarck's last years until his death in 1898 were spent in spiteful sniping at his old master—a petty end to the life of a great man.

BISMARCK AS A GREAT LEADER

Otto von Bismarck had recognized early that the creation of a strong, centralized Germany was vital to the maintenance of stability in Europe. A balance of power, with the German Empire at its center, was the only workable prescription for the maintenance of European stability and peace. Beginning in 1873, Bismarck had attempted to reconcile Austria and Russia, becoming a party to the *Dreikaiserbund*, or League of the Three Emperors. By assuring two old enemies that Germany was the guarantor of fair treatment for both, he helped to ensure the peace. In 1879, Bismarck offered Austria an alliance directed against Russian attack. At the same time, he made it plain to the Russians that he was not engaged in any plot against them and that he wished to renew the *Dreikaiserbund*. In 1882 he created the Triple Alliance by admitting Italy into the system, assuring Rome that Germany would defend Italy against French aggression. At the same time, he assured the French that he had no aggressive designs against them, if they kept the peace. He assured all that Germany had no imperial ambitions in the Middle East, the Balkans, or North Africa and that everyone could expand at the expense of the Ottoman Empire, if they kept the peace. One of the keys to the maintenance of a central European balance of power was the Reinsurance Treaty that Bismarck negotiated in 1887. The treaty guaranteed Russian neutrality in the event of a Franco-German conflict. This served to isolate France and discourage revanchist tendencies to compensate her for losses she had incurred in the Franco-Prussian War. At the same time, Russia's interests in Bulgaria, which were challenged by Austria, were recognized, while Austria's existing boundaries, possibly enlarged to include Serbia, were reaffirmed. The effect of the Reinsurance Treaty was to preserve the balance of power on the European continent while placing ultimate control over possible territorial changes in the hands of the German chancellor. Indeed, William II's failure to renew the Reinsurance Treaty after Bismarck had left office was one of the critical steps in the gradual disintegration of the latter's European balance-of-power system, a failure that climaxed in the outbreak of World War I.

In his domestic policies, as in his foreign policy, Bismarck maintained a spirit open to ideas of growth and change, albeit one that was buttressed by fundamentally conservative political persuasions. In the face of parliamentary opposition from the right and from the left, he implemented advanced ideas on social insurance that anticipated policies introduced in Western democracies half a century later. During most of his chancellorship, he weathered parliamentary crises by forming temporary coalitions with opposition parties; without a parliamentary majority of his own, he skillfully wove coalitions, centered about the National Liberal Party, that permitted him to govern without being forced into long-term ideological commitments that would have limited his freedom of action. He was a consummate political leader who exhibited imagination, foresight, determination, courage, and overwhelming persuasive powers. He never lost sight of his objectives, and he pursued his political vision with single-minded dedication wedded to an imagination that exhibited unlimited adaptability and flexibility.

BISMARCK THE TYRANT

As a nation-builder, Bismarck's concept of his role was demanding in the extreme: for the sake of his nation's security and long-term interests, he felt compelled to respond with unyielding force, with devious Machiavellianism if need be, to the challenges that faced him. The doctrine of *raison d'état* or *Realpolitik*, which he invoked in his memoirs, placed the welfare of the state ahead of any moral consideration. Bismarck had spoken of the scientific imprecision of policymaking, and that very imprecision enabled him during his stewardship to be the sole judge of the direction and costs of German policy.

The quest for unlimited political power could easily degenerate into an outbreak of military conflict, and indeed Bismarck did not shrink from applying Clausewitz's famous dictum that war is the continuation of policy by other means. In his *Reflections and Reminiscences*, he recalled that, when he decided on launching the Austro-Prussian War of 1866, he thought he heard "the footsteps of God" at the moment he ordered his Prussian troops into action. In retrospect, it is clear that if Bismarck had moral qualms over the inevitable loss of life his policy had caused, he suppressed them in the belief that his political ends justified the bloody means he had chosen: building a prosperous, secure, and peaceful empire in the center of a prosperous, secure, and peaceful European continent warranted the most extreme means that he might deem necessary. He did not imagine that the elaborate and costly structure of balances would be only partially, temporarily successful, nor did he anticipate that it would collapse less than twenty years after his death. In hindsight, the question whether the outcome justified the sacrifice of "blood and iron" that Bismarck exacted remains open.

Bismarck's pragmatic approach to domestic politics often did not keep him from indulging in excesses born of his conservative prejudices. When his definition of state interest was challenged, he asserted himself by putting in motion repressive policies, such as the persecution of German Catholics in the *Kulturkampf*. This conflict arose when the ecclesiastical authorities demanded that the state dismiss from teaching posts in state schools all

"Old Catholics," that is German Catholics who had refused to accept the decisions of the Vatican Council of 1870.

In league with the National Liberal Party, Bismarck introduced measures in the parliament to place education and marriage outside the control of the ecclesiastical authorities. Legislation was also introduced to control what could be preached from pulpits, how the clergy was to be educated, and how monastic orders were to be regulated. When the pope ordered Catholics to disobey these laws, Bismarck directed that salary payments be withheld from Catholic teachers and members of the clergy; he also ordered the expulsion of Jesuits from the German Empire. These restrictive laws were pushed through the parliament, notwithstanding the objections of a significant part of the Catholic population in South Germany. Bismarck had served notice that he was prepared to resort to the most draconian measures, even at considerable political risk, in order to assert the primacy of the state against all competing interests.

SUGGESTIONS FOR ADDITIONAL READING

Craig, Gordon A. *From Bismarck to Adenauer: Aspects of German Statecraft.* Baltimore: The Johns Hopkins University Press, 1958.

Crankshaw, Edward. *Bismarck.* Hammondsworth: Penguin, 1983.

Eyck, Erich. *Bismarck and the German Empire.* New York: W. W. Norton, 1964.

Gall, Lothar. *Bismarck, the White Revolutionary.* Translated by J. A. Underwood. Boston: Allen & Unwin, 1986.

Meinecke, Friedrich. *Machiavellism: The Doctrine of Raison d'Etat and Its Place in Modern History.* Translated by Douglas Scott. New York: Frederick A. Praeger, 1965.

Pflanze, Otto. *Bismarck and the Development of Germany; The Period of Unification.* Princeton: Princeton University Press, 1963.

Stern, Fritz. *Gold and Iron: Bismarck, Bleichröder and the Building of the German Empire.* New York: Vintage Books, 1979.

Taylor, A.J.P. *Bismarck, the Man and the Statesman.* New York: Knopf, 1955.

———. *The Struggle for Mastery in Europe, 1848–1918.* Oxford: The Clarendon Press, 1954.

Eric A. Belgrad

Fidel Castro (Fidel Alejandro Castro Ruz) 1926–

Cuban Chief of State, 1959–

The intensity of responses evoked by the name Fidel Castro has few parallels among world leaders, and the volumes written about him, considering that he is still alive, are truly impressive. This enigmatic figure effected a radical transformation in Cuba, then projected that small island nation to the center of global politics and kept it there for three decades despite efforts to destroy him. Furthermore, he came to play a role in international politics far out of proportion to Cuba's size or resources. The story of Cuba between 1959 and 1989 reflects, in many ways, the story of Fidel Castro's personal, seemingly quixotic schemes that resulted in his coming to power in the first place.

Identifying himself as a liberal and a patriot who was intolerant of the corruption that had come to characterize Cuban leaders, Castro launched a campaign to overthrow Fulgencio Batista. He narrowly escaped with his life on a number of occasions and finally succeeded in driving Batista from power. Fiercely nationalistic, Castro sought to end Cuba's dependence on the United States by embracing the Soviet Union and communism. Then, faced with what seemed like the inevitable invasion of Cuba by the United States, Castro invited Nikita Khrushchev to place nuclear missiles in Cuba. This would result in heightened Cold War tensions that brought the world to the brink of nuclear conflict. In the end, the island was assured that the United States would not invade, and Cuba became the recipient of substantial aid from the Soviet Union. Amid all the glory showered on Fidel Castro as liberator of Cuba and champion of Third World interests, many have attested to his tyrannical rule and have sought to hasten his demise. In addition, Castro's objective to create a fully independent Cuba has proven to be elusive.

BIOGRAPHICAL BACKGROUND

In 1926, Fidel Alejandro Castro Ruz became the fifth of nine children born to Angel Castro y Argiz and the third of seven to Lina Ruz Gonzalez. Angel

Castro was a Spanish immigrant who had become a successful planter through his entrepreneurship in his adopted country. His first two children were born to his first wife prior to his divorce and subsequent marriage to his housemaid, Lina. Despite Fidel's middle-class status his roots were solidly anchored among the have-nots of Cuba. Lina's father and two brothers drove oxcarts to transport sugarcane to mills, and the family's story is one of rags to riches.

Young Fidel Castro was given the best education that Cuba had to offer. He attended Jesuit schools in Santiago and in Havana where self-discipline, dignity, and tenacity were highly valued. As a young man Fidel was an outstanding athlete and fond of the outdoors. He also showed early signs of strong leadership skills, deep and abiding interest in politics, and genuine concern for the poor.

In 1945, at the age of nineteen, Castro was enrolled in the law program at the University of Havana, where he soon became involved in student politics. The university had become widely known for its involvement in national politics since the 1920s. Indeed, the campus was at the center of the 1933 revolutionary current that saw Fulgencio Batista's rise to power.

In 1933 Batista, a sergeant and stenographer, emerged as the leader of noncommissioned officers. Supported by striking workers and university students, he led a successful revolt against dictator Gerardo Machado and became Cuba's strong man for the next twenty-six years. U.S. envoy Sumner Welles worked with Batista in order to establish a government suitable to Washington, but since Washington's goals were largely incompatible with those of the revolutionary students, the Batista/Washington partnership was seen by them as a subversion of the revolution. From the rebels' perspective, this was especially conspicuous when the United States refused to recognize the new revolutionary government led by university professor Ramon Grau San Martin.

To Castro and many of his peers the betrayal of the people's 1933 revolution was only another U.S. circumvention of Cuban aspiration. In 1898 when Cubans fought for independence from Spain, the United States had entered and forced protectorate status on the island. The Platt amendment, which was imposed on Cuba by Washington, not only made the island's economy heavily dependent on the United States, but it sought to secure U.S. strategic interest by establishing a military base on the island's Guantanamo Bay. The ultimate insult of the amendment was the right claimed by the United States to intervene in Cuba to "protect Cuba's independence." To nationalists like Castro the maneuvers by Welles, which caused the fall of Grau's government, were a bitter reminder that Cuba's destiny was influenced more by men in Washington than by Cubans.

Despite the perception among revolutionaries that Batista had betrayed the 1933 revolution, the politics of Cuba's strong man between 1933 and 1951 gave the opposition little real ammunition to mobilize mass support against him. In fact, when Batista first held direct power, in 1940–1944, he implemented some significant reforms. However, after he staged the 1952 coup and again assumed the Cuban presidency, his political fortunes declined steadily.

As a student leader Castro demonstrated discipline, zeal, tenacity, and unyielding commitment to political change in Cuba as well as in all of Latin America. Among Castro's first revolutionary exploits, he participated in an armed expedition aimed at overthrowing the Dominican Republic dictator Rafael Leonidas Trujillo-Molina in 1947. The expedition was aborted, but the following year Castro found himself in the midst of another foreign uprising. It occurred in Bogota, Colombia, where the assassination of the popular leader of the Colombian liberal party, Jorge Eliecer Gaitan, sparked a spontaneous mass protest while Castro and other Cubans were attending a congress of Latin American students. Castro's involvement in this event demonstrates his proclivity to supporting rebel causes, based on a conviction that Latin America needed to be liberated from the dominance of the colossus to the north.

Among Castro's heroes were José Martí, the father of Cuba's struggles for independence, and Eduardo Chibas, a contemporary politician. Like Simon Bolivar, liberator of Latin America, Martí had warned against U.S. dominance, and Chibas agitated against Cuba's economic dependence and against political corruption under U.S. guardianship. After Castro graduated with his doctor of law degree from the University of Havana in 1950, he became a member of Chibas' Ortodoxo party. The following year Chibas took his own life, allegedly to awaken Cubans to their political plight. Batista would underscore this plight with his March 1952 coup, preempting the June elections in which Castro was a candidate for the House of Representatives. This dashed any faith Castro might have had in the electoral process.

Concluding that force was necessary to fight against Batista, Castro planned a daring and ill-fated attack on the Moncada military barracks on July 26, 1953, a date adopted as the name of his organization, the 26th of July Movement. This attack was easily crushed, and although Castro escaped to the mountains, he was captured and imprisoned. At his trial he gave the famous speech "History Will Absolve Me," which would later be printed and widely circulated. The speech invoked the names of José Martí and Eduardo Chibas and called for reform in what some of his biographers describe as the liberal tradition.

Castro's fifteen-year sentence was commuted, and after spending nineteen months in jail he was released. Fidel Castro would later travel to the United States to raise funds, then to Mexico where he completed plans for a new assault against Batista, who was alienating increasing numbers of the Cuban population. In 1954 and again in 1958, for example, Batista staged mock elections in which he ran unopposed for the presidency. His military was well equipped with weapons from the United States, but to many Cubans his administration lacked legitimacy. Therefore, although he was able to defuse the military coups plotted against him, a general state of disorder persisted in the country.

Castro and over eighty other revolutionaries arrived in Cuba's Oriente province from Mexico early in December 1956 aboard a small yacht called the *Granma*. Their arrival, however, was poorly timed. Instead of a quiet landing, which was to have been ensured by the distractions of allies, they met the force of Batista's military. This disastrous encounter left all but about a dozen of Castro's revolutionaries dead. Castro and the few remaining leaders of his 26th of July Movement barely escaped to the Sierra Maestra mountains, from where they recruited followers, then organized and waged a successful guerrilla war against Batista's military machine.

By all accounts the limited support Castro had when he landed in Oriente could easily have been crushed by Batista. Batista thought he had done just that when early reports claimed that Castro was among those killed. The problem for Batista was that internal as well as external support for his government continued to erode as accounts of his men's ruthlessness were reported. Not the least of his supporters, the United States, decided to delay a shipment of weapons and munitions in the fall of 1957, and in the spring of 1958 Washington announced an arms embargo against Cuba.

As support for Batista diminished, Castro's stature as a credible liberator increased, and by 1958 his leadership was unrivaled. When, therefore, Batista escaped to the neighboring Dominican Republic early on January 1, 1959, leaders from various sectors of Cuban society threw their support behind Fidel Castro, who promised rapid and profound change. It is doubtful whether anyone, including Castro himself, could have anticipated the dramatic changes that the next two years would bring.

CASTRO AS A GREAT LEADER

While Castro had many admirers in the United States, the Eisenhower administration was not sure what to make of the bearded, charismatic rebel. However, when he visited Washington shortly after the revolution in 1959 and expressed no interest in U.S. aid, some politicians became concerned that he might be difficult to control. Their concerns would be confirmed when Castro returned home and put in place his agrarian reform law, reduced rents in urban areas, and concluded a sugar-for-oil agreement with the Soviet Union. The latter would be the catalyst for destroying an already strained relationship with the United States. On the advice of the State Department, U.S. oil companies operating in Cuba refused to refine Cuban oil obtained from the Soviet Union. In response, Castro nationalized those companies. Washington responded by cancelling its sugar quota agreement with Cuba. Castro then stepped up nationalization of both foreign- and domestic-owned companies. Washington played its last diplomatic card by imposing a trade embargo against Cuba and severing diplomatic relations in October 1960. Support for an invasion to overthrow Castro would follow in 1961. But numerous factors worked in Castro's favor, giving him a major victory in the April 1961 Bay of Pigs invasion. This victory enabled him to unify and mobilize the Cuban people around his plan for radical change. It also forced him into the Soviet orbit, resulting in an unprecedented escalation of the Cold War conflict.

Although Castro's military under his personal command overwhelmed the invaders at the Bay of Pigs, he understood that the United States could reverse this victory virtually at will. He therefore arranged with the Soviet Union to place missiles on Cuban soil as a deterrent to a possible U.S. invasion. Not surprisingly, the nature of the conflict quickly changed into a global confrontation between the two superpowers. The result was the 1962 Cuban missile crisis, which brought the world dangerously close to a nuclear confrontation. President John Kennedy and Premier Khrushchev managed to reach an agreement and avert a nuclear war after many tense hours of uncertainty.

Khrushchev did not consult Castro before he agreed to remove the missiles from Cuba. However, he had received assurance that the United States would not invade the island nation. Despite this embarrassment for Castro, he would come to play a significant role in world politics during the 1970s and 1980s. For example, Castro would send troops to Angola and to Ethiopia; he would send advisers, educators, and medical professionals to these and a number of other countries including Nicaragua and Grenada. Indeed, Castro would become a highly admired figure in many developing countries.

While Castro expanded his influence in the developing world in partnership with the Soviet Union, Cuba succeeded in eradicating traditional forms of corruption, illiteracy, gross inequity, and dependence on the United States. The country has also made progress on the questions of gender and racial equality, which has won him strong support among women and reduced chances of racial tension. In addition, Cuba has made impressive gains in the areas of health care, biotechnology, and education. Developments in the manufacturing and agricultural sectors, however, have been disappointing. Furthermore, Castro exchanged dependence on the United States for dependence on the Soviet Union and its Eastern European allies. Thus the unforeseen collapse of communism in Eastern Europe and the former Soviet Union coupled with the U.S. embargo have proven disastrous for Cuba.

Many who have long hoped for and worked toward Castro's fall from power came to believe that the economic and political impact of the dramatic decline of communism would bring about the imminent collapse of socialist Cuba. That his power in Cuba appears to be yet unshaken is testimony to Castro's undeniable skills as a political leader. He continues to enjoy the status of a hero among many Cubans and is not generally blamed for Cuba's current plight. His daily contact with Cubans, his continued demonstration of personal interest in their welfare, his method of solving problems informally, blaming his own bureaucracy at times for inefficiency, and the ever-present reminders, in the form of posters and slogans, that he saved Cuba from the United States, continue to endear Fidel to Cubans, particularly the older ones. Many Cubans have responded to the call to make adjustments, to make sacrifices, and to be innovative, as their leader steers the state in turbulent and uncharted waters.

CASTRO THE TYRANT

Castro's tyranny was most evident during the period shortly after the revolution when he set out to consolidate power. The public trial and execution of Batista supporters who were accused of bombing civilians, particularly peasant villages, seemed appalling to outside observers. Also, Castro's dealings with his enemies or those whose ideas come in conflict with his, have generally been carefully calculated to ensure public support. He has been known to try and convict high-ranking officials in the streets at mass rallies where his spellbinding rhetoric and charismatic appeal to people's trust and sense of loyalty have always proven successful.

The revolution received the support of various sectors of the population. This included the middle class as well as elements of the business elite. The naming of a highly respected judge, Manuel Urrutia Lleo, as president of the provisional government was an acknowledgment of this fact. In addition, before the overthrow of Batista, Castro promised to conduct elections within months of destroying the repressive dictatorship. Not only did Castro postpone the elections indefinitely but, when Urrutia announced publicly that communists were infiltrating the administration, Castro used mass support to force his resignation.

Like Urrutia, Huber Matos Benitez was opposed to increasing communist influence in the new administration. Matos, a Sierra Maestra rebel hero, was governor of Camaguey province, but Castro mobilized the military and the masses to remove him as a threat to the revolution. Matos' imprisonment created some difficulty for Castro, but since his opposition coincided with opposition from the outside, Castro was able to link them and sway the crowds in his favor.

To those who believe in the ownership of private property and the European order established in the Americas after 1492, among the most telling acts of tyranny by Fidel Castro is the massive confiscation of property that he carried out in the name of the revolution. Foreigners as well as Cubans lost land and businesses without compensation. This course of action represents the fundamental systemic change that has subordinated individual interest to that of the community in Castro's Cuba.

With the collapse of communism in the former Soviet Republics and Eastern Europe leaving Castro somewhat isolated, Cuba is forced to make significant modifications to its standard of living, its way of doing business, and its relationship to capitalism. This might well prove to be the greatest challenge in Castro's political career. Although many observers have commenced the requiem for Castro's leadership in Cuba, this author's visit to that country in 1991 did not reveal definitive support for any such conclusion. Castro continues to enjoy wide support among the Cuban masses, who can point to substantial gains as a result of the revolution. Whether the economic crisis the country faces and the mellowing of its leader will lead to the demise of the Cuba he created after 1959 is a chapter yet to be written by time and events.

SUGGESTIONS FOR ADDITIONAL READING

Aguila, Juan M. del. *Cuba: Dilemmas of a Revolution.* Boulder, Colo.: Westview Press, 1988.

Balfour, Sebastian. *Castro.* London: Longman, 1990.

Bourne, Peter. *Fidel: A Biography of Fidel Castro.* New York: Dodd, Mead & Company, 1986.

Castro, Fidel. *In Defense of Socialism: Four Speeches.* Edited by Mary-Alice Waters. New York: Pathfinder, 1989.

Draper, Theodore. *Castro's Revolution, Myths and Realities.* New York: Frederick A. Praeger, 1962.

Matthews, Herbert. *Fidel Castro.* New York: Simon and Schuster, 1966.

Quirk, Robert E. *Fidel Castro.* New York: W. W. Norton & Company, 1993.

Suarez, Andres. *Cuba: Castroism and Communism, 1959–1966.* Cambridge, Mass.: The MIT Press, 1967.

Suchlicki, Jaime. *Cuba: From Columbus to Castro.* Washington: Pergamon-Brassey's International Defense Publishers, 1987.

Szulc, Tad. *Fidel: A Critical Portrait.* New York: William Morrow and Company, 1986.

Gersham A. Nelson

Catherine the Great

1729–1796

Empress of Russia, 1762–1796

INTRODUCTION

Catherine the Great was undoubtedly one of Russia's greatest rulers, though she was a German by birth. Possessed of extraordinary energy, she is described by contemporaries as capable of working through the greater part of twenty-four hours without exhaustion. Writers of fiction have capitalized on her sexual promiscuity. Historians, more conservative by nature, have usually stopped just short of describing her as a nymphomaniac. Any modern psychoanalyst would, however, have to relate her extraordinary physical appetite to the rest of her frenetically energetic life. That she could conduct wars, repress rebellions, and concern herself with the mundane aspects of governing an empire, while carrying on a voluminous correspondence with admirers in all Europe, make her "a wonder of the world." That she also wrote serious treatises in philosophy that were dignified by the serious attention of great scholars, puts her in a special intellectual class.

On a superficial level, the empress may be called "Great" because during the thirty-four years of her reign she destroyed the Kingdom of Poland and annexed the greatest part of that realm. She may deserve the accolade because she seized a segment of the Turkish Black Sea coast and created a new seaport at Odessa, further opening isolated Russia to the world. Perhaps her role as a founder of a world-class navy is worthy of note. It is certainly a colorful addition to mention that at her death, the Russian flag flew in Europe, Asia, and in Alaskan North America. She also continued the process briefly interrupted after the death of Peter the Great, of westernizing the Russian aristocracy, and pasting a thin veneer of Western European culture and behavior over all of Russian society. Perhaps it is more important that she managed to persuade such hardened cynics as Voltaire, that she was truly an *enlightened despot* worthy of adulation.

BIOGRAPHICAL BACKGROUND

Sophia Augusta Fredericka was born a princess of Anhalt-Zerbst at the Prussian port of Stettin on May 2, 1729. Her father, Prince Christian August, served as a Prussian major general and later as a field marshal. Her mother, Johanna Elizabeth, was a princess of Holstein-Gottorp. In 1744, accompanied by her mother, the fifteen-year-old princess was invited to St. Petersburg by Empress Elizabeth of Russia. The motive for the journey, understood by all parties, was to betroth the young princess to Grand Duke Karl Peter Ulrich of Holstein, heir apparent to the throne of Russia, as a nephew of Empress Elizabeth and a grandson of the late tsar Peter the Great. The bridegroom, who was to reign briefly as Peter III in 1762, was of limited intelligence and immediately alienated his bride by the sort of impulsive behavior which included policy decision-making entirely divorced from reality and public dalliance with mistresses. The fact that he also sat propped up in bed, playing with toy soldiers, did nothing to build respect.

At her marriage, the bride accepted the Russian Orthodox faith, abandoning her native Lutheran Church. She also took the baptismal name Catherine. With her new religion and name, she devoted the rest of her life to being thoroughly Russian.

Even while Empress Elizabeth was alive, Catherine, neglected by her husband, began her series of notorious love affairs with a succession of men. It may be speculated that Grand Duke Paul, her son, was not the son of Peter III, and that in fact the later tsars had no Romanov blood in their veins. She bore at least one other illegitimate child, Alexei Bobrinskii, alleged to have been Alexei Orlov's son.

At the death of Empress Elizabeth in 1762, Peter III reigned for only two months, then was forced to abdicate, after which he was murdered. His widow was immediately proclaimed Empress Catherine II and was invested with sovereign power. She reigned in her own name, thenceforth, excluding her son Paul from any share in power. There is no doubt that the ruin of Peter III was engineered by Catherine's friends, but she was carefully protected from any direct involvement so that she could play the role of a grieving widow.

Catherine took pride in being a truly enlightened despot, cultivating men of letters who were rewarded handsomely for public paeans of praise about her. When the great French philosopher Voltaire proposed to write her biography, and asked leave to visit her to make her acquaintance, she discouraged him from making the journey, expressing concern for his health. In actual fact, the empress probably feared that the "king of the philosophers" would discover the ugly truth, and that his adulatory tribute might become a vitriolic condemnation. Voltaire wrote his biography, and Catherine emerged unscathed.

The empress died on November 6, 1796, at Tsarskoe Selo, at the moment when Napoleon Bonaparte was winning his first great victories in Italy. She was buried at St. Petersburg, in the imperial Romanov mausoleum at the Peter and Paul Fortress.

CATHERINE AS A GREAT LEADER

As a German princess who had become a Russian empress, Catherine prided herself on being an enlightened rationalist. By eighteenth-century definition, a rationalist was a person who avoided making decisions based on emotion, trusting only those impressions that were confirmed by the test of the five physical senses. If a sovereign such as Empress Catherine had pretensions to being a rationalist, it was assumed by eighteenth-century *philosophes* (philosophers) that she would apply rationalism to all the crises of government, offering her people the advantage of "Enlightened Despotism." Tyranny was not regarded as evil, provided that it was adopted for the good of a sovereign's subjects. She completed the work of Peter the Great in making St. Petersburg a model "Western" city. Her art collection at the Hermitage Palace made it one of the world's great museums. She cultivated the personal acquaintance of western *philosophes* such as Grimm and Diderot, and was accepted as a serious philosopher by a giant such as Voltaire. When a smallpox vaccine was developed by Dr. Jenner, she had her family vaccinated but did not share the favor with anyone of lesser rank.

Her *Great Instruction* of 1767 was saluted by Voltaire as the "finest monument of the century." It provided the blueprint that led to the reform of provincial government in 1775. In 1762 and 1785 she completed the process of making the nobility a purely hereditary social class, rather than a "service nobility" with inherent rights to form part of the administration of the empire. It may be debated whether the transformation of thousands of people into parasites is creative or destructive. However, there is no doubt that thereafter the tsars were autocrats in fact, as well as title, with no one to challenge them for power.

Consistent with Catherine's announced enlightenment, she proposed early in her reign to end serfdom. Pursuant to that goal, she imported skilled German farmers to train the primitive Russian peasants. When she abandoned peasant emancipation following the Pugachev Revolt, all that remained of her grandiose scheme was a vast colony of Germans living on the shores of the Volga River. The Volga Germans have had an often unhappy two-century career under successive Russian governments.

Through her participation in the major wars occurring during her reign, Catherine forced all Europe to reckon with a new major power. She enlarged Russia in Finland, at the expense of Sweden. She annexed additional Black Sea frontage, at the expense of Turkey. It was Catherine who made Odessa a major seaport.

More importantly, the Treaty of Kutchuk Kainardji of 1774, which ended her first Turkish War, gave the tsars two important claims. The first was that Russia joined Britain and France, which ever since the sixteenth century had claimed capitulatory rights. This meant that their consuls stationed on Turkish soil could serve as judges adjudicating the legal claims of their own nationals against one another. The second claim was based on a vaguely worded clause of the treaty which Russia interpreted to mean that the tsar was the protector of all Greek and Russian Orthodox Christians living anywhere in the Ottoman Empire. Certainly Russian expansion in the Middle East profited mightily, thenceforth, from those pretensions.

Catherine was the European sovereign who was directly involved in all three partitions of Poland, in 1772, 1793, and 1795. While wiping that country off the map, Catherine took care to annex only those parts of Poland inhabited by Russian- or Ukrainian-speaking populations. Only Lithuania constituted a Roman Catholic and non-Russian prize stolen from the ravaged kingdom by Russia. It was to be her grandson, Alexander I, who, in 1815, annexed the greater part of Catholic Poland.

Finally, it was Catherine the Great who carried Russian expansion in Alaska almost to its extreme extent. At her death, the Russian flag flew over Europe, Asia, and North America.

CATHERINE THE TYRANT

In 1773–1774, in the midst of her Turkish War, Catherine confronted a rebellion that purported to be in the name of her dead husband. A pretender named Emilien Pugachev, actually a Don Cossack, claimed that he was Peter III and had survived assassination. He was supported not only by Cossacks, but by Tartars, numerous Mongoloid tribes, by convicts and exiles, as well as by a great part of the peasantry. As the revolt seriously threatened the empress, Pugachev had to be made an example. When he was captured, he was placed in an iron cage too low for him to stand in and too narrow for him to lie in. His public execution was followed by brutal measures against his followers. Whether or not the empress had ever intended to end serfdom, the revolt remained her pretext for reducing the status of serfs to chattel property.

Under Catherine, the Ukrainians lost the last vestiges of sovereign self-government as a people. The Jews who had previously been Polish subjects were confined to a Pale of Settlement and prohibited from residing beyond that line. Catherine's repression of the Jews set a model for her successors until the Russian Revolution, with the exception of the relatively liberal reign of her great grandson, Alexander II, during 1855–1881. Thus, at the very moment when Western European Jews were eagerly assimilating into general society, Russian Jews remained a solid bloc of Yiddish-speaking isolates, cut off from Russian society.

Catherine tolerated no opposition from any element in her realm. Her son Paul, denied any part of his rightful role as tsar, came to the throne only at his mother's death, a deeply resentful, frustrated, and bitter man.

SUGGESTIONS FOR ADDITIONAL READING

Alexander, John T. *Catherine the Great: Life and Legend.* New York and London: Oxford University Press, 1989.

Dukes, Paul. *Catherine the Great and the Russian Nobility.* Cambridge: Cambridge University Press, 1967.

Ilchester, Earl of, ed. *Correspondence of Catherine the Great with Sir Charles Hanbury Williams.* London: Thornton Butterworth, 1928.

Kluchevsky, V. O. *A History of Russia.* Vol. 5. New York: Russell and Russell, 1960.

Madariaga, Isabel de. *Catherine the Great: A Short History.* New Haven, Conn.: Yale University Press, 1990.

———. *Russia in the Age of Catherine the Great.* New Haven, Conn.: Yale University Press, 1981.

Raeff, Marc. *Catherine the Great: A Profile.* New York: Hill and Wang, 1972.

Ransel, David L. *The Politics of Catherinian Russia: The Panin Party.* New Haven, Conn.: Yale University Press, 1975.

Reddaway, W. F., ed. *Documents of Catherine the Great: The Correspondence with Voltaire and the Instruction of 1767.* Cambridge: Cambridge University Press, 1931.

Arnold Blumberg

Count Camillo Benso di Cavour

1810–1861

Prime Minister of Sardinia-Piedmont and Italy from 1852 to 1859 and from 1860 to 1861

The two dominating principles of the nineteenth century were the ideas of nationalism and Liberalism. Cavour's life was dominated by the idea that people who shared a common language and common geographic area had a right to govern themselves. The political life of Cavour fits almost exactly into the same time frame as the struggle for Italian unification. The importance of Cavour cannot, therefore, be separated from the issue of Italian unification. The problem, however, is how Cavour influenced unification. Much historical controversy exists over some key issues concerning Cavour's role. The debate over Cavour's leadership skills centers on whether he planned and controlled events from 1854 to 1861 or merely reacted to them. One of the major controversies surrounds the efficacy of Cavour's planning of the revolts in the central Italian duchies. Would they have occurred without his inspiration? To what extent were they the carefully planned creations of Cavour and his faithful supporter, Giuseppe La Farina? Another, larger controversy surrounds his prior knowledge and support for the Garibaldian expedition to Sicily. This dichotomy can best be seen in the work of Denis Mack Smith and Romeo Rosario. Early histories of Cavour leaned toward hagiography, whereas more recent studies, especially those of Mack Smith, have tried to show Cavour less as the great organizer, and more as the statesman reacting to events. A contemporary Italian historian, Rosario stands in stark contrast to Mack Smith by arguing for the planned continuity of Cavour's actions. The argument over Cavour's leadership lies not so much in what he did to advance Italian unification, but rather in whether his methods and goals were noble and prearranged, as Rosario claimed, or selfish and haphazard, as Mack Smith would argue. Cavour's early death deprived historians of examples of his leadership abilities apart from Italian unification, thus further kindling the debate.

BIOGRAPHICAL BACKGROUND

Count Camillo Benso di Cavour was born in Turin on August 1, 1810, to a Savoyard-Swiss aristocratic family. Enamored of the English, he became a strong supporter of both economic and political Liberalism. Drawing on British examples, he wrote exhaustively on agriculture, Ireland, and the English Poor Law. Consequently, Cavour supported the revolts of 1848 and convinced the Piedmontese king, Charles Albert, to support the Milanese in their attempt to oust Austria from Lombardy.

First elected to parliament in 1848, Cavour became prime minister of Piedmont on November 4, 1852, and held that office, except for a brief episode, until 1861. During the Crimean War, Cavour joined the Anglo-French alliance against Russia by contributing 15,000 Sardinian troops, thereby meriting a place at the Paris peace conference. Cavour achieved few tangible results other than getting the European Powers to recognize the problem of maladministration in the Papal States and the Kingdom of Naples.

In July 1858, Cavour gained more concrete results for Italian unification at a secret meeting at Plombières, where he and Emperor Napoleon III of France agreed to a war against Austria. The two conspirators agreed that after Austria had been ousted from the peninsula, an Italian federation of four states under the presidency of the pope would be established. With a formal alliance, Cavour provoked the Austrian attack of April 29, 1859, and the Franco-Piedmontese forces were able to defeat the Austrians, first at Magenta, then at Solferino, thereby forcing them to retreat to the Quadrilateral fortresses and abandon Lombardy. For reasons of his own, Napoleon broke the alliance and concluded a separate truce with Austria at Villafranca, on July 8, before the liberation of Venetia. When King Victor Emmanuel II of Sardinia-Piedmont agreed to the truce, Cavour resigned in protest.

During the war, Cavour had carefully engineered rebellions in the central Italian states against their Bourbon, Habsburg, and papal rulers. When Cavour returned as prime minister, he arranged what he hoped would appear to be "spontaneous" requests from the central Italian states for annexation to Piedmont. Soon after uniting upper and central Italy, Cavour was faced with another potentially threatening situation. The Italian republican and revolutionary, Giuseppe Garibaldi, with his army of one thousand "Red Shirts," captured Sicily and Naples. Cavour, by moving troops into the Papal States to crush a rebellion and in the process annexing papal territory, was in a good position to defend against Garibaldi's advance. All of this was done in secret collusion with Napoleon III. When the Piedmontese forces met Garibaldi's army, Garibaldi surrendered his conquests to Victor Emmanuel without a fight.

The Kingdom of Italy was proclaimed on March 17, 1861. The only major exclusions were Rome and Latium, still controlled by the pope, and Austrian Venetia. It is ironic that Cavour died suddenly, on June 6, 1861, in Turin, less than three months after the birth of his beloved united Kingdom of Italy. With his usual foresight, Cavour had exacted a pledge from his parish priest to give him Extreme Unction, regardless of Pope Pius IX's manifest displeasure. The priest kept his word and was disciplined by his superiors after Cavour's funeral.

CAVOUR AS A GREAT LEADER

What distinguished Cavour as a great leader was his concern for the Italian people, his vision, and his determination. Contemporaries saw Cavour as the great statesman of the middle path leading Italy between foreign Habsburg autocrats and demagogic republicans like Giuseppe Mazzini. Cavour's Italy would be a Liberal constitutional kingdom under the House of Savoy. It had to be a Liberal and a constitutional regime because his studies of English politics convinced him that this was the best possible system—free enough to allow influence to those who had a stake in the country, but paternalistic enough to protect the great mass of Italians who needed to be shielded from the seductive voices of republicanism. So intense was his commitment to Liberalism, that in 1831 Cavour resigned his commission in the Piedmontese army rather than support what was then an absolutist regime. Cavour later founded a newspaper, *Il Risorgimento*, which during the 1848 revolts lent King Charles Albert essential support as he moved toward the creation of a constitutionalist monarchy.

Although the Revolutions of 1848 brought a constitution to Piedmont, they failed to oust Austria from the Italian peninsula. Cavour, however, did not abandon the dream of a free and united Italy. Unlike Mazzini, he realized that "Italy cannot make itself." Cavour was thus wise enough to see that achieving Italian unity would need European help. Like most good leaders, he was able to use events to his advantage. Thus, during the Crimean War, although Piedmont had no real interest in the Crimea, he aided France and Britain, to get their support for Italy. As he put it, "Italy will be made from Russian mud."

While critics in Turin castigated Cavour for not achieving more tangible results for Italian unification at the Paris peace conference, Cavour left the fledgling power an even greater legacy. By signing the 1856 Treaty of Paris which regulated the "Eastern Question," Cavour and later Italian statesmen were able to use that treaty to insinuate themselves into the European Concert. Cavour claimed a voice in the settlement of Syrian problems in 1860. Before the outbreak of the Italian War of 1859, he demanded that Sardinia-Piedmont be represented on an equal footing with the Great Powers at the congress to be called on the Italian Question. Cavour also gained admittance to the Conference on the Danubian Principalities in 1858. This legacy is one of Cavour's greatest contributions to Italy's growth as a great power.

Realizing further that Piedmont's presence at the Congress of Paris would not be enough to unify Italy, Cavour sought out Napoleon's help at Plombières. As a skillful and shrewd diplomat and statesman, he not only was able to get Napoleon to agree to an alliance but also succeeded in manipulating Austria into being the aggressor in order to comply with the terms of the alliance. Committed to a free and united Italy, when Napoleon ended the war before the liberation of Venetia, Cavour felt betrayed and resigned as prime minister in July 1859. Yet, being a greater leader, he could not easily be replaced and was recalled by the king in January 1860.

Committed to unification, Cavour even sacrificed part of his own country to ensure the birth of a united Italy. According to the Plombières agreement, Piedmont was to cede to Napoleon both Savoy and Nice in exchange for help in liberating Lombardy and Venetia. Napoleon at first declined the cession because Venetia was not liberated, but later, when Sardinia annexed the central Italian duchies, he changed his mind and agreed to accept both regions. In order to achieve the cession, Cavour had to overcome the resistance not only of Victor Emmanuel, since Savoy was the ancestral home of the ruling family of Piedmont, but also of the British and the Prussians, who objected to the increase in French power.

What distinguished Count Cavour as a great leader was his concern for the Italian people, his vision, and his determination. His concern for the Italian people can be seen in his commitment to a Liberal constitutional regime for Piedmont and Italy. His vision was to unify Italy and make it a great power. His determination can be seen in the way he used events to forward Italian unity and greatness.

CAVOUR THE TYRANT

Niccolò Machiavelli, in *The Prince*, established the qualities of a successful ruler who could unify Italy. Today, Machiavelli's "prince" has become the archetypal tyrant. Cavour exhibited many of the qualities of Machiavelli's "prince." Among these qualities were the retention of power at any cost, the emphasis on war as the ruler's main occupation, and the determination to maintain the façade of virtue but not the reality. Therefore, using these criteria, Cavour could be classified as a tyrant.

During his first tenure in the Piedmontese cabinet in 1851–1852, Cavour secured the portfolios of Agriculture, Navy, and Finance and became one of the most powerful members of the cabinet, rivaling the prime minister, Massimo d'Azeglio. So power hungry was Cavour that he arranged the *connubio*, or marriage, of the Left-Center and Right-Center parties to elect Urbano Rattazzi as head of the Chamber of Deputies without the consent of the prime minister. Forced to resign over this action, Cavour was soon recalled to head his own ministry from March 1852 until he resigned in protest in July 1859. His return to power in January 1860 was only cut short by his untimely death in 1861. As prime minister, Cavour held the reigns of power tightly. In his first administration, he personally controlled the portfolios of Foreign Affairs, Finance, Agriculture, and Commerce, and from 1859 the Ministry of War as well. Similar conglomerations of power marked his second administration. Cavour's political style left Italy another long-lasting legacy. Cavour's use of the *connubio* to arrange power coalitions favorable to himself was continued by his successors and led to the weakening of the Italian political party structure. Thanks to Cavour's attempt to keep power at any cost, Italy suffered for decades with the instability of weak political coalitions.

For Machiavelli, the main occupation of the ruler should be the art of war. War is the surest way to increase the power of the state, and it was through force that Cavour was able to achieve his goal of Italian unification. The most obvious example was the conquest of Lombardy from the Austrians. The less obvious example of Cavour's tyrannical behavior can be found in the central Italian duchies. The Bourbon and Habsburg dukes were deposed by supposedly "spontaneous" demonstrations of the inhabitants during the 1859 war. Cavour had orchestrated ahead of time with Giuseppe La Farina, head of the National Society, to start these revolts at the proper time so that these duchies could be annexed to Piedmont. According to the Plombières Agreement, the central Italian duchies were to be joined into a separate central Italian kingdom; according to the Treaty of Zurich, based on the Truce of Villafranca, the central Italian duchies were to be restored to their legitimate rulers. Cavour, seeing that none of these alternatives suited his designs, violated all three agreements by annexing the central Italian duchies. In 1860, Garibaldi sailed with his army from Genoa with the secret support of Cavour, Victor Emmanuel II, and the National Society to conquer Naples and Sicily for "Italy." Cavour's support of the Garibaldian conquest of Southern Italy is an excellent example of how Cavour disregarded international law, diplomatic agreement, and his own personal dislike of republicans in order to achieve his ends through the use of armed force.

Cavour was a consummate diplomatist with a keen sense of when to keep his word and when to break it. The ability to maintain the façade, but not the reality, of virtue is the third Machiavellian trait that labels Cavour a tyrant. He had developed his Liberal constitutional views from his studies of the English. While outwardly supporting constitutionalism, he did not hesitate to sidestep these principles. It was at the Congress of Paris that Cavour realized that while he admired the British, they would be of little material support in ousting the Austrians from Italy. Cavour chose, therefore, the autocratic Napoleon III over the Liberal British as the surest means to his ends. While abandoning the British, however, Cavour had not abandoned the appearance of Liberal constitutionalism. In order to give the appearance of self-determination to the conquered regions, plebiscites were held. In truth, it was Napoleon III who urged the use of plebiscites to lend the appearance of genuine support for popular sovereignty.

The first was held in the central Italian duchies, where Cavour had orchestrated the "spontaneous" revolts. The results were, of course, overwhelmingly in favor of annexation to Piedmont. The second plebiscite was held after the conquest of Naples; the ballot read, "Yes, Victor Emmanuel, King of Italy." With these plebiscites, Cavour could claim that he was acting on the will of the people and for the good of Italy.

Cavour fit the mold of the "prince" whom Machiavelli had said would be needed to unify Italy. By making war his main concern, Cavour was able to unify Italy with the help of French arms and planned revolts. His use of the *connubio* allowed him, and his successors, to keep power at any price. Cavour maintained the façade of Liberal constitutionalism through the use of plebiscites, while in reality achieving unification through deceit, conquest, and broken promises.

SUGGESTIONS FOR ADDITIONAL READING

Blumberg, Arnold. *A Carefully Planned Accident; The Italian War of 1859*. Cranbury, N.J.: Associated University Presses, 1990.

Delzell, Charles, ed. *The Unification of Italy, 1859–1861: Cavour, Mazzini, or Garibaldi?* New York: Holt, Rinehart and Winston, 1965.

Mack Smith, Denis. *Cavour*. London: Werdenfeld and Nicolson, 1985.

———. *Cavour and Garibaldi 1860: A Study in Political Conflict*. London: Cambridge University Press, 1954.

———. *Victor Emmanuel, Cavour, and the Risorgimento*. London: Oxford University Press, 1971.

Thayer, William R. *The Life and Times of Cavour*. Boston: Houghton Mifflin, 1911.

Whyte, Arthur. *The Political Life and Letters of Cavour 1848–1861*. London: Oxford University Press, 1930.

Lawrence P. Adamczyk

Charles I (Charles Stuart)

1600–1649

King of England, Scotland, and Ireland, 1625–1649

Charles I, more than any British monarch before or since, believed that he ruled by the divine will of God. This divine authority, however, did not simply assure him of wealth and privilege; it obligated him to preserve the order of the realm, the central role of the church within that order, and the succession of God's anointed. These obligations were for Charles Stuart not simply the ephemeral notions of a political ideal; they were the basis for every decision he made as king, including the decision to die rather than negotiate terms with a Parliament which would have compromised his authority and thus his ability to fulfill his responsibilities to God and to his people. Such single-mindedness often thwarted Charles' judgment about the practical details of government—not the least of which was his selection of advisers—and made him incapable of understanding, or trusting, the motives of those who would question either his authority or the manner in which he exercised it. The very irony of history is that so resolute a king would ascend the throne of Great Britain at a time when social and economic forces were determined to dismantle all the institutions, both practical and philosophical, that might have underpinned Charles' rule; that he resisted these forces created the image, which has become his legacy, of an unmovable, at times cruel and tyrannical, monarch. A further irony is that at that moment when he, against his own will, gave in to Parliament and allowed the execution of his most capable adviser, the Earl of Strafford, Charles Stuart lost the services of the one man perhaps capable of protecting him against the assault that would follow. Charles I carried his guilt over Strafford to his grave; he may never have grasped the practical consequences of that loss.

BIOGRAPHICAL BACKGROUND

Charles Stuart was born on November 18, 1600, at Dunfermline, Scotland, the second son of James VI of Scotland, later James I of England, Scotland,

and Ireland, and Anne of Denmark. The sickly child, who seemed in danger of living only briefly, was created Duke of Albany at his baptism and given to the charge of Lord Fyvie and his wife. In 1604, he was taken to London to join his family, his father having ascended the English throne the year before. In London, Charles was placed in the charge of Lady Carey, who nurtured the boy who by temperament, and perhaps as a result of his frail condition, was withdrawn and somewhat overwhelmed by life at court.

As a result of his shy personality, Charles was the opposite of his elder brother Henry, the heir designate and the one of James I's children who, because of his imposing physical stature and lively temperament, seemed destined to rule a great nation. Charles admired his brother greatly and, rather than living in his shadow, thrived on the attention he received from Henry, as well as the tender affection of his sister, Elizabeth. In 1612, however, Henry died suddenly, leaving Charles, the heir presumptive to the throne, in deep mourning. It was a role he had not been prepared for; it was a role he had never envisioned for himself. And yet the diligent and serious Charles, who had battled his weak physical condition by engaging in rigorous exercise, took seriously the role now confronting him. From the very beginning of his political career, Charles I considered himself obligated by God and circumstance to the role he must play, and this conviction remained throughout his life.

Discussions had taken place in 1613 about Charles' marriage possibilities, mostly concerning the French princess Christina. In 1614, these were expanded to include the Infanta Maria of Spain. Charles, as heir to the English throne, was a desirable match for both countries; he and his father, realizing this, were determined to use this fact to their advantage in continental politics and delayed action to keep their position of control. After Charles became Prince of Wales in 1616, he was ready to marry, but the continuing power shifts in Europe made the English cautious about where to commit themselves. Very likely Count Gondomar, the astute Spanish ambassador, had no intention of marrying Catholic Spain to Protestant England, but was merely striving for a treaty that would end the long war which had been fought intermittently since 1587. Nonetheless, in 1623, the prince, accompanied by the Duke of Buckingham, went to Spain to woo the Infanta. The Spanish found the two young Englishmen less than diplomatic, and Charles was frustrated by the coolness of his hosts, particularly regarding his desire to secure their help in the Palatinate. Negotiations ended abruptly. The English celebrated this break with their traditional Catholic adversary, and the possibility of a French marriage became all-important. Shortly after, King James I died and Charles ascended the throne in 1625. He married the French princess Henrietta Maria by proxy in June and soon after met his first Parliament as king. Almost immediately, Charles I experienced problems with the House of Commons as his principal adviser, Buckingham, came under criticism and attack. He disbanded this Parliament but soon found that his need for funds required him to call a second Parliament in 1626, but the result was the same. Parliament, using opposition to the king's advisers as an excuse, was persistent in its unwillingness to cooperate with Charles. By 1628, the king's financial position, largely because of ill-advised interventions in Europe and ill-tempered assaults on Spain, was so bad that he tried a third time to work with Parliament, again in vain. For the first time in history, Parliament refused to grant the king the tariff income known as tonnage and poundage for life. Instead, Charles was given that crucial money on an annually renewable basis. Also in this year, Buckingham was assassinated, leaving the king with no adviser whose judgment he trusted completely. Combined with the ongoing disputes with the Commons, the loss of Buckingham caused the king again to disband Parliament, preferring instead to rule on his own. Thus began the eleven-year personal rule.

Between 1629 and 1640, Charles used a variety of measures to raise revenues without the aid of Parliament, including the sale of titles, the extending of ship money to inland counties, and the exercise of the crown's traditional control over forests and common lands. Such measures, taken without Parliament, created significant hostility in England, especially with the country gentry who were most affected. Also, Charles began to have difficulties in Scotland. He was crowned in Edinburgh in 1633, but in 1637 introduced the modified *Prayer Book* which was opposed by Scottish Presbyterians who banded together under the national Covenant to oppose the king's meddling in religious matters. Even before this, the authoritarian policies of Archbishop William Laud had embittered Anglo-Scots relations. Charles' response was to subdue Scotland, where he hoped to find a secure base from which to deal with his opponents in England. The Bishops Wars of 1639 and 1640, however, proved to be disasters for the king and left him with a Scottish army on English soil with which he had to come to terms. To meet these terms, Charles was forced to call Parliament, but old animosities combined with new grievances to create hostility. Charles disbanded the "Short Parliament," now looking more and more to his chief adviser Thomas Wentworth, Lord Strafford, whose Irish army offered him alternatives. But during the Long Parliament that followed, Wentworth was accused of plotting to bring that army to England, tried for treason, and executed—with the king's consent—for his crimes. Charles had lost his best counselor, and he suffered a guilt that made him see the events of the English Civil War that followed as the result of his abandoning his most able adviser and devoted servant.

The war that followed saw early victories for the king and an uprising of popular support despite dissension in the ranks over the influence of Charles' nephew, Prince Rupert. However, as the war continued, the wealth of London which he had abandoned, the zeal of his adversaries—including the Scots—and the inability to resolve matters in Ireland and free his army there to come to England combined to turn the tide against Charles. In 1645, Parliament reorganized its forces as the New Model Army under the command of Thomas, Lord Fairfax, who was supported by the brash but capable Oliver Cromwell, whose ability won battles at Marston Moor and Naseby. After Rupert lost Bristol, the last Royalist harbor that could land a force from Ireland, Charles fled north and in 1646 delivered himself into the hands of the Scots at Newcastle. The negotiations that followed were difficult and even included an escape attempt by the king—but led to the Scots turning the king over to the English army in 1648. Charles was tried for treason in 1649, at which time he pressed his points with uncanny ability. He was, nevertheless, condemned and executed in front of Whitehall on January 30.

CHARLES I AS A GREAT LEADER

In her excellent biography of Charles Stuart, Pauline Gregg titles the chapter dealing with the period immediately after the king disbanded his third Parliament, "Peace." She has not used a misnomer, for in many respects almost the entire period of Charles' personal rule, certainly until difficulty with the Scots began, was characterized by calm, albeit a foreboding one. Without Parliament providing funds, the kind was required to limit expenditures. He therefore altered his foreign policy to accommodate his budget. He halted his efforts to punish Spain for his lingering resentment over the failed marriage embassy years earlier. He also came to terms with the French, not so much because of his wife's desire to do so as because he could ill afford continuing conflict. Most telling, Charles had given up his efforts to intervene on his sister's behalf in the ongoing struggles in the Palatinate (Elizabeth's husband, Frederick, had been the original initiator of the Thirty Years' War) and thus his father's image of England as the primary Protestant power in European affairs. Charles simply could not afford to continue foreign policy as he and Buckingham had envisioned it, but the resulting peace allowed the king to turn his attention to more domestic matters.

Foremost among his new concerns was making his court a center of culture. Charles had long been interested in acquiring art and toward that end now brought Rubens to London and commissioned work from him as well as from court painter Van Dyke. He sponsored masques by Ben Jonson and Inigo Jones, who also designed buildings and improvements in existing structures. The Cavalier poets flourished at the court of Charles and Henrietta Maria, and the theater in London continued its success. In short, with the political difficulties that had been foremost in Charles' mind temporarily covered, his one significant achievement, that of creating a center of artistic energy, took shape.

To ignore Charles the politician here completely would be in many ways inappropriate, although on balance he failed miserably to lead England during this period. After his failed policy dealing with the Scots and calling Parliament back in 1640, Charles made several concessions that stripped him of his power base and allowed England to move toward a government balanced between Parliament and monarch. The Star Chamber and ecclesiastical courts were gone, advisers were presented to him from Parliament, and revenue measures established during the personal rule were retracted. When his authority over the church was challenged, as it had been by the Scots, and when Parliament sought control of the military, the period of cooperation ended. Charles was willing to give up neither, and thus began the Civil War. But for a few moments in history, he did attempt to work with Parliament, albeit with the belief that he would soon recover all he lost once his position had been secured.

CHARLES I THE TYRANT

At least in political terms, the period during Charles I's reign when he would have earned a reputation for tyranny was that between 1629 and 1640, when he attempted to rule without Parliament, that period to which historians refer as his personal rule. Ironically, Charles elected to rule without Parliament because in 1629, at his third Parliament, the Commons passed the Petition of Right, which challenged the traditional prerogatives of the crown and the king's exercise of those prerogatives. Charles quietly accepted Parliament's attack; he needed their support in his efforts to raise revenue, but when the next step was for the Commons to challenge the ecclesiastical order of the state and those who ruled it, the king acted. He disbanded Parliament and, feeling that he had been the "victim" of tyranny, responded in kind.

The term "personal rule" seems most appropriate to the type of "tyranny" Charles I practiced. After the loss of Buckingham and the break with Parliament, he took no close confidants, surrounding himself with advisers to work not so much on policy but rather implementation of the policies he desired. Most of these were policies for raising revenue. The most controversial of these measures was the imposition of ship money on inland communities. Traditionally, the levy of ship money—funds that were used to maintain the English fleet—had been limited to coastal areas that were most directly protected by naval power. The king argued in 1634, however, that the trade which benefited all England needed a strong fleet and thus extended this levy. That he did so created bad feelings with the country gentry; that he did so without consent of Parliament left Charles open to the charge of tyrannical rule. Much the same was said when he further increased crown revenues by enforcing long-neglected forest laws, demanded payment from those who had earned money by the sale of woodland products, and enclosed the common lands that gave livelihood to many of the nation's rural poor. The measures were unpopular, but that the king enacted them without Parliament's approval added significantly to his reputation as an authoritarian monarch who ruled beyond his proper scope.

Even had Charles I been able to avoid problems with economic measures, he faced another stern challenge to his authority, this regarding the church. The demand for religious reform was widespread and heartfelt in seventeenth-century England; yet the king and his principal architect of religious policy, Archbishop Laud, felt that order required conformity, specifically conformity to Laud's ecclesiastical policies concerning worship and the king's claim to head the church. Charles was unwilling to accept overt challenges to authority and saw such attacks as assaults on the political order of the realm. His response to vocal opponents was swift, certain, and often brutal. William Prynne, most noted for the attacks against the stage he published in *Histriomastix* (1633), was a particular object of the king's wrath. His claim that women who performed in plays were "notorious whores" was deemed an attack on the queen for her performances in masques. Prynne was, therefore, fined in 1634 by the Star Chamber, driven from Lincoln's Inn, and placed in the pillory at Westminster, where both ears were shorn. These public exhibitions preceded his life imprisonment. Interestingly, after supporting the Parliament during the war with his gift for words, Prynne later turned against the cause because of the abuses of the army and was then imprisoned by those whom he had supported against the king; from prison he attacked the trial of Charles I.

Prynne was only one of many whom Charles I persecuted; others included defenders of Puritanism, Henry Burton and John Bastwick, and the distinguished pamphleteer John Lilburne, who faced the Star Chamber in 1637 for his attacks on the bishops, for which he was publicly whipped and imprisoned. Released by Parliament but then captured during the war, Lilburne again fell victim to the king's wrath and was saved only by negotiation with Parliament. Like Prynne, with whom he often disagreed, Lilburne later fell victim to the fears of the army regime of Cromwell.

The fact that so many who opposed Charles before war broke out, and against whom he then retaliated, were later persecuted by Parliament and the army suggests that the times themselves contributed to the reputation Charles Stuart has assumed as a tyrannical leader. The times saw a significant transition in power and social temperament; by resisting change, and being willing to wage a war in an effort to assure long-term stability—even to die in that effort—Charles I was as much a victim of history as he was a victim of his own emotional and intellectual weaknesses.

SUGGESTIONS FOR ADDITIONAL READING

Brookes, Joshua. *A Vindication of Charles I.* London: Hurst and Blackett, 1934.

Donald, Peter. *An Uncounselled King: Charles I and the Scottish Trouble, 1637–1641.* Cambridge: Cambridge University Press, 1990.

Gregg, Pauline. *King Charles I*. Berkeley: University of California Press, 1981.
Kenyon, J. P. *Stuart England*. London: Penguin, 1978.
Reeve, L. J. *Charles I and the Road to Personal Rule*. Cambridge: Cambridge University Press, 1989.
Wedgwood, C. V. *The Trial of Charles I*. London: Collins, 1964.

Gerald W. Morton

Charles V

1500–1558

Duke of Burgundy, 1506–1555
King of Spain, Charles I, 1516–1555
Holy Roman Emperor, 1519–1555

By the accident of birth, Charles of Habsburg inherited great and wealthy realms from each of his parents and grandparents. As king of Spain, he became the recipient of the gold and silver of Mexico and Peru. His realms almost surrounded France, his greatest rival. Indeed, at one point he held the king of France as a prisoner for ransom.

Nevertheless, by the age of fifty-five he saw all of his dreams reduced to dust and ashes, as the Protestant religious revolt threatened the unity of his beloved church. He saw the Moslem Turk advance to the gates of Vienna, as Turkish ships sailed boldly in the western Mediterranean, with the collusion of Catholic France. Indeed, Charles was forced to make the pope a prisoner when the papacy became too friendly to France.

How effective was Charles as a great leader? How effective was he as a tyrant?

BIOGRAPHICAL BACKGROUND

The fifteenth century was ending as Charles of Burgundy was born on February 24, 1500, in Ghent. His mother was Joanna the Mad, daughter of King Ferdinand of Aragon and Queen Isabella of Castile. His father was Philip the Handsome, Duke of Burgundy (contemporary Belgium) and the Netherlands, son of the Habsburg Holy Roman emperor, Maximilian I. Charles was the second of six children, and the oldest son. At birth he was modestly titled count of Luxemburg.

But his family set his destiny. In 1504 Queen Isabella died, leaving Joanna next in succession, and Charles the male heir to the throne. In 1506, when Philip the Handsome died, Charles inherited the Habsburg holdings in the Netherlands, Burgundy, Austria, and Italy, becoming the next Habsburg candidate for the throne of the Holy Roman Empire (the German states of Central Europe). In 1506, Charles was proclaimed Duke of Burgundy. In 1516 King Ferdinand died, and the Spanish *Cortes* (the assembly of notables) proclaimed the boy Charles I, the first Habsburg King of Spain. Since his mother, Joanna the Mad, still lived, she was co-ruler.

He had barely begun to make contacts in Spain when Maximilian I died, and through persuasion and bribes, he won election in 1519 as Charles V, Holy Roman Emperor. Thus, in the short space of three years, the young man obtained power over the greater part of Western Europe and the lands of New Spain in the western hemisphere. His youthful sense of self-importance was evident in his choice of titles: "King of Rome, future emperor, always Augustus, King of Spain, Sicily, Jerusalem, the Balearic Islands, the Canary and Indian Islands as well as the mainland on that side of the ocean, Archduke of Austria, Duke of Burgundy, Brabant, Steier, Carinthia, Carniola, Luxemburg, Limburg, Athens and Neopatria, Count of Habsburg, Flanders, Tirol, Viscount of Burgundy, Hennegau, Rousillon, Baron in Alsace, Prince in Swabia, Lord in Asia and Africa."

Charles had been carefully groomed for his role. When his insane mother was confined in Spain in 1506, Charles remained in Flanders in the care of his very capable aunt, Margaret of Burgundy. He studied Spanish and French as well as Flemish. His tutor, a Catholic deacon who later became Pope Adrian VI (1522–1523), imbued him with the passionate Catholic faith that was the hallmark of his reign. Charles tenaciously overcame childhood illnesses to excel in athletics, tourneys, and shooting. Margaret's chancellor, William de Croy, rigorously trained him in courtly politics, ritual, and diplomacy, underscoring the strategic importance of dynasty by arranging his successive engagements with seven hopeful young women. Charles himself chose Princess Isabella of Portugal, whom he married in 1526. The couple had seven children, only three of whom survived childhood, before Isabella died in childbirth in 1539.

As King and Emperor, Charles V confronted important leaders of the sixteenth century. His contemporaries included Henry VIII, King of England (reigned 1509–1547), whose scorned first wife, Catherine of Aragon, was Charles' aunt; Martin Luther (1483–1546), whom Charles denounced and outlawed at the imperial Diet of Worms for his religious pronouncements, setting off the Reformation struggles of Germany; and Suleiman I the Magnificent, sultan of the Ottoman Empire (1520–1566), who defeated the Hungarians at the Battle of Bohács in 1526 and marched on to besiege the Austrian capital of Vienna in 1529. Lesser known but more frustrating was the opportunistic King of France, Francis I (1515–1547), at war with either Charles V or Henry VIII throughout his reign.

Although the Spanish *Cortes* expected Charles to reside in Spain, his far-flung imperial duties kept him almost constantly on the move. The Protestant Reformation in Germany troubled him greatly. After the Knights' War (1522), he made his younger brother, Ferdinand of Austria, regent and heir of his German possessions, hoping that Ferdinand could gain support from the Catholic southern princes. But the Peasants' War (1524–1525) in south Germany indicated that the heresy had spread to all levels of society. In 1526 the Protestant princes in the north formed the League of Torgau.

With Charles preoccupied with Germany, Francis I of France fought from 1521 to 1529 to gain the northeastern province of Navarre and parts of Habsburg Italy. Captured in 1525, he agreed in the Treaty of Madrid (1525) to abandon his claims to Italy and cede French Burgundy to Spain. But on his return home, Francis I broke his word and resumed his attacks until, at the Treaty of Cambrai (1529), he relinquished his claims to Naples in exchange for the return of Burgundy.

Meanwhile, Suleiman the Magnificent also began a campaign into Europe by capturing Belgrade in 1521. Turkish assaults continued, defeating Hungary in 1526, and pressing against the gates of the Austrian capital of Vienna by September 1529. Although forced to retreat, Suleiman continued his war with the empire until 1532, when he made peace with Ferdinand of Austria.

Because of all these problems, Charles had to wait until 1530 for his imperial coronation. He traveled to the Italian city of Bologna for the honor. He was the last of the Holy Roman emperors to be crowned by the pope. From there he went to Augsburg, Germany, to preside over the imperial diet at which the Protestant spokesman, Melanchthon, outlined the tenets of the Lutherans in the Augsburg Confession. The diet issued a decree forbidding all deviations from the Catholic faith, including now the Anabaptist and Zwinglian sects as well as the Lutherans. The Protestants responded by forming the Schmalkaldic League, a defensive alliance of princes and cities to resist the imperial forces. But a renewed Turkish threat led to temporary truce in 1532, and even Protestants joined the army of 80,000 with which the emperor himself forced the Turks to retreat.

In 1535 Charles V attacked the Turkish forces in Tunis with the Spanish fleet under the command of *Andria Doria.* After Ferdinand and Isabella had conquered the last Muslim state in Spain in 1492, Spain dominated the Moslems in North Africa, forcing them to pay tribute. Charles V continued this crusade with a bloody three-day massacre at the city of Tunis.

When Charles V inherited Milan in 1535, Francis I renewed his war with Spain. Charles retaliated by invading Provence in southern France. Francis allied with Suleiman, who sent troops into Hungary and fleets to attack the Italian coast. The Treaty of Nice (1538) ended the war without resolving the issues. A fourth Franco-Spanish war (1542–1544) brought Henry VIII of England to Charles' aid against Francis and Suleiman. The Treaty of Crespy (1544) ended the conflict with an agreement that Francis' son would marry an imperial princess and receive Milan. With that Francis and Charles gave up their claims on each other's kingdoms.

Freed, at last, of foreign intervention, Charles turned his attention once again to the Reformation conflict. In 1545, at the Diet of Worms, he urged German support for the Council of Trent, convened by Pope Paul III to reform the Catholic Church. But Charles had decided to end the conflict by destroying the Protestant league. The Schmalkaldic War (1546–1547) was a disaster for the dissenters, yet ended any chance of Christian unity within the empire. The small concessions of Charles' compromising "Augsburg Interim" of 1548 brought them no closer to reconciliation. The Protestants were as opposed to imperial domination as they were to the Catholic Church and religion.

Yet, by 1548, Charles' position seemed stronger than ever. Luther died in 1546; Henry VIII and Francis I in 1547. The Council of Trent had begun the Catholic Counter Reformation. The emperor had a few years of respite, but in 1552 the Protestant princes again rebelled, supported by King Henry II, the new monarch of France. Charles was even forced to flee, but the war continued. Finally, both sides spent, they met in Augsburg, Germany, in February 1555. After negotiation for half a year, they agreed upon the principle *Cuius regio, eius religio*, "he who owns the land determines its religion," allowing Catholic and Lutheran states to co-exist in the empire.

The compromise protected and extended the cohesion of the Holy Roman Empire, but Charles was exhausted by the years of struggle. His mother, and co-ruler in Spain, had died in April, and Charles considered affairs of the dynasty. In October 1555 he announced his abdication and the division of the Habsburg holdings. Spain, America, Italy, Burgundy, and the Netherlands went to his son, who was crowned Philip II. His brother, Ferdinand, who succeeded to the German lands, was unanimously elected Holy Roman emperor. Charles retired to an estate in San Yuste, Spain, and died on September 21, 1558.

CHARLES V AS A GREAT LEADER

Charles V was the last of the great medieval dynastic rulers of Europe. In the early Renaissance, while Henry VIII and Francis I were consolidating authoritarian national monarchies out of formerly feudal states, Charles was virtually alone in looking back toward the model of the medieval European synthesis of church and state as the two interlocking cornerstones of society. Confronted with the Protestant Reformation, the expansionist threats of the Ottoman Turks, and the treacherous ambitions of the French monarchs, Charles nonetheless maintained the multinational Habsburg dynastic holdings and honor throughout the first half of the sixteenth century.

Raised in the tradition of chivalry, Charles V granted Martin Luther safe conduct and a full hearing at the Diet of Worms (1521). To the Pope's excommunication of Luther, Charles added the imperial ban, declaring him outlaw throughout the Holy Roman Empire. He deemed those princes who supported and sheltered Luther as treacherous traitors to their oaths as well as heretics, making their suppression doubly necessary.

Yet he was willing to consider means besides war to keep the Holy Roman Empire intact. He made his younger brother, Ferdinand, regent and heir in the Habsburg German holdings (1522) in order to provide more accessible leadership and opportunities for negotiation. This seemed all the more necessary after the Peasant War (1525–1526) boded continuing social unrest in the empire. His willingness to attempt peaceable solutions is reflected in his use of the imperial diet as a forum, at Speyer (1526) and Augsburg (1530), and he did not resort to arms until the Schmalkaldic War (1546–1547). The Peace of Augsburg (1555) was also a compromise designed to prevent further bloodshed in the empire.

Similarly, Charles' view of Christendom involved him in struggles outside his own realms. He was regarded as the savior of Europe for driving off Suleiman in 1529 and for leading the Holy League (Charles, Pope Clement VII, and Venice) against the Turks in 1538.

Charles had world ambitions. In 1519 he sent Ferdinand Magellan off on his voyage of exploration, the first circumnavigation of the globe. He ordered the consolidation of the conquest in Mexico (1521) and Peru (1534). In 1524 he reorganized the Council of the Indies, which administered New Spain, to add judicial and ecclesiastical functions. When it appeared that Spanish colonial landowners were mistreating the Indians, the crown issued the New Laws (1542–1543) to correct the worst of the abuses. The earliest American universities were established (1551) in Mexico City and Lima, Peru, during his reign.

When he realized that the Habsburg dominions were too diverse to be ruled by one man, he effected the division himself rather than have their cohesion destroyed by a foreign power. In 1555 he also arranged a dynastic marriage of his son, Philip II, to Mary Tudor of England (reigned 1553–1558).

Despite the turmoil of the era, Charles V reigned over the beginning of the golden age of Spanish culture. There were some exceptional Spanish historians, including Bartolomé de las Casas (d. 1566), who provided so much information about New Spain. Religion was an important element. Spaniard Ignatius de Loyola founded the Society of Jesus (Jesuits) in 1534, and Santa Teresa de Jesús wrote her mystical autobiography and reorganized the Carmelite convents.

CHARLES V THE TYRANT

Charles V derived his title from the Holy Roman Empire, but squeezed the funds to maintain it from Spain, where he was the first Habsburg and first king to unite the country. The Spaniards preferred his brother, Ferdinand, raised in Spain, but the laws of primogeniture made Charles heir to the thrones of Aragon and Castile. Surrounded by Flemish courtiers who were contemptuous of Spain, Charles pressed the Spanish for funds to support his candidacy for the imperial throne. He so offended Spanish tradition and practice that major cities, like Toledo, rebelled against him. He suppressed the *Comuneros* Uprising of 1520–1521 ruthlessly and ordered its leaders executed. He thus dealt a heavy blow to the political ambitions of Spain's bourgeoisie.

Other severe measures suggest that Charles would not brook resistance from any quarter. When the Treaty of Madrid (1526) gave him considerable land and power in Italy, Francis I, Pope Clement VII, Venice, and Florence formed a coalition to oppose him. Charles defeated them and, despite his deep religious convictions, ordered his mercenaries to sack Rome. Clement VII was captured and humiliated and the city devastated. Charles' similar treatment of Tunis in 1535 destroyed that Muslim city and drove Suleiman the Magnificent into an alliance with Francis I of France.

Charles was only slightly more restrained in dealing with the Protestant states of the Holy Roman Empire. His intense personal Catholicism and his rigidity made it impossible for him to compromise with Lutheranism and the princes who supported it. Although the Protestants showed their loyalty to the empire by fighting against the Turks in 1532, Charles was determined to crush their religious and political rebellion. When the Anabaptists took over Münster, his armies routed them, tortured the ringleaders, and suspended them in cages from the marketplace church. In 1546, when France and Turkey were quiet, he attacked the Schmalkaldic League and led the imperial forces into Saxony, where his armies fought pitilessly.

Charles' medieval conception of state and his rigid mentality made him increasingly out of place among the rulers in Renaissance Europe. He created his own opposition. In the end he had to compromise on the religion of the empire and divide the Habsburg holdings. His efforts to build a unified Catholic Europe had failed, and had bankrupted both Spain and Germany in the process.

SUGGESTIONS FOR ADDITIONAL READING

Alvarez, Manuel Fernández. *Charles V: Elected Emperor and Hereditary Ruler.* London: Thames and Hudson, 1975.

Bradford, William, ed. *Correspondence of the Emperor Charles V. and His Ambassadors at the Courts of England and France.* London: Richard Bently, 1850.

Brandi, Karl. *The Emperor Charles V: The Growth and Destiny of a Man and a World Empire.* Trans. C. V. Wedgwood. Atlantic Highlands, N.Y.: Humanities Press, 1968.

Elliot, John H. *Imperial Spain 1469–1716.* New York: New American Library, 1964.

Elton, G. R. *Reformation Europe 1517–1559.* London: Collins, 1963.

Holborn, Hajo. *A History of Modern Germany*, Vol. I, *The Reformation.* New York: Alfred A. Knopf, 1959.
Robertson, William. *The History of the Reign of the Emperor Charles the Fifth.* Boston: Phillips, Sampson, & Company, 1857.
Rosenthal, Earl E. *The Palace of Charles V in Granada.* Princeton, N.J.: Princeton University Press, 1985.
Seaver, Henry Latimer. *The Great Revolt in Castile: A Study of the Comunero Movement of 1520–1521.* New York: Octagon Books, 1966.

Eleanor L. Turk

Oliver Cromwell

1599–1658

Dominant Officer in the Army Council, 1646–1653
Lord Protector of the Commonwealth, 1653–1658

Few historic figures are as enigmatic as Cromwell. There is every likelihood that he was entirely sincere when he spoke in theological terms to justify political actions that can only be described as amoral service to the state. Cromwell fought a civil war in the name of the rights of Englishmen. He killed a king whom he described as a tyrant. Nevertheless, once triumphant, Oliver Cromwell created a dictatorship more complete than any of England's kings had ever designed.

It is little wonder that after the monarchy was restored by Charles II, Thomas Hobbes in his classic work *The Leviathan* denied the right of subjects to rebel against effective authority. He argued that the only duty of society is to provide for its own survival; that the rights of individuals do not count; and that revolution is vain because it only begets new tyranny.

BIOGRAPHICAL BACKGROUND

This first and only English republican dictator was born to a family of the lesser gentry at Huntingdon, England, on April 25, 1599. Oliver Cromwell's father, Robert, and his mother, Elizabeth (née Steward), sent their son to a free grammar school in Huntingdon. In 1616, however, Oliver was admitted to Sydney Sussex College of Cambridge University. There he obtained a gentleman's education, though he never took a degree. More significantly, his days at Cambridge made him a devout Puritan at the same moment when King James I was threatening to expel such extremist troublemakers from England. Indeed, later, young Cromwell very nearly decided to go to Massachusetts, or to the Calvinist Dutch Reformed Netherlands, where so many Puritans took refuge.

At the death of his father, he was summoned home to supervise the family's property, and though briefly a student of law at the Inns of Court in London, he seemed destined to live the quiet life of a country gentleman, far from significant theological disputation.

In 1620 he married Elizabeth Bourchier, the daughter of a London businessman. The marriage ultimately produced eight children. Cromwell first emerged from the obscurity of his life at Huntingdon when he was elected to Parliament in 1628. He immediately made a name for himself by resisting King Charles I. Although all the English sovereigns since Edward I had received the income of Tunnage and Poundage, or Tariff and Customs due for life, the parliaments of Charles I had granted those essential royal moneys in increments extended one year at a time. Worse than that from the king's viewpoint, parliament used the annual battle over tunnage and poundage to coerce the king into surrendering established royal prerogative rights. Faced with the loss of what he regarded as his rightful income unless he surrendered his essential powers, the king had recourse to extraordinary means of raising money.

Edward I had practiced Distraint of Knighthood in the thirteenth century, selling that once honored chivalric title in exchange for fees paid to the royal treasury. Cromwell, however, declined to pay for knighthood, and acting thus in direct defiance of the king, found himself paying a substantial fine instead.

From 1629 to 1640, the king attempted to govern his disaffected realm without Parliament. During the Personal Rule, Cromwell was forced into retirement in the country. However, at the death of his uncle, Sir Thomas Steward, he inherited a sizable estate that made him independently wealthy by 1638. For the rest of his life he was free to pursue his goals unencumbered by financial restraint.

He was elected to the Long Parliament in 1640. That body gained its name because for twenty years it was never dissolved and was still officially in office when, in 1660, King Charles II performed one of his first acts as king by dissolving it and calling new elections. In 1640–1641 Cromwell made himself particularly obnoxious to Charles I by urging a statute that would have required annual meetings of Parliament, and another that would have "purified" the Anglican Church of Roman Catholic influence by eliminating the offices of bishop and archbishop. It is scarcely surprising that when the king entered the House of Commons in January 1642, supported by an armed guard, Cromwell was one of the five men whom he tried, unsuccessfully, to arrest. However, as the king remarked, "the birds have flown." That act precipitated the Civil War. The king withdrew from London, and summoned loyal members of Parliament to join him. Most of the Lords and about one-third of the Commons did so. Those who remained at London became recreant rebels.

Cromwell had had no previous military experience. However, like most of the country gentry, he was a skilled horseman and swordsman. Quite naturally, he took a major role in training a cavalry regiment known as the "Ironsides." In addition to inculcating a code of iron discipline in the ranks of his troopers, he punished blasphemy, immorality, and political dissent as offenses worthy of court-martial. This army of saints rode into battle singing hymns, convinced that they were doing the Lord's work.

By 1645 he was virtually in command of what Parliament called the New Model Army. From 1644 to 1646 the discipline and greater resources of the parliamentary army at last began to tell. Cromwell's victories at Marston Moor and Naseby, his seizure of Oxford, and the king's retreat to Scotland gave Cromwell the leeway to return to the political sphere, dominating Parliament as well as the army. When, in 1647, the king was surrendered to the English by the Scots, there began that awkward minuet in which the king, Parliament, the army, the Scots, and the French each conducted very complex negotiations in which each betrayed the others with aplomb.

By 1648, Cromwell was able to write that although no one could harm the sacred person of the king, if the king persisted in resisting the religious and political concessions demanded of him, it could be taken to mean that his condemnation was divinely predestined.

In November 1648 Colonel Thomas Pride stationed his troops at the entrances to Parliament and carefully excluded 140 Presbyterian members, thought to be loyal to the king, from entering the building. Pride's Purge created a Rump Parliament, dependably subservient to the army. The Rump then formally brought forward charges that the king had been guilty of treason. The fact that the king's secret correspondence with the French had been intercepted made a strong case for the king's guilt.

Cromwell took the lead in composing a bank of judges whose verdict was predetermined. The trial took only three days, during which the king declined to speak on his own behalf, except to deny the jurisdiction of the court to try a king who is "the source and fount of all power." Cromwell took an active role in coercing individual judges to make themselves parties to regicide. On January 30, 1649, Charles I was beheaded on a scaffold erected in front of Whitehall Palace.

From 1649 to 1653 Cromwell was merely the first among equals in a Council composed of military men theoretically subject to that Rump Parliament which they themselves had created. They were actually the architects of a republican military dictatorship. In 1653, however, Cromwell sent the Rump Parliament home, and on December 16 was named Lord Protector of the Commonwealth. Although he was ultimately named hereditary Protector, he declined the title of king that he might have had. Haunted by bad health, he died on September 3, 1658. He was briefly succeeded by his son, Richard.

Upon the return of Charles II, at the Restoration of 1660, Cromwell's body was disinterred and beheaded, as a punishment for regicide.

OLIVER CROMWELL AS A GREAT LEADER

From 1649 to 1653, Cromwell was responsible for the exercise of executive power in the British Isles. He was, however, slightly inhibited by the Rump Parliament, which dared, occasionally, to dissent. From 1653 until his death in 1658, as Lord Protector of the Commonwealth, he so overawed his old military comrades on the Council that he was a dictator from whose decisions no dissent was possible. Certainly Cromwell brought a final end to those remnants of feudalism and manorialism which had survived the Middle Ages and Renaissance.

Notwithstanding his reputation as a sour bigot, Cromwell believed in religious toleration, in principle. The important qualification to his tolerance is that he judged all other religions by their willingness to concede primacy to that specific form of Calvinist Protestantism known as Anglican Puritanism. Thus he favored suppression of the Levelers because their messianic emphasis on the immediate advent of Christ in judgment seemed presumptuous, to him. He resented also their social egalitarian views, particularly because he was deeply committed to a class-oriented society.

He opposed Scots Presbyterians in spite of their close affinity to Puritanism because they were as unwilling to yield primacy as he was. He was bitterly hostile to Irish Roman Catholicism because he viewed the Irish as more of a military threat than a theological rival. At the same time, he tended to be hostile to the Netherlands although the Dutch Reformed Church was very close in principle to Puritanism. Though Cromwell would not have verbalized it, he undoubtedly regarded the Netherlands as a naval and commercial rival, hence a threat to be checked.

Thus, in spite of his brutal hostility to Irish Catholics, whom he consistently called idolaters, he was perfectly prepared, as occasion offered, to work with Catholic Spain against France or Catholic France against Holland. In coming to an understanding with France's Cardinal Mazarin, Cromwell jettisoned his support for French Huguenot Calvinist Protestants who were ideologically close to Puritanism. Conversely, Mazarin had no scruples about forcing the exiled King Charles II to take refuge in Holland, even though Charles II's mother was the sister of France's Louis XIII.

Seen from the distance, it is clear that Cromwell chose his friends with a view to advancing what he regarded as England's permanent interests, which formed a continuum whether a Stuart king or a Puritan Lord Protector ruled at Whitehall.

In 1653 he received Rabbi Menassah Ben-Israel at London to discuss the admission of Jews to the British Isles. No Jews had lived in England legally since Edward I's edict of expulsion of 1290. Cromwell was prepared to avert his eyes if Jews returned to England, allowing them to worship openly but discreetly. He gave Rabbi Ben-Israel no assurances of permanent refuge in England, but he was sufficiently welcoming that in 1654, a small congregation of Dutch Jews founded the first synagogue in London since 1290. Fundamentally, Cromwell saw no threat to Puritanism in a Jewish restoration. He may have even hoped that the arrival of Dutch Jewish merchants would assist England in its rivalry with Holland for commercial supremacy. Typically, however, when asked why he tolerated Jewish residence, he took refuge in theological subterfuge, saying, "Christ will not come to give judgment until the Jews are scattered to the four corners of the earth."

Cromwell divided the British Isles into six military commands, pretty much bypassing civilian restraints on authority. In effect he imposed that very sort of martial law which the Parliament of 1628 had forced King Charles I to renounce in the Petition of Right.

OLIVER CROMWELL THE TYRANT

After the execution of King Charles I, Cromwell led an army into Ireland in 1649–1650 and utterly crushed that country. The English massacre of an Irish Catholic garrison at Drogheda, after they tried to surrender, and Irish resistance to the last man, at Wexford, defined a war in which no quarter was given. By 1650, for the first time, Ireland was entirely reduced to submission. Thousands of Irish soldiers were transported as slaves to the West Indian plantations. Perhaps the worst blow to Irish self-respect came when Cromwell appropriated Irish estates and replaced Catholic country gentry with English Protestant landlords who rarely visited their Irish properties, but regarded them only as sources of income. Breaking the tie of human sympathy between Irish peasant and landlord created problems that haunted Ireland until the twentieth century.

In 1650–1651 Cromwell defeated young King Charles II, struggling to seize his father's realm with Scottish support. After his impressive victories over the Scots, Cromwell treated the Kingdom of Scotland as a mere province of England, one of the six military commands subject to him.

Cromwell closed the theaters, forbade horse races, bull baiting, cock fighting, and other traditional forms of popular amusement. He was not so much concerned with the immorality associated with the theaters, or the cruelty to animals associated with blood sports, as he was preoccupied with the conviction that gambling, idleness, and frivolity are keys to damnation. Cromwell's suppression of the relatively innocent pleasures of the common folk make it easy to understand the absolute abandonment to immorality which marked the Restoration of 1660.

Cromwell's sober "Roundheads" smashed the magnificent stained-glass windows of innumerable churches, regarding them as relics of "papist" idolatry. Cromwell's attempt to police extravagance in dress, hair style, public behavior on Sundays, and free speech provide surface evidence of a tyrannical regime that destroyed the freedoms the Civil War had been fought to ensure.

SUGGESTIONS FOR ADDITIONAL READING

Ashley, Maurice. *The Greatness of Oliver Cromwell.* New York: Collier Books, 1962.

Capp, Bernard. *Cromwell's Navy.* Oxford: Oxford University Press, 1989.

Fraser, Antonia. *The Lord Protector.* New York: Knopf, 1973.

Hill, Christopher. *God's Englishman: Oliver Cromwell and the English Revolution.* London: Weidenfeld and Nicolson, 1970.

Howell, Roger, Jr. *Cromwell.* Boston: Little, Brown, 1977.

Morrill, John S., ed. *Oliver Cromwell and the English Revolution.* London: Longmans, 1990.

Roots, Ivan, ed. *Speeches of Oliver Cromwell.* London: Dent, 1989.

Arnold Blumberg

Charles de Gaulle (Général de Gaulle)

1890–1970

President of the French Fifth Republic, 1958–1969

Charles de Gaulle was involved in history from 1914 to 1969. Twice, in 1940 and 1958, he was the lone and crucial force in support of France. Both times the situation was so extreme as to suggest that a less willful and tyrannical personality would not have been effective, so that it becomes difficult to distinguish the leader from the tyrant. Furthermore, the knowledge and understanding of his extraordinary deeds of 1940–1944 provide him with the credentials that no other Frenchman possessed in his lifetime. With the passing of time, and his work mostly completed, his tyrannical side became a liability. Then he quickly resigned before he could be pressured to retire.

BIOGRAPHICAL BACKGROUND

Charles-André-Marie-Joseph de Gaulle, second son of Henri de Gaulle, a history professor, and Jeanne Maillot-Delannoy, a passionately patriotic and religious woman, was born in Lille, in northern France, on November 22, 1890. He entered the Military College of Saint-Cyr with first rank. When World War I broke out, he served as a lieutenant, then a captain, was wounded three times and made a prisoner, following which he escaped three times. After the war, he married Yvonne Vendroux, daughter of a wealthy industrial family, taught history at Saint-Cyr, lectured at the École de Guerre, and distinguished himself early by his views, which clashed head-on with conservative theories on military warfare. He held his first command post in the Rhineland, then was sent to Beirut.

Upon his return to France in 1930, he was attached to the Conseil Supérieur de la Défense Nationale, where he clashed more and more with the proponents of defensive strategy, led by the respected Marshall Pétain. In 1934 he published a book, *The Future Army*, a passionate plea for a more effective defense system, based on a permanent force of technically trained men, equipped with the latest weapons, including armored tanks, his own specialty, new at that time.

In 1933, Hitler seized power in Germany, and from then on a series of aggressions and annexations made war seem more and more inevitable, in spite of futile efforts to stop him on the part of France and England. In 1939, Germany attacked their ally, Poland, overrunning that country in two weeks. Very unprepared, France and Great Britain had to declare war to honor the alliance. In the spring of 1940, Germany launched a massive offensive on Norway, Holland, Belgium, and finally France, invading through the northern plains and making useless the Maginot line of fortification on the Rhine. De Gaulle, now a brigadier general, fought a losing battle with his tank unit, then was called to the post of undersecretary of war in the last government of the Third Republic, which retreated with the armies from Paris to Bordeaux. There Marshall Pétain was asked to form an emergency government, and on June 17 he announced that he had taken steps to surrender and seek an armistice, actually on German terms, in violation of some provisions of the alliance with Great Britain. The armistice took no account of remaining assets, like "vast overseas territories, guarded by large forces, and one of the principal navies of the world!," as de Gaulle would define them later.

Refusing to accept the defeat and the shame of the deal with the enemy, General de Gaulle flew to London and obtained from Winston Churchill use of the BBC to broadcast an appeal to the French, on June 18. By coincidence, on the same day, Churchill made his famous speech, "the finest hour," to the House of Commons. De Gaulle's appeal stated forcefully that France had lost a battle, but the war was not lost because "it is a world war and France is not alone." It invites all French officers, soldiers, engineers, and workers in England and elsewhere to join him in the fight for the future of the world, "for the flame of French resistance must never be extinguished, and it will not be extinguished."

This was the beginning of a four-year uphill fight in which he single-handedly "assumed the burden of France," spreading his message throughout the empire, assembling a sizable French force under Allied command and building the foundation of a postwar political system. This background was the base of his future power, and constituted the formidable credentials that in fact enabled him to dominate, directly or indirectly, French history from 1940 to 1969.

After the war, he was made head of a Provisional Government, but found himself unable and unwilling to deal with a divided and traumatized country, in a Fourth Republic that fostered division and instability. He resigned and started working on his memoirs, while France embarked on an uncertain course with mostly uncertain leaders, doing very well on the job of reconstruction, and very poorly on adapting to a new era, with colonies a thing of the past. The loss of Indochina in 1954, and the continuing Algerian war, so exacerbated existing differences that the nation was on the brink of civil war in 1958. The army was in open rebellion and ready for a coup in order to keep Algeria at all cost. At that point, de Gaulle's supporters rallied public opinion to call on the general, the only man who could save France again.

De Gaulle accepted this second call by stating he was available, providing there would be an orderly passing of power from M. René Coty, president of the dying Fourth Republic, a drafting of a new, American-type constitution, and a referendum to adopt it and himself as president. The process was completed in the fall of 1958, and thus de Gaulle found himself in a position of unprecedented strength and facing another giant task, that of making France fit into a new, dangerous world where she no longer was a leading force and yet wanted to retain her independence and identity. All of the measures he promoted in the ten years of his mandate were controversial to some degree, with one party or another, although none was rescinded after him. However, the strain of time, a massive students' and workers' upheaval in 1968, and an inconsequential referendum lost in 1969, made him feel he was no longer in touch. He quickly resigned, died in November of 1970 at his country home, and was buried in a simple military ceremony according to his wishes.

DE GAULLE AS A GREAT LEADER

In 1940, France's capital, Vichy, became another country, strange even to its own inhabitants. Everywhere, German uniforms reminded them that they no longer had control of their land. On everything official, the words "République Française" were replaced by "État Français." Basic liberties were suspended, and life became a routine of rules and regulations, rationing for food, clothing, fuel, and even paper, curfews, restrictions on travel, and controls by French and German police. The whole economy was working for the Nazi war machine, while, said the Vichy government, Germany was defending France against mortal enemies: communism, capitalism, and the Jews. New politicians appeared, some known as leaders of the right, others unfamiliar. Jews lived in fear, and their friends feared for their safety. Old Maréchal Pétain gave frequent talks, lecturing the French on their sins and promised better days under his slogan "Travail, Famille, Patrie."

The country settled down, grimly, for the ordeal of national survival, the hardest part of which was not the lack of material necessities, but the crushing collective lack of self that resulted from the military disaster and the collapse and enslavement of the state. However, the mood of France did not reflect that of the Vichy regime. For instance, a simple folk song like "En passant par la Lorraine" became immediately a substitute national anthem, because Lorraine is the disputed frontier province and the land of Joan of Arc. Because England continued the fight, William Shakespeare was immensely popular. The Resistance began organizing, with the support of the British, who used it for intelligence purposes, air-dropping supplies on deserted spots at night. The climate of resistance at first prevailed largely with the younger and more liberal set, but it always existed. Mounting Nazi atrocities, corresponding repressive measures from Vichy, and the general course of the war made collaboration a terrible and hideous thing, abhorred by most people.

Once the climate of occupied France is understood, it is not too difficult to see why de Gaulle was immediately recognized for the man of destiny he thought he was. Few people, in fact, heard his June 18 appeal, but somehow, the news of the words and their substance traveled like wildfire in the confusion of an initially fluid situation. The badge of Free France, the Cross of Lorraine, needed no explanation, and the name de Gaulle was magic: a general from Gaulle, the ancient Celtic land now called France! The distant romance, danger, and anguish of those years also explain the hold de Gaulle had on public opinion when he was asked to become president in 1958, the devotion of the men who had shared with him the adventure of Free France and the Resistance, and the fading of his popularity when new generations brought their preoccupations to the foreground.

In 1940, de Gaulle was facing a giant task. There was mutual recognition of greatness between him and Sir Winston Churchill, whom he called the great artist of a great history. But the British would have preferred a French contingent directly under their command. Some men came from France, by way of Spain and Portugal, some came in fishing vessels, but by and large, the bulk of the Free French were troops and ships that had been stationed in the empire. It is also the empire that gave de Gaulle his first legal recognition, when Félix Éboué, the black governor of Chad, declared allegiance to Free France in August 1940. Meanwhile, the British Cabinet having recognized de Gaulle as the leader of the Free French, he was able to obtain loans to finance his operation, and he set out on a course of crisscrossing the territories of the empire, rallying military and political support, repeating everywhere his message of hope and freedom.

France reentered the war in June 1942, when the British, fighting German General Rommel, "the Desert Fox," called on a Free French brigade to hold Bir Hakeim in Libya, which they did heroically. From then on, the Free French Forces, numbering fifteen divisions toward the end, participated in the war, especially in the bloody campaign of Italy and the liberation of France.

Thus de Gaulle returned in triumph and was made head of a Provisional Government that the United States recognized on July 11, 1944, after the Soviet Union had done so.

Undoubtedly the interior Resistance would have taken place without him, because it rose instantly in every subdued country of Europe. However, the strength and steadfastness of his message and his presence next to the British, and later the Americans, gave it great impetus and a sense of unity. The men and women of the Resistance were a very heterogeneous lot; patriots, communists, intellectuals, Catholics, Jewish refugees, and students, they numbered 200,000 by 1943. But it took another man, Jean Moulin, a former administrator for the fallen Republic, to give his life to coordinate all the underground efforts for ultimate linkage with the Allies. This mysterious, handsome, and self-sacrificing man was hunted by the Gestapo and finally caught and tortured to death under the infamous Klaus Barbie, but not before he had a meeting with de Gaulle, who was made aware of the complexities in occupied France, and sent him back as his official delegate.

In 1958 he received the powerful mandate of an 80 percent vote for himself and the new constitution, which features a strong executive, with checks and balances and is action-oriented to overcome the paralysis of the previous regime. The "De Gaulle constitution" remains a major accomplishment, along with the seldom mentioned independence of fifteen Black African colonies, which was negotiated amicably between 1958 and 1962. Relinquishing the empire, a source of pride in the past, and of salvation recently in war, was not easy, but in Algeria the situation was embittered by the closeness of France and the presence of one million French settlers born there and called *pieds-noirs*. What de Gaulle did here in the midst of controversy, violence, terrorist attempts on his life, and an aborted military putsch, is equivalent to turning a ship around in a storm. Perceiving that the sole modern solution was complete independence, and despite initial public opinion to the contrary, he entered into negotiations with the Arab leadership. They culminated in the Evian Agreements of 1962, followed by a referendum approving it in both France and Algeria. The *pieds-noirs*, who were compensated upon return to France, called him a traitor, but on the whole the French people were relieved after this masterful operation of "arm-twisting" rather than tyranny.

Having liberated France from the bondage of the past, President de Gaulle proceeded to make her, in his words, "espouse her century." This included building a nuclear capability in both industrial and military fields, and producing a matching line of intermediate-range bombers called *mirages*, which were sold around the world. Modernizing the economy to make it cost-efficient was not a small task but a necessity since France, having taken a lead already in the European Economic Community (Common Market), had to maintain her place right behind Germany. These endeavors, often taking place in a climate of French reluctance, and in the international nervousness of the Vietnam War years, were made possible by the strength of his personality, and the power of the elected Gaullist majority in the National Assembly. The fact that the next president, Georges Pompidou, was a Gaullist, the next one Valéry Giscard d'Estaing, a former cabinet member but not a Gaullist, and François Mitterrand, a Socialist, proves that Gaullism existed mostly in direct relationship to de

Gaulle, and to the drastic situations France was in during his times. However, since none of his major actions have been revoked, it seems that he was, once again, although less dramatically than before, of service to his country.

DE GAULLE THE TYRANT

During his presidency, de Gaulle and his tyrannical nature became the target of satirists, comedians, and cartoonists. This tall man, who was like a walking statue, frequently talked about himself in the third person and was so domineering that people automatically called him "mon général" rather than "monsieur le Président." He was hard on all who knew him, from the start. The one person who endured the most was probably Madame de Gaulle, who developed such an aversion for divorced men that her influence was blamed for several broken political careers.

However, there is a difference between saying, "De Gaulle is not of the right or the left, he is above!" and grabbing power by force, or running a police state, or ordering atrocities. First it must be remembered that he always operated in situations that were extreme as in 1940, or urgent as in the 1958 threat of civil war, or contrary like the conflicting interests with Great Britain and the United States. These conflicts were genuine. For instance, one big issue with the British Command was the fate of the French fleet, part of which was bombed and sunk by the R.A.F. in the North African port of Mers-El-Kebir in 1940, because of fear that it might fall to the Germans. Churchill experienced the full weight of a personality that was inflexible because the man, as he said, had so little. The differences with the United States were much worse. It seems that President Roosevelt and the State Department recognized the government at Vichy because it was useful to have an embassy reporting to Washington from Nazi-dominated territory. However, much damage was caused by the misperceptions and reports of the American ambassador, Rear Admiral William D. Leahy, whose 1950 book *I Was There* makes astonishing reading today. After Pearl Harbor, the United States became extremely sensitive about French Indochina, occupied by the Japanese (the fate of which had to be resolved after the war), the French islands of St. Pierre, and Miquelon near Newfoundland, in the submarine-infested North Atlantic, which were liberated peacefully from Vichy by the Free French, causing an uproar in Washington. President Roosevelt also wanted to impose on the Free French a leader of his own choosing, a General Giraud of small French credibility. France was excluded from the wartime conferences among Stalin, Roosevelt, and Churchill, and de Gaulle was not given full information about the Allied landing in Normandy. These frictions surely influenced his obstinate striving for national independence within interdependence: building a separate nuclear force, dismissing American bases on French soil (while remaining in the defensive NATO alliance), and protecting the economy against dangerous potential partners like the British with their huge Commonwealth countries.

On the homefront, it seems that everything he did was absolutely necessary—from severing all colonial bonds, a sort of radical surgery, to modernizing the country—but was mostly resented because of his haughty, uncompromising manner and because of the national temperament. "How do you propose to govern a country that has two hundred and forty-six varieties of cheeses?" De Gaulle most certainly made difficulties for his allies and partners, he certainly outstepped his bounds in the Québec incident of 1967, when he spoke and acted as if in a sovereign state. But he was also the lone voice of dissent in a Cold War world in which two giants, capable of total destruction, dictated the fate of a whole planet. He conceived of France as the center of a *Third Force* capable of balancing and checking the ambitions both of the United States and the USSR.

SUGGESTIONS FOR ADDITIONAL READING

Churchill, Winston S. *The War Speeches of Winston Churchill.* Boston: Houghton Mifflin Company, 1953.

Crawley, Aidan. *De Gaulle.* Indianapolis: Bobbs-Merril, 1969.

de Gaulle, Charles. *War Memoirs.* Vol. 1, *The Call to Honor.* New York: The Viking Press, 1955. Vol. 2, *Unity.* New York: Simon and Schuster, 1959. Vol. 3, *Salvation.* New York: Simon and Schuster, 1960.

Gavin, Catherine Irvine. *Liberated France.* New York: St. Martin's Press, 1955.

Lacouture, Jean. *De Gaulle: The Rebel 1890–1944.* New York: W. W. Norton, 1990. *The Ruler 1945–1970.* New York: W. W. Norton, 1990.

Macridis, Roy. *De Gaulle: Implacable Ally.* New York: Harper & Row, 1966.

Lucile Martineau

Elizabeth I (Elizabeth Tudor)

1533–1603

Queen of England, 1558–1603

There is no doubt that Elizabeth I was one of the great actresses of all times; a mistress of disguised motives and pretense. From the moment that she ascended the throne, she busied herself in finessing the major problems that faced her. At Christmas Mass in 1558, a little more than a month after inheriting the throne, she was still a practicing Roman Catholic, as she had been during her sister Mary's reign. However, she instructed the priest not to elevate the Host during the Mass, and walked out of the chapel when he did so anyhow. At the same moment, she was writing to the pope, assuring him of her unshakable loyalty to the Roman Church. Her royal titles included the honorific "Supreme Head of the Church," but she allowed "et cetera, et cetera" to be used in place of that title. Ultimately, she became the head of an *Ecclesia Anglicana* or English church which was Catholic in appearance but close to Lutheran in doctrine. All of this was accomplished by the passage through Parliament of a statute of thirty-nine articles, effecting a religious revolution without the queen having to admit that she fully understood the fine points of these theological changes.

She was perfectly aware that as the last Tudor she was expected to marry and beget heirs. She therefore spent almost thirty years pretending to intend marriage, keeping Catholics, Protestants, and even the Russian Orthodox tsar Ivan the Terrible of Russia, awaiting the acceptance of marriage offers. Only when her Protestant cousin, and heir apparent, James VI, King of Scotland, reached his twenty-first birthday in 1587 could she risk executing her prisoner, James's mother, Mary Queen of Scots, precipitating war with Spain. She could then end the "marriage game."

BIOGRAPHICAL BACKGROUND

Elizabeth Tudor, the only child of King Henry VIII and his second wife, Anne Boleyn, was born on September 7, 1533, at Greenwich Palace, near

[redacted]

London. Although she was declared heiress presumptive in March 1534, when Parliament passed an Act of Succession, it was presumed that her mother would shortly bear a male child who would displace her. Instead, Anne Boleyn suffered two miscarriages. When Elizabeth was two and a half years old, her parents' marriage was annulled and she was declared illegitimate. On May 19, 1536, Anne Boleyn was beheaded for treason, having been found guilty of adultery. King Henry married Jane Seymour the next day. On October 12, 1537, the long-awaited male heir was born and christened Edward. Ten days later, Queen Jane, Elizabeth's first stepmother, died. Henry VIII married his fourth wife, Anne of Cleves, on January 6, 1540, but six months later the union was annulled. That same month he married Catherine Howard, cousin of Anne Boleyn. On February 13, 1542, Queen Catherine was beheaded for treason after being convicted of adultery. On July 12, 1543, Henry VIII married his last wife, Catherine Parr. These events had little direct effect on Elizabeth, living far from court, ignored by her father and his entourage.

During her early years, Elizabeth's meager household barely supplied her daily needs. At times she lacked some common comforts which even a poor man's daughter might expect. Her solace during these bleak years was learning, at which she distinguished herself. Throughout her life she was very proud of her triumphs in the schoolroom and enjoyed demonstrating her erudition to all and sundry. Catherine Parr brought Elizabeth back to court, and for a few years was a mother to all three of her husband's children. Elizabeth and her younger stepbrother developed a genuine affection as they shared tutors and competed academically. With Elizabeth's stepsister, Mary, there was nothing but a cool civility.

On January 27, 1547, Henry VIII died, and in his will named Elizabeth his heiress after her brother, now Edward VI, and Mary. A month after her father's death, Elizabeth received her first serious marriage proposal, from Thomas Seymour, one of the brothers of Queen Jane, and Lord High Admiral of England. She refused, but when he wed Dowager Queen Catherine (the former Catherine Parr) later that year, Elizabeth accepted their offer to live with them. In 1548, Princess Elizabeth, now fifteen, set up her own household at Hatfield. Although Elizabeth was closely questioned a year later during the treason trial of Thomas Seymour about her benefactor's improper advances, she survived this tribulation with her status unimpaired. After this rather harrowing experience, her life was relatively quiet until her brother's death on July 6, 1553.

Lady Jane Grey, a great-niece of Henry VIII, was proclaimed queen on July 10, 1553, but within ten days the coup collapsed and Mary ascended the throne. Lady Jane Grey was executed for treason on February 12, 1554, having been implicated in the failed rebellion of Sir Thomas Wyatt. On March 18, Elizabeth was committed to the Tower of London under threat of similar charges, but nothing could be proved against her, and on May

19 she was transferred to Woodstock near Oxford, where she remained under house arrest until December. Her release from prison and subsequent restoration to favor were probably due to the intercession of Philip of Spain, whom Queen Mary had recently married. Elizabeth was allowed to return to court; relations with her sister did not improve, however, and her repeated requests to retire to Hatfield were finally granted in October 1555. There she lived quietly with her books, seemingly content to be far from the center of power, but she was kept informed of events by loyal friends like Sir William Cecil, later Lord Burghley. Queen Mary died on November 17, 1558, and Elizabeth ascended the throne, having survived parental and filial rejection, privation, numerous intrigues, and threats of death.

Crowned at Westminster Abbey on January 15, 1559, Elizabeth opened her first Parliament ten days later. Her realm was divided by religious strife that pitted neighbor against neighbor. The economy of England, which had been the envy of Europe in the reign of her grandfather, Henry VII, was in shambles. England was regarded by the rest of Europe as a second-class power. Elizabeth was determined to reverse the decline of her kingdom while securing her place among her fellow rulers. She succeeded in all her endeavors and left England stronger and wealthier than even Henry VII might have thought possible.

During long years of adversity, Elizabeth I had developed a keen understanding of men and women, and was wary of following any counsel save her own. Blessed with the rare gift of choosing subordinates who were both talented and loyal, she never shared her authority with anyone. The servants of the crown, either in Parliament or in the council chamber, served the queen's pleasure and not their own ambitions.

Elizabeth I was confronted with a number of problems at the beginning of her reign that might have daunted a lesser monarch; she accepted these challenges and sought solutions in ways modern political theorists might describe as pragmatic. In the chaotic world of the sixteenth century, hesitation could prove fatal to a timid ruler. Elizabeth I was neither timid nor hesitant.

Throughout her reign she was threatened by a number of plots, most involving attempts to place her Roman Catholic cousin, Mary Stuart, the Queen of Scotland, upon the English throne. On January 26, 1569, Elizabeth committed Mary to protective custody after the Scottish queen fled her own kingdom following the successful rebellion of her Protestant subjects. However, Mary of Scotland was no less dangerous to Elizabeth as a prisoner than she had been as a reigning monarch. After the official excommunication of Elizabeth by Pope Pius V on February 25, 1570, Roman Catholics were actively encouraged to assassinate her. Elizabeth retaliated with the full severity of the law. On June 2, 1572, the Duke of Norfolk was executed for his involvement in the Ridolfi Plot. Finally, in February

1587, Elizabeth ordered the execution of Mary Queen of Scots for her involvement in the Babington Plot.

The death of Queen Mary as well as Elizabeth's continued encouragement of his rebellious Dutch subjects provoked Philip II of Spain to attempt the conquest of England. On August 8, 1588, Elizabeth I had the pleasure of addressing English troops after the retreat of the Spanish Armada. This event started the long struggle between England and Spain, but the devotion of the English to their sovereign never wavered.

Elizabeth died on March 24, 1603, after a short illness and was succeeded by her cousin, James VI of Scotland, the only child of Mary Queen of Scots. On April 28, 1603, Elizabeth was buried in Westminster Abbey in the same crypt with her sister, Queen Mary.

ELIZABETH I AS A GREAT LEADER

When at the end of her life, Elizabeth was celebrated by poets and artists as if she were a divine personage, few took issue with such adoration. The queen had, during a reign of almost forty-five years, become the symbol of the nation, England's icon. She made no attempt to discourage this veneration and indeed encouraged it, not merely out of vanity, although that played a part in her policy, but from an understanding of the value of symbolism in creating national unity. She had inherited a realm torn by faction; she bequeathed a united one to a successor ignorant of the subtleties of statecraft.

With an economy on the verge of collapse, Elizabeth was forced to institute policies that, though initially unpopular, would prove ultimately successful. In 1560, on the recommendation of Sir Thomas Gresham, her chief adviser on economic matters, she ordered the complete recoinage of the entire silver circulating medium, thus removing debased coins that had encouraged bullion speculation and counterfeiting. Her father had repeatedly debased the coinage to combat inflation, and whether from ignorance or timidity, the advisers of Edward VI and Mary had failed to solve England's economic woes. Within two years Elizabeth's recoinage was complete, and England's money was once again respected at home and abroad. Coins of proper weight and fineness which pre-dated the debasement began to reappear, a sure sign that public confidence was growing. Throughout her long reign, Elizabeth I promoted monetary policies that stimulated trade and encouraged industry while moderating the effects of worldwide inflation, which was due in part to the influx of vast amounts of gold and silver from the new world.

While certainly religious, Elizabeth, unlike many of her contemporaries, was neither a zealot nor a bigot. She preferred a more comprehensive and less exclusive national church. Thus the Anglican faith that evolved during her reign was truly a bridge between the extremes of Catholicism and Calvinism. Her solution to the religious problems confronting England was sound, but not without its critics. Elizabeth attempted to incorporate differing ideas into her policies governing religion, but she also permitted a great deal of latitude to the individual Christian. If her successors had continued her tactics, the disastrous civil wars of the next century might have been avoided.

Difficulties were encountered by Elizabeth in the area of religion, such as the operation of the Jesuits in England, but the queen tended to approach them as political, not ecclesiastical matters. She had little patience with her subjects, be they nobleman or commoners, who sought to force their religious prejudices on their fellow Englishmen. Thus, while she reigned, there was relative religious peace in England.

Like her father, brother, and sister, Elizabeth was caught up in the rivalry between the royal houses of Valois and Habsburg. Unlike her predecessors she knew how to gain advantage from the international situation. Until 1568, when her cousin Mary sought a haven in England, Scotland posed problems for Elizabeth. The close ties between France and Scotland had troubled a number of English monarchs, but with Mary under house arrest Elizabeth could establish a rapport with the new Scottish rulers, who hated the French Catholics as much as Elizabeth distrusted them.

From 1567 until 1585 Elizabeth was allied with France. Both nations feared the growing power of Spain, and even the infamous massacre of thousands of Protestants on St. Bartholomew's Day, August 24, 1572, did not destroy the union. The outbreak of civil war in France in the late 1580s, however, offered Elizabeth the chance to terminate the alliance.

The real enemy of England was Philip II. Fortunately his interest in a marriage alliance with his former sister-in-law gave Elizabeth time to prepare for the ultimate conflict with a seemingly invincible Spain. Elizabeth secretly tried to undermine Philip's position by encouraging and supporting the Protestant rebels in the Netherlands. She only mildly reprimanded the English captains who preyed upon Spanish commerce. King Philip endured Elizabeth's duplicity until the Queen of Scots' execution in 1587. The following year Philip sent the Great Armada against Elizabeth, only to see his enormous fleet destroyed by a combination of English skill and inclement weather. The defeat of the Armada signaled the beginning of a war between England and Spain that lasted until 1604, and marked the beginning of Spain's decline as a world power and England's ascent to greatness.

Elizabeth survived most of her contemporaries, but when she died, on March 24, 1603, the national sense of loss was somewhat mitigated by the novelty of being ruled by a king after a half century. Once James I arrived in England, the fascination of his new subjects quickly dissipated, and as decade succeeded decade, Englishmen longed for the return of the golden age and the Virgin Queen who still dwelled in the memory of her people.

ELIZABETH THE TYRANT

To those whom she favored Elizabeth was a kind and sometimes generous mistress, but for those who displeased her she was a virago. Members of her household, and particularly her ladies-in-waiting, were subject to her whims and fits of temper. She dominated their personal lives with the same tyrannical control she exercised over their public appearances. Elizabeth treated men, particularly those who were young and handsome, like pets. She spoiled them, coddled them, and often punished them with equal pleasure. When forced by circumstances to do something she found distasteful, like the ordering of the execution of her Scottish cousin, Elizabeth often shifted the blame to hapless subordinates. The fact that she often "forgave" them was of small comfort.

Although she probably never intended to marry, Elizabeth kept several eligible royal and noble bachelors dangling for years. When pressed by Parliament to marry and produce an heir, the queen often replied with an outburst of her famous temper. There were certain topics that members might not discuss under pain of arrest, and her private life was one of them.

Elizabeth sought to manage Parliament using a blend of charm and Tudor coercion, but throughout the reign her royal power was eroded by both houses of the legislature as they sought to augment their role in the making of national policy. The deterioration of Tudor absolutism brought repeated disputes between the queen and her loyal Commons, but there was no open breach between them because both combatants were keenly aware of the need for cooperation to challenge successfully the power of Spain. Perhaps the most important change initiated by the alliance of monarch and legislature was the Poor Law of 1601, which determined England's social system until the nineteenth century. It was typical of Elizabeth that even in her social policy she sought to shift the burden from the national purse to that of the localities composing her realm.

Elizabeth's chief failure in the area of foreign policy was her handling of the Irish question, a problem complicated by the animosity between Catholics and Protestants. Repeated uses of force only aggravated the situation and prepared the way for the atrocities that characterized both sides in the next century.

SUGGESTIONS FOR ADDITIONAL READING

Bassnett, Susan. *Elizabeth I: A Feminist Perspective.* New York: St. Martin's Press, 1987.

Erickson, Carolly. *The First Elizabeth.* New York: Summit Books, 1983.

Haigh, Christopher. *Elizabeth I.* London: Longman, 1988.

Haigh, Christopher, ed. *The Reign of Elizabeth I.* Athens: University of Georgia Press, 1985.

Jenkins, Elizabeth. *Elizabeth the Great.* New York: Coward, McCann, 1959.

Maccaffrey, Wallace T. *Queen Elizabeth and the Making of Policy, 1572–1588.* Princeton, NJ: Princeton University Press, 1981.

Neale, John E. *Elizabeth I and Her Parliaments.* 2 vols. New York: St. Martin's Press, 1953–1958.

Ridley, Jasper G. *Elizabeth I; the Shrewdness of Virtue.* New York: Viking, 1988.

Rowse, A. L. *The Elizabethan Renaissance: The Cultural Achievement.* (Vol. 3, part 2 of *The Elizabethan Age.*) New York: Scribner, 1972.

Smith, Lacey Baldwin. *Elizabeth Tudor: Portrait of a Queen.* Boston: Little Brown, 1975.

Strong, Roy. *The City of Elizabeth; Elizabethan Portraiture and Pageantry.* London: Thames and Hudson, 1977.

Williams, Neville. *The Life and Times of Elizabeth I.* New York: Doubleday, 1972.

Clifton W. Potter, Jr.

Francisco Franco y Bahamonde

1892–1975

Spanish Chief of State, 1936–1975

The Spanish Civil War, 1936–1939, which brought General Franco to power, is considered by some historians as the opening round of World War II. While British and Americans tried to be neutral, leftist France and the Soviet Union aided the Republic, and the Axis Agreement was born in Spain with Adolf Hitler and Benito Mussolini helping Franco.

The civil war in Spain certainly weakened a politically divided France and helped lead to its defeat in 1940. Fear of communism in Britain and France bolstered appeasement, and the dictatorial anti-communist governments of the fascist powers enabled the Axis to take an early offensive in both the Spanish Civil War and the first phase of World War II.

From 1936 to 1943, Franco for the most part was considered a dictator in charge of a fascist state. Unlike his mentors Hitler and Mussolini, he survived World War II, and he ruled Spain as a reactionary and despotic international pariah from 1943 to 1953. But by 1953 he had openly repudiated his earlier fascist associations and had metamorphosed into an anti-communist ally of the United States. President Dwight Eisenhower in 1959 paid a courtesy call on Franco, signaling the Spanish dictator's rehabilitation in the democratic and capitalist worlds after more than twenty years of hostility. In 1959 the Spanish dictator opened up Spain's faltering, supposedly self-sufficient economy to NATO's capitalists, and economic boom ensued in Spain. Ironically, the new economic prosperity created new Spanish middle classes, which began to yearn for democracy and association with the European Economic Community (EC) even before Franco's death in 1975. In 1977, Spain held its first democratic elections since 1936, and today Franco is generally repudiated as a man of the past. Economically, since 1975 Spain has faced similar problems as the EC and the United States: a stagnating economy and ecological damage with chronic unemployment, despite the computer revolution and a boom in tourism and service industries.

BIOGRAPHICAL BACKGROUND

Francisco Franco y Bahamonde was born on December 4, 1892, son of a Spanish naval paymaster in El Ferrol, Galicia province on the Atlantic. After studying at Toledo's infantry academy, he was commissioned an army second lieutenant in July 1910.

The youthful officer fought from 1912 to 1917 in Spanish Morocco, where he won rapid promotion and was severely wounded in mid-1916. As a war hero, Franco was named second-in-command of the Spanish Legion in North Africa in 1920 and commander in 1923. The cool and calculating Franco loyally served the dictator, General Miguel Primo de Rivera; in Franco's old age he would become increasingly like Primo. After fighting with the Rifs (North African Moslem rebels) finally ended, in 1926 Franco returned to the mainland.

In January 1928, ambitious Brigadier General Franco, reputedly the youngest general in Europe since Napoleon, was appointed commander of Spain's new military academy at Zaragoza, in connection with which he observed maneuvers and visited military schools in Berlin and in Paris. From 1928 to 1930, Franco introduced textbook reforms to educate young Spanish officers in the major lessons of World War I. He was convinced, for example, that artillery would have more importance in future campaigns, while the infantry would have less.

Early in 1931 Franco presided over the court-martials of republican army officers who had tried unsuccessfully to overthrow the monarchy. But after Alfonso XIII fled in April 1931, the accommodating Franco served various republican ministers of war from 1931 until mid-1936, believing that a counterrevolution to return the monarchy was not worth the spilling of blood. Meanwhile, his younger brother, aviator Ramón, was considered a "red anarchist," while his brother-in-law Ramón Serrano Suñer, educated in law in fascist Italy and a member of the Catholic Confederación Española de Derechas Autónomas (CEDA) party, was elected a deputy in the conservative Cortes of October 1933.

Despite Franco's prudent silence, he was "exiled" by the first liberal republican government of 1931, first to Corunna and then to the Balearic Islands. Under the subsequent conservative government, Franco headed the repression of the Asturian miners' strike in October 1934, in which he employed Moroccan mercenary troops, the first time in centuries that Muslims had fought in Spain. The cautious Franco demanded supplies and military facilities for an army several times the size of the one he commanded. This resulted from his long experience of campaigning under primitive African conditions, and foretold the cautious strategy that characterized him during the Spanish Civil War. In May 1935 he became chief of staff for the CEDA minister of war, José Gil Robles. Their major ambition was to purge the army hierarchy of leftist sympathizers.

After the leftist Popular Front victory in the elections of February 1936, the new liberal minister of war "exiled" Franco to the Canary Islands. Although other army officers had talked about a coup d'état against left-wing coalition governments since May 1931, Franco avoided involvement. He considered joining General José Sanjurjo's conspiracy in August 1932, but rejected the notion after discovering that Sanjurjo was planning poorly. Immediately after the February 1936 elections, Franco toyed with the idea of seeking a seat in the Cortes as a political Catholic, but chief of the Falange José Antonio Primo de Rivera, son of the 1920s dictator, and Gil Robles vetoed the bid.

Following the Popular Front elections, generals Emilio Mola and Sanjurjo began secret talks with all elements of the Spanish conservatives. Obviously, this included the church hierarchy, Catholic political leaders, and Spain's own version of Fascists, the Falange. Leaving no stone unturned, Mola and Sanjurjo even consulted with the rival monarchist camps. These were the Carlists, who were loyal to a monarchial pretender descended in a direct male line of succession, from Louis XIV of France's grandson, the first Bourbon King of Spain. Their rivals, the Alfonsists, accepted royal claimants descended from King Alfonso XIII, who sprang from a female branch of the Bourbon line. While all of these elements were becoming involved in a rightist rebellion, the shrewd Franco, aware of these plots against the government, held back from making any commitment.

In the end, Franco decided to join the July 1936 conspiracy—but why? Was it from political opportunism, to protect the officer caste, from dislike of the anarchist threat to property or the atheist threat to the church? Did he fear Russian contacts with the Communist Party of Spain or imagined "Jewish-Masonic ties" to the liberals? All these factors probably influenced him, but Franco's motives remain obscure.

From the beginning Franco knew that anti-Soviet and anti-communist views were widely held in Western Europe. In his first speech after the rebellion, Franco appealed for order, for the unity of the Spanish nation, and charged that the spirit of revolution was being exploited by Soviet agents. At the time the charge was rhetorical. However, on October 10, when Franco learned that five Russian ships with fifty tanks were actually proceeding to Spain, the rebel general could claim, "I not only face a red Spain, but also Russia."

Public order and countering revolution were more basic to Franco's goals than promoting Catholicism, or opposing Stalinism and the Soviet Union. Despite his militant nationalism, General Franco needed foreign help to win.

For tactical reasons, General Franco benefited most from the foreign aid he requested of Hitler and Mussolini. As commander of the Army of Africa with German and Italian weapons and advisers, he began the reconquest of southern Spain at the beginning of August 1936. In late September, nine other insurgent generals agreed that Franco be named Generalissimo. He was also elevated to be chief of government on October 1, 1936.

While consolidating his supremacy, Franco put together a group of militarists, fascists, and reactionaries to rule Spain. After José Antonio Primo de Rivera was shot by Republicans in November 1936, the Generalissimo made the dead man into a martyred hero and "saint" of the fascist movement, which rapidly gained members throughout the Nationalist zone. Franco had the Carlist leader Manuel Fal Conde exiled; CEDA leader Gil Robles fled to Portugal in July 1936. A plane crash had killed General Sanjurjo at the outset of the coup. A possible rival for power, General Mola, chief conspirator of the July uprising, died in a mid-1937 airplane accident. By an April 19, 1937, decree, Franco forced the unification of the Carlists and the Falange into the one totalitarian party of Spain with himself proclaimed Caudillo. On January 30, 1938, he became chief of state, thus dashing the hopes of Spain's monarchists.

Franco gradually won his war by sheer military attrition. Stopped outside Madrid in December 1936, he turned his attention to the north, which fell to his armies in the summer of 1937. In April 1938 the Republic was split in two when Franco's Nationalist armies broke through to the Mediterranean. After fighting on the Ebro River, and a decisive campaign in Catalonia beginning before Christmas 1938, Franco closed the last frontier to France in February 1939. Isolated Madrid surrendered on March 31, 1939, ending the Spanish Civil War.

The Nazi dictator in Berlin and the fascist dictator in Rome sent the Legion Condor and the Corpo Truppe Volontarie to assist Franco's Nationalist movement beginning in late July 1936. Without the $569 million worth of arms and troops (16,850 Germans and 80,000 Italians) that eventually came from the Axis dictators, Franco could not have triumphed. Franco's victory, in part, resulted from a series of complex diplomatic maneuverings by the five great powers, in which Hitler came out on top in Europe in 1939.

Between April 1939 and the outbreak of World War II in September, Franco managed, in view of his war-torn economy and growing Anglo-German hostility, to hold both Britain and Germany at arm's length. Upon Britain's declaration of war on Germany in September 1939, Franco declared neutrality. After Hitler's invasion of the Soviet Union on June 22, 1941, Franco sent the Blue Division (with an eventual total of some 47,000 troops) to aid Hitler on the Eastern Front. The Anglo-American victory in Tunisia in 1943 silenced the most powerful pro-Axis voices in Spain, and Franco pledged neutrality again in October 1943.

Ostracized by the victorious Allies after August 1945, Franco consolidated his power domestically. As chief of state for thirty-nine years, from 1936 to his death in 1975, Franco's major political problem was to hide numerous inconsistent promises made to the Alfonsists, Carlists, Falange, and other Spanish rightist factions. A 1947 referendum effectively established Franco as regent for life for Alfonso's grandson Juan Carlos, now the king of Spain.

With the cooling of relations between the United States and the USSR, in 1953 Franco agreed to the establishment of American air and naval bases in Spain. Economic autarky, a fascist ideal, ended by 1959 when private investment from abroad, previously held back, was welcomed. Hesitantly, Spain moved toward economic union with Europe. Franco retained power for an additional sixteen years, until his death on November 20, 1975.

FRANCO AS A GREAT LEADER

Generalissimo Francisco Franco ruled Spain for nearly forty years; his was the longest "reign" since that of Philip II. He will always be considered greater in Spain than in Europe and America. As a military leader, Franco followed in a long Spanish tradition. Spanish capitalists are indebted to him for helping to repress labor unions and opposition parties during and after the civil war.

Franco's World War II foreign policy turned out to be successful, wavering between commitment to the Axis and a nonbelligerent, malevolent neutrality toward the Anglo-American allies. Perhaps Franco's sphinx-like stance at his first and only meeting with Hitler—at Hendaya in October 1940—was forced upon him by economic circumstances. Or perhaps it was the fruit of a narrow nationalist vision. Either way, the Caudillo proved to be a shrewder diplomat and economist than Mussolini, at least between 1936 and the end of World War II. By delaying, Franco effectively denied Hitler's impulse to take Gibraltar. Franco thus understood Europe's classic balance-of-power system.

Whether the Roman Catholic Church will regard Franco as a great man is more controversial. Popes Pius XI and Pius XII gave him their blessings because of their fear of communism. The new liberation theologians who came to prominence during the pontificate of John XXIII, which began in 1958, did not, however, regard Franco as a Christian hero. By 1975, when Franco died, a generation gap had developed within the Spanish church about Franco and his crusade of 1936–1939.

After the late 1950s, Franco surprised the world by bending with the winds of change. Behind the new course were ministers who belonged to the Opus Dei movement. These committed Catholic lay technocrats showed up among Franco's advisers particularly after 1957.

Franco's American connection ultimately led to the downfall of almost every idea that he had espoused as a counterrevolutionary. The fact that Eisenhower was a military man fooled Franco as much as Franco's brand of anti-communism had fooled the American president. On the one hand, the Generalissimo badly needed American military technology and money.

Yet the economic boom of U.S. capitalism spreading to the Common Market would mean that the expanding middle and lower middle classes in Spain would eventually Europeanize their cultural tastes. In 1966, censorship was greatly moderated, and a new organic law attempted to harmonize and update the regime's major legislative statutes. With Franco's death, his protégé Juan Carlos became a democratic king of Spain and parliamentary government was established.

FRANCO THE TYRANT

Franco's early politics were conservative to reactionary, but generally cautious. From his parents he learned to hate the Masons and the United States for "stealing" Cuba. The anarchist-Catholic confrontation during the Barcelona strike of 1909 convinced Franco that conservatives should always head the Spanish government. He claimed that Spaniards who belonged to an "international Masonic conspiracy" sought to weaken the fatherland. Like most other officers in neutral Spain during World War I, Franco sympathized with militaristic Germany rather than with Spain's historic enemies, liberal Great Britain and radical France. A cold-blooded survivor of the bloody war in North Africa, General Franco emerged as a military professional who elected to remain silent on political questions. Yet, by 1930, he could be considered well read for a Spanish officer of the time—having read Machiavelli's *Prince*, the life of Napoleon, and other works on history and politics in French.

During the Second Spanish Republic, Franco voted for no republican party and never shouted "Viva la Republica." For Franco, the Spanish "reds" included all the parties of the Popular Front—Communists, anarchists, "Spanish Marxists" (Leninists or Trotskyites), both the revolutionary and the reform socialists, plus the three liberal or republican parties, and the "separatists"—Basque and Catalan—whom he termed "anti-Spanish." Franco's conception of Spain was counterrevolutionary, and he longed for a revival of the glories Spain enjoyed during the Reformation and the Siglo del Oro. To Franco in 1936, a bigger "red" threat to the army came from Spanish socialist leader Francisco Largo Caballero than from the small Spanish Communist Party or from the Soviet Union. One of Franco's first acts of repression when he came to power was to outlaw pro-British and pro-French Masons. Franco saw Paris, where President Manuel Azana had been educated, as the center of Spain's problem of order, not Moscow. Paris had given birth to the French Revolution of 1789 and most recently to the Popular Front idea.

Psychologically, Franco's personality was secretive—more like Stalin than the flamboyant orators Hitler and Mussolini. But in imitation of Mussolini, giant photos of Franco and José Antonio Primo de Rivera were displayed with a slogan designed to deceive the illiterate: "One State! One Country! One Chief!"

Franco's thirty-year resistance to a restored monarchy began with advice given to him by Mussolini. The Duce called a dictatorship with a monarchy (such as ruled Italy when he was dictator from 1922 to 1943) "a two-headed monster."

The human cost of Franco's vindictive victory included 43,000 to 70,000 battle deaths of Nationalists and some 87,000 to 125,000 Republicans killed in combat. Cruel and unforgiving, Franco was also responsible for the deaths of an estimated 40,000 to 200,000 political prisoners through starvation, overwork, and disciplinary executions during and after the war. The repression did not slacken for some years. The exact number of informal class and ideological executions carried out in both zones from 1936 to 1939 remains one of the most controversial of historical problems. Although patience and discipline were Franco's hallmarks, he lacked tolerance. On several occasions even Italian fascists and German Nazis appealed on the basis of common sense to Franco to slow down the executions.

Religiously, Franco's attitude was subordinate to politics. In Morocco he permitted the heads of executed enemies to be paraded on bayonets. Franco did not allow the anti-Nazi papal encyclical "Mit Brennender Sorge" (May 1937) to be published in Spain. He blamed Jesuits and the Vatican for the failure of the Basques to support the rebel cause.

Franco's regime was hostile to the Jews—more on religious than on ethnic grounds. The fictitious *Protocols of the Elders of Zion* was published in Nationalist Spain, pleasing the Nazis. Franco, from 1936–1939, hated Jewish internationalists for backing the Republic. On the other hand, in 1942–1944, Franco, who was no racist, accepted into Spain thousands of Jewish refugees, particularly those of Sephardic Spanish descent.

Despite general caution during the European war, Franco made three rash foreign-policy decisions. The first was following Mussolini and abandoning neutrality for nonbelligerency on June 12, 1940—a public endorsement of the triumphs of Nazi Germany. The second was his invasion of the international city of Tangiers in North Africa, assuming that France was permanently defeated and that Britain would soon collapse. His third plunge into the world war came after Hitler's invasion of the Soviet Union in June 1941, when Franco agreed to send the Blue Division to the Eastern Front. Like Hitler, Franco thought it would be a short and victorious campaign, after which he would be in a better bargaining position for Mediterranean territorial concessions in French Africa. Spanish military participation in the east encouraged Hitler to take German pressure off the Pyrenees. Possibly Franco sought revenge on Stalin for the Soviet dictator's intervention in the civil war; Serrano's pro-fascist press certainly thirsted for revenge. Eventually 47,000 Spaniards fought in the Soviet Union, and about 4,500 of them died there.

It is part of the genius of Francisco Franco that he managed to make these relatively minor concessions to his German and Italian allies, while making truly significant gifts to the United States. If Franco had not been cooperative, the Anglo-American invasion of North Africa in 1942 could not have succeeded. It is only thus that we can understand the ease with which Franco survived World War II, the only Fascist dictator, to do so. Franco remains an enigmatic but vital twentieth-century leader.

SUGGESTIONS FOR ADDITIONAL READING

Coles, S. F. A. *Franco of Spain.* London: Spearman, 1955.

Crozier, Brian. *Franco.* Boston: Little, Brown, 1967.

Ellwood, Sheelagh. *Spanish Fascism in the Franco Era.* New York: St. Martin's, 1987.

Fusi, Juan Pablo. *Franco, a Biography.* New York: Harper & Row, 1987.

Hills, George. *Franco the Man and His Nation.* London: MacMillan, 1967.

Payne, Stanley G. *The Franco Regime 1936–1975.* Madison: University of Wisconsin Press, 1987.

Preston, Paul. "The Discreet Charm of a Dictator: How Franco's Personae Hid His Neurosis, Cruelty, and Corruption." *Times Literary Supplement* (5 March 1933): 13–14.

Trythall, John W. D. *El Caudillo: A Political Biography of Franco.* New York: McGraw-Hill, 1970.

Whealey, Robert H. "Francisco Franco, 1892–1975," in James A. Moncure, ed., *Research Guide to European Historical Biography, 1450–Present.* Washington, D.C.: Beacham Publishing Co., 1992.

———. "Franco," in James Cortada, ed., *Historical Dictionary of the Spanish Civil War.* Westport, Conn.: Greenwood Press, 1982.

Robert H. Whealey

Franz Joseph I

1830–1916

Emperor of Austria, 1848–1916
King of Hungary, 1867–1916

The historian István Deák has characterized Franz Joseph as "Europe's last *grand seigneur.*" In his personal qualities, he was "punctual, considerate, honest, reliable, unimaginative, boring, and, most important for his peoples, religiously and ethnically tolerant." He indulged his authoritarian instincts only during the first decade of his long reign; thereafter, while he remained an autocrat at heart, he tended to rely on compromise and moderation to preserve the Habsburg dynasty and his multinational empire. By the turn of the century, as the only monarch that most of his fifty million subjects had ever known, he became a symbol of Austria-Hungary, personifying the Dual Monarchy's positive aspects as well as its fatal weaknesses.

BIOGRAPHICAL BACKGROUND

Franz Joseph was born on the outskirts of Vienna at Schönbrunn, the summer palace of the Habsburg, on August 18, 1830. He was the eldest son of Archduke Franz Karl and Sophie of Bavaria; his father was the second son of Emperor Franz I. Franz Joseph's younger siblings included Ferdinand Maximilian, later Emperor Maximilian of Mexico (1832–1867).

In 1835, on the death of Franz I, the crown passed to Franz Joseph's mentally handicapped uncle Ferdinand and the governing power to a regency including Prince Clemens von Metternich. Ferdinand married but produced no heirs. Franz Karl, dull-witted and dominated by his strong-willed wife Sophie, was little more competent to rule. Thus, from an early age, Franz Joseph appeared destined for the throne. The revolutions of 1848 merely hastened his rise to power.

The initial uprising in Vienna forced Metternich to resign; thereafter, revolutions almost tore apart the multinational Austrian Empire. The Habsburg family twice had to flee the imperial capital and was at Olmütz (Olomouc) in Moravia in November 1848, when Prince Felix zu Schwarzenberg became minister-president and foreign minister. Recognizing that the monarchy could not survive with an incompetent monarch, Schwarzenberg persuaded Ferdinand to abdicate and Franz Joseph's father, Franz Karl, to renounce his right to the throne. On December 2, in a brief ceremony in the archbishop's palace at Olmütz, the eighteen-year-old Franz Joseph became emperor. If not for the crisis of revolution, his accession might have been delayed for decades: Ferdinand, sound in body if not mind, lived on until 1878.

Late in his reign, Franz Joseph remarked that Schwarzenberg had been the ablest of all his ministers, but the prince's term of office was brief: he died in 1852. Under his guidance Austria survived the revolutions intact and recovered its pre-1848 position in Germany and Italy. Throughout the 1850s Franz Joseph pursued an autocratic domestic policy, while in foreign affairs Austria's costly armed neutrality during the Crimean War offended Russia and left the empire dangerously isolated.

The 1850s were an eventful decade in the personal life of Franz Joseph. In 1853 he survived the only serious assassination attempt of his reign. The following year he married Elizabeth, his sixteen-year-old Bavarian first cousin. The union produced two daughters before the birth of Rudolf, their only son, in 1858; a third daughter was born later. The unhappy marriage was plagued in its early years by the bitter rivalry between Elizabeth and her mother-in-law, Sophie, and eventually by the fundamental personal incompatibility of the emperor and the empress.

Austria's defeat at the hands of France and Sardinia-Piedmont in the war of 1859 was traumatic for Franz Joseph. His youthful self-confidence deserted him, never to return. The bureaucracy he erected during the 1850s survived to provide the governmental backbone of the empire, a role it continued to play until 1918, but in the political realm Franz Joseph abandoned neo-absolutism in favor of representative government. In 1861 he established an elected Reichsrat, only to have a Hungarian boycott render it ineffective. After four years Franz Joseph suspended the new parliament and opened direct negotiations with Hungarian leaders to produce a new constitution.

With this procedure under way, Austria suffered its ultimate exclusion from German and Italian affairs. After being allied as recently as 1864 in a brief campaign against Denmark, Austria and Prussia went to war in 1866. Their contest for hegemony over Germany ended in a Prussian victory, after which Bismarck chose aggrandizement at the expense of the pro-Austrian German states rather than Austria herself; thus he paved the way for the unification of Germany without Austria, achieved in 1871, while leaving open the possibility of a future alliance between the German and Habsburg empires. Italy, Prussia's ally in 1866, received Venetia, Austria's last substantial Italian possession, after the war. Thus, for better or worse, the conflict resolved the German and Italian questions that had long dominated Austrian foreign and domestic policy. The following February, the Compromise of 1867 resolved the Hungarian question by transforming the Austrian Empire into the Dual Monarchy of Austria-Hungary.

After 1871 Franz Joseph accepted Austria's exclusion from Germany as an irreversible fact, and Habsburg foreign policy became receptive to Bismarck's overtures of friendship. The formal alliance of the two powers, concluded in 1879, lasted until the end of World War I. The two empires were also linked with Italy in the Triple Alliance of 1882–1915. Franz Joseph acquiesced in Austria-Hungary's role as junior partner of Germany in the international arena.

The eventful year of 1867 also brought the first of many tragedies in Franz Joseph's family life: his brother Maximilian, abandoned to his fate in Mexico by Emperor Napoleon III of France, was executed at Queretaro. In 1889 his son, Rudolf, committed suicide at Mayerling. Nine years later his wife, Elizabeth, was assassinated in Switzerland by an Italian anarchist. In 1914, at Sarajevo, the assassination of his nephew and heir, Franz Ferdinand, by a Serbian nationalist, Gavrilo Princip, touched off the chain of events that led to World War I.

On July 28, 1914, Franz Joseph signed Austria-Hungary's declaration of war, the first in almost half a century. After coming to power amid warfare and revolution, he had led Austria into wars in 1859, 1864, and 1866; thereafter his quest to preserve the dynasty and the empire took a peaceful course. Never optimistic about the prospects for victory, he consoled himself with the notion that Austria-Hungary at least would die a dignified death: "If we must perish, we should do so with honor." Franz Joseph died on November 21, 1916, at Schönbrunn, the same palace where he had been born eighty-six years earlier. In the uncertain hands of his great-nephew Karl, his dynasty and empire lasted another two years.

FRANZ JOSEPH THE TYRANT

Franz Joseph owed his early accession to the maneuvering of Schwarzenberg, but by the time of the prince's death the young emperor was already siding with his political opponents. At the end of 1851, influenced by court conservatives, he suspended Schwarzenberg's constitution of March 1849 and ushered in the era of neo-absolutism. After Schwarzenberg's death Franz Joseph served as his own minister-president, chairing meetings of the council of ministers. Under neo-absolutism the empire had a unitary administration for the only time in its history. Known as the "Bach system" after the interior minister, Alexander von Bach, its authoritarian approach and lack of political vision reflected the emperor's own instincts and weaknesses. Above all, centralization only worsened the nationality problem. By placing all groups on an equal footing—for example, treating the Croatians, who had remained loyal in 1848–1849, the same as the Hungarians and Italians—it was shortsighted to the point of stupidity.

Systematic tyranny ended with the abandonment of neo-absolutism following Austria's defeat in the war of 1859. Thereafter Franz Joseph suppressed his authoritarian instincts, but the policies he promoted or supported continued to reflect a shortsightedness that ultimately would be fatal both for the Habsburg dynasty and the empire. The greatest example was the Austro-Hungarian Compromise of 1867, which created two states, each with its own parliament and prime minister, economic policy, and reserve military formations. They shared a common foreign policy, regular army and navy, and of course a monarch, Franz Joseph.

The Compromise of 1867 appeased the Hungarians but produced a constitution that, in effect, could not be amended. Worse yet, the arrangement did not solve the empire's nationality problem: it established the German Austrians and Magyars (ethnic Hungarians) as the dominant nationalities, but together they accounted for less than fifty percent of Austria-Hungary's population, and separately neither constituted a majority even in its own half of the empire. But any revision of the Compromise of 1867 would require the consent of both governments, and plans to grant other nationalities, most notably the Czechs and South Slavs, a status similar to that of Hungary always foundered on the opposition of Budapest. Within Austria parliamentary rule prevailed, eventually with universal male suffrage and equal rights for all nationalities, while Hungary retained a restrictive franchise, kept political power firmly in Magyar hands, and in various ways pursued a policy of cultural "Magyarization."

For a dozen years after 1867, Franz Joseph accepted the domination of German Liberals over Austrian politics. Reforms included the elimination of most censorship, secularization of education, and legal enforcement of religious toleration. But after the Liberals stumbled in the elections of 1879, Franz Joseph appointed his boyhood friend, Count Eduard Taaffe, minister-president. For the next fourteen years Taaffe headed a bloc of conservative and Slavic parties, the so-called "Iron Ring," which stemmed the tide of official anticlericalism and kept a lid on the nationality problem while doing nothing to solve it. Franz Joseph and Taaffe succeeded in breaking the German Liberals, but in the process drove the German Austrian electorate toward new parties with agendas that were to varying degrees revolutionary: the Christian Socialists, Social Democrats, and German Nationalists. All three supported programs incompatible with the Compromise of 1867. The fragmentation and alienation of the German Austrians, who should have been the foundation of stability, led to political chaos once the nationalist movements of the Czechs and other Slavic groups experienced a revival just before the turn of the century. Parliamentary coalitions became impossible to maintain, ministries changed hands frequently, and Franz Joseph often resorted to rule by emergency decree under Article 14 of the Austrian constitution of 1867.

Meanwhile, Franz Joseph handled the Magyar ruling elite with great care, fearful of a crisis that would prompt Hungary to secede from the empire. Except for the Croatians, who received a fixed minority of seats in the Budapest parliament, non-Magyars were excluded from Hungarian politics. The kingdom's education system and cultural policies denied to non-Magyars many of the same rights that all nationalities enjoyed in the Austrian half of the monarchy. But Franz Joseph's patience had its limits. In 1905, Hungarian elections were won by liberal nationalist Magyars who pressed for the division of the regular army and for Magyar to replace German as the language of its Hungarian half. Franz Joseph did not consider the unity of the regular army or its German language of command to be negotiable.

Matters came to a crisis in February 1906, when the emperor ordered troops in Budapest to disperse the parliament. The popular revolutions that some of Franz Joseph's generals feared did not materialize, exposing the undemocratic parliament's narrow base of support. Some advisers urged the emperor to exploit the situation and force the Hungarian leadership to grant reforms; instead, Franz Joseph hastened to mend fences with the leading Magyars. They accepted a continuation of the status quo within the regular army in exchange for an expansion of the Hungarian reserve (*Honvéd*). Thus, late in his reign, Franz Joseph still demonstrated a willingness to behave in a tyrannical manner when the issue at stake was near to his heart. But he resorted to tyranny only to maintain the existing order, and could not be persuaded to employ this device in the cause of change.

Bosnian Muslims traditionally have considered the Austro-Hungarian occupation of the Turkish province of Bosnia-Hercegovina in 1878, and its formal annexation in 1908, as great acts of tyranny by Franz Joseph's government. Most Muslim and Yugoslav accounts have been critical of Habsburg rule in Bosnia-Hercegovina, but the period remains a subject of debate. Austria-Hungary promoted industrial development, infrastructure improvements, and a Bosnian cultural identity, enough to upset Serbian nationalists who hoped for an eventual Serbian annexation of the province. While Bosnian Muslims naturally have cherished the historical memory of the centuries of Ottoman rule before 1878, they certainly fared better during the ensuing four decades of Austro-Hungarian rule than under the domination of their non-Muslim fellow Yugoslavs after 1918.

FRANZ JOSEPH AS A GREAT LEADER

In June 1867, four months after the conclusion of the Austro-Hungarian Compromise, Franz Joseph went to Budapest to be crowned king of Hungary. The ceremony was an act of reconciliation with a nation that had been in open rebellion against him when he first assumed the throne. He received the crown of St. Stephen at the hand of Count Gyula Andrássy, a Magyar aristocrat who had once been condemned to death for his role as a revolutionary in 1848–1849. In 1867 Andrássy became the first minister-president of Hungary, and four years later, foreign minister of the Dual Monarchy. Upon his coronation in Budapest, Franz Joseph issued a general amnesty to all former Hungarian revolutionaries not yet pardoned individually. Coronation gifts were dispensed to veterans of the rebellion, and to the widows and orphans of those who had not survived. Few rulers in history have been willing to make such gestures to former rebels for the sake of peace. Unfortunately, as we have seen, the appeasement of the Magyars came at the expense of the goodwill of every other nationality in the Hungarian half of the monarchy.

While the constitutional structure of 1867 did not satisfy most parties and nationalities, on an individual basis the subjects of the Dual Monarchy enjoyed the rule of law. The most dramatic example came after the assassination of Franz Ferdinand, when Gavrilo Princip was not given the death penalty because he had been nineteen at the time of the murder—a minor under imperial law! In an era of growing intolerance, ethnic and confessional tensions, Franz Joseph assumed the role of the tolerant patriarch. In the words of István Deák, "it made no difference to him whether a subject was a German, Hungarian, or Slav, so long as the subject did his duty. With the same humility and grace that he accepted the blessings of the pope, he accepted the blessings of a rabbi or of a Muslim cleric."

At times Franz Joseph resorted to tyrannical methods in the service of these better instincts, the most dramatic case being his attempt to block the election of Karl Lueger, leader of Austrian Christian Socialism, to the post of mayor of Vienna. Lueger's staunchly Catholic party—anti-liberal, anti-capitalist, anti-Marxist, and anti-Semitic—supported the Habsburg monarchy but not the Austro-Hungarian compromise (Lueger's targets included the "Judeo-Magyar" regime in Budapest). His message found favor among all sectors of Viennese society, from the aristocracy to the working class, and by the mid-1890s his party controlled two-thirds of the city council. But to Franz Joseph, Lueger was a rabble-rouser, a Jew-baiting demagogue whose popularity depended on his skill in manipulating the worst fears and prejudices of his subjects. The emperor went so far as to admit that he admired most aspects of the Christian Social program but found their anti-Semitism repugnant. Twice in 1895 and again in 1896 he used his imperial veto to block Lueger's election as mayor of Vienna. In the spring of 1897, when the council elected Lueger for a fourth time, Franz Joseph finally relented and allowed him to take office. Lueger served as mayor until his death in 1910; along with the German Nationalist leader, Georg von Schönerer, he became a political role model for the young Adolf Hitler.

SUGGESTIONS FOR ADDITIONAL READING

Bled, Jean-Paul. *Franz Joseph*. Translated by Teresa Bridgeman. Cambridge, Mass.: Blackwell Publishers, 1992.

Crankshaw, Edward. *The Fall of the House of Habsburg*. New York: Viking Press, 1963. (Paperback edition: Penguin, 1983.)

Deák, István. *Beyond Nationalism: A Social and Political History of the Habsburg Officer Corps, 1848–1918*. New York: Oxford University Press, 1990.

May, Arthur J. *The Habsburg Monarchy*. Cambridge, Mass.: Harvard University Press, 1951.

Murad, Anatol. *Franz Joseph I of Austria and his Empire*. New York: Twayne Publishers, 1968.

Rothenberg, Gunther. *The Army of Francis Joseph*. West Lafayette, Ind.: Purdue University Press, 1976.

Sked, Alan. *The Decline and Fall of the Habsburg Empire, 1815–1918*. London: Longman, 1989.

Taylor, A. J. P. *The Habsburg Monarchy, 1809–1918: A History of the Austrian Empire and Austria-Hungary*. Chicago: University of Chicago Press, 1948. (Paperback edition, 1976.)

Lawrence Sondhaus

Indira Nehru Gandhi

1917–1984

Prime Minister of India, 1966–1977, 1980–1984

Indira Nehru Gandhi, who would become the first woman prime minister of India, was born in Allahbad, India, on November 19, 1917. She was the only child of Jawaharlal Nehru, the first prime minister of independent India, and his wife Kamala.

From earliest childhood, Indira saw her politically and socially prominent Indian family's active support on behalf of Indian independence. While her family was quite wealthy, her grandfather Motilal Nehru was a renowned and successful attorney, and Indira suffered no deprivation. The family's open opposition to British rule was fraught with danger. At any time family members, as well as friends, could be arrested and imprisoned for long periods for their participation in the independence movement. Virtually every member of her immediate family, including her grandfather, father, mother, and aunts, was imprisoned at one time or another during her childhood. Her father was first imprisoned when she was only four years old.

Indeed Mrs. Gandhi's emotional aloofness as an adult is often attributed to the insecurity she experienced as a child and to her deep-seated need to become self-reliant as a defense against these early separations from the people she loved. Undoubtedly, the difficult circumstances of Indira's relationship with her mother were also a factor.

BIOGRAPHICAL BACKGROUND

Mrs. Gandhi's mother, Kamala, was a shy, retiring woman who had married into a family much more socially prominent than her own. Unlike the other Nehru women, she had received a traditional Indian upbringing and was often poorly treated by her mother-in-law and sisters-in-law. Her husband, Jawaharlal Nehru, apparently made no attempt to protect his wife from their hostility and criticism.

Always frail, Kamala Nehru was sick during most of Indira Gandhi's childhood, although she did manage to share her husband's interest in the Congress Party. In 1926, Mrs. Nehru was taken to Switzerland for treatment for tuberculosis. Indira was placed in a Swiss school. Her later tendency to withdraw from people first became noticeable at this time.

In October 1930, just before she turned thirteen, her father was again arrested, only a week after his release from a six-month prison term. At this time her grandfather, who was ill, had already been in prison for two months. Shortly after her thirteenth birthday, Indira's mother, despite her ill health, was imprisoned for the first time. A month later her grandfather died, and before the end of 1931, her father was imprisoned for the fifth time. In fact, between 1931 and 1935, Jawaharlal Nehru remained in jail almost continuously. Finally, in 1935, Kamala Nehru died when Indira was only eighteen years old.

After her mother's death, Mrs. Gandhi went to England to study history at Oxford. Her performance as a student was lackluster, and after several years Indira, still without prospects for a degree, decided to return to India to support the growing struggle for Indian independence. In February 1941 she sailed home from England with a fellow student and future husband, Feroze Gandhi.

A month later, at the age of twenty-four, Indira married Feroze Gandhi against her father's wishes. Feroze, a son of a Parsi retail merchant of Allahbad (no relation to Mohandas Gandhi), had known Indira since he joined her mother as a teen-age Congress Party volunteer. The class-conscious Nehru family could not reconcile themselves to the idea of her marrying someone below her social status and opposed the marriage. Unfortunately, Mr. Gandhi was unable to overcome his in-laws' skepticism and did not succeed in holding any job for any period of time. He was finally elected to Lok Sabha, the lower house of parliament, in the 1951–1952 general elections and served there until his death in 1961.

Soon after their marriage the couple was jailed by the British for eight months for participating in the "Quit India" movement. After their release from prison, Mrs. Gandhi seems to have decided to put politics aside and settle down to domestic life as a wife of a sometime journalist.

However, Indira Gandhi's family life in Lucknow, a city 270 miles from Delhi, was dramatically disrupted when India received its independence on August 15, 1947, and her father, Jawaharlal Nehru, became its first prime minister. By 1950 the social responsibilities of her father's office forced her to move with her two sons, Rajiv, aged six and Sanjay, four, to his residence to serve as his official hostess.

Despite that role, Indira Gandhi did not really show any personal interest in public office until she became prime minister on January 16, 1966 at the age of forty-eight. Until then she held only one major party position, the presidency of the Indian National Congress Party in 1959. She occupied the post for less than a year but decided to forego political responsibility in favor of her maternal obligations. Subsequently, she regularly declined invitations to run for parliament.

After her father died in 1964, Mrs. Gandhi turned down suggestions that she succeed him as prime minister. Later, when Lal Bahadur Shastri became prime minister, she at first refused all offers of cabinet positions and only reluctantly accepted the Ministry of Information and Broadcasting, a minor post, after being subjected to a great deal of pressure.

It was only after Prime Minister Shastri's sudden death two years later that Mrs. Gandhi agreed to become the head of government. Her decision was prompted by Kumaraswami Kamaraj, president of the Indian National Congress Party. He urged her to accept because he wanted to prevent a power struggle among strong party leaders and because he also thought Mrs. Gandhi would be easy to control. Indeed, during her first three years as prime minister, she did very little and was considered only a mediocre leader and politician. However, by 1969 Mrs. Gandhi began to consolidate her political power, which resulted in the ultimate split in the Congress Party in 1970. Suddenly there was a new Congress Party (Congress-I) with Mrs. Gandhi at its helm, and over a relatively short period of time a body of significant legislation was enacted. More than half of the thirty-five constitutional amendments added since the constitution's adoption in 1950 were passed within a nine-year period beginning in 1966. Mrs. Gandhi also nationalized fourteen major commercial banks and abolished the "privy purses" and other privileges enjoyed by the descendants of former native Indian rulers; both these actions were extremely well received by the Indian public, and her popularity rose to a new high.

Riding the crest of her popularity, Mrs. Gandhi called for national elections in 1971 and state elections in 1972, and led the new Congress Party to power in a landslide victory that surprised many. She polled over 66 percent of the vote, compared to less than 26 percent for her major opponent.

The election victories of 1971 and 1972 confirmed Indira Gandhi's nationwide popularity, and for a time it seemed that all of the factions of her Congress Party were revitalized and resolutely united behind their leader. Victory over Pakistan in the war over East Pakistan (now Bangladesh) in December 1971 and the Simla Agreement with Pakistan of July 1972 only added to Mrs. Gandhi's stature. Many expected that her resounding triumphs would open the way to significant social, political, and economic change, consistent with her campaign promise of *Garibi Hatao* (abolish poverty).

To fulfill her campaign promise, Mrs. Gandhi embarked on an economic policy of nationalizing many industries. In May 1972 the coking-coal industry was nationalized; in August 1972 the management of the Indian iron and steel company, one of the two largest steel-producing companies, was taken over by the government without compensation, and in September

1972 general insurance companies were also nationalized. During 1971–1972 shipping, gold, and copper were nationalized, and in October 1972 management of forty-six textile mills in twelve states was transferred to the state-owned Textile Corporation, pending nationalization. Finally, after the food riots in the summer of 1972, Mrs. Gandhi decided that public agencies would take over the wholesale trade in wheat, starting with the winter crops, and rice, starting in the following summer.

However, 1972 also saw the most serious economic crisis faced by any Indian government and ultimately led to the establishment of emergency rule in 1975. Although the Congress Party was returned to power in most elections in 1972, from that time forward the political fortunes of the prime minister and the Congress Party took a backward slide, reflecting the worsening economic situation and the accompanying public discontent and disillusionment.

After five years of good monsoons, the summer monsoon of 1972 was very poor, producing an extensive drought that lasted through the spring of 1974. By mid-1972, as agricultural output began to slacken and prices started to rise, the economy also felt the inevitable strain of the ten million refugees who had fled East Pakistan during the Pakistani civil war in 1971. Also the tremendous burden of India's war with Pakistan was increasingly evident, and the inflationary pressure of rising world oil prices dealt yet another serious blow to the already devastated Indian economy.

The Gandhi government seemed increasingly ineffective. Agitation was widespread and violence, street demonstrations, and charges of corruption against the government officials became common. In one of the Indian states (Madhya Pradesh) a coalition of small parties opposed to the Congress government defeated the Congress Party in statewide elections. This coalition, led by prominent Indian leader J. P. Narayan, became the rallying point for the anti-Congress movement. In March of 1975 at Mr. Narayan's behest, a massive rally was held in New Delhi drawing an anti-government crowd estimated at more than 250,000.

Adding to Mrs. Gandhi's woes, the June 24, 1975, judgment of the Supreme Court of India upheld a lower court decision that had found Mrs. Gandhi guilty of corrupt election practices in the 1971 ballot. Mrs. Gandhi was convicted of using a government employee as a campaign worker and of having local police help in organizing rallies.

The opposition parties immediately called for Mrs. Gandhi's resignation, and Mr. Narayan proclaimed a nationwide campaign of passive resistance to her government. In the face of mounting opposition and her own rapidly deteriorating position, Mrs. Gandhi launched a preemptive strike.

At dawn on June 25, 1975, police arrested virtually all opposition politicians as well as some members of the Congress Party. Simultaneously, Mrs. Gandhi's government declared a state of emergency under the "Defense of India" provision of Article 352 of the Indian Constitution. Emergency rule lasted nearly two years until March 1977, when elections were finally held and Mrs. Gandhi was swept from office by a coalition of opposition parties that united to form a new party called Janata.

The Janata coalition, however, was fragile and unable to remain united once they gained power. It quickly began to disintegrate, leading to the triumphant return of Mrs. Gandhi to power in the elections of January 1980. Her party captured 351 out of 542 seats in the Lok Sabha (the lower house of parliament) and the governments of eighteen out of twenty-two states.

However, Mrs. Gandhi's government was again beset by problems both at home and abroad. In 1980 her favorite son, Sanjay, who had exercised tremendous influence on her administration, was killed in a plane accident. Massive and sometime violent demonstrations continued in various states including Punjab, where Sikh nationalists began to agitate for an independent state of Khalistan. They would often carry out terrorist activities resulting in hundreds of deaths and then retreat to the Golden Temple in Amritsar, the holiest shrine of the Sikh religion, for sanctuary. In June 1984, Mrs. Gandhi ordered an assault on the Golden Temple by Indian troops to capture the extremists and destroy their headquarters. Later that same year, on October 31, Indira Nehru Gandhi was assassinated by two Sikh members of her own security service.

GANDHI AS A GREAT LEADER

India's economy improved significantly during Mrs. Gandhi's first term in office. The defense forces and defense production grew, and there was a steady trend toward economic self-reliance. Economic indicators responded positively, mainly because of expanded agricultural production, remittances from overseas Indians, and skillful economic diplomacy.

By 1970, food production had increased to 100 million tons compared with 55 million tons in 1950, and India reached the point where it no longer needed imports of food grains. Further, economic improvements were achieved in the areas of irrigation, steel production, electric production, life expectancy, and the number of children in schools.

During Mrs. Gandhi's first term in office, India's armed forces were expanded in number and were more widely deployed. The supply of equipment increased and the quality and diversity of weapons systems improved as domestic defense production rose. The process of modernizing the military started when India's border conflict with China erupted and was accelerated by the humiliation suffered in the 1962 war. Expenses on defense, however, were kept down to approximately 3.5 percent of the GNP and about 20 percent of the budget.

Despite the limits on defense spending, India became a military power of some consequence. India's army of approximately one million men was the fourth-largest in the world. The Indian air force grew to over six hundred combat aircraft of increasing sophistication and many were manufactured in India. The navy, though small, had a broad strategic perspective and was equipped with an air wing and submarines. As a consequence, India's might in South Asia could not be ignored in the 1970s and 1980s by either regional or outside powers.

From 1972 to 1980 India's Space Energy Commission upgraded its program of rocket research to produce sophisticated varieties of rockets and satellites. Communication satellites were devised and launched in cooperation with NASA. It was also during Mrs. Gandhi's term in office that India joined the nuclear club by exploding the so-called peaceful nuclear device.

In foreign policy, unlike her father, Nehru, who often articulated India's national interest in idealistic phrases of world peace and cooperation, Indira Gandhi was much more of a pragmatist. She stressed security, territory, and prestige as integral parts of India's national interest. She wanted India's representatives to strengthen the weakest links in India's foreign policy, namely export markets and public image.

GANDHI THE TYRANT

The declaration of emergency powers in June 1975 saw Indira Gandhi at her worst. When it became obvious that she might lose her seat in the parliament because of the agitation by the opposition parties calling for her resignation after the June 24, 1975, decision of the Supreme Court, Mrs. Gandhi decided to hold on to power by whatever means necessary. At dawn on June 25, police arrested nearly 700 prominent public figures on record as opposing Mrs. Gandhi, including J. P. Narayan and Morarji Desai, a one-time finance minister in her own administration. Even many members of the Congress Party were arrested because they allegedly had shown a lack of support for her government. In the following weeks, thousands were arrested, public meetings were banned, and a rigid censorship was imposed on the Indian press. Measures to control prices and protect the farmers were also adopted, in part to soften the character of repression.

These actions were taken under constitutionally provided emergency powers that, Mrs. Gandhi alleged, had been invoked because of a conspiracy threatening national unity and stability. However, very few individuals took her conspiracy charge seriously, and it was clear that opposition to her rule was growing. Thus with stunning swiftness the nation that had often loudly proclaimed itself the world's largest democracy was changed overnight from an open society to a tyrannical one in which to oppose or criticize Mrs. Gandhi was to court arrest.

With the opposition either in jail or thoroughly intimidated, the Indian parliament proved to be very accommodating. In July 1975 it endorsed the government's assumption of sweeping emergency powers, and in August parliament took action to bar the courts from interfering with any of the emergency decrees. Parliament also changed the law under which Mrs. Gandhi was convicted of election fraud. Finally, to ensure that no similar legal embarrassment would occur in the future, the offices of prime minister, president, vice-president, and speaker of the house were exempted from any future judicial sanctions. The constitution was amended to allow only a parliamentary commission to inquire into the election of the prime minister. This meant that there would be no scrutiny into the electoral activities of the prime minister, because the prime minister is the head of the majority party in parliament.

In January 1976 a bill to introduce compulsory sterilization was introduced. The government decreed that all government employees have no more than two children. In September there were additional constitutional amendments to give greater power to the prime minister. For instance, the prime minister would be able to alter the constitution by requiring the president of India to issue an executive order to that effect.

This sudden turn of events produced shock waves throughout much of the world. There was strong criticism of Mrs. Gandhi from leaders of the Western democracies. Eventually, faced with criticism at home and abroad, Mrs. Gandhi, in January 1977, called for general elections to be held in March. The result was a sweeping victory for the opposition and restoration of democracy in India.

Although Mrs. Gandhi was returned to power for a second time in 1980 as a result of the opposition's listless performance, her own leadership was equally uninspired. Her government continued to flounder until the fateful decision to attack the Golden Temple, which ultimately culminated in her assassination on October 31, 1984.

SUGGESTIONS FOR ADDITIONAL READING

Bhatia, Krishan. *Indira*. New York: Praeger, 1974.

Carras, Mary C. *Indira Gandhi: in the Crucible of Leadership*. Boston: Beacon Press, 1979.

Jayakar, Pupul. *Indira Gandhi: A Biography*. New Delhi: Viking (Penguin India), 1992.

Masani, Zareer. *Indira Gandhi: A Biography*. New York: Thomas Y. Cromwell, 1975.

Mansingh, Surjit. *India's Search for Power: Indira Gandhi's Foreign Policy 1966–1982*. New Delhi: Sage Publications, 1984.

Nanda, B. R. *The Nehrus: Motilal and Jawaharlal.* Chicago: University of Chicago Press, 1962.

Vasudev, Uma. *Indira Gandhi: Revolution in Restraint.* New Delhi: Vikas, 1974.

Vasudev, Uma. *Two Faces of Indira Gandhi.* New Delhi: Vikas Publishing House, 1977.

Peter Merani

Mikhail Sergeevich Gorbachev

1931–

General Secretary of the Communist Party of the Soviet Union
President of the Soviet Union, 1985–1991

Twentieth-century Russia is a nation scarred by the vicissitudes of despotism, war, and socio-economic chaos. Its brief flirtation with democracy in 1917 was wedged between the oppressive regime of Russia's last tsar, Nicholas II, and that of Lenin. As a result, Russia had few democratic traditions to remember or honor. Over the next seventy-four years, an increasingly oppressive Soviet police state emerged, built primarily during the long years of Stalinist rule between 1927 and 1953. After Stalin's death, there were mild attempts by Nikita Khrushchev to moderate some of the more harsh aspects of the Soviet police state. After his fall in 1964, the Soviet Union drifted into a mafia-type system of dictatorship and slowly degenerated. In 1985, Mikhail Gorbachev emerged from this abyss and began to lead his country and the Soviet empire away from the autocratic traditions that had dominated it for over six decades. During his brief six years in office, he oversaw the transformation of his nation, Europe, and the world. Tragically, his popularity at home waned in the face of pressure from reactionaries who sought to preserve the USSR's outdated Stalinist traditions, and radicals who felt he should push the country along a more daring path of reform. Gorbachev lent support to certain actions designed to preserve the territorial integrity of the Soviet Union that smacked of some of the tyrannical behavior of earlier Soviet dictators.

BIOGRAPHICAL BACKGROUND

Mikhail Sergeevich Gorbachev was born on March 2, 1931, in the small, northern Caucasian village of Privol'noye, in the Stavropol Krai, where his father, Sergei Andreevich, drove a combine-harvester. Gorbachev initially attended school in Privol'noye, but transferred to a school in another town when war broke out in 1941. Gorbachev was unable to attend school for a year during the war, but resumed his studies and won a prize. In 1945 he joined the Komsomol, the Communist youth organization, and worked alongside his father, a war veteran and Communist Party member, in the fields. Gorbachev was awarded the Order of the Red Banner of Labor in 1949, an award usually reserved for older workers, which enabled him to earn a spot as a gifted farm youth to the law faculty of the prestigious Moscow State University. Gorbachev won a silver medal for his academic achievements upon graduation from high school in 1950.

Gorbachev began his legal studies that fall, and the following year applied for candidate membership in the Communist Party of the Soviet Union (CPSU). In 1951 he was elected *komsorg kursa*, or Komsomol organizer for his law class, and in 1952 became *komsorg kursa* for the entire law faculty. He acquired full membership in the CPSU the same year and married Raisa Maximova Titorenko in 1954. Upon graduation with a law degree in 1955, Gorbachev returned to Stavropol and began to do political and propaganda work for the city's Komsomol organization. In 1956 he became first secretary of the Stavropol city Komsomol and was appointed to the regional Komsomol's Propaganda Department. Soon he became second secretary of the Stavropol regional Komsomol, and in 1960 its first secretary, which earned him a seat on the Krai's Communist Party Committee.

He was a delegate to the XXI Party Congress of the CPSU in 1961, and the following year was appointed the party's political organizer in one of the Stavropol's new agricultural administrative units. Gorbachev began to take correspondence courses from the Stavropol Agricultural Institute, and in 1962 was made a member of the Stavropol party's organizational department. In 1966, Gorbachev became effective mayor of Stavropol when he was made first secretary of the city's Communist Party Committee. He traveled to the German Democratic Republic and France in 1966, and the following year received a diploma in agricultural economics from the Stavropol Agricultural Institute.

In 1968, Gorbachev became second secretary of the Stavropol party committee and head of its agricultural department. A year later he was selected as a delegate to the Supreme Soviet in Moscow, where he served on its environmental committee. He visited Czechoslovakia the same year, and in 1970 was made first secretary of the Stavropol Krai Communist Party Committee, which put him in charge of the entire region. He attended the XXIV Party Congress in Moscow in 1971, and was elected a full member of the CPSU's Central Committee. He traveled officially to Belgium in 1972, West Germany in 1975, and France in 1976.

During this period, Gorbachev began to acquire a reputation for toughness and honesty among prominent Soviet leaders such as party ideologist Mikhail Suslov and Yuri Andropov. In 1977, Gorbachev oversaw a successful grain-harvesting experiment in his Ipatovsky district, which won him the Order of the October Revolution. In 1978 he was given the agricultural post on the Central Committee previously held by his old mentor, Fyodor Kulakov.

In 1979, Gorbachev became a candidate member of the ruling Politburo, and eleven months later was elevated to full, voting membership. He was soon elected to the Supreme Soviet and represented the Altai region of Siberia. In 1982 he became party ideologist after Suslov's death, which made him the number-two man in the Kremlin behind his new mentor, former KGB head Yuri Andropov. After Andropov's death in 1984, Gorbachev became the power behind the Soviet throne as the Kremlin's new leader, Konstantine Chernenko, struggled with the ravages of emphysema. As the new chairman of the Foreign Affairs Committee of the Supreme Soviet, Gorbachev began to acquire an international reputation with a visit to Great Britain at the end of 1985. Within months he replaced the dead Chernenko as the Soviet Union's new leader.

Gorbachev's six-year tenure as head of the Soviet Union began inauspiciously. Throughout 1985 he gave hints of significant change, though it was the Chernobyl nuclear accident on April 26, 1986, that gave Gorbachev the first real opportunity to test the new dimensions of change that he had talked about since he had come to power. Though it took him almost three weeks publicly to respond to the catastrophe, he used the growing public disillusionment over his handling of the crisis to launch a campaign of *glasnost* (openness) in the Soviet press, followed by his program of *perestroika* (restructuring). Symbolically, he announced the withdrawal of six Soviet regiments from Afghanistan and freed Soviet dissident Andrei Sakharov. In early 1987, the year he was named *Time* magazine's "Man of the Year," Gorbachev announced a new wave of political reforms and struck out against political corruption. He initiated new economic reforms that summer, and in December signed the INF nuclear limitation treaty with President Ronald Reagan.

Gorbachev began 1988 with the announcement of a full Soviet withdrawal from Afghanistan over the next year, and introduced new electoral and legislative changes. He met with President Reagan in Moscow and New York, and was troubled by the violent Armenia-Azerbaijani conflict in Nagorno-Kharabakh and an earthquake in Armenia. He also was plagued by growing conservative disaffection with his reforms, but introduced further political reforms that called for the creation of a presidency, a position he later assumed, and a new legislature for the Soviet Union. In December 1988 he addressed the United Nations and pledged that the Soviet Union would trim the size of its military by half a million troops by the end of 1990.

The year 1989 was a watershed in European and world history as the Soviet empire began to become unwound. As numerous East European states left the Soviet fold, new Popular Front and independence movements began to change the Soviet Union's political landscape. Gorbachev, who won the Nobel Prize and was named *Time*'s "Man of the Decade" in 1990, found himself trapped between liberal and conservative factions who demanded diametrically opposed changes in all facets of Soviet life and politics. Intensified public disorder in Georgia, Estonia, Latvia, and Lithuania marred his international reputation, while domestic confidence in his abilities waned. Gorbachev's appointment of Boris Pugo, the former head of the Latvian Communist Party and KGB, to head the Soviet Interior Ministry, was a gesture to conservatives who wanted a restoration of public order. On December 20, 1990, Eduard Shevardnadze, Gorbachev's reform-minded foreign minister, resigned and warned of an imminent dictatorship.

Gorbachev's decision to initiate a military crackdown in the Baltic republics in early 1991 produced worldwide protests and seriously eroded his remaining domestic support. A successful March 17, 1991, referendum on the future of the USSR prompted Baltic declarations of independence, while Boris Yeltsin emerged as Gorbachev's principal political rival. Elected the Russian Republic's first president on June 12, 1991, Yeltsin and Gorbachev tried to hammer out a workable power relationship for the country. On April 23 they created a Union treaty for the USSR that gave republics the right to secede. Growing concern among party conservatives about the deterioration of the economy, the military, and the country were exacerbated by Yeltsin's efforts to neutralize the Communist Party on July 20. Ten days later, Gorbachev met with President George Bush in Moscow, and then began his summer vacation in the Crimea. On August 18, 1991, he was arrested in a coup that faltered three days later. Gorbachev returned humiliated to the Soviet capital on August 22, where he reconfirmed his faith in communism. Increasingly bullied by Yeltsin, who had bravely stymied the conspirators, Gorbachev was politically dead. As Yeltsin pushed for the formation of a new Commonwealth of Independent States, Gorbachev vowed to resign if the plan was accepted by other Soviet republics. Once eleven republics chose to follow this path, Yeltsin and Gorbachev agreed that the Soviet Union would cease to exist on January 1, 1992. On December 25, 1991, Mikhail Gorbachev resigned as the country's president and became a private citizen.

GORBACHEV AS A GREAT LEADER

In the broad scope of Soviet Russian history, Mikhail Gorbachev occupies a unique position as a reformer and truly visionary leader. His remarkable accomplishments during his brief six years in power transformed not only the face of his country and Europe, but the world. Gorbachev's achievements are particularly amazing given his Stalinist-era upbringing and his career in the ideologically bankrupt regime of Leonid Brezhnev. In fact, overcoming these traditions became his biggest challenge, while his opponents' commitment to them eventually helped bring about his downfall.

While Gorbachev accomplished many things concretely during his years in power, his greatest achievements lay in the dramatic spirit of *glasnost* and *perestroika* that enveloped the Soviet Union and its empire in Eastern Europe. Though the seeds for this greater openness can be traced to Andropov and earlier Soviet leaders such as Khrushchev and Brezhnev, it was Gorbachev who took these concepts to new limits and was willing to experiment with their untried dimensions. The Chernobyl incident was his first test of true *glasnost*, and though he reacted initially with typical Soviet reticence, he quickly learned the value of truth and public honesty. Interestingly, Gorbachev found a deeper response to his new policies in the international community than he did at home. Soviet citizens had been along this path before, and were deeply suspicious of Gorbachev's real commitment to legitimate change.

Gorbachev's decisions to free Andrei Sakharov and to pull Soviet forces out of Afghanistan were symbolic and helped set the domestic tone for his policies. But his greatest test came in Eastern Europe, where growing independence movements challenged the traditional Communist leadership and threatened totally to undermine Soviet power in the region. Gorbachev gave passive blessing to the collapse of his nation's empire in Eastern Europe by not responding to its demise. In so doing, he changed the course of history. Sadly, these changes came so quickly that he was unable to prepare the Soviet people for their rapid passage from international greatness to domestic insecurity. He was also unprepared for the impact of these international changes on the Soviet Union, and the threatening reaction of party conservatives. The decision of the Baltic republics to follow the path of their East European neighbors came to symbolize many things to many people in the Soviet Union. As Gorbachev struggled to maintain power and find a political middle ground between the growing factionalization in the Soviet Union, he found himself increasingly neutralized. The unsuccessful coup in August 1991 symbolized the nation's disillusionment with his leadership, a sad end to an era that rates as one of the most significant in the course of twentieth-century history.

GORBACHEV THE TYRANT

In classical Greece the *tyrannos* or lord was a dictator brought to power in many of the city-states in an effort to check the power of the landowning aristocracy. It is only in this classical sense that Mikhail Gorbachev can be seen as a tyrant. More precisely, as a creature of the dictatorial and oppressive Stalinist-Khrushchev-Brezhnev political system, Gorbachev exhibited some of their characteristics during his last years in power, though he can never be placed in the same category as some of the USSR's legitimate tyrants. In some instances, tyrannical acts associated with Gorbachev, such as the violent attacks on peaceful demonstrators in Tblisi, Georgia, on April 9, 1990, were instigated without his knowledge.

The most damaging events in his illustrious career came at the end, when he was faced with the decisions of Estonia, Latvia, and Lithuania to secede from the Soviet Union. Stimulated by Popular Front movements that traced their roots back to the early Gorbachev years, the spirit of Baltic separatism and later independence fed off similar developments in Eastern Europe. Initially, Gorbachev tried to counter this spirit with the appointment of reform-minded Baltic Communist leaders, but later tried to put a brake on Baltic reforms when they began to move toward full independence. The collapse of the Soviet empire in Eastern Europe in late 1989 and early 1990 traumatized Soviet Communist Party conservatives, who came increasingly to view Baltic separatist movements as symbolic of everything gone awry in the Soviet Union. When Lithuania voted to secede from the USSR in the spring of 1990, Gorbachev responded with a raw materials embargo. As a gesture to party conservatives, he appointed the former head of Latvia's Communist Party and KGB, Boris Pugo, to head the Soviet Interior Ministry. By the end of 1990, Pugo initiated a violent, deadly crackdown in Riga, Latvia, that resulted in a number of deaths, followed by similar moves in Lithuania. An international outcry prompted Gorbachev initially to blame Lithuanians for the violence, though by the end of January 1991, Pugo promised to withdraw most of the special forces responsible for the violence. More deadly crackdowns came in Lithuania and Latvia in late June 1991, followed by further deaths in Lithuania on the eve of Gorbachev's meeting with President Bush in Moscow in late July. Party reactionaries followed up their growing crescendo of violence with a coup against Gorbachev on August 18, 1991, that ultimately led to his downfall later that year.

SUGGESTIONS FOR ADDITIONAL READING

Aslund, Anders. *Gorbachev's Struggle for Economic Reform.* Ithaca, NY: Cornell University Press, 1991.

Bialer, Seweryn, ed. *Politics, Society, and Nationality: Inside Gorbachev's Russia.* Boulder, Colo.: Westview Press, 1989.

Crowe, David M. "Baltic Separatism under Gorbachev," in Joseph L. Wieczynski, ed., *The Gorbachev Encyclopedia: The Man and His Times.* Salt Lake City: Charles Schlacks, Jr., Publisher, 1993, pp. 49–57.

Dallin, Alexander, and Condoleezza Rice, eds. *The Gorbachev Era.* Stanford, Calif.: Stanford Alumni Association, 1986.

Gorbachev, Mikhail S. *Gorbachev: Mandate for Peace.* Toronto: Paperjacks, Ltd., 1987.

Hartgrove, Joseph Dane. "Gorbachev, Mikhail Sergeevich," in Joseph L. Wieczynski, *The Gorbachev Encyclopedia: The Man and His Times.* Salt Lake City: Charles Schlacks, Jr., Publisher, 1993, pp. 162–185.

Kaiser, Robert G. *Why Gorbachev Happened: His Triumphs, His Failure, and His Fall*. New York: Simon & Schuster, 1992.
Morrison, Donald, ed. *Mikhail S. Gorbachev: An Intimate Biography*. New York: Time Incorporated, 1988.
Sheehy, Gail. *The Man Who Changed the World: The Lives of Mikhail S. Gorbachev*. New York: HarperCollins Publishers, 1990.
Sydorenko, Alexander. "Mikhail Gorbachev," in James A. Moncure, *Research Guide to European Historical Biography*. Washington, D.C.: Beacham Publishing, 1992, II, 812–832.

David M. Crowe

Henry VIII (Henry Tudor)

1491–1547

King of England, 1509–1547

Henry VIII has always fascinated the writers of fiction because his six marriages provide generous material for sensationalism. His six wives and their fates were: Catherine of Aragon (annulment), Anne Boleyn (execution for adultery and treason), Jane Seymour (death following childbirth), Anne of Cleves (annulment), Catherine Howard (execution for adultery and treason), Catherine Parr (outlived Henry).

Serious historians, however, have found him even more fascinating because of the contradictions in his policy. Notwithstanding his break with the Roman Catholic Church, he always maintained that he remained a Catholic who simply refused to recognize the pope but was in every other way loyal to his natal faith.

If he was truly determined to bequeath Henrician Catholicism to England, why did he permit Thomas Cromwell to use Acts of Parliament to tamper with Catholic theology? Was his last will and testament, signed and sealed on his deathbed, the honest fulfillment of his principles? Could it have been a forgery, or was it fobbed off on a dying man who no longer understood what he was doing?

Why did he name Sir John Cheke, a scholar with known Protestant sympathies, tutor to the nine-year-old Prince Edward? Why did he designate the boy's uncles, the Seymour brothers, to head the regency council when they too had Protestant views? Less mysteriously, he legitimized his three children and designated Edward, Mary, and Elizabeth as heirs to the throne, even though it was obvious that Mary would return to Roman Catholicism if she was ever in a position to do so.

We are left wondering whether Henry's creative acts were purposeful and whether his tyrannical deeds were part of a planned policy. Could the king's life work be dismissed as impulsive behavior, aggravated by premature illness and increasingly frequent loss of emotional control?

BIOGRAPHICAL BACKGROUND

Henry Tudor, second son of King Henry VII and Elizabeth of York, was born at Greenwich on June 28, 1491. At the time of his birth, Henry's father had been king of England for less than six years, and the Tudor claim to the throne was still quite tenuous. Henry VII faced repeated challenges to his authority from subjects who refused to accept the outcome of the battle of Bosworth Field, where the first Tudor had triumphed over the Yorkist Richard III. The memory of the fifteenth-century Wars of the Roses and the dynastic instability that this protracted conflict signaled was to guide the more momentous decisions of Henry VIII's reign in a compelling manner. When Henry's elder brother Arthur died unexpectedly in 1502, the new heir apparent was created Prince of Wales and contracted by his father to marry his deceased brother's widow, Catherine of Aragon. A dispensation was secured from the pope for the marriage, and soon after his father's death in 1509 the eighteen-year-old monarch married Catherine, now aged twenty-five.

Henry was an exceptional student in the tradition of Renaissance humanism. His intellectual accomplishments, praised by the great Dutch humanist Erasmus, were matched by an equal dedication to bodily exercise and chivalric pursuits. Unhappily, the latter proclivity for martial exploits and the ideal of the knightly quest directed the youthful king into a series of expensive and, from a strategic point of view, fruitless engagements against the French during the first two decades of his reign. In the process, Henry managed to squander the considerable inheritance his father had amassed through scrupulous avoidance of foreign military engagements and a rigorous domestic revenue policy. This overseas financial profligacy on the part of Henry VIII would later contribute to his attacks on the wealth of the church during the Reformation in the 1530s.

Henry's principal adviser during these early years was the powerful archbishop of York and papal legate to England, Cardinal Thomas Wolsey. The son of a butcher from East Anglia, Wolsey's rise to power under Henry was deeply resented by the traditional aristocracy, who saw in this pretentious social upstart a direct challenge to their own monopoly on power at the highest levels. Wolsey's enormous wealth and lavish life style also engendered the hostility of those elements of the population eager to reform abuses within the church by pointing up the disparity between the spiritual pretensions of clerics like Cardinal Wolsey and the worldly pride and insensitivity of priestly bureaucrats who thought little about the material and emotional needs of their flocks.

By 1527 it was becoming increasingly apparent that Henry's union with Catherine of Aragon would not produce the male heir that the king so desperately desired. While a daughter, the princess Mary, had been born in 1516, Henry was convinced that a female monarch would be incapable of winning the respect of the barons and ruling effectively. Fearful lest the Tudor peace break down and the country return to the chaos witnessed during the previous century of dynastic struggle, Henry turned to Wolsey in order to secure a papal annulment of his marriage. Citing the Old Testament injunction in Leviticus against a man taking his brother's wife as the reason for his inability to produce a healthy male heir with Catherine, Henry insisted that conscience was his guide in the entire affair. The pope, while sympathetic to Henry's dilemma, was at the time the virtual prisoner of Charles V, King of Spain, Holy Roman Emperor, and, unfortunately for Henry VIII, nephew of Catherine of Aragon. The emperor was not about to permit Pope Clement VII a free hand in settling the English king's marital difficulties.

After protracted negotiations, in 1530 the king had concluded that nothing less than a break with the Roman Catholic Church could accomplish his ends. Calling Parliament and enacting into law a series of unprecedented statutes during the course of the 1530s, the king succeeded in creating an independent church in England that not only declared his marriage to the guiltless Catherine null and void, but which also redefined the relationship of church and state in a manner that unequivocally favored the power of the temporal magistrate over the spiritual leadership of the clergy. However, Henry's second marriage, in 1533, to Anne Boleyn proved to be as unrewarding in terms of offspring as the first: the birth of the princess Elizabeth (the future Elizabeth I) was an enormous disappointment for a king who had sacrificed so much for a legitimate son and heir. There would be four more wedding days for Henry VIII, and a male successor named Edward was born in 1537 at the cost of his mother's life in childbirth; but the beloved prince was never very healthy and would himself reign for a brief five years after the death of his father in 1547.

After the turbulent 1530s had come to a close, and once the king's agents had confiscated monastic lands and stripped the church of much of its considerable property holdings, Henry's tenure on the throne of England was marked by an undistinguished return to the failed policy of foreign adventurism and financial irresponsibility. Church lands were sold off to aspiring gentry and aristocracy in a process that eventually undermined the power of the crown to impose its will on the political community. Henry also attempted to slow the call for genuine doctrinal reform within the Church of England, clinging tenaciously to the hierarchical and conservative structure he had forged during the first stages of the Reformation. But powerful forces for social and theological change had been set in motion by a king who had broken with the church in Rome purely for political and administrative reasons. Henry had inadvertently sown the seeds of a Puritan reform movement that would become an intractable problem for his second daughter, Elizabeth, during the second half of the sixteenth century.

HENRY VIII AS A GREAT LEADER

Henry VIII's most important contributions to the future of the English state and English society were byproducts of the king's break with Rome in the 1530s. Unlike its Continental counterpart, the English Reformation under Henry VIII was not a doctrinal or ecclesiological affair; the king intended no wholesale revision of traditional religious ideas and practice. Indeed, at the close of the Reformation decade in 1539, the Parliament secured "An Act for Abolishing Diversity of Opinion," which reaffirmed the importance of a celibate clergy, communion in one kind, the practice of formal confession, and the efficacy of transsubstantiation, all central to the historic Roman Catholic rite. Together with the maintenance of church courts, the episcopal and archiepiscopal administrative system, and a church ceremony that differed little from its Catholic predecessor, the king worked to secure the integrity of an independent national church, a unified Catholic communion in England devoid of papal overlordship.

It was in the creation of this national church that Henry and his chief adviser, Thomas Cromwell, had their most lasting impact on English society. For in the process of separating from Rome, and more specifically through the passage of the 1533 Act in Restraint of Appeals, which mandated that all spiritual cases were to be henceforth handled on English soil without recourse to an appeal process ultimately adjudicated by Rome, Henry had created a new phenomenon in Christian Europe: the sovereign state. The language utilized in the act is significant, for its authors insist that by "divers sundry old authentic histories and chronicles it is manifestly declared and expressed that this realm of England is an empire . . . governed by one supreme head and king." Clearly the king and his ministers were committed to the notion that history was on their side, that papal overlordship was an unwarranted innovation and intrusion into the affairs of a nation where the king represents God's vice-regent on earth. Both civil and spiritual authority over England now rested with the monarch, and never again would the international pretensions of the church in Rome, or any other European authority, interfere in the affairs of the island kingdom.

Henry also had a keen eye for workmanlike and creative advisers, and none was more important than the man responsible for framing many of the Reformation statutes: Thomas Cromwell. Whereas Wolsey seemed more interested in the challenges of international politics and with enlarging his own personal power base at home, Cromwell was the first of a new breed of secular, pragmatic administrator-bureaucrats whose vision for a modern England was unprecedented. As the king's principal secretary from 1534 until his execution in 1540, Cromwell created a number of new royal offices distinguished by their efficiency and rational structure and responsible for financial, legal, and administrative matters throughout the kingdom.

In the process of declaring England's independence from Rome, Henry brought Parliament into the governing process in a dramatic and significant way. His father's twenty-four-year reign had been typical of previous practice in that it was not marked by legislative activity. Henry VII called a total of seven Parliaments, and these bodies passed 192 statutes, most of them acts of attainder and restitution. This inactivity was in keeping with a widespread belief that, as a creature of the crown, Parliament would only be called in times of financial or political crisis. Prior to the sixteenth century, few members of Parliament looked on government as a constructive engine for change, and even fewer viewed their role as analysts of impersonal factors that were disrupting the social, political, and economic fabric of the state. The evils of the day were more often than not thought to be the product of personal immorality and sinfulness, the failure to obey God's specific mandate in one's personal life. One can see an example of this type of critique in Thomas More's famous *Utopia*, in which the ills of rising prices and enclosure are attributed solely to avaricious landowners who have callously abandoned the interests of the commonwealth in the pursuit of personal advancement. The solution offered is one of personal reform and renewal, complemented by an exhortation to avoid the sorts of sinful behavior that will imperil the immortal soul. The near-universal call is to return to an earlier age of harmonious relationships when everyone knew their place and fulfilled their obligations within a rigidly defined hierarchical order.

Henry VIII's Reformation Parliament, on the other hand, met for seven consecutive years and approved 137 statutes, many of which fundamentally altered the role of the state in the lives of English men and women. With the monarch's approval and leadership, Parliament began to play an active role in the transfer of church lands into lay hands, in the shaping of doctrinal articles for the church, and in assisting the establishment of the proper line of succession. This empowerment of a body hitherto called into session only to forward a royal policy, strengthened a nascent sense of institutional identity that would result in the emergence of a parliamentary agenda by the close of the century. Parliament gradually lost its dependent status and began to set its own reform program, a program that was not always in unison with the wishes of the crown. Henry's perspicacity lay in his recognition that there was no better way to win support for his break with Rome than to join in alliance with a strongly anti-papal Parliament, thus enabling the king to present the Reformation as the expression of a united national will.

HENRY THE TYRANT

Henry's nascent state was not only inviolable but infallible as well. The Act in Restraint of Appeals may have secured the autonomy of the nation in a world of hostile and competing powers, but it also confirmed that the supreme magistrate was endowed with "plenary, whole and entire power, preeminence, authority, prerogative and jurisdiction" in order to establish justice on all questions related to the security and preservation of the polity. By the mid-1530s, anyone who refused to accept the changed circumstances brought about by Henry's quarrel with the papacy was to be treated as a treasonous subject.

Undoubtedly the most infamous illustration of the king's intolerance and tyrannical tendencies can be found in the violent elimination of Thomas More. Appointed chancellor of England after Wolsey's fall from power in 1529, this well-known Catholic humanist and scholar had supported Henry's government throughout the early years. But when More resigned his office in 1532, unable to reconcile Henry's vision of a federation of independent European nation-states with his deep commitment to the unity of Christendom under the leadership of the pope, the king would not rest until his former friend would acknowledge the legitimacy of the Reformation statutes. More's silence on the matter was not enough to protect him in a state where the temporal magistrate was now also Supreme Head of the Church of England. Executed in 1534 after the conclusion of a show trial distinguished only by the perjury of the victim's accuser, More's refusal to recognize the omnicompetence of the state echoes even still in our own violent century.

Overall, some 330 English men and women were executed for treason by action or word during this period. Henry spared neither Catholics nor extreme Protestants in his efforts to impose uniformity, and when, in the fall of 1536, a rising in Lincolnshire and Yorkshire against the dissolution of the monasteries, rising taxes, and enclosure of lands briefly threatened to expand into a larger rebellion, Henry's duplicitous response was to hint at concessions, only to later break his promise and execute some two hundred of the participants. Opponents of the royal policy found themselves without recourse in a state where the king's wrath meant death. In terms of the number of lives lost during the Reformation and its aftermath, Henry VIII's actions against his own subjects were quite modest when compared to later revolutions. But perceived martyrs to a cause involving religious principles always galvanize opinion and heighten disdain for the alleged perpetrator. The royal effort to stamp out diversity in public opinion may have facilitated the development of the nation-state concept, but Henry's reputation has unquestionably suffered as historians continue to explore the impact of decisions made in pursuit of national sovereignty.

SUGGESTIONS FOR ADDITIONAL READING

Bindoff, S. T. *Tudor England.* Harmondsworth: Penguin Books, 1978.

Dickens, A. G. *The English Reformation.* New York: Schocken Books, 1964.

Elton, G. R. *Reform and Reformation: England, 1509–1558.* Cambridge, Mass.: Harvard University Press, 1977.

———. *The Tudor Revolution in Government.* Cambridge: Cambridge University Press, 1953.

———. *The Tudor Constitution: Documents and Commentary.* Cambridge: Cambridge University Press, 1960.

Guy, John. *Tudor England.* Oxford: Oxford University Press, 1988.

Miller, H. *Henry VIII and the English Nobility.* Oxford: Oxford University Press, 1986.

Pollard, A. F. *Henry VIII.* London: Longmans, Green, and Co., 1902.

———. *Wolsey.* London: Longmans, Green, and Co., 1929.

Scarisbrick, J. J. *Henry VIII.* Los Angeles: University of California Press, 1968.

Smith, Lacy B. *Henry VIII: The Mask of Royalty.* Boston: Houghton Mifflin, 1971.

W. M. Spellman

Herod the Great

c. 75–4 B.C.E.

King of Judea, 39–4 B.C.E.

Herod has the distinction of being equally execrated in Jewish and Christian sources. In Christian scriptures he is the monstrous instigator of the Massacre of the Innocents. In the Talmud, Jewish tradition describes him as the brute who murdered his beloved wife Mariamne, then preserved her body in honey and continued to have carnal intercourse with the cadaver. His executions of his closest kinsmen constitute a tale of horror.

Nevertheless, he was one of the great builders of his era, and the physical relics of his imagination and enterprise survive to this day. The huge Herodian stones, uniformly grooved at all the margins, still proclaim his enterprise as a creative leader at the *Kotel*, the surviving western wall of the Second Temple at Jerusalem. The remains of his pleasure palaces at Herodian and Massada fascinate tourists. Even at Hebron, the burial places of the biblical patriarchs and matriarchs still testify to the lavishness of Herod's beautification of a major Jewish religious shrine, even if partially obscured by the mosque built over the site after the Moslem conquest of Palestine in 637.

BIOGRAPHICAL BACKGROUND

Herod was born to a family of Idumean or Edomite origin that had been compelled to accept conversion to Judaism by the Hasmonean king, John Hyrcanus. His descent from Esau was never forgotten when he became king of the descendants of Jacob. The fraternal hatred between the twin brothers, described in the Book of Genesis, was both valid and current when Rome imposed Herod on the Judean Kingdom, as its puppet.

Herod's father, Antipater, had been a successful soldier of fortune and political opportunist. He had risen in the goodwill of the Roman overlords of Judea by switching his loyalties, without moral compunction, as Pompey, Anthony, Julius Caesar, or Cassius seemed to be the winner in Rome's long civil war.

Mirroring the Roman political struggle, the Jews of Judea fought an equally bloody civil war, as princes of the Hasmonean or Maccabean royal house struggled for the kingship. Antipater had managed to have himself named Administrator of Judea by the Romans, until it could be determined which Hasmonean prince was the king most acceptable to Rome. At the assassination of Antipater, his son Herod, a client of Rome's leading contender for power, Cassius, inherited his father's primacy in Judea.

That embattled land had the additional misfortune to be caught in the war zone between Rome and its principal foreign rival, Parthia. When the Parthians briefly captured Judea, they mutilated the Hasmonean king Hyrcanus, and carried him off as a captive. Instead of recognizing Hyrcanus' principal Hasmonean rival, Antigonus, Herod hastened to Rome to see the temporarily ascendant Anthony.

Describing himself as a loyal friend of Rome, and as a victim of Parthian aggression, Herod persuaded Anthony to become his advocate. Anthony, knowing little of Judean politics, convinced the Roman Senate to make Herod king of Judea.

In the spring of 39 B.C.E., Herod landed in Judea backed by a Roman army, intent on driving out Antigonus. The Jewish population was horrified to find themselves handed over to a descendant of Esau. What followed was a bitter war in which eleven Roman legions, plus as many as thirty thousand foreign mercenaries in Herod's service, looted and pillaged the land, raping and massacring the inhabitants. Even Herod realized that he would have gained nothing if he became king of a totally destroyed and depopulated land. Therefore, in July 37 B.C.E., he paid the Romans a fortune to withdraw from Jerusalem and its environs. He then executed Antigonus, the leading Hasmonean pretender.

Knowing how much he was despised by his Jewish subjects, Herod married Mariamne, granddaughter of Hyrcanus, the original Hasmonean pretender to the throne. As will be noted hereafter, he spent money lavishly to enhance the beauty of Jewish religious shrines. He attempted, at first, to conform to Jewish religious practice.

As he grew older, however, his fear of treason and assassination, not without justification, drove him to excesses of brutal repression. In his final years his behavior can only be described as psychotic. His chief biographer, instructor, and ambassador, Nicholas of Damascus, fully documented all of Herod's excesses.

His death from intestinal cancer in 4 B.C.E. occasioned no rejoicing because, from his deathbed, he ordered one final act of barbarity. Jewish zealots who had prematurely torn down the eagle erected by Herod in the Temple precincts, were ordered burned alive. The rabbis, however, who had been arrested and condemned by Herod in his last days, were spared when he died.

HEROD AS A GREAT LEADER

When Herod came to power, lawlessness reigned everywhere, taxes were unbearable, and the government was in chaos. Herod immediately made his government a model of efficiency. The country was divided into nineteen provinces, and the governor of each province reported directly to Herod.

During Herod's brief alliance with Anthony, the latter's paramour, Queen Cleopatra of Egypt, had managed to annex territories that had traditionally been Judean. Once Augustus Caesar was securely in power, Herod recovered what had been lost to Egypt, as well as the districts of Ituraea, Trachonitis, Auranitis, and Batanea.

In the all-important area of religious practice, the Hasmonean kings had had an advantage. As they were direct descendants of Aaron, the brother of Moses, they belonged to the hereditary priesthood. Thus the Hasmonean kings could be heads of state, and high priests simultaneously. Herod had no such priestly descent, and even he could not tamper with membership in the priesthood. He did, however, undertake to choose the high priests and to supervise the Temple and its great wealth.

He took land from the old aristocracy and used their confiscated wealth for his own administrative expenses. At the same time, he created a new and loyal aristocracy, obliged to him for all favors received. Banditry was ruthlessly suppressed, so that humble farmers could live in peace. In his earlier years, when he still sought popularity, he reduced taxes. In years of economic depression, he sold his own plate and furnishings to help the needy, taking care to do it as ostentatiously as possible.

In his building enterprises he was both extravagant and dramatic. Mount Moriah, on which the relatively modest Second Temple stood, Herod had surrounded with huge retaining walls within which great amounts of stone, earth, and debris were deposited until the flat area at the height of the mount had been multiplied many times. Herod then undertook to build a greatly enlarged temple, which the historian Josephus later described in these terms: "When the morning sun burst upon the white marble of the Temple, Mount Moriah glittered like a hill of snow; and when its rays struck the golden roof of the sacred edifice, the whole mount gleamed and sparkled as if it were in flames."

Herod constructed a splendid new port at Caesarea, named in honor of his patron. Ironically, with all of the effort he devoted to making himself loved among the Jews of Judea, he remained always the hated Idumean outsider. He was popular among the Hellenized pagan population in the Galilee and Samaria. Jews living throughout the Diaspora also appreciated him because he defended Jewish interests wherever there was friction with the Romans.

HEROD THE TYRANT

Eight years before becoming king, Herod was already well launched on his career as a tyrant. When his father, Antipater, was governor of the Galilee, he had had to suppress a Jewish rebellion. Herod had all captured rebels executed without trial in 47 B.C.E. For this high-handed and illegal measure, the Jewish religious high court in Jerusalem condemned him. When he was at last securely in power, he had forty-five judges of the high court executed.

Throughout his life he killed all members of the Hasmonean dynasty who had any claim to the throne. His victims included not only his wife, Mariamne, but two of their sons, as well as another son whose mother, Doris, was Herod's second wife.

Although Herod knew the value of winning popularity by lowering taxes, he was pitiless in taking what he regarded as due to the state. Towns that held back taxes were razed and the inhabitants sold into slavery. The spectacle of a Jewish king selling Jews into slavery reinforced the suspicion with which religious Jews regarded their "Idumean" king.

Herod's secret police roamed everywhere. Certainly no plot against him ever escaped undetected. Unfortunately, Herod's paranoia saw seditious plots where none existed. He died, universally hated by his Jewish subjects.

SUGGESTIONS FOR ADDITIONAL READING

Dimont, Max I. *Jews, God and History*. New York: Signet Books, 1962.

Graetz, Heinrich. *History of the Jews*, Volume II. Philadelphia: Jewish Publication Society of America, 1893.

Margolis, Max L. and Alexander Marx. *A History of the Jewish People*. Philadelphia: Jewish Publication Society of America, 1927.

"Herod." *Encyclopedia Judaica*. New York: Macmillan, 1972.

Langerkvist, Par. *Herod and Mariamne*. New York: Alfred A. Knopf, 1968.

Markham, Gervase. *A Critical Edition of the True Tragedy of Herod and Antipater*. New York: Garland Publishers, 1979.

H. W. Basser and Aaron Lichtenstein

Toyotomi Hideyoshi
1536–1598

Supreme Daimyo of Japan, 1590–1598

Toyotomi Hideyoshi is one of a trio of men who brought about the unification of Japan in the late sixteenth century after over a century of warfare among feudal barons who answered to no central authority. The first of the three, Oda Nobunaga, brought almost a third of Japan under his sway before his assassination in 1582. Hideyoshi, commander of one of Nobunaga's armies, quickly avenged the death of his master, consolidated his power over rival forces, and left a unified and peaceful Japan to the third of the trio, Tokugawa Ieyasu. Hideyoshi completed the conquest of the nation by 1590 and ruled Japan as a military dictator until his death in 1598. Thus his career was mainly that of a warrior, for only in the last decade of his life was he primarily a political leader.

Much of Hideyoshi's fame derives from the rags-to-riches nature of his career. In a nation where lineage counts for much, Hideyoshi's phoenix-like rise to power was due to his own ambition, abilities, and character—and to a touch of luck. Because of his lowly birth, he did not possess a family name (only the court nobility, military clans, and leading merchant houses had surnames), and during his ascendance to power he took on one then another family name. It is largely for this reason that he was and is mainly known merely as Hideyoshi.

BIOGRAPHICAL BACKGROUND

Hideyoshi was the son of a poor farmer who once served as a foot soldier under the Oda clan in Owari province in central Japan. When he was eight years old, his father died, and when he was only thirteen, Hideyoshi, an unruly child with an aversion to study, set out "to see a bit of the world." Penniless, he turned to begging, then joined a band of robbers, then was apprenticed to a blacksmith, then to a carpenter, but never for long. Restless, energetic, and self-reliant, Hideyoshi sought challenge, and finally, after having impressed a particular samurai (warrior) in the service of the *daimyo* (feudal baron) Oda Nobunaga with his intelligence and his martial skills, the young adventurer was made a samurai. Thus he began his military career at twenty-two years of age as a lowly attendant to the warring Nobunaga, under whom he would serve for the next twenty-four years.

Although the facts of Hideyoshi's early life are hardly known, fables served up by his resourceful biographers tell us of his legendary exploits and of examples of his acumen, courage, and craftiness that account for his rapid rise in the ranks of Nobunaga's army. While much of his hallowed heroism may be exaggerated, there is little question that he was unusually gifted as a courageous and loyal warrior, as a military strategist, and as a leader of men, and that his elevation was the result of his remarkable successes in service to Nobunaga. Ultimately, he was made a general and placed in command of Nobunaga's campaign that set out in 1582 to conquer all rival daimyo west of the imperial capital of Kyoto. It was Hideyoshi's good fortune to hitch his star to a man driven to bring the entire country under his command. He was wise enough to remain loyal to the ambitious Nobunaga and to restrain his own ambition to become the master of the nation.

Hideyoshi was quick, however, to turn the assassination of Oda Nobunaga (for which he bore no responsibility) to his advantage, first by avenging his death, thereby securing the allegiance of Nobunaga's other loyal retainers, then by subduing all remaining rival daimyo in battle. Thus did Hideyoshi progress from becoming first among loyal generals in 1582 to supreme commander of all daimyo of the nation by 1590. He then confirmed the approximately two hundred daimyo of the nation in their powers as feudal rulers of their domains and required them to swear allegiance to him. His authority rested on military conquest, but he legitimized his power by obtaining appropriate titles from the emperor in Kyoto, whose rule was ceremonial but was the legal basis for governing authority. By issuing decrees bearing the seal of the emperor, Hideyoshi instituted a new order and laid the grounds for lasting peace. Hideyoshi's principal measures for organizing the peace included re-establishing a stable feudal relationship between the daimyo and his new central authority, conducting a nationwide disarmament of all commoners, confining the right to bear arms only to the samurai class, and restricting occupational change and travel.

In 1592, Hideyoshi launched an invasion of Korea, which he envisioned as the first step toward the conquest of the Chinese empire. But his military adventurism ultimately failed when, after a long truce, Japanese troops returned without victory in 1598 upon the death of the would-be Japanese emperor of China. Hideyoshi's plans for the succession of his young son would also prove unsuccessful, despite the exacting preparations he made for it.

HIDEYOSHI AS A GREAT LEADER

The violent age of ferocious warfare that produced an Oda Nobunaga, notorious for turning battles into bloodbaths, also produced a Hideyoshi, who, after succeeding Nobunaga and defeating powerful rivals in battle, was comparatively conciliatory. After having built a reputation as a warrior and as the mastermind of many of Nobunaga's victories, Hideyoshi would ultimately be noted most for his pacification of warring daimyo and his building a new political order. The search for security supplanted the drive for conquest. Unlike Nobunaga, who exterminated his enemies, Hideyoshi spared them, treated them generously, and enlisted their support in battles against still other daimyo to be subdued. His battle in 1587 against Satsuma, the most powerful opponent in western Japan, is a case in point. In this, the longest battle of his career to date, Hideyoshi, after finally beating down Satsuma's defense, held back his eager troops from crushing the enemy in his grasp, granting him a generous peace, including the right to retain his domain. He thereby secured the active support of this important daimyo.

Hideyoshi chose to preserve the feudal domains in exchange for his own national hegemony. He recognized that he stood to gain by conciliation and winning the allegiance of daimyo, and they realized that they stood to gain by participating in the new political settlement. Therefore, rather than eliminate daimyo, Hideyoshi reinforced their feudal powers and made them more secure in the rule of their own domains.

Hideyoshi thus restored peace and civility to a country that had been engulfed in war and treachery for over a century. His new order of peace, a federation of feudal rulers who submitted to the new hegemon's authority, was embraced by his able successor, Tokugawa Ieyasu, and maintained by fifteen generations of Tokugawa rulers. Within a generation after his death, war had become a distant memory and the military class was itself becoming an anachronism.

The underlying purpose of Hideyoshi's various reforms was to solidify the status quo. A cornerstone of his national policy was the undertaking of a nationwide land survey (the first since the eighth century) and a new system of taxation, which, by its uniform enforcement, served as an effective instrument of political control. Perhaps the most important of his reforms, the one that would have greatest impact long after his passing, was the "sword hunt." His edict ordering the disarming of the peasantry and other commoners was undertaken as "the foundation of the safety of the country and the happiness of the people." As an inducement, Hideyoshi proclaimed that the weapons collected were to be melted down and used for the construction of a huge statue of Buddha, which would serve to safeguard the disarmed people in their lives beyond death. The sword hunt, together with another edict prohibiting both social and geographic mobility, was designed to freeze the social order. It not only deprived the peasants of arms but deprived samurai of an independent base of power or a tie to the land, and it resulted in the enduring separation of peasants and warriors. The ultimate effect of these measures, which were retained during the Tokugawa period (1600–1868), was to provide security and stability for the central government, the daimyo, and the society over which they ruled in peace. Hideyoshi's brief rule was therefore a major turning point in Japanese history, during which the nation made passage from the brutality of the warring-states period to an era of peace and tranquillity lasting for almost three centuries.

Another enduring legacy of Hideyoshi's rule is his rebuilding of the imperial capital of Kyoto, a city that has remained to this very day one of the world's treasured cities. During the long warring-states period the city fell into disrepair while the imperial house languished in poverty. Nobunaga, in a wrathful revenge against Kyoto nobles who defied him, burned the city, reducing over half of it to ashes. Hideyoshi, who made it a point to seek legitimation for his authority from the imperial court, saw it necessary to restore the grandeur of the court and of the city where it resided. Moreover, Hideyoshi made Kyoto his own monumentally beautiful capital city. Thus he undertook numerous large construction projects, including his own magnificent residence, Jurakudai; a commercial city center with wide avenues, bridges, moats, and river dikes many of which remain intact today; a twenty-two-kilometer-long wall surrounding the city (its first and last wall); a massive statue of Buddha (using the melted weapons); many of the Buddhist temples and monasteries that survive today in the same sites within the city and in the hills to the east of it; and a grand castle at Momoyama just to the south of the city (and a still more massive one in the nearby city of Osaka). Kyoto endures yet today as a testament to Hideyoshi's munificence.

HIDEYOSHI THE TYRANT

As a warrior in command of large armies engaged in many colossal battles during Nobunaga's reign of terror, Hideyoshi contributed his share to the carnage. Although never the tyrant that Nobunaga was, he, like other leading warriors in that era of unbridled warfare, believed that "the end justifies the means." On one occasion he resorted to diverting a river to flood his enemy's castle in order to force his surrender. In quest of victory Hideyoshi did not hesitate to take the heads of thousands of enemy soldiers and to put the lives of as many of his own men on the line.

When he defeated his last rival in 1590 and attained ultimate power, the supremely confident Hideyoshi was already accustomed to wielding the awesome power of a military dictator. To ensure the loyalty of daimyo, Hideyoshi did not rely on oaths alone; he ordered them to destroy all fortifications save for their own residential castle, threatened to confiscate all or part of their fiefs, and ordered them to deliver their wives and children to Kyoto as hostages. Though many of his reforms were constructive, his methods were stern and despotic, and his manner arrogant and audacious. His edicts were replete with threats of awful punishments for offenders. In his edict forbidding the harboring of armed men who were not retainers of a daimyo, he called for collective punishment for offenders, stating that "if you violate these laws and permit such a person to go free, three heads will be cut off and sent [to the previous master] in place of that one man."

As a tyrant he drafted large numbers of laborers from the ranks of peasants and townsmen and drove them harshly in his enormous building projects. Hideyoshi's appetite was for the colossal, and he insisted that his castles and other construction projects be completed with dazzling speed. Insisting on astonishing results, he caused immeasurable pain and hardship to the tens of thousands of laborers he assembled. His attitude toward peasants is summed up in a saying attributed to him: "Treat peasants like sesame seeds; the more you squeeze, the more you get." On one occasion he applied the squeeze, not by raising the tax rate, but by decreasing the size of the unit of measure being taxed.

Though generally conciliatory and judicious in his rule, Hideyoshi occasionally, especially near the end of his life, displayed incredible cruelty. One instance of this was his abruptly ordering the crucifixion of twenty-six Roman Catholic priests in 1597, after having earlier giving indication of his tolerance of the foreign religion and its missionaries. In another instance, when some scribbling was detected on the gate of his own palace, Hideyoshi condemned the twenty detected culprits to be crucified.

Hideyoshi's assault on Korea provides still more evidence of his viciousness. It was an act of aggression and aimed at nothing less than conquest of the Chinese empire, and it resulted in a carnage of the Koreans. He may not have been directly responsible for the savage acts of his armies in Korea, but his orders seem to have prompted them. Hideyoshi enjoined his soldiers to cut off the noses and ears of slain Koreans as trophies with which he promised to build a huge mound in Kyoto. Not only were Koreans the victims of his wrath, but on several occasions he executed high-ranking Japanese officers who failed to execute his orders or questioned his policies or even those who delivered to him unfavorable reports from Korea.

Also extraordinary was his ordering the death of the famous tea ceremony master Sen no Rikyu. Inexplicably, Hideyoshi suddenly turned against this noted man of art who had long been associated with him, presided over his tea parties, and designed tea huts for him. First he exiled him, then ordered his return for punishment, which took the form of ritual suicide.

Hideyoshi's most brutal deed was done in relation to the issue of succession. This was perpetrated against his nephew, Hidetsugu, and his family. In 1591 after the death of his only son, Hideyoshi named the twenty-three-year-old Hidetsugu his heir. Half a year later, however, another son was born quite unexpectedly, and Hideyoshi, the proud father, showered affection on the child, Hideyori, and began scheming to make him heir. But succession had been arranged for Hidetsugu, who had already inherited Hideyoshi's court titles and was installed in Jurakudai palace as Hideyoshi moved to the new castle he had built to the south of Kyoto. Suddenly, in 1595, acting on a suspicion of Hidetsugu's infidelity, Hideyoshi ordered him into exile and then ordered his suicide. Next, Hideyoshi had Hidetsugu's wife and young children (two sons and one daughter) and concubines (thirty-one women in all) publicly executed in Kyoto after carting them through the streets. Their bodies were thrown into a pit over which a stone was erected on which was inscribed the words "Tomb of Traitors."

While there is no agreement among Hideyoshi's biographers on the reasons for his committing these inhuman acts in the final years of his life, many explain simply that he had lost his sanity. Madness would seem too simple an answer, and there is, in any case, insufficient evidence to substantiate it. But it would seem that he did become obsessed with the matter of succession after the birth of his son, and this may help to explain, but not excuse, his annihilation of the family of the would-be heir. Obsessed or not, Hideyoshi was to the end a tyrant whose power knew no bounds.

SUGGESTIONS FOR ADDITIONAL READING

Berry, Mary Elizabeth. *Hideyoshi.* Cambridge, Mass.: Harvard University Press, 1982.

Boscaro, Adriana. *101 Letters of Toyotomi Hideyoshi.* New York: Oxford University Press, 1975.

Dening, Walter. *The Life of Toyotomi Hideyoshi.* 3rd ed. London: Kegan Paul, Trench, Trubner & Co., 1930 (1st ed., 1888).

Yoshikawa, Eiji. *Taiko.* Translated by Williams Scott Wilson. Tokyo: Kodansha International, 1992.

Wayne C. McWilliams

Ho Chi Minh (Nguyen Tat Than)

1890–1969

President of the Democratic Republic of Viet Nam, 1945–1969

The paradox of Ho Chi Minh is that he was at once a gentle, sensitive Confucian gentleman and the leader of a revolution that terrorized when it could not convince and assassinated when it could not recruit. The Chinese and Vietnamese have traditionally interpreted their cosmos in terms of dyads—linked opposites as illustrated by the *yin-yang* symbol. Good-evil, light-dark, male-female, benevolence-cruelty are connected, and each is necessary for the existence of the other, although one is "better" than the other. This thought formed the assumptions of Ho's generation, despite the new Marxist-Leninist ideology, so "Uncle Ho" could be gentle and brutal without causing the least surprise to his followers. He did not adopt the name Ho Chi Minh until 1941. It means "Ho who Enlightens."

BIOGRAPHICAL BACKGROUND

Ho Chi Minh was born Nguyen Tat Than on May 19, 1890, in his mother's village, Hoang Tru, and grew up in his father's village, Kien Lin, Nan Dan district, Nghe An province, in central Viet Nam. Nghe An, one of the poorest provinces in the country, had traditionally produced not only large numbers of Confucian scholars, but rebels as well. His father, Nguyen Sinh Huy (1862–1929) was both. The son of a peasant and a "woman of the second class" (the daughter of a concubine), Huy worked as a farm laborer while studying the Confucian classics in preparation for the imperial exams. He married the daughter of his teacher, the landlord Hoang Duong, and passed both the provincial and metropolitan exams to achieve the *Pho Bang* degree (doctor of literature, second class).

Both Ho's parents had friends and relatives in the anti-French guerrilla movement, and the boy grew up on tales of heroic Vietnamese resistance to foreign invasion. While Huy was secretary to the Imperial Board of Rites, the family lived in the capital, Hué, where his mother died in 1905.

There Ho attended the nationalist school (*Quoc Hoc*) of Ngo Dinh Kha (1905–1910), where the curriculum included Vietnamese history and literature, French language and culture, science, and mathematics. Other students of the *Quoc Hoc* included Kha's son, Ngo Dinh Diem, future president of South Viet Nam, and Vo Nguyen Giap, military architect of the Communist victory.

Fired by the French from a district magistracy for obstructionism, Ho's father became a wanderer. He taught, wrote letters for illiterates, and practiced traditional medicine. His influence on his children was profound. All three became revolutionaries, and Ho too became a wanderer, in search of a new world-ordering philosophy to replace Confucianism.

In 1911, Ho went to work on a French liner as a mess boy. By the time he returned to his homeland in 1941, he had seen the world's misery and had been converted, in a stroke of Ch'an Buddhist enlightenment, to Leninism.

Legend has it that Ho was working in London in the Hotel Carlton kitchen under the famous French chef Escoffier when he decided to move to Paris in 1917. There he immediately immersed himself in leftist politics while supporting himself as a photo retoucher and forger of Oriental antiquities. Assuming the name Nguyen Ai Quoc (Nguyen the Patriot), he wrote anti-colonial articles and founded and edited the journal *La Paria* (*The Outcast*). Failing to interest the Versailles Peace Conference in civil rights for Viet Nam, he moved further to the left. He was a delegate to the 1920 Socialist Congress at Tours and became a founder of the French Communist Party.

In Moscow in 1923, he trained at the University of the Toilers of the East and embarked on a twenty-year career as an agent of the Communist International (Comintern). Sent to Canton, China, with Comintern advisers, he organized revolutionary Vietnamese émigré associations while hiding his communism under the guise of nationalism, a task at which he became a world master. After Chiang Kai-shek's purge of Communists in 1927, he moved his émigré activities to Thailand, often wearing the saffron robe of a Buddhist monk. He merged the three newly formed Vietnamese Communist parties into the Indochinese Communist Party in 1930. Arrested in Hong Kong the same year, he slipped away from a prison hospital where he was being treated for tuberculosis and fled to Moscow. On his return to China in 1938, he visited Mao Zedong's headquarters in Yenan before joining a Red Army mission to the south to teach guerrilla tactics to Chiang's nationalist army.

After the French defeat by the Axis (1940), Pham Van Dong, later premier of the Democratic Republic of Viet Nam (DRV), and Vo Nguyen Giap fled Viet Nam to join Ho in China, where they formed the Viet Minh nationalist front (1941) and trained Vietnamese in guerrilla tactics before infiltrating them back into Viet Nam. Ho himself returned to Viet Nam in

1941 after an absence of thirty years. Developing a base near the border, organizing villagers and training them for a war of national liberation, and spending some time in a Chinese nationalist prison (1942–1944), Ho secured aid from both the nationalist Chinese and the Americans. The tactics of guerrilla warfare he and Giap developed were a mixture of traditional Vietnamese practice and Maoist theories of protracted war, both of which derive from traditional Chinese methods found in Sun Tsu's fourth-century B.C. classic, *The Art of War*.

Realizing that the Japanese must soon surrender, Ho called for a general uprising in August 1945; in control of Hanoi by the end of the month, he declared Vietnamese independence on September 2 and soon assumed the presidency. After the Japanese surrender, a temporary British and Chinese occupation led to the return of the French, and no amount of negotiation could budge them from the country, so Ho and the Viet Minh retreated to their mountain bases in 1946 to fight. Ho obtained Chinese Communist and Soviet recognition of the DRV in 1950. The Chinese advice and aid that followed were instrumental in the defeat of the French in 1954. Ho's work was not over, however, for the country was partitioned by the Geneva Conference. From 1954 to 1959 Ho "built socialism" in the north, while the United States tried to build a viable government in the south.

In the south, the war resumed in 1957; Ho's government began sending advisers and materiel down the Ho Chi Minh Trail in 1959. Behind a façade of noninvolvement, the DRV planned and controlled the Viet Cong insurgency. Shortly after American troops arrived, Ho also sent increasing numbers of northern troops. Through all this, Ho Chi Minh led the government. In the minds of most Vietnamese and many others, "Uncle Ho" personified the Vietnamese revolution.

He died in September 1969, without seeing the success of the revolution that he, more than anyone else, had created.

HO CHI MINH AS A GREAT LEADER

Ho Chi Minh is arguably the greatest leader in Vietnamese history. He combined the achievements of Tran Hung Dao, who vanquished the Mongols in 1288; Le Loi, who, in a ten-year guerrilla war, expelled the Ming Chinese after a quarter-century of occupation; and Nguyen Anh, who reunited the nation in 1802 after three hundred years of division. With superb talent as organizer, strategist, and teacher, he led through personal example.

During a revolutionary career of half a century, Ho never wavered in his goal of liberating and reuniting his country. His frugal, moral life, joined with his kindly personality and subtle intelligence, made him a revolutionary version of the Confucian sage, a superior/enlightened man working in the dust of the world for the benefit of the people. A man of "virtue"

(Chinese: *te*), that mysterious innate knowledge of what to do and when to do it, he was also a man of action; he thus exhibited the characteristics traditional society required in a leader. When the emperor Bao Dai abdicated his throne in August 1945 in favor of Ho's revolution, all Viet Nam knew the Mandate of Heaven had passed to a new leader.

Ho's personality made him *Bac Ho*, Uncle Ho, to his people. *Bac* is the title given to a paternal uncle. In the Confucian hierarchy a father is second only to the emperor in dignity, one who must be revered and obeyed. An uncle, however, could be warm and loving as he guided a youth to his proper place in the world of rites and morality. Uncle Ho, therefore, is a title of affection and trust and not merely a propaganda device in Ho's "cult of the personality."

The most cosmopolitan of Communist leaders, Ho combined a knowledge of the West with a deep understanding of his people, which made him an organizer of rare ability, whether as a Comintern agent founding the Indochinese Communist Party out of three rival factions or, back in Viet Nam, as a revolutionary leader elaborating the political-military structure of *dau tranh* (struggle), which emphasized political organization of the peasants in the villages before training or deploying them as soldiers. The committee government he gave the DRV survived his death without the turmoil seen in successions in other Communist countries.

His ability to choose the right man for the job may be seen in his choice of the brilliant but headstrong young Vo Nguyen Giap as his military lieutenant. His eye for the right moment in human affairs made him a superb strategist, a man who knew himself and his enemy, and therefore a man who, in the words of Sun Tzu, could achieve victory. He opened the revolution to people of talent and involved the masses in the political process for the first time. In doing so he tapped the vast energy of the Vietnamese peasant.

His profound awareness of his people's need for a new philosophy that would re-connect them to the Tao, the Way of the Universe, made him a superb teacher. As the anti-colonial writer Nguyen Ai Quoc, he sustained and enlightened his people during the dark days between the world wars when liberation seemed very far away. As a revolutionary propagandist, he understood the ancient values of the village, which enabled him to teach the peasants to understand socialism in a way that seemed to recreate the traditional village social community, previously destroyed by the French introduction of a money economy. In this way he linked past and future in a typically Sino-Vietnamese fashion, which made it possible for his people to move from the past into the future.

As only great leaders can, Ho Chi Minh gave his people the strength and unity to endure a thirty-year struggle for liberation.

HO CHI MINH THE TYRANT

If Ho Chi Minh, more than any other, was the architect of victory, he is also responsible, more than any other, for the present lamentable state of Viet Nam, as the *Lao Dong* (Workers' Party) clings grimly to a failed system. It was Lenin and his "Theses on Colonialism," not Marx, that drew Vietnamese radicals to communism. It is Lenin's one-party government to which they cling. Ho brought Viet Nam one-party government and communism, not the socialism he had described to the villagers.

Like the indivisibility of the yin-yang, leadership and tyranny are not easily separated in Asia. Confucianism allows actions in time of disorder that would not be considered moral at other times, for the maintenance of unity and order are of paramount importance. If Confucianism allows cruel actions, revolution demands them. While the system Ho devised may seem tyrannical to a person nurtured in a parliamentary democracy, it may not seem so to the Vietnamese. The imperial Vietnamese government was authoritarian and sometimes arbitrary, but it was also distant from the village. The emperor's law stopped at the bamboo hedge. Behind the hedge, the village notables ruled by customary law. Only in criminal matters did the central government penetrate into the village. The revolution's first priority was to penetrate the village to reorganize it for revolutionary struggle. From the outset, Ho's men killed uncooperative notables and formed revolutionary committees to govern in their place. They mobilized traditional village organizations for revolutionary action and formed new groups. Control of the villages was vital—and more important than military victory—for whoever controls the villages controls Viet Nam. Ho's kindly face concealed a will of steel; he routinely ordered the ruthless liquidation of his opponents.

A Westerner might regard Ho's clandestine communism disguised as nationalism, his eternal front organizations secretly controlled by communists, his pretense that the north was not running the southern insurgency, as dishonest, if not immoral. His compatriots might not. Secret societies are traditional in Viet Nam. The Sino-Vietnamese system had no formal channels for political opposition. Dissent had to be covert; to tell the truth would be fatal to the cause. In any case, a leader in the Vietnamese tradition is supposed to be opaque and mysterious; it is part of his virtue.

Linked in a dyad with dishonesty, however, is the important neo-Confucian concept of "sincerity," the ability of a man to make his actions fit his words. The betrayal of promises to his followers may be more important to them than any charge of tyranny. His land collectivization program (1954–1956), which raised rebellion in Ho's home province, had to be curtailed, and Ho publicly apologized for its excesses. Still, the transformation of the village collectivity, where each family tilled a private plot, into collective farms was not what the peasants had understood the revolution was about. Ho had promised land to the landless.

The betrayal of the National Liberation Front in the south was also a serious matter. Members of the Viet Cong apparently believed the DRV's promise of southern autonomy and gradual unification, but in 1975 the country was united by force, and Viet Cong veterans today claim they do not get even the small benefits that go to northern veterans. It happened after Ho's death, but it was part of his plan.

Marxist central planning and the command economy introduced after 1954, possibly necessary steps in Viet Nam's modernization, brought the whole weight of the central government to bear on the individual in a way that the country had not seen even under the French. The regimentation of every facet of life was new to the Vietnamese peasant, who was accustomed to the ancient autonomy of village life. There was no channel for opposition to the policies of this government, either. Along with rebellion, flight and noncooperation have been traditional Vietnamese responses to tyranny. The number of Boat People who have fled the country testify to widespread dissatisfaction with the new order.

Such betrayals and intrusions may not add up to tyranny in the minds of the Vietnamese, but neither are they signs of a government ruling by virtue, a Confucian concept likely still remembered. The brutal re-education camps for the South Vietnamese and the ill-planned New Economic Zones in the malaria-infested mountain jungles, where camp graduates and other unlucky souls were sent to colonize lowland Vietnamese among the tribesmen and open up new land, came after Ho's death, but they are part of the system he inaugurated. He conspired for forty years to root out the old system and impose upon his people the new system he had found to replace Confucianism, Marxism-Leninism. If that system is tyrannical, so was he.

For the Vietnamese, however, to characterize Ho Chi Minh as *either* a great leader *or* a tyrant would be foreign to their thought processes. From the time of the first Chinese emperor (221 B.C.), great leadership has included great tyranny.

SUGGESTIONS FOR ADDITIONAL READING

Chen, King C. *Vietnam and China, 1938–1954.* Princeton, N.J.: Princeton University Press, 1969.

Duiker, William. *The Communist Road to Power.* Boulder, Colo.: Westview Press, 1981.

Fall, Bernard. *Ho Chi Minh on Revolution; Selected Writings, 1920–1966.* New York: Frederick Praeger, 1967.

Vo Nquyen Giap. *Unforgettable Months and Years.* Ithaca, N.Y.: Cornell University Press, 1975.

Hoang Van Hoan. *A Drop in the Ocean; Hoan's Revolutionary Reminiscences.* Beijing: Jiefangjen chubanshe, 1987.

Kobelev, Yevgeny. *Ho Chi Minh.* Moscow: Progress Publishers, 1983. English translation, 1987.
Lacouture, Jean. *Ho Chi Minh, a Political Biography.* New York: Vintage Books, 1968.
Our President Ho Chi Minh. Hanoi: Foreign Language Publishing House, 1970.
Sainteny, Jean. *Ho Chi Minh and His Vietnam; a Personal Memoir.* Chicago: Cowles Book Co., 1972.

Marilynn M. Larew

Ivan IV, the Terrible

1530–1584

Grand Prince and Tsar of Moscow, 1533–1584

The seven churches that still stand at the Kremlin in Moscow have their origins in the memorialization of the victories won by Ivan IV in his conquests. This tsar, undoubtedly insane, at least in his later years, left his mark on Russia in other meaningful ways. It was he who opened the way for Russia to cross the Urals and to begin its march across Siberia to the Pacific Ocean. It was he who broke the power of the *boyar* nobility, which had arrogant memories of having sprung from the same roots as the tsar himself. Ivan created a new nobility of humbler origin, which did not dare to claim equality with the tsar. When the first Russian ambassador was sent by Ivan to the court of England's Queen Elizabeth I, the diplomat crawled the length of the throne room on his hands and knees, humbly to kiss the hem of the queen's gown. Elizabeth was amused at the self-abasement of a Russian envoy. In Russia, the difference between the Autocrat of all the Russias and any of his servants was not at all amusing.

BIOGRAPHICAL BACKGROUND

Ivan Vasil'evich, better known as Ivan IV or Ivan the Terrible, was born on August 25, 1530, at Kolomenskoe, near Moscow. He was the son of Grand Prince Vasilii (Basil) III, the titular ruler of what was still known then as the Kingdom of Muscovy, and Ielena Glinskaia, member of the well-known *boyar* (princely) family of Glinskiis. His family claimed descent from the medieval Novgorodian prince, Alexander Nevskii and Rurik, the legendary founder of Rus'. Ivan's father died when he was but three years old and his mother and her lover, Prince I. Ovchina-Telep'ev Obolenskii, ruled as regents until 1537, when apparently she was poisoned by boyar plotters. Four of Ivan's uncles were also murdered, along with other important personages at the court, by jealous boyars. Some of these killings took place in Ivan's presence, traumatizing the young boy for life.

In 1543, at the age of thirteen, Ivan manifested some of the qualities for which he later earned the name *Groznyi* ("Stern," or more commonly, "the Terrible"), when he ordered that the leader of the boyar clique, Andrei Shuiskii, be summarily executed in his presence. Later he ordered that a nobleman, who was apparently rude to him, have his tongue cut out. There were other similar incidents and only the Metropolitan of Moscow, Makarii, could restrain some of these excesses. Still, during his minority the kingdom was ruled by the Glinskii family. Ivan spent his days hunting and traveling, being particularly fond of visiting remote monasteries.

On January 17, 1547, he was formally crowned as Muscovy's first "tsar" (a derivation of the title "Caesar") in the Kremlin's great hall. In this he was consciously laying claim to the imperial Byzantine legacy, evoking the formula of "Moscow, the Third Rome" set forth earlier by a Muscovite cleric. Shortly thereafter he married Anastasia of the Romanov clan. The marriage was a happy one, since Anastasia calmed Ivan's violent temper. The happy marriage and youthful optimism characterized the first—the "good"—period of Ivan's reign (1547–1560). During that time Ivan surrounded himself with progressive advisers, including Metropolitan Makarii, Prince Andrei Kurbskii, the priest Silvester, and a gifted young adviser, Aleksei Adashev. Together they came to represent an informal cabinet, the "Chosen Council," entrusted with various administrative and military reforms. Particularly significant were various measures to curb the power of the boyar class, historically a very disruptive element. Ivan summoned also a series of councils, such as the *zemskii sobor* (Assembly of the Land) in 1549 and various church councils. In 1550 he promulgated a new code of laws, the *Sudebnik*, which reinforced central authority and promoted the service gentry. He established new departments, the *prikazy*, which functioned as state ministries.

Ivan was also very active in matters of foreign policy and military affairs. In 1548 he launched his first campaign against the Tatars of the Khanate of Kazan', one of the remnants of the Golden Horde of Batu, which had devastated the medieval Kievan Rus' and had dominated Russian lands for two centuries. Kazan' was finally taken by Ivan in 1552. From there, he moved against the Khanate of Astrakhan', eventually taking over the entire Volga River basin. Under his initiative, Muscovy also expanded eastward, into and beyond the Ural Mountains, thus beginning the rapid conquest of Siberia. He subsequently moved into the Baltic region, precipitating in 1558 the Livonian War. It lasted twenty-four years, an exhausting yet futile struggle that ended only with the intervention of Pope Gregory XIII in 1582. During this conflict, Muscovy experienced one of the most devastating raids by the Tatars of Crimea, who sacked and burned the city of Moscow in 1571.

Gradually, Ivan's reign began to sour, bringing his "good" period to an end. The palace intrigues intensified as Ivan's wars dragged on. Part of the problem was the boyars' resistance to Ivan's centralizing, autocratic ideals. Some of his close associates grew disillusioned with Ivan's growing capriciousness—his friend Andrei Kurbskii later defected to Lithuania, whence he bombarded Ivan with bitterly critical letters. Although weakened by the rise of the service gentry, the boyars still represented a formidable force against the modernization of Muscovy.

In 1553 Ivan fell gravely ill. Believing that he was dying, he ordered the boyars to swear allegiance to his son Dimitrii, but many refused. He never forgot the betrayal. He shortly broke with his "Chosen Council," insinuating treachery. In 1560 his beloved Anastasia mysteriously died, perhaps poisoned. Shortly thereafter, Metropolitan Makarii, who also exerted positive influence on the tsar, died too. This, together with the desertion of many of his associates, seemed to make his mind snap. In 1564 he suddenly left Moscow for his estate at Aleksandrovskaia Sloboda sixty miles away. He then sent letters to the Metropolitan of Moscow, denouncing the boyars and the clergy and expressing his wish to step down from the throne. In consternation, the people of Moscow marched to Ivan and begged him to return. He agreed on two terms: that they recognize a new subdivision of the tsarist state, the *Oprichnina* (from the Russian word *oprich*, meaning "aside" or "apart"), to be administered only by him; and that they endorse his right to punish the traitors and evildoers in their midst.

Ivan's return to Moscow in early 1565 began the peculiar period still known in Russian history as the *Oprichnina*. Strictly speaking, it referred to a private domain of the tsar, a state within the state, consisting, at its height, of one-third of the Muscovite realm. It was supervised by the *oprichniki*, a private tsarist force dressed in black and whose symbols were a broom and a watchdog. But the *Oprichnina* soon became a euphemism for terror. Boyar estates were seized by force, whole towns were devastated, and widespread tortures and mass executions were carried out. One prominent target was the city of Novgorod, which Ivan accused of treason and terrorized in 1570. Estimates of the number of people killed by the *Oprichnina* vary, ranging from four thousand to tens—possibly hundreds—of thousands. In 1572, for no apparent reason, Ivan ended the bloody purges.

Following the death of Anastasia, Ivan remarried six times (two of his wives were sent to a nunnery). It is said that at one time he even proposed marriage to Queen Elizabeth of England. When she refused, he then proposed marriage to her lady-in-waiting, Mary Hastings, who also refused. Ivan had a special affinity for the English: he carefully cultivated good relations with England, opened Russia to English trade in 1555, and at one time even considered relinquishing the throne to live in England. But his last years, especially after 1581 (when he murdered his own son and heir), proved unhappy, spent between bouts of illness, madness, and solitude. He died during a game of chess on March 19, 1584, at the age of fifty-four.

IVAN THE TERRIBLE AS A GREAT LEADER

While historians disagree in their assessment of Ivan the Terrible, it is clear that he was one of the most significant and fascinating figures in Russian history. He had numerous accomplishments to his credit, particularly during his "good" period (1547–1560). He was the first crowned tsar of Muscovy, thus transforming the largely feudal and often chaotic Grand Principality of Moscow into a strong, centralized, and autocratic state. In order to accomplish this he had to overcome the powerful resistance of the Muscovite landed aristocracy, the boyars, who, like all feudal elites, had carved out large estates and had reduced early rulers to impotence. Moreover, they had consistently mismanaged Muscovy and had plundered its wealth. Ivan courageously neutralized their influence and gradually began to replace them with loyal gentry servicemen of lower ranks.

Ivan, therefore, formulated the theoretical and the practical dimensions of Russian autocracy, which technically lasted until 1917. He chose to crown himself tsar, claiming the imperial legacy of Byzantium. He believed that he ruled by divine appointment and that he was responsible to God alone. The affirmation of the unity of the state was central to his reign. This proved a consistent policy and it was backed by extraordinary will.

Ivan's geopolitical and military outlooks were expansionist. Under his initiative, Muscovy gained huge territories during the 1546–1564 period, laying the basis for the colossus subsequently associated with the concept of "Russia." By moving against the Tatars of Kazan' and Astrakhan', he opened the entire basin of the River Volga—so central in modern Russia's psyche—to his control. His wish to expand southward, to absorb the Tatar Khanate of Crimea, was frustrated by difficulties with logistics and the growing presence of Zaporozhean Cossacks. He also launched Russia's eastward expansion, into the Siberian land mass and the Pacific coast. Ermak, a cossack-commander, was the titular "conqueror" of Siberia, but a stronger impetus was provided by the renowned Stroganov family, who developed large-scale commercial concerns beyond the Ural Mountains.

Anticipating the future policies of Peter the Great, Ivan also advanced the "Westernization" of Muscovy. He attempted to open a window to Europe in Baltic Livonia. Western neighbors, however, did not relish the idea of an expansionist Muscovy, which was still regarded as a "rude and barbarous" Asiatic kingdom. This led to the prolonged Livonian War with Poland and Sweden, which ended unfavorably for Muscovy in 1582. In the end, Ivan had to abandon his dream of an outlet to the west. Still, the push westward remained a consistent theme in Russian history. Ivan also encouraged cultural, technical, and commercial contacts with Western countries. He sent students abroad to acquire useful skills and information. He introduced printing and other Western innovations, such as military organization and technology, including artillery and gunpowder. These were first used—with modest success—during the siege of Kazan' in 1552. He inaugurated the *streltsy* (musketeers), an elite military corps, later crushed by Peter the Great for insubordination. He also invited foreign specialists to work in Muscovy, but few came because of opposition from the Hanseatic League and Livonian Knights. Still, in 1553 the English captain, Richard Chancellor, reached the Russian White Sea and arrived at Moscow, formally to open longstanding direct Anglo-Russian diplomatic and trade relations.

Finally, Ivan's rule also coincided with a splendid artistic and literary flowering in Russia. Muscovite writers, architects, and icon painters created magnificent expressions of Orthodox spirituality. One of the most enduring examples of the works commissioned by Ivan was the famous St. Basil the Blessed Cathedral on Moscow's Red Square (completed in 1561). It is said that Ivan, to make the feat unique, ordered the blinding of its architect. Although very devout, he was remarkably well read and cultured. He composed church music, wrote prayers, and dabbled in theology. He corresponded extensively, writing even to Queen Elizabeth of England. But his most famous and historically relevant letters were to his former adviser, Prince Andrei Kurbskii, who had fled to Lithuania. These letters are not only remarkable for their rhetorical refinement and biting sarcasm, but for their political sophistication. They suggest that Ivan was familiar with the political philosophy of classical antiquity. Given their sophistication, some modern scholars have suggested the possibility that they were seventeenth-century forgeries. On the other hand, Ivan has also been characterized as a student of Machiavelli's theories of statecraft and thus should be viewed, both in spirit and in practice, as a Renaissance prince.

IVAN THE TERRIBLE THE TYRANT

Even the most cursory cataloguing of Ivan the Terrible's misdeeds delineates a fascinating, albeit melancholy historical figure. Prince Andrei Kurbskii, his former associate, was harsh in his evaluation, seeing Ivan as a bloody tyrant intent to destroy the flower of the Muscovite aristocracy. Perhaps his cruelty and disregard for life were a result of the traumatic experiences of his childhood, when he was forced to witness acts of wanton violence at the court. Ivan demonstrated his personal affinity for violence quite early, at the age of thirteen, when he ordered the killing of the hated boyar Andrei Shuiskii. From then on, no one was safe in Muscovy.

Given the realities of the time, violence and brutality were not exclusive to Ivan's "barbarous" Muscovy—note the celebrated St. Bartholomew Massacre in "civilized" France. Violence was often simply used as an instrument of state policy. Thus the summary execution of Shuiskii and others at the court could be seen as crude but effective object lessons for the incorrigible boyars. Ivan's violence, however, had overtones not only of cruel megalomania, but also of paranoid sociopathic manifestations of an imbalanced personality. Similar tendencies were also evident in Joseph Stalin, who, incidentally, idolized Ivan the Terrible. Unlike Stalin, however, Ivan was tormented by guilt and remorse.

In his later years he would spend long hours on his knees praying for the souls of his many victims and for God's forgiveness of his crimes. Once he sent to various monasteries a 3,000-long (apparently incomplete) list of his victims, along with large sums of money, for the monks to pray for their salvation in memorial services. He killed his own son and heir, Ivan, in a fit of fury, hitting him repeatedly with his heavy staff. The incident became the subject of the famous painting by the nineteenth-century painter Illia Repin, which still hangs at the Tretiakov Gallery in Moscow: it depicts Ivan, with an expression of insane despair in his eyes, cradling the helpless body.

The most notable example of Ivan's violence, of course, was the seven-year *Oprichnina* (1565–1572), the veritable reign of terror conducted by his overzealous *oprichniki*. In recent times, Marxist historians have viewed the *Oprichnina* as a carefully planned policy of "class struggle," targeting the reactionary boyar class. Hence they saw it as a "progressive" process of state-building, meant to eradicate Muscovy's pernicious "feudalism." Even the epithet *Groznyi*—rendered as "Terrible" in English—was regarded not as a condemnation but as a positive attribute. Evidence suggests, however, that the *Oprichnina* was not a product of some Machiavellian scheme, but a manifestation of Ivan's morbid paranoia and vindictiveness. For one thing, it victimized not only the boyars, but all classes. Indeed, the *oprichniki* themselves—some 1,000 to 6,000—were represented by elements from all social groups, including the boyars.

Whatever the motive, the results were tragic. Notable boyars and even royal relatives and close friends were executed at first. Then the circle of victims widened, to include their immediate families, clerics and even servants. When the Metropolitan of Moscow, Filip, protested, he was incarcerated and murdered. Estates and villages were confiscated, plundered, or burned. Towns, such as Torzhok, Klin, and particularly ancient Novgorod (1570), were sacked. No one knows for certain the extent of the devastation or how many people perished during this period, but when Ivan suddenly put a stop to the terror, the entire country was on the verge of civil war and total collapse.

The consequences of Ivan's fury were disastrous for Muscovy. There was massive depopulation (not entirely caused by the terror, but significantly exacerbated by it). Moreover, much of the active elite was wiped out, depleting Muscovy of leadership for a generation (the newly elevated service gentry was still politically and numerically insignificant). No less momentous was Ivan's failure to leave a clear line of succession on the throne: his murder of the able son Ivan in 1581 placed the other son, the feeble Feodor, in the line of primogeniture. When Feodor's young son, Dimitrii, died in childhood, the Muscovite Rurikid line became practically extinct. Far more consequential, however, was the ensuing struggle for power, which erupted some twenty years after Ivan's death. Known as *Smuta* (literary meaning "sorrow") and as "Time of Troubles," this crisis involved Muscovy in a wider conflict involving foreign powers, ending only in 1613 with the election of Michael, the first Romanov tsar.

Finally, Ivan became the embodiment of the idea of imperial Muscovite autocracy. He did not introduce absolutism in Muscovy—this was largely the handiwork of his predecessors, particularly Ivan III, the Great (1462–1505). No one before him, however, had practiced it on such a scale and with such ruthlessness. While the rise of autocracy provided both Muscovy and eventually the Russian empire with centralized power, it came largely at the heavy price of the reduction of free peasants to serfdom. Universal Russian serfdom, abolished only in 1861, along with unrestricted tsarist power, rendered Russia historically backward and a veritable prison of peoples and nations.

SUGGESTIONS FOR ADDITIONAL READING

Berry, Lloyd and Robert O. Crummey. *Rude and Barbarous Kingdom. Russia in the Accounts of Sixteenth-Century English Voyagers*. Madison: University of Wisconsin Press, 1968.

Cherniavsky, Michael. "Ivan the Terrible as Renaissance Prince," *Slavic Review* 27 (1968): 195–211.

Crummey, Robert O. *The Formation of Muscovy*. London and New York: Longman, 1987.

Fennell, J.L.I., ed. *The Correspondence Between Prince A. M. Kurbsky and Tsar Ivan IV of Russia*. Cambridge: Cambridge University Press, 1955.

Grey, Ian. *Ivan the Terrible*. Philadelphia and New York: J. B. Lippincott, 1964.

Kennan, Edward. *The Kurbskii-Groznyi Apocrypha*. Cambridge, Mass.: Harvard University Press, 1925.

Platonov, S. F. *Ivan the Terrible*. Gulf Breeze, Fla.: Academic International Press, 1974.

Norretranders, Bjarne. *The Shaping of Tsardom Under Ivan the Terrible*. Copenhagen: Munskgaard, 1964.

Skrynnikov, Ruslan. *Ivan the Terrible*. Gulf Breeze, Fla.: Academic International Press, 1975.

Yanov, Alexander. *The Origins of Autocracy. Ivan the Terrible in Russian History*. Berkeley: University of California Press, 1981.

Alexander Sydorenko

Bohdan Zynovyi Khmel'nyts'kyi (Bohdan Khmelnytsky)

c. 1595–1657

Hetman of the Ukraine, 1648–1657

A Cossack is, by definition, a Russian warrior who has resisted becoming a serf bound to the service of a landlord. By the seventeenth century the Cossacks of Zaporozhia, having a well-established tradition of freedom from Tatars, Poles, and Russians, were uniquely in a position to lend their services to anyone whose interests happened to coincide with theirs at a given moment. The greatest *Hetman* or elected leader of the Zaporozhian Cossacks managed to make himself the father of Ukrainian national independence. That he committed errors of judgment, which doomed his cause to defeat, has marred his historic reputation. If, however, he remains a hero to this day among Ukrainian patriots, he is stained with the reputation of a bloodthirsty tyrant among modern Poles. Because he probably murdered more Jews than anyone prior to Adolf Hitler, memorial prayers are still recited for his victims in many synagogues to this day.

BIOGRAPHICAL BACKGROUND

Bohdan Zynovyi (Fedir) Khmel'nyts'kyi was born in 1595 or 1596 in at an undetermined locality in the Chyhyryn district in Ukraine. Son of Mykhailo Khmel'nyts'kyi, he was by birthright a member of the lesser nobility of what was then still the Polish Commonwealth. His mother was of Cossack descent. Little is known about his early life. He apparently received an elementary education in the Ukraine and higher education at the Jesuit college at L'viv (Lvow). He eventually acquired a broad knowledge of world history, jurisprudence, diplomacy, politics, and foreign languages (he was fluent in Polish, Latin, French, Turkish, and Tatar). He had his first military experience in the Polish Cecora campaign against the Turks in Moldavia (1620), where his father was killed. At Cecora, Khmel'nyts'kyi himself was taken prisoner by the Turks. Tradition has it that he participated in diverse Polish-sponsored campaigns against the Turks, Tatars, and

Muscovites. He belonged to the "Registered" Cossacks (as distinguished from the "Free" Cossacks of the Zaporozhia), whose numbers and rank were sanctioned by the Polish crown. Sometime between 1625 and 1627 he married his first wife, Hanna Somko, the mother of all his children. After her death he married twice.

Khmel'nyts'kyi rapidly became a prominent figure in Cossack circles. He participated in various Cossack campaigns against the Turks and the Poles in the 1630s. In 1637 he attained the high office of military chancellor. At this time he favored an autonomous Zaporozhian Cossack Host within the Polish realm. While Polish policies precluded such an understanding and Cossack discontent increased, Khmel'nyts'kyi's prominence in both Ukrainian and Polish circles grew. In 1645 he accompanied a large detachment of Cossacks to France in the service of Cardinal Mazarin and participated in the famous siege of Dunkirk. Subsequently, the king of Poland, Wladyslaw, personally asked him to procure Cossack support for a coalition against Turkey. In 1648 he was a member of a high delegation to Warsaw demanding the restoration of Cossack privileges.

His intimate associations both with the Polish king and Cossacks rendered him suspicious to the Polish *szlachta* (landed magnates). In his own district of Chyhyryn a powerful clique of Polish landowners led by Crown Hetman Zolkiewski, conspired to deprive Khmel'nyts'kyi of his royally endowed estate at Subotiv. The vice-regent Danylo Czaplinski, an old archfoe, raided and plundered Subotiv in his absence, tortured his young son publicly, and humiliated his wife, leading to her premature death. His efforts to redress these grievances before Polish courts proved futile. Instead, an order for his arrest and execution was issued, forcing Khmel'nyts'kyi to flee in 1647 to Sich, the legendary Cossack stronghold in Zaporozhia.

In Zaporozhia Khmel'nyts'kyi played a pivotal role in the Cossack uprising against Poland. In customary Cossack fashion, he was elected *Hetman* (leader) of the Host in January 1648. Through a series of appeals, Khmel'nyts'kyi summoned all Ukrainians to rise in rebellion against Polish oppressors, to free Ukrainian lands, and to defend the Orthodox faith. The response was overwhelming, especially among the peasants, recently reduced to serfdom by repressive Polish magnates. Khmel'nyts'kyi also secured the alliance of the Turkish sultan and his vassals, the Crimean Tatars—a decision he later bitterly regretted. At Zhovti Vody and Korsun', the Cossack-peasant armies crushed the flower of Polish military aristocracy. Other victories followed and soon all of Poland lay defenseless before the massive army of Khmel'nyts'kyi. But contrary to the advice of his commanders, the Hetman chose not to crush Poland and granted an armistice. Soon the hostilities erupted anew and once again the Polish armies were crushed, notably at Zboriv (1649). But as the war dragged on and the Poles regained momentum, he suffered some serious reverses, notably at Berestechko (1651), where he was betrayed by his Tatar allies. That same year he was forced to accept a Polish peace at Bila Tserkva.

Poland and Ukraine, albeit both near exhaustion, continued the bloody conflict. The vicissitudes of war and the prospect of a wider conflict led Khmel'nyts'kyi to seek the help of the Muscovite tsar, Aleksei Romanov, to break the stalemate. Diplomatic contacts with Moscow, maintained by Khmel'nyts'kyi throughout the entire war, were intensified in 1653. In October 1653 a Muscovite *zemskii sobor* (assembly of the land) approved the tsar's will to take the Ukraine under his protection. On January 18, 1654, a fateful Cossack *rada* (council) was held at Pereyaslav, at which the majority of Khmel'nyts'kyi's regimental colonels agreed to accept the tsar's protection. Subsequently, an oath of allegiance was sworn, with the notable exception of some prominent Cossack officers, who protested the decision by their absence.

The Treaty of Pereyaslav of 1654 proved momentous, since it gave Muscovy (later Russia) its symbolic claim on the Ukraine. While its precise terms remain a subject of controversy—Russians see it as a "reunion of two brotherly peoples," the Ukrainians as a military alliance between two sovereign nations—it clearly guaranteed, among other things, the preservation of "Cossack liberties"—a euphemism for Ukrainian autonomy. But Moscow almost immediately began to violate the terms, leading the disillusioned Khmel'nyts'kyi to reconsider his relationship with Muscovy. He began negotiations with Sweden, Hungary, and other European powers to free the Ukraine from Moscow's growing interference in the internal affairs of the Cossack Hetmanate. But he died at his capital of Chyhyryn before he could change the course of events and was buried on August 25, 1657, in the St. Elijah's Church, which he had built himself at Subotiv. He was succeeded in the Hetmanate by his general-secretary, Ivan Vyhovs'kyi, who was antagonistic to Moscow.

KHMEL'NYTS'KYI AS A GREAT LEADER

It is very difficult to overestimate Khmel'nyts'kyi's impact on Ukrainian history. The epoch of the great national war of liberation is associated with his name, *Khmel'nyshchyna*. His contemporaries respectfully called him "*Bat'ko* (Father) Bohdan." Although modern historians compare him in stature to such contemporaries as Cromwell of England and Wallenstein of Bohemia, the comparison does not account for the psychological impact that Khmel'nyts'kyi has exerted on the Ukrainian national psyche. He stands, along with the nineteenth-century national poet Taras Shevchenko, as the founder of the modern Ukrainian nation and its aspirations for independence.

Khmel'nyts'kyi's greatest accomplishments lay in his leadership during the war of liberation against Polish rule and in his state-building endeavors.

He proved a man of extraordinary skills in such diverse areas as administration, finance, diplomacy, and culture. He proved, despite some crushing setbacks, a master of military strategy and tactics. With consummate mastery he channeled the anarchic energies of the Zaporozhian Cossacks to constructive ends and united all classes. Moreover, he was the founder of an independent Cossack state, the Hetmanate (formally abolished by Empress Catherine II in the 1780s), combining military and civilian administration under an elected Hetman. The Hetmanate, with its inherent Cossack democratic ideals, has become the historical and psychological basis for modern Ukrainian national identity, political ideology, and a quest for independent statehood.

Indeed, under Khmel'nyts'kyi's able leadership, the Ukraine ceased to be a geopolitical vacuum, a frontier outpost, renowned for its "Wild Prairie," Cossack anarchy, and infinite opportunities for rapacious Polish magnates to carve out huge estates and enserf free Ukrainian peasants. Instead, a legitimate national state began to merge, with a distinct national ethos. Under Khmel'nyts'kyi, Ukrainian cities, freed from the oppressive Magdeburg Law favoring foreigners, became centers of learning and budding urban culture. Kiev, for example, boasted of the famous Mohyla Academy, the first major institution of higher learning among the Eastern Slavs. Indeed, students and faculty of the Kiev Academy participated in the triumphal reception given Khmel'nyts'kyi in Kiev in 1649, hailing the Hetman as "the second Moses" and "liberator of his people from Polish slavery."

Significantly, the Ukraine also ceased to be the battleground for debilitating confessional conflicts involving Roman Catholicism, Protestantism, and Orthodoxy, which in the past had threatened national suicide. Khmel'nyts'kyi, under very difficult wartime conditions, was instrumental in fomenting a national consciousness and a sense of unity among the disparate political, class, and religious interests. He was instrumental in the advent of a civil society in Ukraine, a politically conscious elite, and a national policy.

The Khmel'nyts'kyi-led rebellion liberated large (but not all) Ukrainian territories from Polish rule and induced significant socio-economic changes in Ukraine. It established a new Cossack-based cosmopolitan elite, comparable to the Polish *szlachta*, with distinct political and social outlooks and prerogatives, crucial to the preservation of national identity during the ensuing unrelenting tsarist policy of Russification. Indeed, the subsequent partition of Ukraine between Poland and Muscovy and other national disasters failed to erase the memory of Cossack liberties in the popular consciousness. Even during the era of the Russian empire, the Cossacks of the Don and the Kuban regions—linear descendants of the outlawed Cossacks of Zaporozhia—enjoyed a special status within the imperial autocratic order.

Khmel'nyts'kyi distinguished himself not only as a brilliant military commander and state-builder, but also as a talented diplomat. During his tenure, the Ukraine cast a wide diplomatic net, establishing relations with all major foreign powers. Clearly, at first he wished to establish a common partnership with the Polish state, but the destructive and expansionist tendencies of the Polish aristocracy precluded this possibility. To assure a lasting victory over hostile Poland, he was forced to seek foreign support. This proved problematic, since it usually involved a high price. While Khmel'nyts'kyi claimed divine right to rule over the Cossacks (his documents included the formula "Bohdan Khmel'nyts'kyi, by Divine grace Hetman with the Zaporozhian Host"), in the seventeenth century the concept of sovereignty of the "people" was not clearly defined. Thus the elected Hetman technically had to recognize the nominal but legitimate suzerainty of an established hereditary ruler as the price for a military alliance. This led him first to consider nominal vassalage to the king of Poland, then the Turkish sultan, and finally the tsar of Muscovy. Still, the Cossack state proved a major player in European politics and military affairs, a force to be reckoned with even by the emerging Muscovy, vying with Khmel'nyts'kyi's Ukraine for the medieval Kievan Russian patrimony.

In light of the subsequent disputes over the precise terms of the Pereyaslav Treaty, compounded by the mysterious disappearance of the original documents, it is important to note that, despite his nominal vassalage to the Russian tsar, Khmel'nyts'kyi retained full state powers over internal and external affairs in Ukraine. He freely entered into relations with foreign powers, which gave the Hetmanate an international recognition as a sovereign state: a 1657 treaty of alliance with Sweden recognized Ukrainians as *pro libera gente et nulli subjecta* ("a free people, subjected to none").

Khmel'nyts'kyi referred to himself as "the master of all Russian lands," claiming even present-day Belorussia. These claims greatly disturbed Muscovy, which began in earnest, in the words of a modern historian, "the struggle of the two Rus's over the third Rus'." But the fundamental conflict involved a struggle between two political philosophies: Cossack democracy, as formulated in Khmel'nyts'kyi's Hetmanate, and Muscovite absolutism, embodied in the autocratic tsar.

Beyond the immediate successes, Khmel'nyts'kyi's legacy rests on his charismatic leadership, which allowed him to accomplish so much against almost impossible odds, as well as on his grip on popular and artistic imagination. His name is invoked in history, legend, and song, while his equestrian statue on St. Sophia's Square in Kiev has become the rallying point during the two incipient affirmations of modern Ukrainian statehood in 1717 and 1991. In the Ukrainian national psyche he remains forever the "Stern Father" of his people and the awakener of the nation.

KHMEL'NYTS'KYI THE TYRANT

For all his personal triumphs and contributions to the Ukrainian cause, Khmel'nyts'kyi's historical legacy is marred by setbacks, mistakes, and follies. Posterity has criticized him for his unwillingness to proclaim full Ukrainian independence at the outset, thus affirming the right of the Ukraine to independent statehood and averting the tragic fate which befell it during the ensuing centuries of Russian domination. His obvious misjudgment of the political and military realities of his time proved crippling to his nation. First, he failed to crush the power of the Polish *szlachta.* After the Battle of Pyliavtsi and the siege of L'viv in late 1648, the Polish Commonwealth lay defenseless before him. But Khmel'nyts'kyi, whose own psychological and social affinities lay with the hated *szlachta,* chose to spare Poland and its volatile aristocracy by offering an honorable armistice. This simply prolonged the bloodbath, which, in the end, destroyed both Poland and the Ukraine.

Second, his stubborn reliance on Turkish and Tatar allies, Ukraine's historical enemies, during the war proved disastrous. The presence of the despised Tatars on Ukrainian soil was particularly disruptive, since they had a long history of plundering cities and villages. Indeed, at the crucial Battle of Berestechko (1651) the Tatars switched sides and joined the Polish army, inflicting a crushing defeat upon the Cossacks. Yet despite their unreliability, Khmel'nyts'kyi continued to court Tatar and Turkish support. In 1654 the Tatars again devastated the towns and villages of Ukraine practically under his nose.

His most serious misjudgment, however, was his fateful decision to submit to the Muscovite tsar. The Treaty of Pereyaslav of 1654 had a profound affect on Ukraine, since, in the end, it led to the three-century Russian domination. He ignored the advice of some of his closest associates, who grasped more fully the tsarist intentions behind the vague terms. The immediate result of the treaty, in addition to placing Ukraine firmly in the Muscovite sphere of influence, was to polarize the Ukrainian elites into pro- and anti-Moscow factions and to unleash powerful centrifugal forces throughout the country. But the long-term repercussions proved even more serious: shortly after his death in 1657, Ukraine plunged into a prolonged internecine conflict commonly known as the "Ruin," from which it never quite recovered, resulting in the loss of independence. For this, the judgment of posterity was harsh. In his political poem, "The Great Cellar," the national poet Taras Shevchenko has the soul of a young girl doomed to eternity because she naively watered Khmel'nyts'kyi's horse when he journeyed to Pereyaslav to sign the fateful treaty with the Russian tsar.

Sadly, even the common masses, who invested their hopes and aspirations in their "Father Bohdan," were, in the end, let down by their leader. At first the Cossack insurrection rested on egalitarian ideals, but in due time the hated Polish *szlachta*, with their latifundia, was generally replaced by the native *starshyna* (Cossack elite). The disregard of the *starshyna* for the plight of the common people fueled the longstanding class conflicts in the Ukraine.

Finally, to the Polish and Jewish peoples Khmel'nyts'kyi's name is synonymous with wanton destruction and butchery. The profound hatred between Poles and Ukrainians, fueled by class and confessional antagonisms, led to unspeakable atrocities committed by both sides. These are well documented in contemporary accounts, such as the "Eyewitness Chronicle." Unfortunately, widespread Cossack pogroms were carried on against the Jews, who, in the popular perception, represented the *szlachta* on the local level. Since the Jews were more vulnerable than the well-armed *szlachta*, their losses were stupefying. Between 1648 and 1656 tens of thousands of Jews (precise figures are impossible to establish) were butchered. To the present day the Khmel'nyts'kyi uprising represents to the Jewish people one of the darkest episodes in their long history.

SUGGESTIONS FOR ADDITIONAL READING

Basarab, John. *Pereiaslav 1654: A Historiographical Study*. Edmonton: University of Alberta Press, 1982.

Braichevsky, Mykhailo. *Annexation or Reunification. Critical Notes on One Conception*. Munich: Ukrainische Institut für Bildungs-politik, 1974.

Gordon, Linda. *Cossack Rebellions. Social Turmoil in the Sixteenth-Century Ukraine*. Albany: State University of New York Press, 1983.

Hannover, Rabbi Nathan. *Abyss of Despair. The Famous 17th Century Chronicle Depicting Jewish Life During the Chmelniczki Massacres of 1648–49*. New York: Bloch, 1950.

O'Brien, C. Bickford. *Muscovy and the Ukraine. From the Pereiaslav Agreement to the Truce of Andrusovo, 1654–1667*. Berkeley and Los Angeles: University of California Press, 1963.

Potichnyj, Peter J., ed. *Poland and Ukraine*. Edmonton and Toronto: The Canadian Institute of Ukrainian Studies, 1980.

Potichnyj, Peter J., and Howard Aster, eds. *Ukrainian Jewish Relations in Historical Perspective*. Edmonton: University of Alberta, 1988.

Subtelny, Orest. *Ukraine. A History*. Toronto, Buffalo, and London: University of Toronto Press, 1988.

Vernadsky, George. *Bohdan, Hetman of Ukraine*. New Haven, Conn: Yale University Press, 1941.

———. *The Tsardom of Moscow, 1547–1682*, Part I. New Haven, Conn.: Yale University Press, 1969.

Alexander Sydorenko

Nikita Sergeevich Khrushchev
1894–1971

First Secretary of the Soviet Communist Party, 1953–1964

During its seventy-four-year existence, the Soviet Union was dominated by five men—Lenin, Stalin, Khrushchev, Brezhnev, and Gorbachev. Three—Lenin, Stalin, and Brezhnev—made terror an active part of rule, while Khrushchev and Gorbachev provided intervals of sanity and reform. It is from this perspective that Nikita Khrushchev should be seen, despite the fact that he was an integral part of the Stalinist police state that dominated the Soviet Union for almost a third of its history. Khrushchev's role in Soviet history is yet to be adequately evaluated, but taken in light of the Gorbachev era (1985–1991) and the ultimate collapse of the Soviet Union, his period of domination must be seen in a positive light, since it marked the beginning of the destruction of the Stalinist state mechanism that had plagued Soviet Russia for so long.

BIOGRAPHICAL BACKGROUND

Nikita Sergeevich Khrushchev was born on April 17, 1894, in the central Russian village of Kalinovka in the former Kursk oblast. As a schoolboy he worked in the fields, but became a miner at age fifteen, working with his father in the coal mines of Yuzovka in the center of the Donets Basin mining region. In time he became a mechanic, which gained him an exemption from the military when World War I broke out in 1914. He married the following year, and in 1917 returned to Kalinovka. He quickly became involved in politics and was selected head of a village committee that was to oversee the redistribution of estate lands to peasants. After Lenin's Bolshevik seizure of power in November 1917, Khrushchev joined the Communist Party. In January 1919, during the Russian Civil War (1918–1921), he enlisted in the 9th Rifle Division of the Red Army. Three years later, after the Communist victory against its White (non-Communist) opponents, Khrushchev returned to Yuzovka, where he became assistant manager of his former mine. He also became a Communist Party cell leader and enrolled in the new workers' faculty of the Donets Mining Technical School to improve his education.

In 1923, school officials made him a *politruk* or political leader. Two years later, during the power struggle between Stalin and Trotsky for control of the Soviet leadership after Lenin's death in 1924, Khrushchev became party secretary of the Petrovsk-Marinsk district as a reward for his support of Stalin. Khrushchev, now under the watchful eye of the head of the Ukrainian Communist Party and his future mentor, Lazar Kaganovich, was also a delegate to the IX Congress of the Ukrainian Communist Party in 1925 and a nonvoting delegate at the XIV Congress of the All-Union Communist Party (AUCP) later that year. In 1926 he became head of the Orgburo (Organizational Bureau) in Yuzovka and was a delegate to the X Congress of the Ukrainian Communist Party and the XV Congress of the AUCP. Kaganovich convinced him to become deputy chief of the Ukrainian Orgburo in Kharkov in 1928. In the following year he got a leave of absence from his post to continue his education at the Industrial Academy in Moscow.

His loyalty to Stalin and his friendship with Nadezhda Alliluyeva, Stalin's wife, won him the position of secretary of the Industrial Academy's Communist Party group and a similar position in Moscow's Bauman district. His successful purge of the academy's party organization earned him the position of secretary of Moscow's most important district, Krasnaya (Red) Presnaya in 1931. In early 1932 Stalin made him second secretary of the Moscow City Party Committee, which was headed by Kaganovich. The following year he acquired the same position with the Moscow Regional Committee, which was also under Kaganovich, and became a candidate member of the Central Committee of the AUCP. When Kaganovich became Stalin's new commissar of transport, Khrushchev replaced him as secretary of the Moscow City and Regional Committees.

Khrushchev inherited from Kaganovich a modernization plan of the Soviet capital that included the construction of the famed Moscow subway system and the Moscow-Volga Canal. Khrushchev so pleased Stalin with his work and loyalty that he awarded him the Order of Lenin in 1935, and three years later appointed him first secretary of the Ukrainian Communist Party, which earned Khrushchev a seat on the Politburo, the supreme governing body of Stalin's Russia. His new job was complicated by the human and economic devastation wrought by years of forced collectivization and purges. Later, after the conclusion of the Nazi-Soviet Pact of August 23, 1939, Khrushchev became responsible for integrating those sections of eastern Poland into the Ukraine, which the Soviet Union seized in September 1939. The following spring he oversaw the integration of Bessarabia and Bukovina into the Soviet Union, when Romania fell victim to Soviet aggression.

When Adolf Hitler invaded the Soviet Union on June 22, 1941, Khrushchev did everything he could to strengthen Russian resistance. He also helped organize the Soviet retreat as the major cities of the Ukraine fell before the German onslaught. For the next three years, Khrushchev served as Stalin's personal representative at military headquarter posts throughout the southern part of the country. Khrushchev received ample rewards for his work throughout the war and achieved the rank of lieutenant general. He entered the Ukrainian capital, Kiev, in the wake of its capture by the Red Army in November 1943, and soon became head of the Council of Ministers (cabinet) of the Ukraine with orders to rebuild the region. Unfortunately, he was unable quickly to repair the severe economic losses suffered during the war, which triggered a devastating famine in 1946–1947. Consequently, Stalin removed him as head of the Ukrainian Communist Party and replaced him with Kaganovich. Khrushchev retained his position as chairman of the Ukrainian Council of Ministers, and regained his post as Ukrainian party secretary at the end of 1947 after new figures showed an improved Ukrainian harvest. Khrushchev argues in his memoirs, though, that his brief political demise was due to illness, not politics. Within two years he was back in Moscow as secretary to the Central Committee and as head of the Moscow city and regional party committees. His return to the Soviet capital was also linked to Stalin's efforts to maintain some sort of balance among his principal underlings.

Khrushchev also became Stalin's spokesperson on Soviet agriculture, though he enjoyed mixed success with some efforts to reform it in the early 1950s. Nevertheless Stalin selected him to deliver one of the two primary speeches before the XIX Party Congress in the fall of 1952. His talk dealt with changes in laws dealing with the Communist Party. The other major talk given at the congress was delivered by Georgi M. Malenkov, soon to be Khrushchev's competitor for Stalin's mantle of leadership.

Joseph Stalin died on March 5, 1953, and Khrushchev became immediately embroiled in a complex, four-year power struggle. During the early days of the struggle, Khrushchev, who had arranged the fallen Soviet leader's funeral, lost his posts as Central Committee secretary and as head of the Moscow city and regional party committees. However, on March 14, 1953, the Central Committee removed Malenkov as first secretary of the party and placed Khrushchev in the party's principal leadership position. He was now the only Soviet leader with positions on the Presidium, which had replaced the Politburo, and the Secretariat, which executed Presidium decisions, and was the party's watchdog. He officially became First Secretary of the Soviet Communist Party in the fall of 1953.

Over the next three years, Khrushchev was able gradually to undermine the collective leadership of other prominent Stalinists and remove his most important opponents from power. As part of this struggle, Khrushchev gambled that a devastating attack on Stalin and his crimes before the XX

Party Congress on February 24–25, 1956, would strengthen his hand and lead the party in a new direction. His talk sent shock waves throughout the Soviet empire. Over the next year, Khrushchev was able to counter efforts to remove him from power, and by June 1957 he assumed full control of the party. During his seven years in power, he promoted domestic destalinization and experimented with new ways to enhance industrial and agricultural output. His domestic policies had mixed results, while his adventuresome forays into foreign affairs proved equally ambitious. He strengthened his hold on power in 1958 when he was made premier, while in 1961 he renewed his anti-Stalinistic campaign at the XXII Party Congress. At the same time, he announced a new party program designed fully to communize the Soviet Union within two decades. Unfortunately, his domestic and international misadventures slowly undermined his authority, and on October 13–14, 1964, he was removed from office.

KHRUSHCHEV AS A GREAT LEADER

The hallmark of Nikita Khrushchev's career was his daring program of destalinization that slowly began to underscore the horrid, dictatorial crimes and abusive policies of Joseph Stalin. It also helped Khrushchev to begin to undo some aspects of the police state regime created by the former dictator from 1927 to 1953. The dramatic starting point for Khrushchev's move was the secret speech he gave before the XX Communist Party Congress in Moscow on February 24–25, 1956. His rambling, twenty-thousand-word talk before prominent Soviet leaders and Communist delegates from throughout the Soviet bloc was as much a forced political maneuver as an effort truly to distance himself from Stalin, whom he had recently praised and served for years. For Khrushchev and other Soviet leaders, the attack on Stalin laid the basis for a new direction in Soviet domestic and international politics and created severe problems in the Soviet family of nations. Five years later, Khrushchev revived his attacks on Stalin at the XXII Party Congress, and had the Soviet dictator's body removed from the shared tomb with Lenin on Red Square. Khrushchev's destalinization efforts brought forth a groundswell of articles and memoirs on the horrors of life under Stalin, particularly in the Gulag, the Soviet prison camp system. The most famous work to emerge from this era was Alexander Solzhenitsyn's *One Day in the Life of Ivan Denisovich*, which was later banned in the Soviet Union.

Khrushchev also experimented with changes in the Soviet agricultural system through his Virgin Lands program. Designed to bring millions of new acres under cultivation in Central Asia, particularly Kazakhstan, it was initially quite successful. However, by the early 1960s a series of bad harvests doomed the program to failure. Khrushchev was somewhat more successful with the development of the Soviet military-industrial complex that produced the space program. On October 4, 1957, the Soviet Union launched the first satellite into space, the *Sputnik*, followed two years later by an unmanned rocket landing on the moon. Two dogs went into space in 1960, and a year later, Major Yury Gagarin became the first man to orbit the earth. Other aspects of the Soviet economy, however, suffered during this period.

Khrushchev was equally aggressive in foreign affairs and initially tried to establish stronger ties with the United States. Perhaps his greatest international triumph was the restoration of the ties with Marshal Tito's Yugoslavia.

KHRUSHCHEV THE TYRANT

At this juncture in the study of Soviet history, we are only beginning to catch a glimpse of the specific involvement of prominent supporters of Stalin during his years in power. Consequently, one can only speculate about Khrushchev's involvement in these crimes, since few records have been released about them. Though Khrushchev's years as Soviet leader have earned him some good marks for the changes he brought about through destalinization, it is important to remember that for Khrushchev the Stalinist, destalinization was a political gamble designed to strengthen his hold on power over a country already in the throes of distancing itself from Stalin's past. Furthermore, from the time that Khrushchev joined the Communist Party until the death of Stalin, his unbending loyalty to the Soviet leader and Stalin's close associates was the principal reason for Khrushchev's climb up the party ladder in the Ukraine and Soviet Union. He had no qualms about implementing a Stalinist purge of Moscow's Industrial Academy, while as a Ukrainian party leader he was very aware and evidently supportive of the horrible collectivization campaign there in the early 1930s that resulted in the death of millions. He also must have been aware of the labor abuses and unnecessary deaths during the construction of the Moscow subway system and the Moscow-Volga Canal in the 1930s. Furthermore, as party chief in Moscow during the Purges, Khrushchev proved to be a ready and loyal supporter of Stalin's war against the party and the military. Stalin's revitalization of the purge mentality after World War II found Khrushchev, desperate to regain his post as secretary of the Central Committee, a willing ally. His talent as a purger and brutal political infighter served him well from 1953 to 1957, when he successfully drove all of his political competitors from power. He had learned his lessons from Stalin well, which perhaps explains his need to so distance himself from the crimes of his former master.

Perhaps the best example of Khrushchev's tyranny in the midst of destalinization came in Hungary in 1956. After months of domestic turmoil stimulated by his "secret speech," Hungary seemed to be moving to a multiparty system and withdrawal from the Soviet-dominated Warsaw Pact. In response, Khrushchev ordered the brutal suppression of the Hungarian "uprising" on November 1, 1956. The Russian move, orchestrated by Moscow's ambassador in Budapest, the future Soviet leader Yury Andropov, resulted in more than 3,000 deaths, 13,000 injuries, and the destruction of over 4,000 buildings. Thousands were sent to Hungarian prisons or Soviet labor camps, while 2,000 Hungarians were later executed for their role in the rebellion.

SUGGESTIONS FOR ADDITIONAL READING

Burlatsky, Fedor M. *Khrushchev and the First Russian Spring: The Era of Khrushchev Through the Eyes of His Advisor.* New York: Charles Scribner's Sons, 1991.

Crankshaw, Edward. *Khrushchev: A Career.* New York: The Viking Press, 1966.

Dmytryshyn, Basil. "Khrushchev, Nikita Sergeevich (1894–1971)," in Joseph Wieczynski, ed., *The Modern Encyclopedia of Russian and Soviet History*, vol. 16. Gulf Breeze: Academic International Press, 1980.

Frankland, Mark. *Khrushchev.* New York: Stein and Day, 1969.

Kellen, Konrad. *Khrushchev: A Political Portrait.* New York: Frederick A. Praeger, 1961.

Khrushchev, Sergei, and William Taubman, eds. *Khrushchev on Khrushchev: An Inside Account of the Man and His Era.* Boston: Little, Brown and Company, 1990.

Medvedev, Roy A., and A. Zhores. *Khrushchev: The Years in Power.* New York: Columbia University Press, 1976.

Talbott, Strobe, ed. *Khrushchev Remembers.* Boston: Little, Brown and Company, 1970.

Talbott, Strobe, ed. *Khrushchev Remembers: The Last Testament.* Boston: Little, Brown and Company, 1974.

Werth, Alexander. *Russia under Khrushchev.* Greenwich, Conn.: Fawcett Publications, 1961.

David M. Crowe

Pierre Laval
(Pierre Jean Marie Laval)

1883–1945

French Premier, 1931–1932 and 1935–1936
Deputy Premier, 1940
Head of Government, 1942–1944

Pierre Laval, twice premier of France during the Third Republic in the 1930s, and twice second in command of the Vichy government under Marshal Philippe Pétain during the German occupation in World War II, has been called a French patriot who tried to save as much as possible from vengeful and ruthless German occupation officials. He has also been seen as an unscrupulous and ambitious opportunist who utilized the tragic circumstances of defeat and occupation for his own personal agenda of power and revenge on his political enemies.

Laval was the one skilled and experienced parliamentary political leader of the Third Republic who retained power in Pétain's authoritarian regime. His political career took him from Socialist beginnings in the early twentieth century to more conservative parliamentary alliances in the mid-1930s and finally to the authoritarian and anti-Semitic, if not openly fascist, Vichy government. Second in command at Vichy, Laval supported a policy of collaboration with the German occupation authorities. It was said of him that his politics was like his name—both could be spelled equally from left to right or from right to left. A skillful political opportunist, Laval always saw himself as a French patriot. When the war turned against the Germans and the imminent collapse of the Vichy government became evident, Laval foresaw that he would be reviled in his own country as a traitor. Tried for treason after the liberation of France, he gave a spirited defense of his intentions and his patriotism but was convicted and executed in 1945.

BIOGRAPHICAL BACKGROUND

Pierre Jean Marie Laval was born June 28, 1883, in the village of Châteldon in the northern part of the Auvergne region of France. He was the son of a hotelier and the youngest of four children. At age twelve, he was withdrawn from school by his father, who wanted him to help with the family business. Laval later returned to school and received his baccalauréat from the Lycée Saint-Louis in Paris in 1901. He next served as a supervisor in several lycées in the provinces before returning to Paris in 1907. In 1903 he joined the Socialist Party and in the same year was called up for military service but was discharged on medical grounds for varicose veins. Laval then turned to the study of law and in 1908 began a practice in Paris.

In 1909 he married Jeanne Eugénie Élisabeth Claussat, who was also from Châteldon, and in 1911 their daughter, Josée, was born. Elected to the French Chamber of Deputies from the working-class constituency of Aubervilliers, north of Paris, in the general election of April–May 1914, Laval was swept out with the defeat of the left in 1919. In 1923 he was elected mayor of Aubervilliers as an independent socialist, affiliated with neither the Socialist nor the Communist parties, which had split from one another after the Bolshevik Revolution. Laval would retain the mayoralty of Aubervilliers until the Liberation of 1944. In 1924 he was again elected to the Chamber of Deputies, as a member of the victorious Cartel des Gauches, again without affiliating with a specific party. His first cabinet post was minister of public works from April to October 1925. Two years later, he shifted from the left to the right in the chamber and, in 1930, he was named minister of labor and national solidarity in the right-wing government of André Tardieu.

In January 1931 Laval was named premier and, later that year, "Man of the Year" by *Time* magazine. He was premier until February 1932, when his government lost a vote of confidence on an electoral reform issue. He became foreign minister upon the assassination of Louis Barthou in October 1934. Hitler had come to power in 1933 and, as foreign minister, Laval supported Mussolini's invasion of Ethiopia in hopes of building a Franco-Italian alliance that might protect France against a resurgent Nazi Germany. From June 1935 through January 1936 he was again premier. Now pursuing a policy of deflation to deal with the deepening economic depression in France, Laval continued to try to forge an alliance with Mussolini against the Germans. His second government fell in January 1936. Laval's deflationary policies were soundly condemned in the Popular Front electoral victory of March 1936, which removed him temporarily from political center stage and which he interpreted as a personal rebuke.

In September 1939, France and England went to war in a vain effort to save Poland from German aggression and World War II had begun. A German offensive in May 1940 sent the French forces reeling and in June a new cabinet, headed by World War I hero Marshal Philippe Pétain, requested and got an armistice from the Germans. Laval became deputy premier. With Paris occupied by German forces, the government fled, first to Bordeaux, then to Vichy where Laval, a skilled and experienced parliamentary negotiator, took the lead in turning the republican government into an authoritarian state and embarked on a policy of collaboration with Nazi Germany. Three-fifths of France, including Paris, was occupied by the

Germans and the government settled in Vichy, in the unoccupied zone. Laval remained deputy premier until December 13, 1940, when he was fired by Pétain for arrogating to himself too much power and negotiating with the Germans behind Pétain's back.

On April 18, 1942, Laval was recalled to office, this time as official head of government, responsible only to Pétain. Attempting to mitigate German demands for French workers to help ease manpower shortages in their factories, Laval created a program in 1942 by which French volunteers could work in Germany. As German losses mounted, this labor program became obligatory. In November 1942, the Allies landed in the French North African empire and the Germans responded by occupying all of continental France, depriving the Vichy government of even the semblance of independence it had held until then. Laval chose to stay on at his post. As late as the spring of 1944, he still supported a German victory in the hope of somehow finessing a role for France to play in a compromise peace settlement and at the same time staving off the Communists. Even after the June 1944 Allied landings in Normandy, Laval attempted to play a mediating role. In August, however, as Allied forces approached Paris, the retreating Germans forced him to travel east with them where they set up a new French government, soon to take its place in German exile, but Laval considered himself a prisoner and refused to exercise his official functions. He spent the period from September 1944 to the collapse of Germany in April 1945 as a prisoner in Germany along with some of the more extreme French collaborators, who play-acted at a government in exile. With the collapse of Germany, Laval sought refuge in Spain, but was turned over to the Americans, who, in turn, handed him over to the new French government of General de Gaulle. Charged with collaborating with the enemy, Laval was placed on trial on October 4, 1945. Amid a tumultuous atmosphere in which he was openly insulted by judges and jurists, he was convicted and sentenced to death. On October 15, 1945, he was executed.

A month after his execution, Laval's remains were moved to the family vault of his son-in-law at the Montparnasse cemetery in Paris. He was survived by his wife Jeanne Eugénie Elisabeth Claussat Laval, his daughter Josée Laval de Chambrun, who wrote a preface to the *The Diary of Pierre Laval* (New York: Charles Scribner's Sons, 1948), and her husband, Count René de Chambrun, who worked assiduously to rehabilitate the memory of his father-in-law in the postwar years.

LAVAL AS A GREAT LEADER

History has not been kind to Pierre Laval. His name has come to exemplify treasonous collaboration in the *Oxford English Dictionary* and the Spanish *Diccionario Basico Espasa*, to name two examples reflecting popular usage. To the end, however, he insisted that he had done no wrong and that he had always acted as a French patriot. He defended his deflationary attempts to cope with the Depression and the attempt to link France with fascist Italy in the mid-1930s, arguing that his policies, had they been supported, would have precluded the rise of Nazi power. When France was defeated by the Germans in June 1940, he depicted himself as a Cassandra whose words of warning and wise policies had gone unheard. Later he insisted that he had collaborated with the Germans to save as much for France as possible and to try to work toward a Franco-German reconciliation that would also remove the threat of Soviet communism. In defense of Laval, it might be said that there were those in France prepared to go even further than he in the direction of collaboration with Nazi Germany and, especially after 1942, he was able to save Jews from deportation and he worked strenuously to lessen the numbers of French workers sent in forced labor to Germany.

Laval argued that he, in fact, had really been a resistor—perhaps the first—against the Germans. Unlike de Gaulle, who was safe in London from the Germans, Laval argued that on a daily basis he had resisted German demands for ever greater concessions as the war went on. "I had no link with the Committee of de Gaulle," he wrote in his diary just before his trial, "but it can well be imagined that we might have been in accord. He in London or Algiers, ready to participate in the Liberation and anxious to hasten V-day, and I in Vichy or Paris to protect the country, maintain our administration and the financial and economic structure of our nation." His political program of domestic order and European rapprochement had roots in nineteenth-century French political figures such as Léon Gambetta, one of the founders of the Third Republic after the fall of Napoleon III in 1870. Gambetta had argued for a moderate republic that would respect the social order and had sought rapprochement with the Germany of Bismarck, which had defeated the French in 1870. Laval's statements on behalf of Franco-German friendship have also been echoed in the postwar Bonn-Paris alliance that has flourished in NATO and the Common Market.

Defenders of Laval have argued that collaborators were but one side of a civil war in Europe where there had been no traitors. This argument maintained that the war had ended for France with the armistice in 1940, when it appeared that Germany had won decisively. Those who, like Laval, had sought accommodation with the victorious Germans were Patriots. As a veteran of the collaboration put it, "One had to get one's hands dirty to save Frenchmen. We made mistakes but we were all honest patriots." Refusal to collaborate by the French, according to historian Patrice Higonnet, might have led Hitler to treat the French as he did the Poles, in which case losses would have been substantially higher. "Ironically," according to Higonnet, "the Vichy regime, by fending off the installation of a ruthless fascist government, may have helped protect those Frenchmen about whom it cared least."

German pressure in late 1943 and 1944 forced Laval to appoint hardline collaborators to his government, but Laval continued to believe he was the indispensable man. Rather than resign, he argued that his presence was needed to somehow keep France from becoming totally a German satellite. To the very end of the Vichy regime, he believed that he could serve as a bridge between the Germans and the Allies, then between Marshall Pétain and de Gaulle's Free French, in the hope of keeping the Communists from power. All this proved illusory. De Gaulle refused to recognize Vichy in any way. Laval was transferred as a prisoner to Germany in September 1944.

LAVAL THE TYRANT

Laval was an opportunistic politician, invariably ready to compromise to gain and hold power. Trying to balance Hitler in 1935, he condoned Mussolini's attack on Ethiopia. His political shifts even before the war made it difficult to see whether he had any enduring political values beyond personal ambition. The resentment Laval felt at having been marginalized politically by the 1936 election was evident in July 1940 when he skillfully stage-managed the death of the Third Republic by helping to engineer an overwhelming vote in which the National Assembly granted special powers to Marshal Pétain to refashion the French state. The result was the establishment of the Vichy government with Laval as a dominant force until he was fired by Pétain in December.

In office in 1940, Laval helped initiate a policy of collaboration with the Germans. He met with Hitler at Montoire in October and helped arrange a meeting between the German leader and Pétain a few days later, after which the Marshal publicly ordered the French to follow his lead in collaboration. Discussions of collaboration often focus on those who wrote or publicly defended their positions and were highly visible. Economic collaboration, however, may have been less visible but was often more important in the greater political scheme. The surrender to the Germans of the French-owned Bor copper mines in Yugoslavia by Laval in the fall of 1940 undoubtedly aided the German war effort more than the activities of many of the more vocal collaborationist journalists in occupied Paris.

Laval also played a significant role in Vichy's anti-Jewish policies. Although in 1940 he opposed the first anti-Semitic legislation that exposed noncitizen Jewish refugees of the 1930s in France to round-ups and deportation to German extermination camps, Laval signed the decree. Returned to power in 1942, he offered up the non-French Jews and tried to save the French Jews. When asked by the Germans for Jews between ages sixteen and forty-five, Laval argued that the children should be deported with their parents. How much Laval knew or cared about the final fate of these victims is unclear, but it appears that he did not want to trouble relations with the Germans by fighting with them over the foreign Jews.

Although his second tenure in power under Vichy was marked by more resistance on his part to German demands, Laval nonetheless continued to supply them with labor and treasure. Many of the French workers sent to fill empty places in German factories did not return. In 1943 he announced publicly that he wished for a German victory in the war because otherwise Communism would be triumphant. He also created the Milice, a governmental paramilitary organization which fought against the Resistance and organized the special sections, kangaroo courts that executed Resistors after quick and secret trials, often in the middle of the night. Milice officials were being tried for crimes against humanity as late as the 1990s.

Hitler's primary goal with respect to occupied France was to utilize her economic resources for his war effort. To do this, he needed to maintain domestic order in France. It was much cheaper for Hitler to have the traditional French governing elites police their own society, than to have German forces do it for him. Laval's personal ambition played into Hitler's hands.

SUGGESTIONS FOR ADDITIONAL READING

De Chambrun, Josée and René, eds. *France during the German Occupation, 1940–1944: A Collection of 292 Statements on the Government of Meréchal Pétain and Pierre Laval.* Translated by Philip W. Whitcomb. 3 vols. Stanford, Calif.: Hoover Institution Press, 1957.

Gordon, Bertram M. *Collaborationism in France during the Second World War.* Ithaca, NY: Cornell University Press, 1980.

Higonnet, Patrice. "How Guilty Were the French?" *New York Review of Books*, December 3, 1981.

Kupferman, Fred. *Laval 1883–1945.* Paris: Balland, 1987. (In French.)

Laval, Pierre. *The Diary of Pierre Laval.* New York: Charles Scribner's Sons, 1948.

Milward, Alan. *The New Order and the French Economy.* Oxford: Clarendon Press, 1970.

Paxton, Robert O. *Vichy France: Old Guard and New Order, 1940–1944.* New York: Alfred A. Knopf, 1972.

Paxton, Robert O. and Michael R. Marrus. *Vichy France and the Jews.* New York: Basic Books, 1981.

Thomson, David. *Two Frenchmen: Pierre Laval and Charles de Gaulle.* London: The Cresset Press, 1951.

Warner, Geoffrey. *Pierre Laval and the Eclipse of France.* London: Eyre and Spottiswoode, 1968.

Bertram M. Gordon

V. I. Lenin (Vladimir Ilych Ulyanov)

1870–1924

Russian Head of State, 1917–1924

Soviet historians before about 1990 were unanimous in their praise for Lenin as the man who created Communism and the first Communist state. Since the fall of the Soviet Union in December 1991, however, most Russian scholars and many ordinary people have blamed Lenin for originating the tyranny that Stalin perfected. Many Western historians since World War II have embraced this negative assessment, although some have argued that Stalin buried Lenin's efforts to create an equitable society, along with the twenty million victims of his state-sponsored terror. These conflicting views arise in part from the political biases of those who hold them, but they also reflect contradictions in Lenin's own character and career. His goal was a society free of repression, filled with productive people living together in harmony, and he believed that the world was destined to achieve that goal, starting in Russia. So utterly did he believe in the righteousness of his cause, however, that he was willing to adopt almost any expediency in pursuing it. He failed to understand that the means he adopted often carried unintended consequences that subverted the goals he embraced.

BIOGRAPHICAL BACKGROUND

Vladimir Ilyich Ulyanov, better known by his revolutionary pseudonym, Lenin, was born on April 22, 1870, in Simbirsk, Russia. He was the third child and second son of Ilya Nikolayevich Ulyanov, a public school inspector, and Maria Aleksandrovna Blank, a well-educated and liberal woman. Young Vladimir graduated with honors from the Simbirsk Gymnasium in 1887 and seemed destined to become a respectable lawyer. The dream died when his brother Alexander was executed in 1886 for participating in an attempted assassination of Tsar Alexander III.

Expelled from Kazan University for joining student demonstrations, Ulyanov read law and revolutionary ideologies. The former effort earned him a law diploma first-class by examination from St. Petersburg University. The latter brought him to embrace Marxist doctrines, which gave shape to his hostility toward all things tsarist and determined his career as a revolutionary.

By 1895, his writing having established a small reputation, he traveled to Switzerland to meet George Plekhanov, the "Father of Russian Marxism," whose Emancipation of Labor group had attracted a formidable group of émigrés. A welcome disciple, Vladimir was soon sent to St. Petersburg with another young radical to organize the Fighting Group for the Emancipation of Labor. Both were arrested within weeks, and Ulyanov spent the years 1897–1900 in Siberian exile. There he married Nadezhda Konstantinova Krupskaya (1898), wrote *The Development of Capitalism in Russia* and other works, adopted "Lenin" as his revolutionary name, and enhanced his reputation as a theorist.

His exile over in 1900, Lenin returned to Geneva, where he became a frequent contributor to *Iskra*, the newspaper of the new Russian Social Democratic Labor Party (RSDLP), which had been organized in 1898. When he published *What Is to Be Done* in 1902, Lenin diverged from the orthodoxy of Plekhanov and most other Russian Marxists by calling for the RSDLP to adopt a conspiratorial structure and policy in order to meet the challenges of the tsarist police state. The Second Congress of the RSDLP (1903) rejected his platform, but he subsequently won control of *Iskra*, in a strong vote that inspired him to call his faction "Bolshevik," or majority. Plekhanov and the rest of the RSDLP became by default the "Mensheviks," or minority.

Save for a few months in 1905, he remained abroad until 1917, writing, and organizing a small but devoted following, both inside Russia and abroad. When war broke out in 1914, Lenin was in Zurich, almost unknown except to socialists, among whom he represented a tiny fraction of the RSDLP, one of the smallest and least influential of European socialist parties. Within little more than three years, however, he would lead the revolution that would enable the Bolsheviks to seize control of the defunct tsarist empire.

Most socialists supported their countries' war efforts, but those who did not organized a conference at Zimmerwald, Switzerland, in 1915. Lenin was there, insisting that the "imperialist war must be turned into a revolutionary war of class against class." His position drew only minority support, but it clearly placed him on the extreme left wing of Marxism. Also in 1915 he published perhaps his most important work, *Imperialism, The Highest Stage of Capitalism*. Lenin argued that the revolution that would destroy capitalism in the name of the proletariat could break out anywhere in the world, and not necessarily in an industrially advanced country ruled by the bourgeoisie. Even Russia could be the chosen country.

When revolution spontaneously erupted in Petrograd in March 1917, Lenin quickly arranged for transportation home, confident that his theories would bring Bolshevism to the fore. Upon his return, he pursuaded his colleagues to adopt a policy of intransigence against the Provisional Government with which liberals and moderate socialists had replaced the tsar. "All power to the Soviets," he cried, referring to the chaotically democratic Soviet of Workers and Soldiers Deputies, whose ideology was socialist. Limited at first, the Bolshevik appeal grew steadily, fed by food shortages, governmental ineptitude, the ill-fated and unsuccessful July offensive, and a pathetic rightist putsch in August. In late October the Bolshevik Central Committee began laying the groundwork for its own revolution.

On November 7, pro-Bolshevik workers and soldiers took control of strategic points all over Petrograd and arrested ministers of the Provisional Government. Next day at the All-Russian Congress of Soviets, Lenin claimed victory for the Communists, as the Bolsheviks now called themselves. As head of the new government, the Council of People's Commissars, he spent the next months drafting social and economic legislation and surrendering to Germany on draconian terms. Those who opposed the new policies were often arrested, and many were sent to labor camps.

In the spring of 1918 the real struggle for power began, a civil war between the Communists and their many opponents—tsarist military officers, liberals, monarchists, anarchists, and moderate socialists. The previous optimism turned into a grim determination to win the armed contest at whatever cost. Worker-controlled factories came under strict central management; democracy in the Red Army disappeared with a new emphasis on rank, corporal punishment, and discipline; concessions to peasants were replaced with forced confiscations of grain. War Communism ruthlessly and often violently mobilized every one and thing under Communist rule for the war effort, antagonizing millions.

Communist victory over the White forces in 1921 unleashed popular unrest throughout the country, which Lenin tamed with ruthless force and liberal reform. The Red Army brutally crushed the revolt of the Kronstadt sailors, who had been staunch Bolshevik supporters in 1917. Simultaneous reforms—the New Economic Policy (NEP)—installed a limited market economy that began slowly to reverse the terrible privations that peasants and workers had suffered under War Communism. Despite the famine that followed in the wake of war, the Soviet economy began to recover, and by 1926 agricultural and industrial productions were back to 1913 levels. But Lenin did not live to see the recovery.

Lenin's first stroke hit in May 1922, forcing him to curtail his activities. Two more strokes in December left him almost an invalid. Over several months he dictated a set of instructions and his observations on the future of the Soviet Union. He called for the New Economic Policy to continue and urged gradual reconciliation of all classes through education. His "Last Testament" weighed the capacities of leading Communists who might succeed him. Toward the end, he instructed Leon Trotsky to engineer the removal of Stalin from all positions of authority for his rudeness and high-handedness, but Trotsky failed the task. After an incapacitating stroke left Lenin bed-ridden in March 1923, he died on January 21, 1924.

LENIN AS A GREAT LEADER

His effective grasp of political tactics, his persistence, and his charismatic personality lent Lenin the aura of the great leader. Prior to 1917, his tiny faction was among the smallest in Europe and was largely comprised of followers living in exile in Switzerland or in Siberia. When World War I broke out, the leaders of Lenin's little band huddled in Zurich, sporadically smuggling propaganda to Russian workers. Among the minority of European socialists who opposed the war in 1914, he led a minority who advocated immediate revolution. When he returned to Petrograd in April 1917, a month after the tsar had fallen, Lenin galvanized his followers and won steadily increasing support among the urban masses. Eight months later, his Bolsheviks were strong enough to take control of the capital and eventually of the entire Russian Empire. While it is certainly true that the Provisional Government was inept, economic conditions disastrous, and other political parties indecisive, Lenin demonstrated remarkable skills of leadership in bringing the Bolsheviks to power. Without his presence, the November Revolution would have been unimaginable.

His tactical genius is most clearly seen by comparing two events during the revolution. After the disastrous July offensive had collapsed with heavy losses, radical workers and soldiers who embraced Bolshevik propaganda demanded that the party seize power from the Provisional Government. Lenin, persuaded that the government still had enough popular support to repress an uprising, argued in vain to dissuade his followers from their rash action. The attempted coup was a debacle; the impetuous radicals were routed, and party leaders were imprisoned for several weeks or forced into hiding. Lenin's judgment had been verified by events.

Three months later, the situation had changed dramatically. An abortive military coup had severely weakened the Provisional Government and its prime minister, Alexander Kerensky, who had appealed for support from the leftists whom he had been trying to suppress. Lenin, who had fled to Finland after the July Days, recognized before any of his Bolshevik colleagues that Kerensky had lost his base of support and was ready to fall. His colleagues feared a reprise of the July Days, however, and ignored his letters insisting that they begin planning a takeover. Only when Lenin returned to Petrograd in October did he persuade party leaders to prepare a new revolution. On November 7 the Bolsheviks took control of Petrograd almost without bloodshed, reconfirming Lenin's acumen.

Once in power, Lenin quickly learned that the problems of governing differed from the problems of creating a revolutionary theory and organizing a strong party. By spring, however, he had consolidated Communist control over most of European Russia, had made peace with Germany, signing the Treaty of Brest-Litovsk, and had begun to reorganize the economy. The outbreak of civil war in April forced Lenin to turn his party's attention to the urgent military situation. Over the next three years, he presided over a wartime government that fought viciously for survival and dealt ruthlessly with dissent. In the name of War Communism, his government took direct control over the economy, seizing food from the peasants without recompense and driving workers mercilessly. The victory over the White armies came at a high cost. The brutality of the war and of Lenin's policies left many people disillusioned by 1921; a new spontaneous revolution threatened to overthrow the Communists.

Lenin reacted energetically and decisively, by pushing through sweeping social and economic reforms (NEP) against the strong opposition of many Communist leaders. Peasants were allowed to expand their lands, hire labor, and sell their goods at market prices, paying only a small tax on their proceeds. Workers received good wages and their working conditions were improved. Those who wished to open retail shops or small manufacturing plants were able to do so. Censorship was even relaxed somewhat. By 1923 the economy was starting to recover from a decade of war, revolution, and civil war.

The failures of War Communism and the promise of the New Economic Policy persuaded Lenin that Soviet Russia could not quickly be transformed into a socialist state. He began to write of the need for education, reconciliation among the people, and gradual economic growth based on the policies of NEP. It is impossible to know what Lenin would have done had he lived another decade, but there is good evidence that he would not have led his country to the horrors of forced collectivization and arbitrary blood purges.

LENIN THE TYRANT

The tyrannical side of Lenin arose from his unshakable conviction that his theories were true and his analysis accurate. Those who had the temerity to reject his theories, like Leon Trotsky between 1903 and 1917, met Lenin's bitter denunciations. He condoned almost any tactical measure that seemed likely to advance his cause. It mattered not that those measures frequently required the death or imprisonment of those who disagreed.

In his theoretical writings, Lenin rejected the terrorism and assassination that had been woven into the Russian revolutionary tradition since the late

1860s, arguing that such activities reflected political naïveté. But expediency sometimes persuaded him to violate his own strictures. During the civil war, food was in short supply both for the Red Army and for the cities. Lenin approved the creation of "Food Brigades," made up of urban toughs who rampaged through the countryside, terrorizing peasants whom they accused of hoarding their grain. Peasants who resisted the seizure of the seed grain they needed for spring planting were often killed on the spot as enemies of the revolution. To be sure, the policy did bring in foodstuffs, but it also contributed to the famine of 1921–1922, in which millions died because of the shrunken harvests.

On December 20, 1917, Lenin ordered a veteran Polish Bolshevik, Felix Dzerzhinsky, to create the All-Russian Commission for Struggle with Counterrevolution and Sabotage, the Cheka. At first, this forerunner of the KGB concentrated on criminals and terrorists, but as civil war heightened political tensions, Cheka officers began arresting persons suspected of hostility toward Communist rule. Although few were executed, many were shipped to newly established labor camps, where overwork and inadequate food and shelter left few survivors. By the end of the fighting in 1921, the Cheka had become a fearsome organization that ignored the niceties of legal procedure and questions of guilt or innocence.

So severe were the hardships of the civil war and so ruthless the government's treatment of real or imagined sabotage, that even some Communists advocated a less rigorous dictatorship. At the X Party Congress in 1921, after introducing NEP, Lenin pushed through a Resolution on Party Unity that seriously curtailed open debate. Communists who organized factions that tried to change policy were warned that they could be stripped of party membership and even arrested by the Cheka. Here was the origin of Stalin's blood purge of the party fifteen years later, when millions of Communists, including most of those who had led during revolution and civil war, were charged with ludicrous crimes and executed.

It must be noted that Lenin's tyranny was minor in comparison to that of Stalin, who led the Soviet Union from 1928 to 1953 and who was directly responsible for the arbitrary deaths of some twenty million Soviet citizens. Scholars have long debated whether Stalin fulfilled Lenin's legacy or violated it. Those who blame Lenin for the tragic purges and terror of the Stalinist era, argue that Lenin's theories and his policies during the civil war provided the model that Stalin emulated. Others view Stalin as an aberration, who used arbitrary terror to ensure his own control. All agree, however, that Lenin was not immune from tyrannical measures.

SUGGESTIONS FOR ADDITIONAL READING

Chamberlin, William H. *The Russian Revolution.* 2 vols. New York: Grosset and Dunlap, 1965 (1935).

Clarke, Ronald William. *Lenin*, New York: Harper & Row, 1988.
Deutscher, Isaac. *Lenin's Childhood*, London and New York: Oxford University Press, 1970.
Fischer, Louis. *The Life of Lenin*. New York: Harper & Row, 1964.
Hill, Christopher. *Lenin and the Russian Revolution*. New York: MacMillan, 1949.
Service, Robert. *Lenin: A Political Life*. Vol. 1, *The Strengths of Contradiction*. Terre Haute: Indiana University Press, 1985.
Ulam, Adam. *The Bolsheviks*. New York: MacMillan, 1965.
Williams, Robert Chadwell. *The Other Bolsheviks: Lenin and His Critics, 1904–1914*. Bloomingdale: Indiana University Press, 1986.

J. Martin Ryle

Leopold II

1835–1909

King of the Belgians, 1865–1909

King of the Congo Free State, 1885–1908

The second king to occupy the throne of modern Belgium holds a unique place in history. As the constitutional, limited monarch of a parliamentary country, he earned a solid reputation for wisdom, restraint, and respect for the institutions of his people. As the absolute monarch of the Congo Free State, he earned worldwide condemnation for his cruel exploitation of his African subjects. In the Belgian homeland he made major contributions to the capacity of his little country to defend itself from foreign threat. Viewing imperialism as a positive "good," he endeavored to expand the role of Belgium as a substantial force in the world's economy.

Like his father before him, he was acutely aware of the importance of building the prestige of a dynasty that was still new to the Belgian throne. Through his father, he was a first cousin to both Queen Victoria of Great Britain and her consort, Prince Albert, the children of Leopold I's sister and brother. Through his mother, he was a grandson of Louis Philippe, King of the French. He himself was married to a Habsburg archduchess. His sister Charlotte was married to Ferdinand Maximilian von Habsburg, brother of the emperor of Austria, who reigned briefly as Emperor Maximilian of Mexico. His father had arranged the marriage of another Saxe-Coburg prince to the queen of Portugal. In his determination to be the cousin of all Europe, Leopold II even arranged the marriage of his daughter to the heir of the House of Bonaparte, after that dynasty had been overthrown and seemed unlikely ever to reign again.

All of this ambitious matchmaking, however, should not obscure one important fact. Leopold II was the embodiment of conservative caution. He took care never to offend his dangerous neighbors, the Great Powers. If he "hedged his bets" by making friends in every corner, he also retreated from confrontations, while doing everything possible to make his little kingdom capable of playing a bigger role in the world than its diminutive size would have made likely.

BIOGRAPHICAL BACKGROUND

Leopold Louis Philippe Marie Victoria was born on April 9, 1835, at Brussels. His father, Leopold I of Saxe-Coburg-Saalfeld was the first king of modern Belgium, a pragmatic Protestant who had agreed to raise his children as Roman Catholics in order to receive the crown of a Catholic nation. Leopold I's wife was similarly a choice made for him by politics, rather than romance. Queen Louise Marie was a daughter of Louis Philippe, King of the French. The great powers of Europe preferred that a French princess mount the Belgian throne, rather than a French prince who might someday seek to unify France and Belgium. With his birth conditioned by such political considerations, young Leopold mastered the fine art of pleasing all the jealous great powers.

In 1846 the heir to the Belgian throne was created Duke de Brabant. In 1853 he was married to Marie Henrietta, daughter of Archduke Joseph of Austria, thereby creating a Habsburg link for the ambitious House of Saxe-Coburg.

From 1853 to 1855 the Duke and Duchess of Brabant made ceremonial visits to India, North Africa, and the Middle East. They attained the distinction of being the first Christians since the Age of the Crusades allowed to visit the Moslem holy places atop the Temple Mount in Jerusalem. At Leopold I's death on December 10, 1865, Leopold II inherited the throne. Throughout his reign, he was acutely aware of the dangers posed to his little kingdom by his neighbors, France and Germany.

Part of Leopold's skill lay in persuading each Great Power that an expanded role for Belgium was preferable to the aggrandizement of any of the other Great Powers. It was thus that he built his African domain and expanded Belgium's position in the economic life of Asia.

Leopold II lost his only son, aged eight, and as no other sons were born to him, his heir apparent through most of his reign was his brother Philippe, Count of Flanders. Inheritance in the Belgian royal family was exclusively through the male line. He was ultimately succeeded by Philippe's son Albert.

In December 1909, Leopold II underwent abdominal surgery. He seemed to be making a good recovery when he suffered an embolism. He died at the palace of Laeken on December 17.

LEOPOLD II AS A GREAT LEADER

On his succession to the throne, Leopold II became a witness to dramatic shifts in the European balance of power. A Danish-German War in 1864 and the Seven Weeks War of 1866 made it plain that Bismarck's Prussia could challenge France for military dominance. Leopold's response was to pull his kingdom into tight neutrality, avoiding any adventures peripheral to Belgian interests. When it became apparent in 1866 that France was about to abandon attempts to conquer Mexico, in the face of military threats from the United States, Leopold also withdrew the Belgian Corps of Volunteers, known as the Empress Legion. This was particularly painful to him because his sister Charlotte was empress of Mexico. Their late father, Leopold I, had been an early and ardent supporter for the ambitions of his son-in-law, Ferdinand Maximilian von Habsburg to become emperor of Mexico. When Charlotte visited Europe in August 1866 to beg for renewed help, she pointedly snubbed Leopold. However, when his unhappy sister became hopelessly psychotic, Leopold sent their brother Philippe to escort her to Belgium, where she spent the rest of her life in seclusion.

Although Leopold did not learn of it immediately, he certainly suspected that Napoleon III was engaged in attempts to obtain Prussian consent for a French seizure of Belgium in 1866. This was intended as a compensation to France for all the small German states that Prussia had annexed after her victory in the Seven Weeks War of 1866. Prussia procrastinated and never gave consent. In 1870, when the Franco-Prussian War began, Bismarck reaped a propaganda victory by leaking the incriminating French proposals to the press, making France appear to be an aggressor, while Prussia was a defender of treaties. Less conspiratorially, France attempted to purchase Luxembourg from the king of the Netherlands, in 1867, but was blocked by German threats of war. The prospect of French expansion into Luxembourg was certainly frightening to Leopold, even if he could not prove that France itself had even more threatening plans to seize Belgium. He thus took a very aggressive role in blocking French attempts in 1869 to buy control of the Belgian railroads.

After the defeat of France by united Germany in 1871, Belgium breathed more freely. Leopold was always alert, however, that German hegemony also threatened his little realm. The new and temporarily more stable balance of power created by German triumph in 1871 gave the king an opportunity to expand Belgium's worldwide economic role.

In 1876 he was host at a Brussels Conference at which the International Association for the Exploration and Colonization of Africa was founded. At the conference, Leopold presented himself as interested only in promoting scientific exploration of Africa for the advancement of knowledge and for the economic benefit of all humanity. That this later developed into Leopold's most conscienceless and tyrannical venture, was certainly not predictable in 1876.

When the United States defeated Spain in the Spanish-American War of 1898, Leopold made aggressive attempts to replace Spain in the Philippines. He desisted when it became plain that President McKinley had his own designs on the islands. Nevertheless, both in China and the Philippines, the king took an active role in promoting the formation of trading companies to exploit those vast markets for Belgian industry.

At home, in Belgium, the king took care to avoid intrusion into purely domestic quarrels between Walloons and Flemings, or between Catholics and anticlericalists. Where he could do so, he always supported laissez-faire capitalism against socialism.

Fearing Belgium's powerful neighbors, the kind did take an aggressive stance on military and diplomatic questions. He had a dominant role in strengthening the fortifications at Antwerp, Liège, Namur, and on the Scheldt and Meuse rivers. Against very strong legislative resistance, he succeeded in introducing conscription to build Belgium's armed forces. The parliament held out for a provision that only one son per family be drafted. There is no doubt, however, that it was Leopold II's firm policy that made possible King Albert's heroic defense of the country when Germany attacked in August 1914.

LEOPOLD II THE TYRANT

Following the Brussels Conference of 1876, the king took a lively interest in African affairs. In 1879 he authorized the American explorer Henry Morton Stanley to begin negotiations with 450 African chiefs, who surrendered their land in exchange for gifts. Whether the chieftains understood the concept of sovereignty and had really surrendered their land to King Leopold is debatable. However, at the Berlin Conference of 1884–1885, Leopold was able to obtain international recognition as king of the Congo Free State. By the same act, the conference denied the rival claims of Great Britain and Portugal. Leopold thereby found himself the sovereign head of two states, linked only by the fact that he was king in both.

In addition to Stanley, the king employed another American, Henry Shelton Sanford, in preparing the economic exploitation of the Congo. Sanford had been the United States minister to Belgium during the American Civil War. He had developed a cordial friendship with the Duke de Brabant. After the war he had returned to the United States and played a large role in building railroads in Florida.

Sanford introduced American business practices and treated the Congo as a profit-making organization. Although the king is credited with ending the Arab slave trade in the Congo, he introduced something equally bad. The Congo was divided into geographic districts, each of which had to fulfill a quota for the delivery of natural resources. African tribesmen were forcibly conscripted to work the lucrative rubber plantations and other enterprises.

When news of atrocities committed against the natives began to reach Europe, an outcry went up, demanding that the king surrender the Congo Free State to the Belgian government. The king resisted yielding one of "his" countries to the other. However, by 1908, one year before his death, the Congo Free State became the Belgian Congo. Leopold II's only experiment in tyranny had met defeat.

SUGGESTIONS FOR ADDITIONAL READING

Aronson, Theo. *The Coburgs of Belgium*. London: Cassell, 1968.

Ascherson, Neal. *The King Incorporated, Leopold II in the Age of Trusts*. Garden City, NY: Doubleday, 1964.

Blumberg, Arnold. "Belgium and a Philippine Protectorate: a Stillborn Plan." *Asian Studies* 10 (December 1972): 336–343.

Brausch, Georges. *Belgian Administration in the Congo*. London: Oxford University Press, 1961.

Emerson, Barbara. *Leopold II of the Belgians, King of Colonialism*. London: Weidenfeld and Nicolson, 1979.

Helmreich, Jonathan E. *Belgium and Europe: A Study in Small Power Diplomacy*. The Hague: Mouton, 1976.

Lichtervelde, Count Louis de. *Leopold of the Belgians*. Translated by Thomas H. Reed and R. Russell Reed. New York: Century, 1929.

Martelli, George. *Leopold to Lumumba: A History of the Belgian Congo, 1877–1960*. London: Chapman and Hall, 1962.

Thomas, Daniel H. *The Guarantee of Belgian Independence and Neutrality in European Diplomacy, 1830's–1930's*. Kingston, R.I.: Daniel H. Thomas, 1983.

Arnold Blumberg

Louis XIV

1638–1715

King of France, 1643–1715

Hyacinthe Rigaud's celebrated portrait of King Louis XIV presents a monarch self-assured and confident, the quintessence of absolute monarchy. His emblem, the sun, suggests power radiating into all corners of the realm; all eyes looked to his palace at Versailles. Here, it would seem, was a ruler who knew exactly what he was doing. One can glean as much from summary written accounts, too.

Within the last quarter-century the Louis XIV that has emerged from scholarly histories is not so absolute as Rigaud's Sun King portrait suggests—and not so sure of himself either. Louis XIV could recall being driven out of his own Parisian residence during the civil wars known as the Fronde; he learned to be suspicious, even fearful, of high personages, the sort that had rebelled against his ancestors. Moreover, as Andrew Lossky has written, the king was less aware than he might appear of where his policies, particularly foreign policy, were leading him. He pursued confused and contradictory aims: While dreaming of a Spanish inheritance for a member of his family (the Bourbons), instead of focusing on that object he meddled in petty politics along his German border for no discernible reason; for a considerable time he followed an anti-papal policy destined to yield him nothing. The results of the wars fought during Louis's personal reign (1661–1715), when viewed in purely territorial or economic terms, hardly reflected the effort expended.

BIOGRAPHICAL BACKGROUND

Born on September 5, 1638, Louis XIV was but four years old when his father, King Louis XIII, died in 1643. For years to come Queen Anne would serve as regent for her son; both would be guided by a powerful chief minister, Jules Cardinal Mazarin—a statesman-diplomat directing French policy in Louis's name in the period 1643–1661.

The quarter-century from 1635 to 1659 witnessed the Franco-Spanish War, concluded with the Peace of the Pyrenees. The 1659 treaty confirmed the fact that France had replaced Spain as the predominant European power. Meanwhile, rebellion at home led to civil wars (1648–1653) collectively known as the Fronde, in which the crown ultimately triumphed. If Louis XIV had learned anything from the Fronde and previous rebellions, it was to trust power neither to mighty noblemen nor to his own relatives but, instead, to rely on himself to govern.

At Mazarin's death in 1661, Louis chose no chief minister to replace him. Although he had deep respect for Mazarin, Louis would tolerate no one else that close to the summit. Until the end the king would remain his own first minister; the period 1661–1715 stands for Louis's "personal" reign.

Each decade of that era had certain discernible characteristics. The 1660s, for example, were a time of financial retrenchment. The king's minister, Jean-Baptiste Colbert, strove to bring the royal finances out of the chaos into which they had sunk during the war and to balance the budget. During the early 1660s a series of trials were the talk of Paris as hundreds of lenders to the crown were imprisoned or fined for alleged fraud.

With Louis's approval, Colbert's range of activity extended well beyond government finances: to establishing royal companies to trade overseas, for example, or subsidizing and regulating industry. In other words, the crown pursued a policy of mercantilism—government intervention to increase the wealth of the king's subjects and fill the royal treasury at the same time. And, as we shall see, the later 1660s witnessed a reform program for Paris.

That same period saw the beginnings of a foreign policy that would become the crown's dominant preoccupation, disrupt French commerce, and force the king to borrow. In 1659, peace with Spain had been signed; in 1667, Louis XIV invaded Spanish lands near the present Franco-Belgian border—a conflict known as the War of Devolution (1667–1668). Louis claimed these lands as part of the inheritance due his wife Marie-Thérèse, daughter of King Philip IV of Spain. Foreigners were alarmed. The Dutch, English, and Swedish governments threatened to intervene against France, thus persuading Louis to agree quickly to peace with Spain and settle for slight territorial gains. A warning for the future was the willingness of foreign powers on this occasion to challenge French aggression.

Another occasion came soon. This time Louis XIV and King Charles II of England had conspired to attack the Dutch Republic. For Louis the main objective was to provoke Spain into war and, thereby, seize at least part of the Spanish Netherlands (modern Belgium). If the Dutch War (1672–1678) yielded Louis a few military victories to boast about, it drew him into protracted conflict against a new coalition of foreign powers. In the end Louis derived little from the Treaty of Nijmegen (1678–1679) that he could not have obtained earlier by much less violent means.

If the 1660s were a decade of relative peace and the 1670s scarred by the Dutch War, dominant themes of the 1680s were confused thinking on the king's part and sporadic violence as, without clear overall objectives, Louis grasped aimlessly at neighboring territories. He seized the city of Strasbourg and Spanish Luxembourg, quarreled with the pope and even invaded papal lands (at Avignon), all the while avoiding full-scale war with anyone until 1688. At that point Louis launched a preemptive strike at a neighboring German fortress and, without intending to, triggered the Nine Years War, or War of the League of Augsburg (1688–1697).

The war was the culmination of years of hostility between himself and Holy Roman Emperor (also ruler of Austria-Bohemia) Leopold I of Habsburg, most prestigious of German princes and widely regarded as protector of other German princes' lands against French aggression. The 1690s proved to be a decade of open war, but again France was checked by a coalition—among them the emperor, Spain, and England. The Treaty of Ryswick (1697) compelled Louis to forfeit a few lands along his eastern frontier, but bigger questions remained to be settled.

For years the great issue facing Europe's diplomats had been the ultimate disposal of the Spanish inheritance. As the Spanish king—Carlos II, also a Habsburg—was destined to die childless at any moment, who would inherit his vast empire in Europe, Asia, and the American continents? It is easy to see now that partition was inevitable. At that time, in fact, Louis XIV and William III, ruler of England and the Dutch Netherlands, realized it too. Their treaty of 1700 would have handed over most of Spain's inheritance to Emperor Leopold's younger son, Archduke Charles, while allowing the French smaller compensation elsewhere. (Both French Bourbons and Austrian Habsburgs had arguable claims in that both were related to the Spanish king.)

But Emperor Leopold disliked the partition pact of 1700 especially because it shut him out of Italy; the Spanish themselves rejected any partition. Meanwhile, when Carlos died that same year, he left behind a will bequeathing Spain's entire inheritance to Louis XIV's grandson, Philip. Louis in turn accepted, abandoning the partition treaty. As we shall see, what really brought on the war was Louis's high-handed actions that followed—along with the emperor's intrasigence over Italy.

The conflict is called the War of the Spanish Succession (1701–1713). It constituted the greatest trial for Louis's military machine since 1661; the French could no longer count on winning battles. France reached a low point in 1709, with its economy a disaster and enemies demanding what amounted to unconditional surrender. Actually the nation's fortunes soon recovered sufficiently to allow Louis to emerge with a negotiated settlement. Yet the Peace of Utrecht (1713), leaving Louis's grandson on the Spanish throne, was small compensation for a dozen years of war.

LOUIS XIV AS A GREAT LEADER

Once Mazarin had ended the Fronde and negotiated the Pyrenees treaty, Louis XIV had free reign to exercise leadership. No enemy at home or abroad posed a serious threat. Not only did the king rule personally in France; for better or for worse he was setting a style for Europe's monarchs to imitate. His reign is regarded as a high point of absolute monarchy, a term implying that power emanated from the king alone but that no king could simply act as he pleased: for example, Louis did not ordinarily interfere with the work of the law courts. Since most high officials owned their offices, the king could not dismiss them without repurchasing those posts—a big order, for the government lacked money to redeem a great number of them. Absolutism had limits.

In the arts, the king was very much the leader and style setter. His palace at Versailles and its gardens became models for lesser monarchs to emulate. There was no clear separation, however, among art, propaganda, and politics. Versailles served not so much the king's comfort and convenience as his politics: an announcement to French and foreigners alike that here reigned the mightiest monarch in Europe. For Frenchmen it constituted a summons to submit to royal authority.

Versailles was a symbol of leadership in another, less symbolic sense, too. Noblemen were encouraged to reside there, where the king could observe them; remaining on their rural estates, they might have plotted against the crown as their ancestors had done. The cult of majesty and court etiquette spelled political control; Louis's very appearance cowed friends and foe alike. It is worth noting that the two kings who succeeded Louis XIV lacked that gift for leadership. Had it been otherwise, the history of France in the 1790s might read quite differently.

Although it was the largest, Versailles was but one palace complex; during his reign Louis employed legions of architects, decorators, musicians, and more as part of a grand scheme to patronize the arts. In theory, at least, the music of a Lully or a Couperin or a statue in an urban piazza contributed to the king's grandeur and reputation.

Louis's administration of the government excelled in diverse ways. It represented an advance in the development of bureaucracy, with organized departments of professionals serving where once small groups of amateurs had sufficed. Within the military sphere, a highly significant development was the emergence of a modern army under the direction of Michel Le Tellier, war minister. No more could undisciplined troops roam the land at will; the new regime meant uniforms, drill, and subjection to orders from the war minister, who in turn served the king. (What Louis chose to do with that army is highly questionable.)

Effective leadership is not necessarily spectacular leadership. If the wars did not obscure our view, we could more easily see Louis XIV's reign as a time of renovation and reform—particularly in Paris, the king's capital and by far the largest city in the realm. Paris acquired a police administration that became the envy of Europe. As the king's main interest was foreign policy, domestic policy was exercised through ministers and other professionals. But it could not have happened without Louis's tacit approval, at the very least—such was the logic of absolute monarchy.

The capital Louis inherited from his forbears was a sewer, so to speak, lacking paved streets and lighting and adequate water. In the 1660s the city worried about a host of problems such as crime and air pollution. Appointment of a chief of police with power to curb proliferation of deadly weapons and secure the food supply, to mention but two examples, signified a bold royal initiative. Setting up several thousand lanterns over thoroughfares no doubt made streets safer. In fact a commemorative medal praised Louis for paving many of the streets. The king and Colbert led a campaign to clean up the city, construct more public fountains, widen routes, and decorate their capital with new boulevards.

Of larger significance perhaps were the establishment of a great tariff-free zone in northern France called the Five Great Farms and the creation of Languedoc Canal in the south, both designed to facilitate commerce. During Louis XIV's reign the crown drew up several law codes, for France the most ambitious project of its kind prior to the Napoleonic Codes.

LOUIS XIV THE TYRANT

Tyranny is less visible in the domestic administration of Louis XIV than one might assume. The king was no Oriental despot. Normally Louis let the law courts dispense justice—justice less arbitrary and draconian than it was once thought to be. Harsh language in criminal codes did not necessarily reflect actual practice in royal courts.

Yet arbitrary justice comes to light in one of the most celebrated cases of the reign. The object of attention was Nicolas Fouquet, erstwhile finance minister and crown lender, whose opulent life style and allegedly treasonable language offended his enemies and apparently frightened the king. In 1665 Louis brushed aside a sentence of exile handed down by a duly constituted court and sentenced the man to life imprisonment on the basis of dubious evidence. Today the king's response seems less a reasoned judgment than a reflection of Louis's fear of rebellion by overmighty aristocrats.

In Louis's dealings with his Protestant subjects, the charge of tyranny is not difficult to sustain. The Edict of Nantes (1598) had guaranteed them toleration. Hoping to establish his credentials at home and abroad as a crusader, Louis revoked the edict in 1685. Religion was hardly the issue; civil disobedience and public relations had far more to do with the revocation. By so acting Louis convinced many Protestants at home and abroad that he was a tyrant; nor did the edict win the king Catholic Europe's support, certainly not the emperor's or the pope's.

In the king's foreign policy, more than strictly domestic actions, the charge of tyranny has weight. Invading the Dutch Republic in 1672 was an act of force, after all, designed to draw Spain into conflict and win Louis a foothold in Belgium. One could also cite Louis's undisciplined conduct in the 1680s and early 1690s: bombardment of Genoa, invasion of Luxembourg, and, most notorious, vandalizing the German Palatinate (1691) as an act of war and terror. Louis would pay heavily for such things in bad will and distrust abroad. Responsibility for the Spanish succession conflict was not exclusively his, to be sure. But sending troops into Belgium to "guard" it for his grandson—reawakening foreigners' distrust of the French king—was one ingredient in an explosive mixture that ignited that European war.

SUGGESTIONS FOR ADDITIONAL READING

Bernard, Leon. *The Emerging City: Paris in the Age of Louis XIV*. Durham, N.C.: Duke University Press, 1970.

Hatton, Ragnhild, ed. *Louis XIV and Absolutism*. Columbus: Ohio State University Press, 1976.

———. *Louis XIV and Europe*. Columbus: Ohio State University Press, 1976.

Lossky, Andrew. "The General European Crisis of the 1680s." *European Studies Review* 10 (1980): 177–198.

Louis XIV. *Mémoires for the Instruction of the Dauphin*. Translated by Paul Sonnino. New York: Free Press, 1970.

Rule, John C., ed. *Louis XIV and the Craft of Kingship*. Columbus: Ohio State University Press, 1969.

Trout, Andrew. *Jean-Baptiste Colbert*. Boston: Twayne, 1978.

Wolf, John B. *Louis XIV*. New York: W. W. Norton, 1968.

———. *Toward a European Balance of Power, 1620–1715*. Chicago: Rand-McNally, 1970.

Andrew Trout

Mao Zedong (Mao Tse-tung)

1893–1976

Dictator of the People's Republic of China, 1949–1976

On any short list of the greatest leaders of the twentieth century you will find the Communist leader of China, Mao Zedong. While he lived and after his death, he was one of the most adored and most scorned men. His detractors would paint a picture of a butcher responsible for the death of millions of his countrymen, a wrongheaded schemer whose political machinations left China in turmoil, and a madman who menaced China's neighbors and threatened world peace.

Yet, during his long career as revolutionary leader and ruler of China, Mao was revered by hundreds of millions of his countrymen. Among his admirers were many who were neither Chinese nor Communist. One Western biographer of Mao exclaims, "Chairman Mao is one of the greatest political leaders in the history of mankind," and another asserts that Mao "influenced more human lives more profoundly than anyone else in our century." His admirers point first to his restoration of China to strength and dignity and then to his many accomplishments as a revolutionary, a patriot, and political leader. In the final years of his life, leaders of many nations of the world, including some who had battled him for years, beat a path to Beijing to pay homage to this titan of the twentieth century.

But not long after death claimed him, his successors in Beijing conducted their own assessment of his leadership, and concluded that he was to be honored as the great revolutionary hero who liberated China, but they repudiated his leadership of China after the Communist victory in 1949, and especially scorned him for his "mistakes" in the Cultural Revolution of the 1960s.

BIOGRAPHICAL BACKGROUND

Mao Zedong was born in a rural area of Hunan province in central China in 1893. Mao, the revolutionary, was always proud of his peasant background although his father owned a modest amount of land. Throughout his life he identified with the toiling peasant masses of China. While still in his teens, Mao was swept up in revolution, for the nationalist revolution broke out in 1911 and quickly spread across China and soon brought down the Manchu monarchy. In 1919 the young political activist ventured to Beijing, the capital, where for the first time he took up the study of Marxism. Only two years later he was among the group of twelve men who founded the Chinese Communist Party (CCP).

It was not until 1935 that Mao was made chairman of the CCP, a position he retained until his death in 1976. In the early 1920s, the infant CCP was ordered by Moscow to join forces with its rival, the Nationalist Party. But the coalition of revolutionary parties lasted only until April 1927, when the Nationalist leader, Jiang Jieshi (Chiang Kai-shek), turned against the Communists, shooting them by the thousands and virtually eradicating them in the cities. Mao, who had already gained valuable experience organizing peasants in his native Hunan, now came into his own, boldly proclaiming that the peasants, not the urban workers, constituted the revolutionary force in China. His strategy of mobilizing the peasants and fighting class warfare in the countryside from rural bases proved extremely successful, and soon his movement became, in his own words a "prairie fire." However, in 1934 the Nationalist Army forced the Communists to abandon their southern rural base and flee to northwestern China. It was during this year-long Long March that Mao outmaneuvered his opponents in the party, was made chairman, and went on to establish the reputation and aura as revolutionary leader that ultimately took him to heights of power in his country.

In his struggle against the Nationalists, Mao's Red Army had adopted the strategy of guerrilla warfare, and when war against Japan began in 1937, Mao employed this strategy brilliantly against the invaders. By fighting the Japanese more effectively than the Nationalists, Mao, in effect, stole the banner of nationalism from them. By the end of the war in 1945, the Communist forces, having grown in manpower tenfold and having established nineteen large rural bases, were in a position to contest the Nationalists for power in the impending civil war. Mediation efforts by the United States were unsuccessful, and Mao rejected Stalin's advice to avoid war with the Nationalists. The first year of the civil war went badly for the lightly armed Communist forces, but Mao reorganized the army, now called the People's Liberation Army (PLA), and led it to eventual victory. By the fall of 1949 the Nationalists were routed, and Jiang retreated with the remains of his army to Taiwan, while Mao celebrated victory in Beijing, announcing on October 1 the founding of the People's Republic of China. Among the factors contributing to the decisive Communist triumph, most important were Mao's successful program for winning the active support of the peasant class and his superior military strategy.

For the next twenty-seven years Mao ruled China as the chairman of the CCP, which maintained dictatorial power over the nation in the one-party system established by Mao.

The major policies of the People's Republic, both domestic and foreign, were of his authorship. It was he who devised and ordered the radical land reform program in the early 1950s involving the eradication of the landlord class, the creation of communes, and the Great Leap Forward program for rapid industrialization in 1958, the policy of political and military reliance on the Soviet Union, and the decision in the late 1950s to abandon the Soviet model and to adopt, instead, a foreign policy of self-reliance. Moreover, he was the author of the ideology that guided China's socialist transformation. Most characteristically Maoist of his various programs and most controversial was the Great Proletarian Cultural Revolution begun in 1966. This program was Mao's last great effort to keep the Chinese revolution from backsliding into a Soviet-like bureaucracy-dominated statism.

MAO ZEDONG AS A GREAT LEADER

Mao Zedong's stature as a great political leader derives mainly from the progress of China during his stewardship, the longevity of that stewardship, and the diversity of leadership he provided. When he became a political activist early in the century, China was the sick man of Asia, a downtrodden nation that had been humiliated for over a century by a series of military defeats and punitive treaties at the hands of the West; but by the end of Mao's political career almost seven decades later, a new China had won recognition and respect as one of the world's most powerful nations. As Mao put it, "The Chinese people have stood up." The man most responsible for liberating China and unleashing the energies of his people was Mao Zedong. He, more than anyone else, is to be credited with the restoration of China's national dignity.

Thus Mao's major claim to fame is as a Chinese nationalist. But his achievements as a patriot involved many dimensions of leadership. Among the more important of these are his roles as a theorist, as a revolutionary, as a military strategist, as a social engineer and an innovator, and as man of the people and egalitarian.

Rarely in history does there appear a great leader who excelled as did Mao Zedong as both philosopher and politician, both visionary thinker and activist. Mao is to be credited with rescuing Marxism-Leninism from its prison of dogma and tailoring it to suit Chinese conditions. He provided an interpretation of the Communist ideology that rationalized a peasant-led revolution for a country where the urban proletariat was still small and the peasants made up almost 90 percent of the population. He pressed for his concept of "permanent revolution" by which he meant the ongoing revitalization of the revolution to forestall the return of capitalism or bureaucratic exploitation of the people. Another feature of Mao's ideology was his emphasis on "volunteerism" rather than merely relying on the Marxian "forces of history."

Theorist though he was, Mao constantly railed against theory-bound Marxists or dogmatists and instead insisted that theory is useless unless and until tested by practice. It was especially as a revolutionary that Mao made history. His finest hours were while organizing the peasant revolution, leading the Long March, creating a new revolutionary regimen at Yanan in the northwest from 1936 to 1946, and planning strategy against the Japanese and later against the Nationalists in the civil war. The major features of the so-called Yanan way—party discipline, "the mass-line," egalitarianism, and self-reliance—were fashioned to meet the exigencies of those difficult years of struggle in the barren northwest and would later be refurbished as elements of the new revolutionary society Mao created after the Communists came to power in 1949.

Closely related to Mao's work as a revolutionary was his role as a military leader. Together with his comrade Zhu De (Chu Te), Mao created the Red Army in 1928 and fashioned it as both a fighting force and as an instrument of propaganda. Together they developed the basic formula of guerrilla war that they employed so effectively: "The enemy advances, we retreat; the enemy encamps, we harass; the enemy tires, we attack; the enemy retreats, we pursue." In addition Mao developed the concept and practice of "people's war." He taught that guerrilla warfare succeeds only if it is fought with the active support of the people and serves their needs. People's war was effective against both the Japanese and the Nationalists, and would serve as a model for other revolutionaries engaged in wars of national liberation. Another of Mao's contributions as a military leader was his emphasis on morale: soldiers must understand and believe in the cause for which they fight. Often quoted was his dictum "Weapons are important in war, but not the decisive factor; it is people, not things, that are decisive." Finally, Mao is recognized for his integration of the army into society, making it both an instrument of revolution and a model for revolutionary commitment and service.

Mao Zedong also stands out among world leaders as a social engineer and innovator. He was especially skillful at keeping the revolution alive by making new alliances and forming united fronts. After liberation (1949) Mao organized the peace and created order where chaos, turmoil, warfare, poverty, and misery had reigned for almost half a century. Swiftly he erased many forms of human degradation while seeking to supplant bourgeois with proletarian culture: new marriage laws were implemented on the basis of gender equality; crime, prostitution, and drug abuse were eradicated; and cities were cleaned and sanitation improved. Much of this was accomplished by the mass organizations that Mao had created (or refurbished) and activated in order to attack practical problems as well as to achieve political mobilization.

Soon after founding the People's Republic, Mao made good on his promise to deliver land to the peasantry by implementing history's largest program of land redistribution. No reform—no social program of any sort—in human history benefited as many people as Mao's land reform program. Some 300 to 400 million Chinese peasants received land.

Perhaps Mao's most significant innovation lay in his ceaseless efforts to de-bureaucratize the Chinese revolution, something the Soviet leaders failed to do. Mao insisted on avoiding the injustices of an entrenched, elitist bureaucracy. It was largely for this purpose that he instituted the Yanan way with its emphasis on the "mass line"; engineered the Great Leap Forward, designed not only to boost economic production but to eliminate the gap between the rulers and the ruled, between urban and rural China, and between mental and manual labor; and led the Cultural Revolution, perhaps one of mankind's most ambitious social engineering projects. In it Mao endeavored to bring about a thoroughly egalitarian society, and to a considerable extent he succeeded, despite the excesses involved in implementation.

Among the great leaders of the world Mao ranks very high as a populist as well as an egalitarian. "Serve the People," the rally cry of Mao's Cultural Revolution, was the standard by which all leadership was to be measured during Mao's herculean effort to eliminate elitism and bring about a genuinely egalitarian society. Although the fervor whipped up by Mao's rhetoric generated a great upheaval and caused many negative consequences, still it can be said that no social experiment in history went as far toward the creation of an egalitarian society as did Mao's Cultural Revolution—and this was undertaken in the most populated nation on earth.

MAO ZEDONG THE TYRANT

If for no other reason, Mao must be branded a tyrant because of the immense violence that he unleashed in China, the suffering and death he brought to so many in the name of achieving utopian ideals. For all his good intentions and accomplishments, there was a very heavy price to pay. Like Stalin, Mao saw it necessary to eliminate resistance by use of force, though it is doubtful that he caused as many deaths as the Soviet dictator. But without reliable data it is useless to indulge in the game of tallying up the corpses.

A distinction should be made, however, between the use of force to fight a revolution against armed opponents in the quest of power, and the use of organized violence to conduct an ongoing revolution once power had been won. It is in the latter capacity that Mao, as ruler of China after 1949, is to be condemned as a tyrant. Chinese Communist leaders and Mao himself often employed several well-known quotations from his earlier writings to condone the continued use of violence. Anti-Maoists abroad also cited those same quotations to condemn him. "Power grows out of the barrel of a gun" was perhaps most often repeated, but another often-quoted passage from an early essay illustrates more clearly Mao's approval of violence as the necessary means to revolutionary ends:

> A revolution is not a dinner party, or writing an essay, or painting a picture, or doing embroidery; it cannot be so refined, so leisurely, so gentle. . . . A revolution is an insurrection, an act of violence by which one class overthrows another. . . . To put it bluntly, it is necessary to create terror. . . . Proper limits have to be exceeded in order to right a wrong.

Mao's theory of "permanent revolution," involving the necessity of maintaining class struggle, justified continued use of revolutionary violence after the Communists seized power in 1949. The major instances of its use were the land reform program, the campaign to suppress counterrevolutionaries in 1951–1952, the anti-rightist campaign in 1957, the Great Leap Forward, and last but not least, the Cultural Revolution of the late 1960s. The first of these, the land reform, was carried out with great zeal against the landlord class. Its objective was not merely to redistribute land, but to eliminate entirely the class enemy, the landlords. Unrepentant landlords were summarily executed, sometimes after charges were made against them in impromptu kangaroo courts conducted by local Communist cadre and peasant associations, but often without any legal proceedings whatsoever. Many of the victims were guilty of nothing more than owning an acre or so of land. Estimates of the number of victims in this bloody purge range widely, but it is generally believed that the count runs well into the millions.

No sooner than the rural revolutionary violence subsided than Mao launched a campaign against suspected political opponents of his regime in the cities. The context was the Korean War, which began in mid-1950 and which the newly established government in Beijing feared would arouse counterrevolutionary action within China. With this perceived threat as the pretext, Mao conducted a series of witch hunts, aimed principally at eliminating Chinese capitalists. It was a campaign of terror not unlike that begun in Russia in 1918, and it took the lives of thousands; perhaps as many as three million.

Mao provided the theoretical grounds for this violence against the enemies of the revolution and issued the orders for it. According to Mao's concept of "the people's democratic dictatorship," which served as the basis of CCP rule, the coalition of four revolutionary classes—the proletariat, the peasantry, the petty bourgeoisie, and the national bourgeoisie—constituted "the people" who ruled "democratically" (since they were represented in government by the CCP) and maintained a dictatorship over other classes and individuals who were not "the people." These "others" were counter-revolutionaries who had no political rights and were to be silenced or ferreted out and eliminated as enemies of the people. Thus it was that Mao's CCP had sole authority not only to eliminate enemies but to define and determine who were the enemies. This was license for conducting unlimited state terror.

Coercion, Mao contended, was necessary to rid people of the wrong ideas, just as "dust never vanishes of itself without sweeping." It was the omniscient CCP guided by Mao Zedong's thought that was to do the sweeping. The largest such sweeping endeavor and the largest scale of violence instigated by Mao was the Cultural Revolution, which continued to cause havoc in China for almost a decade (1966–1976). This was the same movement that was proclaimed in the name of the loftiest of ideals, to bring about a utopian egalitarian society utterly free of class exploitation. Such was the contradiction between ends and means in Mao's communism. The youthful Red Guard (students freed by Mao from the universities he closed) were commissioned by Mao to go out and "bombard the headquarters," which is to say purge the ruling CCP of elitists and return the revolution to the people. Their rampage resulted in enormous disruption, including work stoppages and a ten-year halt to higher education. Their excessive fervor soon rendered the Cultural Revolution a terrifying witch hunt that not only destroyed the political order in China but caused untold terror, suffering, torture, and death for countless millions of people.

Mao's tyranny was also a tyranny of the mind. The man who earlier in his career railed against dogmatism ended up the ultra-dogmatist. Mao was an absolutist with an ideological fixation. As the exalted head of the infallible CCP, he arrogated the right to control ideas and correct "wrong thinking." Intellectuals were especially victimized. Purges and "May 7th Schools," which combined manual labor and brainwashing, awaited those who needed "re-education." Thought control involved complete control of all media of communication, censorship, and indoctrination in schools. The quest for ideological conformity was conducted with fever-pitch intensity during Mao's Cultural Revolution when all Chinese shrunk in fear of being targeted as enemies of the revolution. Rather than liberating the Chinese people, Mao terrorized and cowed them. In the end, only good Maoists were safe in Mao's China; if only one could be certain about just what constituted a good Maoist—this week.

SUGGESTIONS FOR ADDITIONAL READING

Ch'en, Jerome. *Mao and the Chinese Revolution.* London: Oxford University Press, 1965.

FitzGerald, C. P. *Mao Tse-tung and China.* London: Hodder and Stoughton, 1976.

Karnow, Stanley. *Mao and China: From Revolution to Revolution.* New York: Macmillan, 1973.

Mao Zedong. *Selected Works*. 4 vols. Beijing: Foreign Language Press, 1961–1965.
Meisner, Maurice. *Mao's China and After: A History of the People's Republic*. New York: Free Press, 1986.
Pye, Lucien. *Mao: The Man in the Leader*. New York: Basic Books, 1976.
Schram, Stuart. *Mao Tse-tung*. London: Penguin Books, 1966.
Wilson, Dick, ed. *Mao Tse-tung in the Scales of History*. London: Cambridge University, 1977.
Zhong Wenxian. *Mao Zedong: Biography, Assessment, Reminiscences*. Beijing: Foreign Language Press, 1986.
Uhalley, Stephen, Jr. *Mao Tse-tung: A Critical Biography*. New York: New Viewpoints, 1975.

Wayne C. McWilliams

Mary I
(Mary Tudor)
1516–1558

Queen of England, 1553–1558

Justifiably or not, Queen Mary has borne the unhappy sobriquet "Bloody Mary" ever since John Foxe published his *Book of the Martyrs* in 1563, only five years after her death. That work commemorates, in gruesome detail, the death of almost three hundred Protestants burned at the stake. Generations of Englishmen read that book, building an angry hatred of Roman Catholicism and of Spain as part of their recollection of Mary's reign. That Mary, left to her own devices, had the intention of being tolerant, gentle, and creative, is usually overlooked. Instead, the creative Mary is forgotten, in favor of Mary the Tyrant.

BIOGRAPHICAL BACKGROUND

The only child of Henry VIII and his Spanish queen, Catherine of Aragon, was born at Greenwich, England, on February 18, 1516. Although a male heir would have been preferred, the infant was welcome because since their marriage in 1509, the royal couple had been unable to produce a baby who survived. The queen, who conceived regularly, lost infant after infant. As it turned out, Catherine never delivered another child who survived. Thus, Mary was heiress presumptive until 1527.

In that year, Henry VIII, guided by Thomas, Cardinal Wolsey, Chancellor of England and Archbishop of York, adopted two fateful decisions. Henry asked Pope Clement VII to annul his marriage to Queen Catherine because she had been married to Henry's deceased brother Arthur. As Roman Catholic Canon Law prohibits a widow from marrying the brother of a deceased husband, such a marriage would be illicit.

Ordinarily, Pope Clement would have had no trouble in accepting Henry's allegation that he had known that Catherine's marriage to Arthur had been consummated, but that he had kept his guilty secret for eighteen years because of his love for Catherine. It was, however, transparently obvious that Henry's sudden crisis of conscience was motivated by his dynastic need for a male heir.

At almost the same moment, in April 1527, Wolsey had pushed England into an alliance with France against Habsburg Spain, Burgundy, and the Holy Roman Empire. The French alliance and the suit for annulment coincided with a military seizure of Rome by the armies of Emperor Charles V of Habsburg. The pro-French Pope Clement became a virtual prisoner under surveillance, and was thus unable to move easily to annul a marriage between King Henry and Queen Catherine, who was Emperor Charles' aunt.

While the adjudication of the annulment dragged on, from 1527 to 1533, Princess Mary was declared illegitimate, by her father, and shared her mother's humiliation and removal from court. The adolescent girl never saw her mother again. As Henry successively married five other women, Mary received varied treatment at their hands, experiencing the kindest reception from the third wife, Jane Seymour, and from Henry's sixth wife, Catherine Parr. Nevertheless, from the age of eleven until she ascended the throne at age thirty-seven, Mary lived in complete social isolation, surrounded by servants who were spies in the service of her enemies. Even those foreign diplomats, such as the ambassador of Emperor Charles V, to whom the princess looked for sympathy and kindness, had their own agenda to pursue, and blithely abandoned her if it would advance Habsburg interests at the English court.

It is scarcely surprising that Mary endured the difficult adjustments of her adolescence, constructing a dream world in which she could preserve her sanity. That world was one in which she was married to a Spanish prince, come from her beloved mother's homeland, who would work with her to restore Roman Catholicism in England.

On his deathbed, in 1547, Henry VIII signed a will, the validity of which is still in doubt. He recognized the legitimacy and rights of inheritance of all three of his children, born to different wives. Thus, although Henry's immediate heir was his only legitimate son, Edward VI, born to Jane Seymour, Mary was recognized as Edward's heiress presumptive if he died childless. Similarly, Elizabeth, Henry's daughter by Anne Boleyn, became third in line of succession if neither Edward nor Mary had children. If we may assume that the dying Henry was fully conscious of what he was doing, he was simply bringing into the line of succession all three of his children, even though both Mary and Elizabeth had been stained with the taint of bastardy at various points in their lives. For Henry and for most Englishmen, the existence of three Tudor heirs minimized the dangerous likelihood of civil war and a contested succession, at some future date.

Henry VIII had finally broken with Rome in 1533–1534 when he had obtained an annulment of his marriage to Catherine of Aragon from his compliant archbishop of Canterbury, Thomas Cranmer, rather than the pope. In 1534, Parliament had passed an Act of Supremacy recognizing the king as the Supreme Head of the Church of England. However, Henry was adamant in his insistence that he remained just as devoted a Catholic as he had been back in 1521, when he had condemned Martin Luther. There is not much doubt that if it had not been for the annulment question, Henry would have remained a stalwart Roman Catholic. He became, in fact, an Henrician Catholic. However much Thomas Cromwell, the successor to the disgraced Cardinal Wolsey, may have tried to push Henry toward true Protestantism, Henry retained the form and content of the church into which he had been baptized.

For Mary the hardest years of her life were passed during the reign of the boy-king, Edward VI, 1547–1553. She was subjected to intense personal surveillance and the complete deprivation of the services of a priest who could offer her valid Catholic sacraments. Henry VIII, though he had broken with the pope, had remained faithful to Catholic theology and the seven sacraments. Edward's reign witnessed a rapid movement from a Lutheran to a Calvinist type of Protestantism.

At the death of Edward VI on July 6, 1553, John Dudley, duke of Northumberland, heading the Privy Council, feared for his head if Catholic Mary inherited the throne. He declared both Mary and Elizabeth Tudor to be bastards, and named his daughter-in-law, Lady Jane Grey, queen. "Queen Jane" was a granddaughter of Henry VIII's younger sister, Mary.

Mary Tudor had no trouble, however, in ending the nine days' reign of "Queen Jane." She approached London riding arm in arm with her sister Elizabeth. Though the sisters had reason to distrust one another, they made common cause against the interloper. The country gentry came riding out to compose Mary's armed guard. They saw a peaceful enthronement for Mary as the best means of avoiding civil war.

In 1553, most English subjects still remembered the Catholic faith and sacraments affectionately. Only a small minority were irrevocably bound to the newly adopted Protestantism of Edward VI. All that really concerned most of the gentry was that they be confirmed in possession of estates confiscated from the church by Henry VIII and sold or given to laymen. Few had any special animus against the queen marrying a Spaniard. Most of the English prayed devoutly that Mary and her consort, Philip II of Spain, would produce offspring. Only thereby could the country be assured of peace. For Mary, her marriage to a man about to succeed to the throne of Spain was a fulfillment of all the daydreams she had spun during her long years of bitter isolation. Philip, six years younger than Mary, and her first cousin once removed, was the closest link to her long lost and beloved mother, and to that Spanish homeland that had grown dear to her, at her mother's knee.

As will be noted, later, Mary's reign might have been a success if she had indeed borne a child to Philip. It was not beyond the realm of possibility that she could have restored Roman Catholicism in England. The fact is, however, that her childlessness rendered hopeless the Catholic cause. Everything else, including the bloody events of a tyranny for which she was not responsible, represented the ruin of her hopes. Even her entry into a bootless war and England's loss of Calais to France must be subordinated to her failure to present England with an heir.

Mary died at St. James Palace in London on November 17, 1558, and was entombed at Westminster Abbey. From her deathbed, Mary had sent her personal jewelry to her heiress, Elizabeth. She enjoined her to "keep the faith." Neither Mary's leadership nor her tyranny could accomplish that result.

MARY TUDOR AS A GREAT LEADER

At her accession to the throne, Mary I showed herself moderate and conciliatory. No one objected to the immediate execution of John Dudley, Duke of Northumberland, who was undoubtedly guilty of treason in his attempt to subvert the succession, by placing Lady Jane Grey on the throne. At first, Mary seemed inclined to spare Jane Grey and her husband, the seventeen-year-old Guilford Dudley, who had been the innocent dupes of Northumberland's ambition. She was even prepared to the spare Thomas Cranmer, Archbishop of Canterbury, though he had been a willing tool of Henry VIII in annulling the marriage of Catherine of Aragon, in the break with Rome, and finally in supporting the adoption of Protestantism during the reign of Edward VI.

Mary gave the most solemn guarantees that she would not persecute Protestants who served her loyally. She assured the gentry and burgesses that she would urge the pope to accept England's submission to the papacy without demanding the return of church property seized by Henry VIII.

In finances, Mary returned to the conservative policy of her grandfather, Henry VII, balancing her earliest budgets and producing a sound currency. Even her insistence on marrying Philip of Habsburg created no serious objection, though there was some sentiment in favor of a native English consort.

In fact, all of these conciliatory good intentions were frustrated by forces she proved unable to control.

MARY TUDOR THE TYRANT

In February 1554, Mary was married by proxy to Philip II of Spain, and again, in person, in July. At the instance of the first marriage ceremony, a revolt led by Sir Thomas Wyatt broke out, but was easily crushed by the loyal army and the support of London's burgesses. Wyatt's support was partially Protestant, but was also composed of peasants who resented having been displaced by great landlords recently come into possession of former church estates. They had enclosed their property with hedges and turned from the traditional farm production involving many peasant families to sheep raising, involving a small number of hired shepherds. As the historian Max Weber remarked later, "It is not so much that the peasants were freed from the land as that the land was freed from the peasants."

Mary panicked after the Wyatt revolt because it seemed to have proved that her early tolerance did not pay. Her fear of Protestant resistance was exacerbated by the arrival in England of a papal legate, Reginald, Cardinal de la Pole, in 1555. Descended from the royal House of York, he was a native Englishman and the queen's cousin. He was destined to be the last Roman Catholic archbishop of Canterbury, after the execution of Thomas Cranmer.

It seems to have been the legate, more than anyone else, who convinced Mary that only the extirpation of Protestantism could ensure England's Roman Catholic future. The queen seems to have abandoned her original intention of being tolerant, in the grip of a paranoia principally fueled by the papal legate. In the next three years, 270 accused heretics were burned at the stake or otherwise executed. Lady Jane Grey, Lord Guilford Dudley, and Archbishop Cranmer were among the victims. The queen's sister, Princess Elizabeth, was spared, after brief imprisonment, only because she was the last Tudor heiress and because she became an ostentatious Roman Catholic convert.

Oddly enough, popular legend has trended to blame Philip II of Spain for the martyrdom of so many people, when actually he urged more restraint upon his wife. Thus the "Black Legend" of Spain became a part of English folklore, especially after the publication of Foxe's *Book of the Martyrs*.

In 1555 and 1557, Mary convinced herself that she was pregnant with a devoutly anticipated Catholic Tudor heir. What she actually carried was probably an ovarian cancer, which eventually killed her.

King Philip, absent on the continent, had to be begged to return to England long enough to initiate the second illusory "pregnancy." The price that he demanded was English entry into Spain's war against France. The queen, in her desperation, used strong measures to get Parliament to vote a war budget. The final result was the ruin of the queen's conservative, sound currency policy. Her reign ended with a growing indebtedness. Even more humiliatingly, England lost its last continental foothold to France. Mary remarked, "When I die, you will find engraved upon my heart the word Calais."

It was melodramatically just that on the day of the queen's death, Reginald, Cardinal de la Pole died as well. With him passed the last English leader who was as determined as Mary to preserve the old faith.

SUGGESTIONS FOR ADDITIONAL READING

Erickson, Carolly. *Bloody Mary*. New York: Doubleday, 1978.
Loach, Jennifer. *Parliament and the Crown in the Reign of Mary Tudor*. New York: Oxford University Press, 1986.
Loades, David M. *The Reign of Mary Tudor: Politics, Government and Religion in England, 1553–1558*. London: Longman, 1991.
Prescott, H.F.M. *A Spanish Tudor: The Life of "Bloody Mary."* New York: AMS, 1970.
Tittler, Robert. *The Reign of Mary I*. London: Longman, 1983.
Waldman, Milton. *The Lady Mary: A Biography of Mary Tudor, 1516–1558*. New York: Scribner's, 1972.
White, Beatrice. *Mary Tudor*. New York: Macmillan, 1935.

Arnold Blumberg

Ivan Stepanovych Mazepa

c. 1632–1709

Hetman of the Ukraine, 1687–1709

The Ukraine has experienced independence only three times in the last three hundred years. The first was in the seventeenth century. The second was for a short period after World War I. The third emerged when the present Ukrainian Republic was proclaimed upon the dissolution of the Soviet Union. However, even during the centuries when the Ukraine was utterly subjugated by Russia, its people continued to have a clear sense of national separateness. Indeed, Stalin insisted that the Ukraine be one of the three Soviet Republics granted seats in the United Nations, even though they were not truly sovereign entities. To understand the emergence of Ukrainian separatism, it would be helpful to consult the following essays in these pages, which will serve as companions to this discussion of Ivan Mazepa. They are the biographies of Catherine the Great, Bohdan Khmel'nyts'kyi, Nikita Khrushchev, V. I. Lenin, Peter the Great, Stenka Razin, and Joseph Stalin.

BIOGRAPHICAL BACKGROUND

Ivan Mazepa was born at his ancestral seat at Mazepyntsy, in the Bila Tserkva district of the Ukraine. The exact year of his birth is uncertain: one tradition dates his birth on March 20, 1632, but some sources suggest that he might have been born in 1639 or 1644. His father, Stepan Adam Mazepa, was a Ukrainian nobleman in the service of the Polish king who later joined Bohdan Khmel'nyts'kyi's war against Poland. His mother, Maryna Mokievsky, member of a prominent family, joined a convent after her husband's death in 1665 but remained a constant influence on her son, Ivan. Mazepa was first educated at the celebrated Kiev-Mohyla Academy, then at the Jesuit college in Warsaw. He became a page at the royal court and between 1656 and 1659 studied in Germany, Italy, and France at King Jan Kazemierz's expense. His studies and travels gave him facility with foreign languages and great familiarity with the issues and personalities of his time. After his return, the king sent him on various diplomatic missions.

In 1663, for unknown reasons, Mazepa's career at the Polish court came to an end and he returned to his family estate in the Ukraine. The reason for his return has been clouded by the famous "Mazepa Legend," traced to the memoirs of the Polish nobleman, Jan Pasek. In that account, Mazepa had an affair with the wife of a nobleman named Falbowski. The latter, once he uncovered the tryst, supposedly punished Mazepa by binding him naked to the back of a horse, which galloped wildly across the steppes until finally stopped by some Cossacks. Later artists imaginatively portrayed the scene. However, there is no evidence to support this tale, and Pasek himself has been dismissed by the historian A. Bruckner as an enemy of Mazepa and an "incredible liar." But the story, subsequently repeated in Voltaire's well-known life of Charles XII, became a standard motif for the Romantic imagination.

In 1669 Mazepa entered the service of the Ukrainian Hetman Petro Doroshenko, whose ambition was to reunite the Left and Right Bank (of the Dnipr River) Ukraine, divided by the Treaty of Andrusovo (1667) between Polish and Russian spheres of influence. Doroshenko, in charge of the Right Bank, recognized Mazepa's abilities and used him as a personal diplomatic envoy. During a mission to the Crimea, Mazepa was taken prisoner by the Zaporozhian Cossacks and dispatched to Ivan Samoilovych, the Hetman of the Left Bank. The latter also fell under Mezepa's spell and made him a chancellor. When Samoilovych was deposed from the office in the wake of an unsuccessful campaign against Crimean Tatars in 1687, Mazepa, with Russian backing, was elected Hetman.

For most of his twenty-one years of rule as Hetman of the Left Bank, Mazepa continued the traditional policies of his predecessors. He issued many land grants to the *starshyna* (Cossack elite), he cultivated the support of the young Muscovite tsar, Peter I, who ascended to the throne in 1689. He assisted Peter in the capture of Azov from the Ottoman Turks in 1697 and also proved a valuable adviser on Polish affairs. This personal association with Peter I proved profitable to Mazepa and allowed him to exploit the Cossack rebellion in the Polish-controlled Right Bank in 1702. Shortly thereafter, he was able to unite the two halves of the Ukraine under his rule.

But the outbreak of the Great Northern War (1700–1721), which pitted Sweden against Russia for the control of the Baltic region, began to put a severe strain on Mazepa's relationship with the Russian tsar. Peter I, in his efforts to "modernize" Russia, began to impose unbearable demands on the Ukraine. Cossack regiments were squandered either as cannon-fodder in the prolonged conflict or as common labor in the draining of marshes for the building of St. Petersburg. Precious resources were seized to support Russian units. Peasants and townspeople were abused by Russian officials, and the tsar seemed intent on abolishing cherished Cossack liberties. It was becoming obvious that the Ukraine, technically an autonomous state, was being systematically plundered and integrated into the tsarist national, administrative, and juridical system. At the same time, it was becoming clear that the Ukraine was marginal to Russia's broader interests. Thus, when the Polish king Stanislas Leszczynski threatened to invade the Ukraine, Mazepa appealed to Peter for help. The latter, preoccupied with other matters, responded, "I cannot even spare ten men: defend yourself as best you can."

This proved the last straw for Mazepa. He entered into secret negotiations with the Swedish king, Charles XII. In 1708, when Charles XII moved into the Ukraine, Mazepa openly went over to the Swedes, hoping to prevent devastation of the Ukrainian countryside. According to the terms, Mazepa was to provide the Swedes with military and material support, while Charles XII vowed not to sign a peace with Peter I until the Ukraine was recognized as completely free from Russia.

Peter, completely surprised by Mazepa's "treason," unleashed the armies of Prince Menshikov upon Mazepa's capital, Baturyn. The city was captured and the entire population (some 6,000 people) was massacred. A reign of terror ensued in other parts of the Ukraine as well. The tsar ordered the election of a new Hetman and, on November 11, 1708, Ivan Skoropadsky was dully elected on Peter's command. Sentiment in the Ukraine was divided, but the Zaporozhian Cossacks openly supported Mazepa.

Throughout the fall and winter of 1708–1709 the gathering armies moved about seeking strategic advantages. Finally, on June 28, 1709, at Poltava, the battle took place. After a close struggle, Peter I prevailed over the combined Swedish-Ukrainian forces. The battle proved momentous: it ended Sweden's domination of northern Europe, allowing for the emergence of the new Russian Empire. For the Ukraine, the Battle of Poltava marked the effective end of a search for independence. For the aging Mazepa, it was a bitter personal defeat and the total collapse of his policies. Pursued by the Russian cavalry, he retreated with Charles XII into Ottoman-dominated Moldavia and died, broken-hearted, at Bender on September 21, 1709.

MAZEPA AS A GREAT LEADER

Mazepa stands as one of the most fascinating personages in Ukrainian history, an elusive and controversial figure who still arouses passion. Ukrainians regard him as a tragic hero who boldly sought to free the Ukraine from oppressive rule. He is perceived as a far-sighted statesman, the principal architect of a broad coalition meant to curb the expansion of Russian power into Europe and thus prevent the establishment of the Russian Empire. The precise details of Mazepa's complex diplomacy remain obscure, but evidence suggests that, at least since 1702, he was deeply embroiled in a scheme involving practically all European powers and the Ottoman Porte. A man of exceptional intelligence and courage, he shrewdly cultivated the trust of the Russian tsar while secretly working to undermine the Treaty of Pereyaslav of 1654, which had placed the Ukraine under the "protection" of Russia. Inasmuch as the terms of that treaty had been repeatedly violated by tsarist authorities, Mazepa had no qualms in breaking with the tsar. Moreover, by opting to disassociate himself from the tsar, Mazepa was asserting his traditional prerogatives as Hetman, set forth by the founder of the Hetmanate, Bohdan Khmel'nyts'kyi, decades before, to choose freely his allies and to promote the interests of his nation. It is the measure of his greatness that he deliberately chose to face the certain tsarist retribution when he could have continued to enjoy a life of privilege and prestige.

Only the vagaries of fortune, brought about by the surprising military blunders of the Swedish King Charles XII, rendered his policies a failure. Although Poltava was both a personal defeat and a national catastrophe, it was not inevitable: with a little luck, Mazepa could have altered the course of history for the Ukraine, Russia, and Eastern Europe.

Mazepa's twenty-two years of rule coincided with the most spectacular cultural outburst of the age, generally known as the "Mazepist" or "Cossack Baroque." This was no mere coincidence, because Mazepa consciously patronized the arts. Seeing himself as the leader of an old and civilized nation, he lavished his vast fortune on the promotion of material and spiritual culture. His largesse was manifest in all areas—education, art, architecture, and the material arts. He endowed the Kiev-Mohyla Academy, the first institution of higher learning in Ukraine, with generous funds and a new academic corpus (which still survives). Indeed, during his Hetmanate the Kiev Academy enrolled over two thousand students—an unprecedented number of participants for that age. He endowed other schools (such as the Chernihiv Collegium) and printing presses, so that "Ukrainian youth may pursue any field of learning." The enhanced cultural and intellectual milieu proved conducive to the publication of both religious and secular literature. It was during his time that the first "Cossack Chronicles" (*litopysy*), including Samuil Velychko's *Litopys Samovydtdsia* ("Eyewitness Chronicle") and Hrabianka's *Skazanie o voine Kozats'koi* ("Account of the Cossack Wars") were produced. They are still extremely valuable historical sources. Moreover, during his tenure a glittering assemblage of Ukrainian scholars, writers, teachers, churchmen, administrators, and craftsmen went to Russia and gave the first impetus to Peter I's westernization of Russian society.

As a defender of the Orthodox faith, Mazepa also endowed monasteries and built numerous churches. Perhaps his most significant project was the restoration of the renowned St. Sophia Cathedral in Kiev. Built by Prince Yaroslav the Wise in 1017, it had fallen into ruins. Under Mazepa's initiative this Byzantine-style basilica was rebuilt in a purely Ukrainian baroque style, with nine cupolas and striking decorations. He also built a series of exquisite churches throughout the Ukraine, most of which (such as the St. Nicholas Cathedral in Kiev) were demolished by the Soviet government during the "anti-religion" campaigns of the 1930s and 1940s.

Finally, Mazepa's personal attributes and peculiarities of character made him both an outstanding representative of the Baroque mentality and a quintessential Romantic hero. The Baroque, foreshadowing the later Romantic *Sturm und Drang* ("storm and stress"), called for the supremacy of feeling over reason, a passionate commitment to life and struggle, grandiose gesture, extravagance of style, and pathos. Certainly his "betrayal" of Peter I, the uneven struggle, and the crushing failure of Poltava must be seen in this light. Moreover, his celebrated affair with Motria Kochubei, the daughter of an important Cossack colonel from Poltava, also deepens the enigma. In the best Romantic tradition, it shocked convention: Motria was forty years his junior. An "autumnal" love affair, it proved an extraordinary complication for an older man deeply involved in more pressing matters. It ended unhappily, but Mazepa's tender love letters to his beloved Motria denote a man driven by delicate yet passionate feelings.

The Romantics found the Mazepa legend irresistible. It loomed prominently in Victor Hugo's *Les Orientales*, Alexander Pushkin's *Poltava*, J. Slowacki's drama *Mazeppa*, Lizst's symphonic poem *Mazeppa*, and so on. But it was with Lord Byron that the legend reached its highest expression. Byron's *Mazeppa* still spun its romantic web about an indiscreet youthful lover punished by a vengeful husband. However, Byron also depicted an older hero, who is "venerable," "calm and bold," comparable to Alexander the Great, whom "thousands of Cossacks would follow everywhere."

Today, in the post-Soviet Ukraine, after centuries of official vilification, Mazepa once again has become a powerful symbol of national defiance and rebirth. The Ukrainian Orthodox Church has formally revoked the anathema imposed upon Mazepa, on Peter I's command, by the Russian Orthodox Church. Young men in Kiev and elsewhere often affect Cossack dress and invoke his legacy as exemplary. There are even proposals to return his bodily remains to the Ukraine. He is regarded as one of the Ukraine's most outstanding national icons.

MAZEPA THE TYRANT

As befits all major historical figures, Mazepa's legacy also includes less commendable aspects. Clearly, Mazepa was guilty of a major miscalculation insofar as his conflict with Peter was concerned. Not only did he miscalculate the depth of anti-Russian sentiment in the Ukraine, but he also failed to inform all potential supporters of his anti-Russian policy. He was completely surprised by Charles XII's invasion of the Ukraine, apparently expecting the battle to take place on Russian soil. Hence, no adequate preparations were made and, at the crucial encounter at Poltava, the Swedish-Ukrainian forces faced the Russians without adequate artillery. While excelling in strategy, Mazepa proved an inept tactician.

Personally, he was driven not only by lofty ideals, but also by the trappings of power and wealth. During his tenure as Hetman, he accumulated great private wealth. He managed to acquire nearly 20,000 estates, which qualified him as one of the wealthiest men in Europe. He also endowed his political supporters with generous land grants, peasants, and privileges. As an aristocrat, he reflected the pre-Enlightenment class exclusivity and privilege. His internal policies tended to favor the much hated Cossack *starshyna*, who, in the wake of the Polish domination of Ukraine, simply replaced the old hated Polish lords. Insofar as the Ukrainian *pospolyt* (commoners) were concerned, Mazepa and his associates proved the immediate enemy. His popularity among common people was consistently low, and Mazepa was also perceived as an instrument of Russian exploitation. Indeed, in 1692 a Cossack, Petro Petryk, led an uprising against the Hetman, intent to free the Ukraine from the "blood-sucking *starshyna*" and to "tear away our fatherland Ukraine from Muscovite rule." The rebellion failed, but the bitterness continued. In the end, the Ukrainian masses remained aloof from the confrontation with the Russian colossus in 1709. In retrospect, this proved a mistake (Empress Catherine II subsequently enserfed the Ukrainian peasants), but at the time the despised Muscovites proved preferable to the oppressive *starshyna*.

Although Ukrainians like to see Mazepa as an unblemished hero and defender of Ukrainian historical rights, it must be noted that he was also prone to personal vanity, aggrandizement, and deception. His talent to win over powerful patrons was legendary. He cleverly mesmerized the young Russian tsar while conspiring against him. It was said that "the tsar would sooner disbelieve an angel than Mazepa." Thus, when colonels Iskra and Kochubei informed the tsar that Mazepa had betrayed the tsar for Charles XII of Sweden, Peter did not believe them. They were tortured and executed while Mazepa remained silent. Hence it is only natural that the tsar, once faced with the facts, took out his full fury not only on Mazepa but also on innocent bystanders. The entire population of Mazepa's capital, Baturyn, was put to death. The Russian also imposed a heavy burden of obligations on the Ukrainians, forcing them to pay dearly for policies not of their making. Peter, not content with Mazepa's total defeat, had him excommunicated by the Russian church. Thus, once a year his name was accursed by priests everywhere. Since that time, Mazepa's name became synonymous with "treachery."

SUGGESTIONS FOR ADDITIONAL READING

Babinsky, Hubert F. *The Mazeppa Legend in European Romanticism.* New York and London: Columbia University Press, 1974.

Ivan Mazepa, Hetman of Ukraine. New York: The Ukrainian Congress Committee of America, 1960.

Mackiw, Theodore. *English Reports on Mazepa.* New York, Munich, and Toronto: Ukrainian Historical Association, 1983.

Manning, Clarence A. *Hetman of Ukraine Ivan Mazepa.* New York: Bookman Associates, 1957.

Subtelny, Orest. *The Mazepists. Ukrainian Separatism in the Early Eighteenth Century.* New York: Columbia University Press, 1981.

Subtelny, Orest. *Ukraine. A History.* Toronto, Buffalo, and London: University of Toronto Press, 1988.

Alexander Sydorenko

Cosimo de' Medici

1389–1464

Head of the Council of the Republic of Florence, 1434–1464

Cosimo de' Medici is the first of that long line of his family, who gradually transformed Florence from a republic into a hereditary duchy, and whose descendants included two queens of France and several popes. He is usually styled *Il Vecchio* (the Elder) to distinguish him from a descendant of the same name. More grandiloquently, he is called *Pater Patriae* (Father of the Fatherland), which ties him to the Roman Statesman Cicero, who bore that title. Cosimo was the quintessential Renaissance man, a Christian who was also a profit-oriented banker, a power-oriented politician, and a man interested in all aspects of the arts and culture. He believed that "God had shed His grace on him."

BIOGRAPHICAL BACKGROUND

Cosimo was born September 27, 1389, to the family of Giovanni de' Bicci de' Medici in the Mugello, a valley near Florence. He was named after Cosmas and Damian, two Christian martyrs. A legend traces the origins of the fame of the de' Medici family and the emblem of their coat-of-arms back to the times of Charlemagne's campaign into Italy and Rome. One of Charlemagne's knights, and supposed ancestor of the de' Medicis, killed a giant who had terrorized people in the Mugello. In this struggle the shield was dented, and the dents are indicated by the balls in the Medici coat of arms. There are other explanations of the family emblem. Cosimo's father, Giovanni, laid the basis of the Medici fortune. His membership in two prestigious guilds, the Arte della Lana and the Arte del Cambio, reflected his economic, social, and political standing. Giovanni also recognized that a successful businessman had to take a share in the government. Thus Cosimo grew up in a prosperous and influential environment. He received his early education in a monastic school. He studied especially languages, German, French, Latin, some Greek, Hebrew, and Arabic. As a young adult he attended lectures presented by the humanist Roberto de' Rossi, whose life was devoted to literature, intellectual friendships, and the youth. Material aspects of life meant little to him. Through Roberto de' Rossi and discussion groups of the convent of Santa Maria degli Angeli, Cosimo was attracted to and had become involved in the humanist movement, which cultivated the knowledge and wisdom of the ancients, especially the Greeks and Romans. In his early twenties Cosimo married Contessina de' Bardi, whose father was an associate of Giovanni de' Bicci's banking enterprise. In the early years of their marriage the couple made the Florentine Bardi residence their home. Here their child Pietro was born. In the meantime Cosimo continued to prepare himself to become the master of the Medici enterprise. He traveled to France and the Holy Roman Empire. In 1415 he witnessed the Council of Constance, at which John XXIII, the would-be pope, suffered condemnation and defeat, but retained the friendship of the Medicis. For three years Cosimo served as bank manager of the Rome branch. Here a slave girl, Maddalena, became his mistress. The relationship resulted in the birth of a son. Giovanni de' Bicci's death in 1429 thrust Cosimo into a crisis. Florence was involved in a struggle with the Duchy of Milan which was pursuing a policy of aggrandizement, as was Florence. Florence failed to conquer Lucca. The then leading oligarchs of Florence, the Albizzi family, blamed Cosimo, their major competitor, for the defeat, resulting in Cosimo's short exile (1433–1434). Through bribery, popular acclaim, and ambivalence Cosimo was invited back to Florence, at which time he became and remained the unofficial head of Florence until his death in 1464. These thirty years were filled with political, economic, and cultural challenges, most of which Cosimo met successfully. Comparing the better-known Lorenzo il Magnifico to his grandfather Cosimo, Francesco Guicciardini, eminent Florentine historian of the late fourteenth century and early fifteenth century, writes, "I believe one can conclude that, all things considered, Cosimo was the more excellent man, and yet through ability and fortune both were so great that perhaps, from the decline of Rome to the present, Italy has never had private citizens like them."

COSIMO AS A GREAT LEADER

Cosimo de' Medici achieved greatness in several interreconnected areas. Greatness in one field created the condition for greatness in the other fields. The foundation for his many remarkable achievements is to be seen in his success as a businessman, as the corporate executive officer and major owner of the Medici enterprises, predominantly the Medici banks. Cosimo was fortunate to be the heir to a financial empire that had been created by his father Giovanni de' Bicci. This empire had its headquarters in Florence and branches in Venice, Naples, Gaeta, Geneva, Brussels, London, Pisa, and at times in Constance, Augsburg, and Lübeck. The most profitable branch was in Rome, where the bank carried out many business activities for the papacy. The actual wealth of the Medici remained a secret. On some of their properties income taxes were paid to Florence; other incomes remained hidden and unreported. Cosimo personally remained in control of the Medici enterprises by never holding less than 51 percent of its shares and also by requiring bank managers located north of the Alps to report to headquarters every second year and those south of the Alps every year. A thorough accounting had to be made of business transactions. Florence shared in the profits of the branches, but often evaded responsibility for bankruptcies. Thus the enterprise prospered, becoming the leading bank in Europe. Being a Christian of the Renaissance rather than the medieval spirit, Lorenzo interpreted his success as a sign of God's grace. Business ledgers carried the heading "in the name of God and profits."

Cosimo's financial success as well as the family's reputation of being on the side of the *populo minuti*, the ordinary people, in contrast to the *populo grossi*, the elite, as well as his personality traits qualified him for political leadership in Florence. Cosimo had the ability to rule successfully, appearing at the same time as not ruling. He gave the impression that others took the initiative whereas in reality he himself exercised the guiding hand. While Florence called itself a republic and had the semblance of such a system, in reality it was directed by Cosimo after he had skillfully overcome the opposition of the Albizzi. Cosimo ran the republic by persuading the *priori* of the *signoria*, Florence's government, by paying favors, or by entertaining its citizens. He adjusted the system in such a fashion that only those served as *priori* found his approval. Special councils were created with extraordinary powers.

Having financial and political strength made it possible for Cosimo to play an active role in diplomacy and to give birth to the modern system of diplomacy. One of Europe's concerns was the growing menace of the advancing Islamic Ottoman Turks. In order to stop their advance by settling the differences between the Roman Catholic and Eastern Greek Orthodox churches, a conference was called for the year 1438 to meet in Ferrara. When a plague broke out there, the meetings continued in Florence, thus adding to the prestige of that city and of Cosimo, who played an active role in attracting the conference to Florence. An additional benefit was the boost that scholars from the Byzantine Empire gave to the growing humanist movement. The conference did result in an agreement between the Roman Catholic and the Eastern Orthodox churches, but did not produce an effective military alliance.

Cosimo's greatest personal success was the diplomatic revolution of the early 1450s. Traditionally the republics of Venice and Florence were allies, as were Milan and Naples, with the papacy shifting its relationships. The *condottiere* (soldier of fortune) Francesco Sforza aspired to overthrow the Visconti of the Duchy of Milan. At the same time Venice was expanding its territory. Cosimo decided to support Francesco Sforza and thus provoked the enmity of Venice, which allied itself with Naples. Sforza's success made the alliance with Florence a significant political-military force, prompting Venice, Naples, and eventually the papacy and the smaller Italian states to conclude the peace of Lodi and later the Holy Alliance, which ultimately created peace in the troubled and strife-torn Apennine peninsula for some forty years. A significant byproduct of changing alliances and the strife among the Italian city-states was the emergence of formal diplomatic relations between the allied states. To coordinate one's political and military steps it was necessary to have resident ambassadors at the seat of government of one's ally. These resident ambassadors enjoyed the confidence of their leader at home and the chief of state abroad. Hence the beginning of the modern diplomatic corps.

Cosimo's economic, political, and diplomatic achievements were one of many reasons for the cultural flowering of Florence. Florence's leader became the great patron of humanism and the creative arts. "To lead means to be human," stated Duke Federico da Montefeltre of Urbino. Leonardo Bruni, a prominent humanist, shaped the concept of the ideal citizen who was to connect the contemplative with the active life. The humanities were worth studying for their own intrinsic value, but they also prepared one for the involved, publicly purposeful life. Cosimo was the embodiment of this ideal. Supporting scholarship and the arts was a natural part of his life. As a trustee of the Studio Fiorentino—the University of Florence—he helped to establish the faculties of moral philosophy, rhetoric, and poetry. To promote classical Greek studies, especially Plato, he founded the Platonic Academy. The academy was to reconcile Platonism and Christianity. To enable scholars to study the Ancients, Cosimo spent large amounts of his earnings in the search for and purchase of ancient Greek and Roman manuscripts, which were then brought to the Medicean Library. Today some ten thousand manuscripts are available to scholars of the world.

With artists such as the sculptor Donatello or the painter Fra Filippo Lippi, Cosimo had a special relationship. He thought that they were entitled to special treatment. Even though Fra Filippo Lippi was in violation of accepted standards of behavior, Cosimo not only forgave his trangressions but continued to shelter and feed and promote him. Donatello was initially given a cash gift for his secure retirement. When this did not please the sculptor, he received from his benefactor a pension for himself and four servants for the rest of his life. Similarly Cosimo sponsored gifted architects such as Michelozzo, the designer of his Florentine palazzo, and Brunelleschi, creator of the architectural plans of the churches of Santo Spirito and San Lorenzo and especially the "crown of Florence," the dome of the Cathedral Santa Maria Del Fiore. Thus through the sponsorship of scholarship and of the arts, Cosimo created a lasting memorial to these famous artists of the fifteenth century, to the glory of Florence and himself.

Cosimo also was thoroughly human. When he conducted a meeting with representatives of the city of Lucca, his grandson appeared asking his grandfather to carve a whistle for him, whereupon Cosimo adjourned the conference until his grandson's wish was fulfilled. When he was growing old, his wife asked him why he talked less and less; he responded that since he was conscious of the fact that he was to leave this earth soon, there was much to think about before he entered the other part of the world. Increasingly he kept his eyes closed to prepare himself for the darkness that awaited him after death.

COSIMO THE TYRANT

While his contributions to the Renaissance and to Western civilization are extraordinary, from a political and economic point of view he was a tyrant, albeit of a special kind. At no time in his life did he openly appear as a tyrant. At the same time, there is no question that Cosimo controlled the affairs of the Florentine Republic for some thirty years, from 1434 to 1464, after he succeeded, through patience, bribery, and a sense of good timing, in defeating the rival family, the Albizzi.

Indeed Cosimo has been compared to American mafia bosses during the 1920s. Once he made up his mind that certain actions needed to be taken to achieve his goals, he left Christian and humanistic morality behind. Anyone he considered the right kind of person—whoever served his goals—would be supported, by devious means if necessary. Even the corrupt, immoral Baldassare Cossa, who had been an anti-pope (John XXIII) until the Council of Constance (1415), was rewarded by Cosimo by having such noted sculptors as Donatello and Michelozzo create an effigy of him, which was placed on top of his tomb in one of Florence's sacred shrines, the Baptistry of San Giovanni, where he rests today. Cosimo's father, Giovanni de' Bicci, had considered the pope-to-be valuable for financial reasons. Cosimo honored the loyal partnership of his father, who had succeeded in having Baldassare Cossa chosen as cardinal bishop of Tusculum. Cossa died in Cosimo's home. Francesco Sforza was an aspiring, power-greedy opportunist *condottiere* intent on gaining control of Milan. Cosimo considered it in the interest of himself and Florence to support Francesco, and so it was done. When it served Cosimo's interests he manipulated the Florentine constitution without regard to established procedures. At one time Cosimo said, "You cannot rule a state through paternosters." Tax evasion was a normal procedure that enhanced the Medicis' fortune, their political power, and their ability to promote scholarship, the arts, and people of their choice.

Perhaps the best way to describe Cosimo de' Medici is to call him an enlightened tyrant who used his considerable talents for the strengthening of Florence and for making it the cultural center of fifteenth-century Italy and of Europe—as Pericles had made Athens the envy of many during the fifth century B.C. Cosimo was a great leader and a successful tyrant.

SUGGESTIONS FOR ADDITIONAL READING

Baron, Hans. *The Crisis of the Early Italian Renaissance.* Princeton, NJ: Princeton University Press, 1966.

Burckhardt, Jacob. *The Civilization of the Renaissance in Italy.* London: The Penguin Group, 1990.

De Roover, Raymond. *The Rise and Decline of the Medici Bank: 1397–1494.* New York: W. W. Norton, 1966.

Goldthwaite, Richard A. *The Building of Renaissance Florence: An Economic and Social History.* Baltimore and London: The Johns Hopkins University Press, 1980.

Guicciardini, Francesco. *The History of Italy.* New York, Collier Books, 1969.

Gutkind, Curt S. *Cosimo De' Medici: Pater Patriae, 1389–1464.* Oxford, Clarendon Press, 1938.

Hibbert, Christopher. *The House of the Medici: Its Rise and Fall.* New York, Morrow Quill Paperbacks, 1980.

Mattingly, Garrett. *Renaissance Diplomacy.* Baltimore: Penguin Books, 1964.

Young, G. F. *The Medici.* New York: Charles Boni, 1930.

Armin Mruck

Clemens von Metternich

1773–1859

Chancellor of Austria, 1809–1848

Fundamentally, Prince Metternich was an eighteenth-century rationalist who regarded the new Romantic notions of nationalism and liberalism as sheer nonsense. He thought it absurd that statesmen should define their loyalties by the language spoken by their people. He considered it equally absurd that illiterate common folk should have any voice in their government.

He therefore pretended to believe that the international community should adopt as its motto "legitimacy and restoration." In actual fact, however, he was not a devoted dynastic loyalist. When it suited him, he was perfectly prepared to dethrone dynasties just as old and "legitimate" as the House of Habsburg.

What was central to him was the preservation of Austria as a great power, strong enough to check the rivalries of France, Russia, and Prussia. Polyglot Austria, with a population speaking eight major languages, could only be preserved if nationalism was rigorously suppressed. The state that ensured the unity of the Danube Valley and the commercial prosperity of all Central Europe, had to define its loyalty by allegiance to the head of the House of Habsburg. The competence of the emperor was of no great significance provided that Metternich could manipulate him.

It is popular, today, to sneer at Metternich as a total reactionary out of touch with his times. It would be appropriate, however, to note that the Europe that Matternich designed in 1815 still possessed a viable balance of power in 1914, at the outbreak of World War I. The splintering of Central Europe, and the creation of so many nonviable states since the war, may give us renewed respect for the pragmatic cynic whose name is forever associated with the years 1815–1848.

BIOGRAPHICAL BACKGROUND

Clemens Wenzel Nepomuk Lothar von Metternich was born at Koblenz on May 15, 1773, the son of Count Franz Georg von Metternich-

Winneburg and Countess Maria Beatrix Aloisia von Kagenegg. He spent his youth at the courts of the archbishop-electors of Mainz, Trier, and Cologne, where his father served as Austrian envoy. Even though he was briefly interested in studying natural science and medicine, he devoted the years 1788–1790 to the study of political science, law, and history at the University of Strasbourg. The violence of the early French Revolution there made him return home.

In 1795 he married Countess Eleonore von Kaunitz, granddaughter of chancellor Prince Kaunitz. His bride brought him great wealth and access to the highest levels of Viennese society. His father's service in the Austrian diplomatic corps and his connections after his marriage brought him appointments as Austrian envoy to Saxony in 1801, to Prussia in 1803, and to France in 1806.

At first he regarded Napoleon as invincible, but as he became aware of the emperor's vulnerability after the French defeats in Spain, Metternich urged the Austrian government to renew its war against France in 1809. Instead, a marriage between Napoleon and Archduchess Marie Louise, daughter of Emperor Franz of Austria, made allies of old enemies. Metternich remained France's ally through the disastrous war of 1812. Reluctantly he changed sides in time for the Battle of Leipzig in October 1813, but it was only Napoleon's continued intransigence that compelled Metternich to agree to the Treaty of Chaumont in March 1814. From September 1814 to June 1815 he presided over the Congress of Vienna.

Further congresses in 1818 at Aachen, in 1820 at Troppau, in 1821 at Laibach, and in 1822 at Verona were held at his behest to deal with rebellion and revolution in Europe. In the German Confederation student unrest lead him to issue the repressive Karlsbad Decrees in 1819. Although Metternich succeeded in putting down feeble revolutions in the German and Italian states in 1830, Emperor Ferdinand refused to give him a free hand in the 1848 revolution. Metternich fled to England and did not return to Vienna until 1851. He died in 1859 without becoming involved in politics again. His mortal remains were put to rest in a mausoleum at his estate in Plass, Bohemia.

METTERNICH AS A GREAT LEADER

Having witnessed the violence of the French Revolution, Metternich in 1794 penned a pamphlet with the title *On the Necessity of a General Arming of the People on the Borders of France, by a Friend of Universal Calm.* It criticized the diplomats of the old school for having "shallow minds" and urged the arming and general rising of the people as the only effective way to combat the French revolutionary armies. Strange sentiments indeed for a man who in later life would be the last great diplomat of the old school, with a dim view of all expressions of popular sovereignty. In Viennese society he became known for his charm and impeccable manner; in Paris he acquired the reputation of a licentious ladies' man.

In his dealings with Napoleon he was wrong several times, but each time managed to produce an advantage for Austria. Though he at first viewed Napoleon as invincible, the events in Spain convinced him of the French tyrant's vulnerability and he urged Austria to join the fray against him. After Napoleon's victory over Austria in 1809, he helped arrange the marriage between Napoleon and Emperor Franz's daughter Marie-Louise, thereby protecting Austria against becoming a French satellite and allowing Austria limited diplomatic freedom. Metternich realized that Austria's financial and military exhaustion left no other course of action. As he explained to Emperor Franz, "we have to be satisfied with maneuvers, evasions, and flattery. Only in this fashion can we survive until the day of reckoning. We have only one option: to save our strength for better days and—regardless of our previous policy—to work on preparing ourselves." Implied in these words was an abiding distrust of Napoleon.

Metternich was equally distrustful of Russian policy, which seemed bent on expansion at Austria's expense in southeastern Europe. Moreover, he was certain that France and Russia would collide and, once more convinced of Napoleon's superiority, decided to back the French.

He was surprised by the war's outcome, but realized that Napoleon's defeat offered fresh opportunities for Austria. The destruction or at least the limitation of Napoleon's power would permit the restoration of Austria's role in Europe. At the same time, though, Metternich was aware that Russia's victory might project its power to Central Europe, where it would interfere with Austria's ambitions. As he wrote to the Prussian chancellor, Prince Karl August von Hardenberg, "a tremendous increase in the power of Russia would be the inescapable consequence of the destruction of the French empire." Thus Metternich was interested in maintaining France as a viable partner on the chessboard of diplomacy and he was perfectly willing to leave Napoleon in charge of France if he could be controlled. Napoleon's actions indicated otherwise, and Metternich no longer opposed his exile to Elba. More fundamentally, the principle of concerted action by the Great Powers in the affairs of Europe as laid down in the Treaty of Chaumont was an affirmation of one of Metternich's basic aims.

Metternich's other major concern at this time was Prussia's growing power. He feared Prussia's emergence as a leading rival in Germany. He solved that problem by offering sovereign status to Bavaria and the other states of the Confederation of the Rhine, encouraging them to pursue their independent aims. Thus they became deaf to the blandishments of a united Germany, and Austria could continue to exert its traditional influence in German affairs.

The Congress of Vienna, from September 1814 to June 1815, was the peak of Metternich's diplomatic career. The states of Europe, great and small, came together to shape a new world order after Napoleon's fall. But instead of pursuing lofty-minded objectives, they quickly reverted to their old ways. Russia wanted all of Poland and Prussia wanted all of Saxony. Metternich triumphed when joined by Prince Charles Maurice Talleyrand of France and Robert Stewart Castlereagh of Britain in opposing Russia's intrusion into Central Europe and Prussia's enlargement. A compromise was reached, with Russia receiving a smaller Polish territory and Prussia obtaining two-fifths of Saxony. Germany was organized as a confederation, dominated by Austria. In Italy, Austria gained Lombardy and Venetia as part of its empire and dominated the rest of the Italian Peninsula through treaties with the Italian princes and the pope, guaranteeing Austria the right of military intervention if revolution threatened the Ancien Régime. The treaties of Vienna were Metternich's greatest achievements. His emperor rewarded him richly with titles, medals, and estates. Among them was Johannisberg on the banks of the Rhine River. Growing excellent wines, the estate is in the possession of the Metternich family to this day, just as to this day it tithes to the Habsburg family as called for in the original feudal contract.

Justifiably Metternich viewed the results of the Congress of Vienna as his own handiwork whose orderly continuation became the chief preoccupation of his diplomacy. Indeed, the statesmen of Europe, led by Metternich, created a stable European order that preserved peace for the next forty years and prevented war involving all of the Great Powers for the next hundred years, an accomplishment unmatched since then.

METTERNICH THE TYRANT

A conservative at the Congress of Vienna, one who preserved the old order because he was convinced that it was the best arrangement for his state, Metternich subsequently showed himself strangely devoid of new ideas. He considered the governance of Germany by a confederation not only as the best but also as the only form of government and thought that "not even nominally should anything ever be changed." There is no reason at all to disbelieve his statement that his life-long aversion to liberalism was generated by the actions of the revolutionary mob in Strasbourg. His visits to Italy in 1815–1817 made him aware of popular discontent and of an economy and a political system in need of reform, but fear of revolution from below paralyzed his reforms from above. The sensible decisions of the 1818 Congress of Aachen, which restored France's sovereignty, were made at Castlereagh's behest against Metternich's opposition.

Similar convictions motivated his policies toward the German Confederation. He was convinced that any changes initiated by liberals or nationalists would harm Austria, whose polyglot multinational composition could survive only through the suppression of liberalism and nationalism. This attitude grew most pronounced in the 1819 Karlsbad Decrees. The liberal and national aspirations of many German students, but especially the assassination of the playwright August von Kotzebue, sent shivers of fear through Metternich. He persuaded the German governments to place their universities under surveillance and to censor the press. Austria and the German Confederation, whose princes he dominated, came to be known for Metternich's repressive police system.

Even though to our modern minds Metternich failed to face the two most important movements of the nineteenth century, liberalism and nationalism, his self-confidence was at its zenith. "Why, among so many millions of people, am I the one who is expected to think where others fail to think, expected to act where others decline to act, write, where others cannot," he said. On another occasion he said, "Twenty times every day I tell myself: Dear God, how right am I and how wrong the others." He had little reason to be so satisfied. In 1822 he convened the Congress of Verona in order to consider the Greek and Spanish revolutions. Metternich was opposed to intervention by the Great Powers on behalf of the Greek revolutionaries—an action that he feared might be extrapolated to other revolutionaries in the Balkans—while George Canning opposed French intervention in Spain for fear that the intervention might be extended to the Spanish colonies in Latin America. Although Canning's attitude signaled the end of Metternich's congressional system, Metternich subsequently remained passive in international politics, erroneously convinced that everything was developing satisfactorily for Austria.

When the July Revolution of 1830 broke out in France and expanded to some German and other European states, Metternich urged intervention but acted only when direct Austrian interests in Italy were affected. Austrian troops restored order in Parma, Modena, and the Papal States. Yet as a result of these upheavals he succeeded in 1833 with his aim of restoring agreement among the three conservative powers, Austria, Prussia, and Russia, to intervene where the public peace was threatened. Once again the "Metternich System," the principle of balance of power, seemed to be secure.

Metternich's attempts to deal with the new ideas of liberalism and nationalism by suppressing them was caused in part by his Emperor Franz, who was even more reactionary than Metternich. But when his feeble-minded son, Ferdinand, succeeded Franz in 1835, the policies did not change, allowing the assumption that the emphasis on the status quo was in fact actually engineered by Metternich.

A policy of drift prevailed. The forces of nationalism and economic and political liberalism continued to spread and, in the face of repression and lack of timely reforms, culminated in the 1848 revolution. As before, Metternich's recommended course of action was to call out the police and the military in order to suppress the revolution, but this time he did not get his way. He resigned his position and then fled for his life to England.

Since his death, Metternich has been assessed from different points of view. Conservatives have praised him, liberals have detested him. Some historians have viewed him as a statesman who earned the right to have the first half of the nineteenth century called the "Age of Metternich." Others have seen him as a good diplomat who achieved his objectives through *technique*; but they deny that his policies had a valuable content.

There is no doubt that his views and policies were determined by his hostility to the French Revolution and its principles. His highest achievement was the Congress of Vienna, at which he pretended to believe in the principles of "legitimacy and restoration," when in fact he sought to protect Austria's interests by the creation of a balance of power. He thought that having such a system in place would serve to avoid repetitions of 1789. But instead of opposing the forces of nationalism and liberalism with ideas of his own, he merely tried to suppress them with censorship and police control. He failed to understand that no society is static, and that the ideas of nationalism and liberalism had become an inherent part of the political organism that he attempted to preserve.

SUGGESTIONS FOR ADDITIONAL READING

Cecil, Algernon. *Metternich, 1773–1859; A Study of His Period and Personality.* 3d ed. London: Eyre and Spottiswoode, 1947.

Herman, Arthur. *Metternich.* New York: Century Company, 1932.

Kissinger, Henry A. *A World Restored: Metternich, Castlereagh and the Problems of Peace 1812–1822.* Boston: Houghton Mifflin Company, 1957.

Klinckowström, Alfons von, ed. *Memoirs of Prince Metternich.* 5 vols. New York: C. Scribner's Sons, 1880–1882.

Kraehe, Enno E., ed. *The Metternich Controversy.* Huntington, NY: Robert E. Krieger Publishing Company, 1977.

Mann, Golo. Secretary of Europe. *The Life of Friedrich Gentz, Enemy of Napoleon.* New Haven, Conn.: Yale University Press, 1946.

Schwarz, Henry F., ed. *Metternich, the "Coachman of Europe"; Statesman or Evil Genius?* Boston: D. C. Heath, 1962.

Treitschke, Heinrich von. *History of Germany in the Nineteenth Century.* 7 vols. New York: McBride, Nast and Company, 1915–1917.

Peter W. Becker

Napoleon I (Napoleon Bonaparte)

1769–1821

First Consul, 1799–1804
Emperor of the French, 1804–1815

Napoleon Bonaparte was one of the most important figures in French history, and there is no dearth of literature on every aspect of the man and his times. The argument remains, however, as to whether Napoleon was a great leader or a great tyrant; the answer has very often depended on the political situation in which the historian is writing. Even before his death, Napoleon was constructing a myth concerning what he had accomplished. Many historians later accepted this myth and saw Napoleon as a great leader, the Heir of the Revolution. Other historians would see in Bonaparte only a great tyrant who destroyed everything that the French Revolution had established. Napoleon was certainly a product of his age and the Revolution, for his military career would not have progressed as far and as fast without it. No matter what their views on other aspects of the Napoleonic era, historians generally agree on the military genius of the "Little Corporal." Whether the Napoleonic myth was something Bonaparte wanted to generate for posterity through his conversations with Las Casas during his exile on St. Helena, or whether his early years of revolutionary and republican fervor later gave way to a power-hungry megalomania, Napoleon remains an enigmatic and controversial personality.

BIOGRAPHICAL BACKGROUND

The island of Corsica, transferred from Genoa to France in 1768, made Napoleone Buonaparte (as he spelled his name until about 1796) a French subject even though he was born of an Italian family of questionable nobility on August 15, 1769. The second son of a large family, Napoleon, who had four brothers and three sisters, was destined by tradition and personal inclination for a career in the military. In September 1785 he entered the royal French artillery, rising to junior lieutenant by June 1786.

During the Revolution, Napoleon rose through the ranks and was promoted to general in 1793 after his valuable service in the defense of Toulon. While working in Paris, he met and married Josephine de Beauharnais in March 1796. He was soon called away to lead the invasion of Italy, where his victory in ousting the Austrians in 1796–1797 made him immensely popular in France. Sent by the Directory to harass the British in Egypt, Napoleon was less successful. After his failure to capture Acre, Napoleon abandoned his army and returned to France in 1799. With the help of his brother, Lucien, president of the Council of Five Hundred, and the Abbé Sieyes, one of the Directors, Napoleon was able to overthrow the Directory in the coup d'état of Brumaire, establish the Consulate, and make himself First Consul. In August 1802, Napoleon decreed that he was extending his tenure as First Consul from ten years to life, and in May 1804 he abolished the Consulate, established the Empire, and proclaimed himself Emperor of the French.

As First Consul, Napoleon had inherited the war of the Second Coalition Against France. During his rule, France would be almost constantly at war. Suffering a second naval defeat by the British at Trafalgar in 1805, Napoleon concentrated on Continental military success. Through a series of great victories, Napoleon defeated the major powers and was able to redraw the map of Europe according to his own designs. He abolished the Holy Roman Empire, replacing it with the Confederation of the Rhine, he established the puppet state of the Duchy of Warsaw, and placed his sister and brothers on the thrones of Holland, Naples, Westphalia, and Spain. By the Berlin and Milan decrees of 1806 and 1807, he established the Continental System to control Europe's foreign trade. He later annexed the Low Countries, Dalmatia, and some Italian states directly to France. In 1810, Napoleon divorced Josephine and arranged an alliance with the Habsburgs, marrying the Archduchess Marie-Louise, who bore Napoleon's only heir, Napoleon Francis Joseph Charles.

Napoleon's power began to decay after his disastrous invasion of Russia in 1812. His retreat from Russia brought in its wake revived threats from Austria, Prussia, Britain, and other powers. Unable to repel their attacks, he was forced to retreat to France, where he abdicated in April 1814. The victorious powers exiled Napoleon to the island of Elba, off the coast of Italy, but he escaped and was able to rally France and the army behind him for the "Hundred Days" in 1815. Defeated at Waterloo on June 18, 1815, Napoleon was exiled once again to the island of St. Helena in the South Atlantic, where he died on May 5, 1821, supposedly of stomach cancer.

NAPOLEON I AS A GREAT LEADER

Napoleon liked to portray himself as the "Heir of the Revolution." The French Revolution, however, went through many phases and meant different things to different people. Throughout the Revolution and until today, the three major themes of the French Revolution of 1789 were Liberty, Equality, and Fraternity. One way to judge whether Napoleon was a great leader, the Heir of the Revolution, would be to determine how well he fostered the ideas of that Revolution.

Liberty, in the context of the Revolution, meant freedom from oppression and the whim of absolutist monarchs. Napoleon was the protector of this liberty. The Directory had abolished universal suffrage and its rulers were concerned with maintaining their own power. His overthrow of the Directory was an attempt to restore the liberty that the Revolution had achieved in overthrowing the Bourbons. In establishing the Consulate, Napoleon told the people that the Revolution had now established the principles which were its base. Napoleon reinstituted universal manhood suffrage. Furthermore, to preserve those revolutionary principles from internal factions and foreign powers wanting to destroy the benefits of the Revolution, the government must be based on a moderate constitutional monarchy which the Revolution had first established. Therefore, even the Constitution of 1804 does not destroy the Republic, but merely entrusts it to the Emperor of the French. Nor was the liberty of the people violated by the change in constitutions in 1799 or 1804, for Napoleon had submitted both actions to the approval of the people through plebiscites. The Consulate was approved by 99 percent of the vote and the Empire was approved by a similar margin.

Equality, the second feature of the Revolution, was also present in Napoleon's Imperial Republic. Equality meant the end of special privileges and the end of seigniorial justice. By his reforms, Napoleon made any return to the feudal system impossible. The Legion of Honor, which Napoleon established in 1802, he considered to be the symbol of equality and a death blow to the old feudal distinctions of knighthood. The Legion of Honor was open to everyone of talent, whether in the field of battle, the arts, the sciences, or government. Unlike the old feudal distinctions, the Legion of Honor would lead to the cohesion, not the struggle, of the classes. The *Code Napoléon* would also foster the new equality. It established the benefits of equal protection under the law throughout France and civil rights for every citizen and resident alien. The code secured the right to protect property from unlawful seizure, yet it also prohibited the renewal of the old feudal concepts of primogeniture and entail. Napoleon's reform of the educational system granted equality of opportunity to all classes. The establishment of *lycées*, a type of secondary school, in the larger cities, and government support of higher education gave all Frenchmen the chance for a better education.

The reform of education and the *Code Napoléon* also fostered Fraternity, the third tenet of the Revolution. With state control of education, students learned patriotism and what is meant to be French, rather than a commitment to a certain trade or community. This fraternity, or brotherhood of all, was granted not only to Frenchmen, but also to those people in countries Napoleon had liberated from the oppression of absolutist monarchs. Napoleon not only established sister republics in Holland (Batavian Republic), Switzerland (Helvetian Republic), and parts of Italy (Ligurian and Cisalpine Republics), but he also spread fraternitiy through the establishment of the *Code Napoléon* in these new republics. This code is still today the basis for civil law in many European countries. In liberating these people from their oppression, he also fostered the growth of nationalism. Not only did he reestablish a separate Polish state, which had been destroyed by greedy monarchs in the 1790s, he nurtured in the Italians, the Germans, and others a sense of nationalism that would blossom into unified states in the second half of the century. Napoleon was thus a great leader because he helped to spread the benefits of the Revolution to others.

Having promoted the principles of Liberty, Equality, and Fraterntiy, Napoleon can be seen to be the Heir of the French Revolution, and thus a great leader.

NAPOLEON I THE TYRANT

If Napoleon fostered the ideas of the Revolution, he could be considered a great leader. On the other hand, if Napoleon only manpiulated those revolutionary principles of Liberty, Equality, and Fraternity to increase his own power, he was not the Heir of the Revolution. Rather, he was merely an absolute ruler, more tyrannical than any of the Bourbon kings, concerned with his own power and not the welfare of his people. Using this definition of tyranny, Napoleon was a great tyrant.

For all its façade, the Napoleonic constitution destroyed liberty, and only served to concentrate power in Bonaparte's hands and not those of the people. While the masses had universal suffrage, they only voted to place members on a communal list. From this list, Napoleon would then choose mayors for French towns. The communal list would choose from their members a departmental list, from which Napoleon would choose the prefects of departments. The departmental list would choose from its members a national list from which Napoleon would choose members of the legislature, in which he initiated the legislation. Napoleon not only destroyed democracy, he also violated liberty of speech and the press. A decree of January 17, 1800, suppressed newspapers that did not support the Napoleonic regime. The number of papers was thus lowered from seventy-three to a more easily watched number of thirteen, and by 1811 the number had fallen to four. Similar constraints were placed on liberty of expression in the theater and the printing and selling of books.

The *Code Napoléon* failed to secure the equality of everyone under the law. Juries, when they were allowed, usually contained members of the upper classes of society, and the Senate could overturn any jury verdict which it deemed to be harmful to the interest of the state. There are instances in which opponents of the regime were imprisoned or executed without proper justice. General Pichegru, who was arrested in an assassination plot, was strangled in his cell. The Bourbon Duke d'Enghien was kidnapped outside of French territory and after a quick nonpublic military trial executed the next morning.

There was also no equality before the law for employers and their workers. Employers engaging in coalitions to lower wages were punished with a maximum jail term of one month and a maximum fine of 3,000 francs. Workers, however, engaged in coalitions for the purpose of striking could be imprisoned for up to five years. Furthermore, the employer's word was to be accepted regarding the rate and payment of salaries while the workers were forced to carry at all times a little booklet, a *livret*, giving a complete history of their employment, thus making police supervision easier.

Women and blacks were also denied equality. The *Code Napoléon* gave the husband far more rights than the wife. Married women were forbidden to carry on many kinds of business without their husbands' consent and were forbidden from entering upon any contracts. Blacks were also denied equality in May 1802, when Napoleon reinstituted slavery, which had been abolished during the Revolution, in French colonies.

In the most blatant attack on the equality brought by the Revolution, Napoleon established an imperial hereditary nobility, rivaling that of the Ancien Régime. In 1804, not only did he make himself Emperor, but granted his family members the hereditary title of French princes, and the eldest son of the emperor, the title of the Prince Imperial. In 1808, Napoleon decreed even further titles of nobility including Duke, Count, and Baron for members of the government, making sure that to support that dignity they had large estates, which along with the title were hereditary by order of primogeniture.

Napoleon also violated the principle of fraternity on which the Revolution was based. After conquering a state he would subordinate its economy and its manhood to the service of his grand scheme of domination. In 1805, Napoleon wrote that his reason for the conquest of Genoa was for the 15,000 sailors which it could provide for the French fleet. His instructions for the occupation of Portugal, in 1807, included a similar mobilization of five to six thousand Portuguese troops, deporting people who were likely to cause trouble, and the collection of taxes for the support of France. Napoleon's Continental System attempted to subjugate all of Europe's economy and commerce to his purpose of preventing British trade with Europe. By the Treaty of Tilsit, in 1807, he forced Russia to close its ports to British commerce. He told his stepson, Eugène de Beauharnais, Viceroy of Italy, in 1810, that his policy should be "France first." Napoleon eventually deposed his brother, Louis, as King of Holland because Louis failed to curb Dutch smuggling in violation of the Continental System. Napoleon was not conquering Europe to spread the Revolution but to feed his own desire for power and control.

Since Napoleon violated the principles of Liberty, Equality, and Fraternity that he claimed to uphold, he was not a true son of the Revolution. Using his power and position for his personal aggrandizement was certainly the sign of a great tyrant.

SUGGESTIONS FOR FURTHER READING

Bonaparte, Napoleon. *Napoleon's Memoirs.* Translated by Somerset de Chair. New York: Harper & Brothers, 1948.

Connely, Owen. *Blundering to Glory: Napoleon's Military Campaigns.* Wilmington: Scholarly Resources, Inc., 1987.

Cronin, Vincent. *Napoleon Bonaparte: An Intimate Biography.* New York: William Morrow & Co., 1972.

Geyl, Peter. *Napoleon: For and Against.* Translated by Olive Renier. New Haven, Conn: Yale University Press, 1963.

Guérard, Albert. *Napoleon I: A Great Life in Brief.* New York: Alfred A. Knopf, 1956.

Holtman, R. B. *The Napoleonic Revolution.* New York: J. B. Lippincott, 1967.

Jones, R. Ben. *Napoleon: Man and Myth.* London: Hodder & Stoughton, Ltd., 1977.

Thompson, J. M. *Napoleon Bonaparte: His Rise and Fall.* New York: Oxford University Press, 1952.

Tulard, Jean. *Napoleon: The Myth of the Savior.* Translated by Teresa Waugh. London: Weindenfeld and Nicolson, 1984.

Lawrence P. Adamczyk

Napoleon III (Louis Napoleon Bonaparte) 1808–1873

President of the French Republic, 1848–1852
Emperor of the French, 1852–1870

The historian Albert Guérard, the warmest contemporary admirer of the "gentle emperor," has cast Napoleon III as a combination of Franklin D. Roosevelt and Benito Mussolini. Undoubtedly, Louis Napoleon Bonaparte never succeeded in reconciling the two *personae* that haunted him. On the one hand, he strove to be a democrat committed to universal suffrage, full employment, personal security for workers, and a vital, self-generating, balanced capitalism. On the other hand, he sought to be a warrior Bonaparte, reviving memories of past glories, carrying France's borders out to their present limits at Savoy and Nice, and fighting limited wars without great risk. Napoleon III's suicidal failure lay in the fact that the revolutionary nationalist and the policeman committed to order, contested for his soul, but neither won. Their contradictions destroyed their host. His romantic idealism made possible the national self-determination of Italians, Germans, and Romanians. Ironically, his political miscalculations and his personal ruin doomed France to a half-century of failed self-confidence and paranoic fluctuations between arrogant aggressiveness and pusillanimous fear.

BIOGRAPHICAL BACKGROUND

Charles Louis Napoleon Bonaparte, known familiarly as Louis Napoleon, was born at Paris on April 20, 1808. He was the third of the three sons of Louis Bonaparte, brother of Napoleon I. His mother, Hortense de Beauharnais Bonaparte, was the daughter of the emperor's consort, Empress Josephine, by her first marriage. He was thus a nephew and a step-grandson of the emperor.

Louis Bonaparte was King of Holland between 1808 and 1810, but so far displeased his brother that Holland was annexed to France and ex-king Louis was "demoted" to the rank of a French prince. After Waterloo in 1815, Hortense separated from her husband, spent some years as a rootless refugee, shunned as a Bonaparte troublemaker. Happily, she ultimately settled down at Arenenberg, Switzerland. There Louis Napoleon and a surviving older brother grew to manhood.

Serving as a captain of the Swiss artillery, he gained his first military experience. In 1830–1831 he saw action in Italy supporting Italian nationalist revolutionaries against Austria. The death of his older brother of fever, during that campaign, followed shortly by the death of his cousin, Napoleon I's only legitimate son, made Louis Napoleon the head of the House of Bonaparte.

In 1836 an attempt to subvert the French army garrison at Strasbourg won him only speedy arrest and exile to New York. In 1840, another attempt to subvert the garrison at Boulogne earned him a public trial and a life sentence to prison at Ham. In 1846 he made an easy escape, and made his way to London via Belgium. In the revolutionary year 1848, as King Louis Philippe was dethroned, the Bonaparte heir hesitated only four months before swearing allegiance to the new republic and accepting election to the Legislative Assembly. On December 10, he was elected president of the Second French Republic by a large majority in a free election. On December 2, 1851, he overthrew the constitution by force and made himself president for ten more years. One year later, he made himself emperor.

He married Eugénie de Montijo y Teba in 1853, and their only child was born in 1856. Napoleon Eugène Louis Jean Joseph Bonaparte, styled the Prince-Imperial, seemed to ensure the future of the dynasty. No one could have foreseen the death of the prince, in 1879, fighting as a British volunteer in the South African Zulu War.

Throughout Napoleon III's reign, France was engaged in a number of limited wars, always carefully selected to ensure victory, without risking popular support for the regime. In 1849 he sent an army to Rome to restore Pope Pius IX after he had been driven into exile by the republican revolutionaries, Mazzini and Garibaldi. Again, with a view to pleasing Catholic sentiment at home, from 1850 to 1853, he attempted to obtain primacy for Roman Catholicism in the Holy Land, at the expense of the Russian-supported Greek Orthodox Church. This led directly to the Crimean War, 1853–1856, which, though fought far from Jerusalem, won France laurels as an ally of Britain and a conqueror of Napoleon I's old Russian foe.

In 1859 he waged an Italian war designed to drive the Austrians from Italy. He stopped short of that goal, but his limited victory permitted Count Cavour, acting in secret collusion with him, to unite the peninsula.

An attempt to conquer Mexico and install Archduke Ferdinand Maximilian of Austria as emperor, ended in disaster when the United States threatened war in 1866. In 1860, France conquered Indo-China, simultaneously supporting war against China itself in alliance with Britain. In that same year, six thousand French soldiers easily pacified Lebanon and Syria.

France was pro-Polish during their rebellion against Russia in 1863, pro-

Danish during their war against the German states in 1864, and neutral during the Seven Weeks War of 1866. In each case, France lost friends without gaining allies. Napoleon resolutely defended the pope against a new Garibaldian attack in 1867, thereby offending Italian nationalists.

Woefully unprepared for war, France could not get Italian alliance because French troops remained stubbornly at Rome to guard the pope. Austria conditioned her alliance on unobtainable Italian support. Entirely isolated, France foolishly went to war in 1870 over the irrelevant and fabricated issue of the candidacy of Leopold of Hohenzollern-Sigmaringen for the Spanish throne. The German victory cost Napoleon III his throne and condemned him to a new exile. He died, during surgery, on January 7, 1873, and was buried at Camden Place, Chiselhurst, England.

NAPOLEON III AS A GREAT LEADER

Louis Napoleon's official title defines the way he wished to be remembered. He styled himself "Napoleon III, by the Grace of God and the Will of the People, Hereditary Emperor of the French." He thus asserted that Bonapartism rested on popular sovereignty. Certainly in the free elections of June and September 1848, he was elected to the republican legislature by four and five constituencies, respectively. In the free presidential election of December 10, 1848, he was elected France's chief executive by more than four million out of the seven million votes cast.

While living in exile at London in 1839, he published the most important of his nine books, titled *Des Idées Napoléoniennes*, which described his cause as a political movement. It maintained that Bonapartism was the inheritance of the French Revolution of 1789, devoted to popular sovereignty, grounded in authority and order. Louis Napoleon evoked the reign of his uncle, Napoleon I, as a happy time when Roman Catholicism enjoyed protection but all religions were equally free. He described the First Empire as having protected the poor from the vicissitudes of laissez-faire capitalism. He painted Napoleon I as a leader who failed to fulfill his program because war was forced on him by jealous despots. Louis Napoleon held out the promise that the opportunity destroyed at Waterloo would reopen under a Second Empire.

A great body of evidence supports Napoleon III's sincerity. Throughout the duration of the Second Empire, the reports of police prefects and departmental administrative officers were systematically summarized, collated and submitted to the emperor as measures of public opinion. During the most repressive phase of the empire, from 1852 to 1862, a minimum of five republican deputies were always allowed election to the legislature and permitted to speak freely, without harassment. After 1867, active legislative opposition and a freer press were tolerated. In 1869–1870, complete freedom of the press, and British style ministries responsible to the legislature rather than the sovereign, were introduced.

Napoleon III was also adept at creating public opinion through the publication of pamphlets expressing his controversial ideas, but signed by ghost writers such as Viscount Arthur de la Guéronniere. Public reaction to such publications as reported by the provincial Procurers-General, permitted the emperor to pursue policies that were popular, and to repudiate those that were not.

In 1844, while a prisoner at the French fortress of Ham, Louis Napoleon had published *Sur l'extinction du paupérisme*, which offered a socialist response to unemployment, by proposing the institution of massive government public works programs.

Under the aegis of Baron Eugène Haussmann, imperial prefect of the Seine, Napoleon III remade the city of Paris, creating great blocs of working-class housing in the suburbs, and designing the tree-lined boulevards that beautify that metropolis to this day. Similar feats of urban renewal benefited almost every French city. France completed a network of railroad lines and telegraph connections. French diplomacy rendered possible such great international enterprises as Ferdinand de Lesseps' completion of the Suez Canal in 1869. Save for rare occasions, France enjoyed full employment under Napoleon III. Labor unions were granted the right to strike, under controlled conditions. The National Pawnshops made inexpensive loans available to the working poor. The Crédit Mobilier made cash available for new enterprises. Napoleon III moved closer to international free trade than any French government prior to World War II.

It is a commentary on the prosperity of the Second Empire that in 1873, just two years after France's defeat in the Franco-Prussian War, a huge indemnity of one billion gold dollars was paid to the surprised Germans.

It is part of Napoleon III's romanticism that he regarded nationalism as a benign force to be encouraged. Both the emperor and Empress Eugenie conceived of great confederations of Catholic or Latin nations that would regard Paris as their center. A century before Charles de Gaulle, a prophetic French diplomat, the Marquis de La Valette spoke of France as the nucleus of a European coalition that would check the Russian colossus to the east and the American colossus in the west.

With such illusions, Napoleon III enthusiastically supported the national unity and independence of such potentially antagonistic peoples as the Italians, Poles, Romanians, Hungarians, Mexicans, American Confederates, and even those Germans who proved to be his nemesis. It is notable that he slowed French colonization of Algeria to encourage the creation of an "Arab Kingdom."

Although France continued its historic role as the protector of Roman Catholicism, imperial prestige was engaged on behalf of persecuted Jews and Protestants. In both the fields of finance and government, the Empire opened free opportunity to religious minorities. The public school system, though obliged to accept a partnership with the Catholic clergy, was open to all males. Education for women made notable advances. By the end of the Empire, Frenchmen were surely the most literate people in Europe.

NAPOLEON III THE TYRANT

There were two periods in Napoleon III's career when he made use of brutal, repressive force to hold power. On December 2, 1851, when he ignored the constitution and asserted his right to an additional ten-year term as president, the army served as a loyal and efficient instrument to crush resistance to the coup d' état. More than 26,000 people were arrested, 10,000 were sentenced to deportation, and nearly as many were driven into exile or enforced confinement to a residence. An estimated three hundred opponents were killed. Victor Hugo, living in a British Channel Island retreat, spewed out his anger at *Napoleon the Little* and the "Crime of December 2."

The second period of repressive military control took place after the emperor and empress narrowly escaped assassination at the hands of Count Felice Orsini on January 14, 1858. Overall military command was given to General Espinasse, who divided France into five military districts and instituted modified martial law. Furthermore, army officers all over the world were "encouraged" to write letters to be published in the "unofficial" columns of the official newspaper *Le Moniteur Universel.* With inspired uniformity, the officers decried the laxity of foreign governments, especially Britain, which allowed suspected assassins to move freely.

Oddly enough, while permitting the army to crush freedom, Napoleon allowed Orsini, doomed to the guillotine, a very public trial, in a courtroom open to the public. Because the emperor wished to know whether public opinion favored French support for Italian nationalism, he allowed Orsini to transform his trial into a plea for Italian freedom from Austrian domination. Napoleon himself wrote part of Orsini's "last will and testament," knowing that the press would publish it verbatim. Orsini's defense lawyer was Jules Favre, one of the five privileged, overt republicans seated in the Legislative Body. Thus, even freedom of expression became a tool used effectively by "Napoleon the Tyrant."

Certainly, Napoleon III's foreign policy, even when conducted in the name of liberal nationalism, rested ultimately on the use of repressive force. In the name of his defense of Roman Catholicism, he overthrew the Roman Republic established by Mazzini and Garibaldi in 1849. Thereby he incurred the unremitting hostility of Italian nationalists even though ultimately he did more to liberate and unite Italy than had anyone else. He entered the Crimean War on the pretext of making Roman Catholicism the premier Christian denomination in the Holy Land, even though Greek Orthodoxy had many more adherents there. His conquest of Mexico was motivated in large part by a desire to control the resources of that country. His ideology, however, shared by his Mexican protegé Emperor Maximilian, was liberal Catholic. He was thus fighting for the cause espoused by Maximilian's enemies, the Juarez republicans, while his only native Mexican monarchist allies were reactionary Catholics.

He attempted to strike bargains with the Prussian leader Bismarck in 1866–1867, under which France could seize Belgium by force or buy Luxembourg from the king of the Netherlands in exchange for Prussia doing as she pleased in uniting Germany. Napoleon's ineptitude, and Bismarck's skill in that tyrannical policy, ended with France getting not a single additional inch of territory inhabited by French-speaking inhabitants, while Bismarck created a united German Empire under the king of Prussia. For good measure, the world condemned Napoleon as the aggressor, when Bismarck leaked news of the intended French seizure of Belgium to the press while applauding Bismarck as a defender of treaties and world order.

SUGGESTIONS FOR ADDITIONAL READING

Barker, Nancy N. *Distaff Diplomacy: The Empress Eugenie and the Foreign Policy of the Second Empire.* Austin: University of Texas, 1967.

Blumberg, Arnold. *A Carefully Planned Accident; the Italian War of 1859.* Selinsgrove, Pa.: Susquehanna University Press, 1990.

———. *The Diplomacy of the Mexican Empire, 1863–1867.* Malabar, Fla.: Robert E. Krieger Publishing Co., 1987.

Bury, J.P.T. *Napoleon III and the Second Empire.* London: English Universities Press, 1964.

Case, Lynn M. *French Opinion on War and Diplomacy during the Second Empire.* Philadelphia: University of Pennsylvania Press, 1954.

Gooch, George Peabody. *The Second Empire.* London: Longmans, 1961.

Guérard, Albert. *Napoleon III.* Cambridge: Harvard University Press, 1943.

Isser, Natalie. *The Second Empire and the Press.* The Hague: Martinus Nijhoff, 1974.

Payne, Howard C. *The Police State of Louis Napoleon Bonaparte, 1851–1860.* Seattle: University of Washington Press, 1966.

Williams, Roger L. *The Mortal Napoleon III.* Princeton, N.J.: Princeton University Press, 1971.

Arnold Blumberg

Kwame Nkrumah

1909–1972

President of Ghana, 1957–1966

Kwame Nkrumah, who led the West African nation of Ghana to independence from Great Britain in 1957, was a prototype, both in his strengths and weaknesses, of many other modern African leaders. Relatively young when he came to power, raised in a small tribe but formally trained by Western teachers, he was energetic, charismatic, and dedicated to achieving a self-reliant nation, whose people were made materially secure by a benevolent socialist state within a united Africa that would lead the nonaligned Third World in the Cold War. But in rushing to achieve his vision, he trampled important cultural traditions, undermined viable economic structures, weakened established legal institutions, heightened tribal, class, and regional conflicts, and antagonized neighboring African states. The result was his political isolation and removal from power in 1966. If his skillful use of protest and compromise leading to the peaceful break with Britain served as a model for other African states, so did the military coup that overthrew his corrupt and unpopular dictatorship, the same way five other African leaders were deposed in 1966.

BIOGRAPHICAL BACKGROUND

Kwame Nkrumah was born in 1909 in the southwest corner of the Gold Coast, then a British colony in West Africa. The son of the senior wife of a goldsmith in the Nzima tribe, he was one of few children allowed to complete seven elementary grades in the local school. From 1924 to 1930 he attended a new teacher training school at Achimota, near the capital, Accra. He then taught at several government schools for five years.

When the Nigerian nationalist, Namdi Azikwe, who had recently returned from a long stay in America, visited Achimota, he urged Nkrumah to continue his education in the United States, rather than in England. In 1935, with passage paid by a distant relative, Nkrumah arrived in the

United States. By 1942 he had received a bachelor's degree from predominantly black Lincoln University in Pennsylvania and a master's in education from the University of Pennsylvania.

Nkrumah's political views were shaped during his ten years in America. His passion for Pan-Africanism was influenced by the writings of W.E.B. DuBois and Jamaica-born Marcus Garvey. He saw the United States, also former British colonies, as a model for a liberated United States of Africa. He began reading Marx, Engels, and Lenin during this time, but his commitment to socialism took more time to develop.

In May 1945 the thirty-six-year-old teacher sailed from New York for London, where he worked for two years among West African nationalists. His reputation as a political organizer spread when he helped arrange the sixth Pan-African Congress held in Manchester, the first to deal primarily with African unity rather than global black unity. The Labor Party had come to power in England in 1945, and many delegates in Manchester hoped the new British government would support independence for her African colonies.

In November 1947, Nkrumah returned home after a twelve-year absence, having taken a job as national secretary of the United Gold Coast Convention (UGCC), a moderately nationalistic group of black African businessmen and professionals. When, in February 1948, anti-British riots broke out in Accra and other coastal towns, resulting in twenty-nine deaths, Nkrumah broke with the UGCC, forming the more militant Convention People's Party (CPP) in 1949. In 1950, when the CPP called for "Self-Government Now" and organized mass marches and a general strike, the British arrested Nkrumah and other CPP leaders, sending them to prison for a year.

With Nkrumah in jail, the British governor, Charles Arden-Clarke, allowed national elections in February 1951, the first ever held in colonial Africa, hoping the more moderate UGCC would win. But the CPP swept to victory and Governor Arden-Clarke was forced to release Nkrumah, naming him chief minister of a semi-autonomous Gold Coast government.

Despite serious differences between Nkrumah's party and more traditional Gold Coast groups, including Ashanti chiefs, Ewe and Ga separatists, and UGCC conservatives, the CPP handily won national elections in 1954 and 1956, paving the way for independence on March 6, 1957. Named Ghana after the eleventh-century African empire that stretched between the Senegal and Niger rivers, and including the northern part of the former Gold Coast, the new nation, with Kwame Nkrumah as prime minister, was the first African colony to win independence, serving as a model for fourteen other African states by 1960.

Nkrumah introduced a new constitution in 1960, which made Ghana a republic within the British Commonwealth and himself an elected president for a five-year term. Voters approved the new constitution by a wide margin but with little enthusiasm, as the joy of freedom gave way to concern about economic decline, government mismanagement, and tribal, class, and ideological conflicts. By 1961, Nkrumah was promoting Nkrumaism, or African socialism, as the only way Ghana could reduce poverty, ignorance, disease, and dependency on European assistance. He supported large-scale state-operated enterprises to provide surpluses for capital investment. The Volta River Project, his most ambitious government venture, was developed to provide irrigation, late-scale fisheries, and cheap power, which, with local bauxite, could make Ghana a major aluminum exporter. The Volta River Project and other government schemes did not produce economic self-reliance, and by 1963, with her major export, cocoa, experiencing declining world prices, Ghana's economy was near collapse.

Despite pressure by Ghanaian businessmen and cocoa farmers to concentrate on the economy, Nkrumah was very active in Pan-African affairs. He provided financial aid to neighboring Guinea, when it was abandoned by France in 1958; he sent troops as part of the United Nations peace effort in the Congo in 1961; he supported the Casablanca group of radical African states that assisted guerrilla groups against white regimes in southern Africa. At great local expense Ghana hosted the 1965 Organization of African Unity (OAU) meeting. Nkrumah offered to send troops to help liberate Southern Rhodesia (later Zimbabwe) from Ian Smith's white rule, but Ghanaian generals strongly opposed military intervention, believing the army too weak and Rhodesia too far away. By late 1965 some generals were planning to topple Nkrumah's regime, which in their view had become corrupt and too friendly toward the Soviets since his state visit there in 1961.

In 1966, with the economic crisis worsening and his reputation as a world leader tarnished, Nkrumah tried to recover some prestige by a quixotic offer to mediate the Viet Nam war. On February 23, 1966, shortly after he had left for Hanoi, Ghanaian troops staged a quick, bloodless coup. Nkrumah went into exile in Guinea, where he spent his last years as the honored guest of Sekou Touré, writing books on neocolonialism and blaming reactionary elements in Ghana and the West for overthrowing his government. He developed cancer in 1970 and died on April 27, 1972, while undergoing treatment in Bucharest, Romania. His body was returned to Ghana in July 1972, where, after lying in state, it was buried in Nkroful, his birthplace.

NKRUMAH AS A GREAT LEADER

Although Ghana is a small country (about 7 million) tucked in the corner of West Africa, Kwame Nkrumah's powerful personality made it one of the leading players in African affairs from the end of World War II to 1966, when he was deposed. His greatest achievement was guiding Ghana to peaceful independence in 1957, the first African nation to win freedom from European control. Neither the British nor local tribal leaders were enthusiastic about Ghanaian independence, having worked out a relationship since 1900 that was mutually beneficial. But Nkrumah, from the time he organized the CPP in 1949, forced the issue, avoiding violent protests and radical rhetoric that would have given Britain an excuse to delay independence.

Nkrumah emphasized nationalism over tribalism, reform over tradition, and freedom over dependence. Keeping his support for a socialist state muted until after independence, he appeared less threatening than more radical CPP elements but more enlightened than the traditionalist opposition.

Raised among the Nzima coastal people, who, for centuries, had contact with traders from faraway places, Nkrumah had a broader perspective than most Ghanaian leaders, who identified with local, regional, or class interests. His strongest supporters in the CPP, the so-called youngmen, were, like him, people of modest background but great ambition; educated commoners, including junior civil servants, primary school teachers, clerks, and shopkeepers, who, rejecting both the British colonial and African traditional systems, saw African unity and socialism as the means to a better future for themselves and the nation.

Nkrumah, in part because of his American experience, carried the concept of African unity beyond his most ardent supporters. For him Nkrumaism, or African socialism, was a necessary means to the ultimate goal of making Ghana a part of a United States of Africa capable of withstanding European hegemony. After the Congo crisis of 1961, where Western powers favored Katangan separatists and the Russians aided Lumumba's radicals, Nkrumah was sure that, if Africa did not stand together, it would be crushed under the weight of the Cold War.

His attempt to benefit Ghana by playing East against West was a dangerous gamble and only partly successful. He guided the Volta River Project from its inception in 1951 to completion in 1964, getting funds from the West despite his close ties with Russia. He cultivated a friendship with President John Kennedy, who kept American funds flowing, although the CIA called Nkrumah a bad risk, a corrupt playboy, who was increasingly dependent on Communist cadres in the CPP.

By the time of Kennedy's murder in November 1963, Nkrumah had survived three assassination attempts, the last and most serious in August 1962, by radicals in his own party. Under attack from all sides, Nkrumah, by the end of 1962, was isolated from the Ghanaian people and ignored by most African leaders. The father of African unity was rapidly declining into a Ghanaian tyrant.

NKRUMAH THE TYRANT

As early as 1958 Nkrumah had shown willingness to use repressive means to achieve political ends. He used state-of-emergency powers to deport dissidents without trial or to have others serve long prison sentences at hard labor. Regional assemblies were reduced to advisory bodies, tribal chiefs had their property seized; an Avoidance of Discrimination Act made all "tribal, religious, and regional" parties illegal; a Preventive Detention Act allowed him to imprison forty-three opposition members of the National Assembly; and in December 1958 all strikes were made illegal. Between 1958 and 1966, Nkrumah had detained without trial more than 1,200 opponents in Nsawam prison. Ghanaians might have accepted his treatment of opponents if the economy had not turned sour. The Volta River Project, like Nkrumah himself, promised more than it could produce. Most of the government projects launched under Nkrumaism lost money. Ghana Airways was a totally uneconomic service via North Africa to Moscow used only by government officials. The government bought a used-up gold mine from a British firm at an exorbitant price. When collective farming was imposed on previously successful cocoa farmers, surpluses disappeared and Guinea and the Ivory Coast replaced Ghana as the leading cocoa exporters. The state-owned National Development Corporation became a major source of public corruption by CPP leaders, including Nkrumah, whose wealth, when deposed, was estimated at $2.3 million. In nine years Nkrumaism had reduced one of the healthiest economies in West Africa to economic bankruptcy.

By 1962 even Nkrumah's claim as Pan-African leader was being challenged. Despite his calls for African unity, Nkrumah was often at odds with more moderate leaders, like the Ivory Coast's Houphouet-Boigny and Togoland's Sylvanus Olympio. His Bureau of African Affairs provided cover for radical African exiles trained by Chinese and East Germans to destabilize moderate governments in Nigeria, Niger, the Ivory Coast, and Togoland. In 1962 African leaders at the Lagos Conference threatened Ghana with diplomatic isolation if Nkrumah did not stop interfering in his neighbors' affairs. But in January 1963 he was thought by many to be implicated in Olympio's assassination. When the Organization of African Unity was formed that year in Addis Ababa, Ethiopia, all of Nkrumah's proposals were rejected and he was criticized by many delegates as a major source of disunity.

After the third attempt on his life in August 1962, Nkrumah became more repressive at home, closing the border, dismissing the Supreme Court chief justice, giving the president power to set aside judicial decisions, and, by 1965, making the CPP the only legal party, with power greater than parliament and the courts.

By 1966 the only institution strong enough to challenge Nkrumah's dictatorial rule was the Ghanaian army. Already disenchanted with him because of cuts in their budgets while the Russian-trained President's Guard were well funded, some generals decided to take action when Nkrumah, in a desperate attempt to regain popularity, informally declared war on Southern Rhodesia. When he left on his abortive peace mission to Hanoi, in February 1963, twenty tanks surrounded Flagstaff House, the president's residence, and with little resistance from Nkrumah's Soviet-led security guard, the coup was completed in twenty-four hours. As CPP cadres were being rounded up, thousands of Ghanaians took to the streets to celebrate the downfall of Nkrumah's regime.

Reactions to the coup were predictable. Many opponents released from Nsawam prison denounced Nkrumah as a corrupt tyrant whose romantic Marxist and Pan-African schemes had nearly destroyed Ghana. Touré and other radical African leaders portrayed him as a revolutionary leader overthrown by Ghanaian traitors working for the CIA and European capitalists.

Since 1966 Ghana has continued to suffer economic and political deprivations under a series of military dictatorships. Many Ghanaians, especially those born since his downfall, have expressed the desire for another Nkrumah. Historians and other African specialists at conferences on Nkrumah's legacy in London (1984) and Accra (1985) emphasized the positive, his vision of a free Ghana and a unified Africa, rather than his failure to sustain and build on Ghana's strengths at independence. Nevertheless, in the 1990s most of Africa is ruled by military strongmen or one-party governments, with stagnant economies and growing hardships, a condition Nkrumah tried to prevent but helped to bring about.

SUGGESTIONS FOR ADDITIONAL READING

Apter, David. *Ghana in Transition.* New York: Atheneum, 1963.

Austin, Dennis. *Politics in Ghana.* London: Oxford University Press, 1970.

Davidson, Basil. *Black Star: A View of the Life and Times of Kwama Nkrumah.* New York: Praeger, 1974.

Fitch, Bob, and Mary Oppenheimer. *Ghana: End of an Illusion.* New York: Monthly Review Press, 1966.

Nkrumah, Kwame. *The Autobiography of Kwame Nkrumah.* Edinburgh: Nelson, 1957.

Rooney, David. *Kwame Nkrumah: The Political Kingdom in the Third World.* New York: St. Martin's Press, 1988.

Thompson, W. Scott. *Ghana's Foreign Policy.* Princeton, N.J.: Princeton University Press, 1969.

Sheldon Avery

Julius Kambarage Nyerere
1922–

President of Tanzania, 1961–1985

From the time in 1955 when he gave up his position as a history master to work full time for Tanganyika's independence, Julius Nyerere was called *mwalimu*, the Swahili word for "teacher." Whether organizing a political party or advocating *Uhuru na kazi*, freedom and work, promoting *ujamaa*, African socialism, or *Uhuru na Umoja*, freedom and unity, Nyerere always put great emphasis on education. He considered raising Tanzania's (its name after merging with Zanzibar) adult literacy rate to 85 percent one of his greatest achievements. Believing that Tanzania's potential could only be realized through African socialism and Pan-Africanism, Nyerere developed a set of principles in the Arusha Declaration (1967) to achieve these goals. His supporters praised Nyerere for remaining faithful to the Arusha Declaration despite enormous difficulties. His critics credit him with leading his country to peaceful independence and creating a stable and unified nation, but they saw his rigid adherence to socialism as undermining Tanzania's chance to become a democratic, self-reliant nation.

BIOGRAPHICAL BACKGROUND

Julius Kambarage Nyerere was born in March 1922 in the village of Butiama, in Tanganyika, East Africa. His mother was the eighteenth wife of the chief of the Zanaki tribe. The Zanaki, whose lands border the west end of Lake Victoria, were a small, poor tribe, whose chiefs had little more material wealth than their subjects.

Typical of African leaders of modest background, Nyerere stood out among his classmates at the local elementary school and was accepted to Tabora Government High School in 1937. He attended Makerere University in Kampala, Uganda during World War II, receiving a diploma in education in 1945. While at Makerere he was baptized into the Roman Catholic faith.

In 1949, after teaching history and biology in a Tabora church school, Nyerere won a scholarship to Edinburgh University, becoming the first Tanganyikan to attend a British university. After receiving a master's degree in 1952, he returned home to become history master at St. Francis School in Pugu, near the capital, Dar es Salaam. He married Maria Magige in 1953 and they had five sons and two daughters.

In the 1950s many college-educated Africans began working for liberation from European colonial rule. In Tanganyika, a British Trust Territory since World War I, many among the black elite belonged to the Tanganyika African Association (TAA). When Nyerere was elected TAA president in 1953, he converted it from a debating society to a political party, the Tanganyika African National Union (TANU).

Small of stature, soft-spoken, and unpretentious, Nyerere's leadership style was based on his experience as an educator. Called *mwalimu*, Swahili for teacher, for his patient but forceful method of presenting ideas, Nyerere won acclaim at home and recognition abroad in 1955 when he presented the Meru tribe's case in a land dispute with Britain at a United Nations Trusteeship Council meeting in New York. Upon his return home, Nyerere resigned his teaching position to devote all his energy to political work for TANU.

An admirer of Gandhi's successful nonviolent campaign in India and Ghana's peaceful evolution toward independence under Kwame Nkrumah, Nyerere guided TANU along a similar path. Following Ghana's independence in 1957, Britain allowed national elections in Tanganyika in 1958, with TANU winning a sizable majority. Working closely with British Governor Sir Richard Turnbull, Nyerere became chief minister of a semi-autonomous Tanganyika in September 1960. After TANU won 70 of 71 seats in the Legislative Assembly, Nyerere was named prime minister in May 1961. On December 9, 1961, Tanganyika became fully independent, the first of Britain's East African colonies to win its freedom. In 1962, Tanganyika became a republic, and in 1964, after merging with the radical island nation of Zanzibar, Nyerere became the first president of the United Republic of Tanzania.

Always a dedicated Pan-Africanist, Nyerere, in 1963, helped create the Organization of African Unity (OAU) at Addis Ababa, Ethiopia. That same year he joined with newly independent Uganda and Kenya to form the East African Community (EAC) for shared currency, airline, and postal service. The EAC collapsed in 1976 from tension between Tanzania and Uganda's stormy dictator, Idi Amin, leading to war in 1978–1979.

In 1985, Nyerere resigned as president after having completed four consecutive five-year terms. He kept the important post of chairman of the only legal party until 1990, when he retired to Butiama and the role of African elder statesman.

NYERERE AS A GREAT LEADER

In his speech to the Tanzanian parliament on July 29, 1985, retiring President Nyerere provided an impressive list of accomplishments since taking office in 1961: the number of children in primary school had risen from 86,000 to 3.6 million, an achievement "unmatched elsewhere in Africa"; adult literacy had risen from 20 to 85 percent, the highest in Africa; access to clean water had increased from 11 to 50 percent of the nation's 20 million people; hospitals had increased 50 percent, rural health centers tenfold, doctors increased from 12 to 782; infant mortality had dropped almost 50 percent and life expectancy had risen from 35 to 51 years, a significant improvement in what was still one of the poorest countries in the world, with an annual per capita income of $250.

During his twenty-four-year reign as president, Nyerere had also made his East African country a major player in African and world affairs. In addition to helping establish the OAU and EAC, Nyerere had offered Tanzania as a refuge and training base for African nationalist rebels seeking to overthrow white rule in southern Africa. Through his South Africa Defense Coordinating Council (SADCC) he backed the Mozambique Liberation Front (FRELIMO) against the Portuguese and set up schools and training facilities for thousands of African National Congress (ANC) cadres fighting apartheid in South Africa. In 1972 he was one of the few African leaders who publicly denounced Uganda strongman Ida Amin for expelling all Asians from his country. When Ugandan troops occupied Tanzanian territory in 1978, Nyerere complained to the OAU that it was tolerating a bloodthirsty aggressor who had killed 500,000 of his own people. When the OAU took no action, Nyerere sent Tanzanian troops into Uganda, forcing Amin and his Libyan advisers to flee in 1979.

Although identified with the nonaligned bloc of nations in the Cold War, Nyerere was a strong advocate of *ujamaa*, Swahili for "familyhood," or African socialism, as the only way for developing nations to become economically self-reliant. His Arusha Declaration (1967) lists the components of *ujamaa*, including villagization (concentrated villages), agricultural collectivism, state industrial ownership, and one-party rule. Nyerere credited *ujamaa* for Tanzania's improved educational and health systems. Since 90 percent of its 20 million people lived in scattered rural areas, Nyerere saw villagization as the most efficient and effective means to provide schools, clean water, and health services. Borrowing from Soviet and Maoist ideas, Nyerere sought to teach Tanzanian farmers to work the land collectively and sell their crops cooperatively. Rejecting capitalism as inappropriate for poor African countries, his *ujamaa* used a system of "parastatals," or national boards in charge of buying foreign goods, selling export crops, like sisal, coffee, cotton, and cashews, and generally controlling the national economy.

Politically, *ujamaa* called for the abolition of all political parties except Nyerere's *Chama Cha Mapinduzi* (Revolutionary Party). In a nation of 123 tribes and four major religious groups, Nyerere argued, a one-party state had the best chance of providing unity and stability.

Tanzania's record of stability, tribal and ethnic harmony, relatively clean record on human rights, and peaceful transition of political power would seem to justify Nyerere's commitment to the Arusha Declaration. "Socialism has served us well," he said in a 1985 interview. "We are a very united country, one of the most stable on the continent . . . because socialism has given hope to our people."

NYERERE THE TYRANT

In the same 1985 interview, Nyerere claimed that his greatest achievement—the establishment of Tanzania—was also his greatest failure. "I never wanted a Tanzania," he said. "What we wanted was a united Africa. We haven't achieved it." Nyerere's dream of a United States of Africa, like that of his mentor, Kwame Nkrumah, was based on extending *ujamaa* to a wider African stage. Only Pan-Africanism through *ujamaa* could save the continent from crushing poverty, economic dependence, and internecine tribalism. But Nyerere's critics see Pan-Africanism as a romantic pipe dream and *ujamaa*, like its East European counterpart, as a fatally flawed economic system. After twenty-four years of *ujamaa*, they point out, Tanzania was still one of the poorest nations in the world.

Although Nyerere got much credit as a leader of Pan-Africanism, the Tanzanian people paid a heavy price. The 1978–1979 war with Uganda that ousted Idi Amin cost Tanzania more than $500 million and left an unstable regime across the border. When the East African Community dissolved in 1976, Tanzania had to spend $200 million to replace the currency, air, and postal services it had provided. By serving as a refuge and training center for left-wing rebels from southern Africa, Tanzania lost considerable investment and assistance from the West, getting instead only the Tanzam railroad built by China.

More harmful to Tanzania's development than Nyerere's Pan-Africanism was his rigid adherence to the Arusha Declaration's socialist agenda. Typical of modern African leaders, Nyerere tried to build a self-reliant industrial state at the expense of the nation's hard-working peasant farmers. His twin agricultural policies of villagization and collectivization undermined the agricultural sector. During the 1970s, in the largest resettlement program in modern African history, 9 million families were rounded up in trucks and moved into 8,000 new centralized villages. Despite better social services, farmers were separated from their land. When the government pressured them to work collectively and sell to parastatals, or national marketing boards, crop production declined 20 percent, as farmers lost incentive to work or sold on the black market.

By 1980 the Tanzanian economy was on the edge of bankruptcy. Payments for imports were six months behind; factories were operating at one-third capacity; foreign reserves were exhausted; and food and consumer goods shortages were chronic. The country was kept afloat by $800 million in foreign aid, the highest level on the continent. Instead of economic self-reliance, after twenty-four years of *ujamaa*, Tanzania was more dependent on Western assistance than ever.

Nyerere had planned to retire in 1980, but because of the economic crisis, he agreed to serve one more five-year term as president. Desperately needing credit, Tanzania had to turn to the International Monetary Fund (IMF). But Nyerere quarreled with the IMF over terms for a new loan. The IMF wanted him to stabilize the economy by cutting government spending, laying off unnecessary government workers, devaluing the currency, selling off or shutting down parastatals, and raising prices paid to farmers. Nyerere, refusing to abandon *ujamaa*, rejected the offer by the IMF, calling it "capitalism's watchdog." As a result the Tanzanian economy continued its steady decline for the next five years.

By stepping down in 1985, Nyerere provided the new Tanzanian government under former First Vice-President Ali Hassan Mwinyi of Zanzibar an opportunity to free itself from *ujamaa*'s shackles. Mwinyi quickly agreed to most of the IMF's terms and credits were released. But Nyerere, as chairman of the Revolutionary Party, could still veto any action by Mwinyi. Until he retired from that post in 1990, public criticism of *ujamaa* was muted.

Julius Nyerere's decision to retire from office while still enjoying good health and national popularity is in sharp contrast with most African leaders of his generation. Tanzania is only the third African nation (the others are Senegal and Cameroon) to have had a peaceful transition of power. Nyerere served his nation well by preparing it for peaceful change. Had he been less rigid in his commitment to socialism and Pan-Africanism, his legacy might have been even brighter.

SUGGESTIONS FOR ADDITIONAL READING

Duggan, William R., and John R. Civille. *Tanzania and Nyerere: A Study of Ujamaa and Nationhood.* Maryknoll, N.Y.: Orbis Books, 1976.

Hatch, John. *Two African Statesmen: Kaunda of Zambia and Nyerere of Tanzania.* Chicago: Henry Regnery, 1976.

Hood, Michael, ed. *Tanzania After Nyerere.* London: KPI, 1987.

Legum, Colin. *Pan-Africanism: A Short Political Guide.* New York: Praeger, 1962.

Nnoli, Okwudiba. *Self-Reliance and Foreign Policy in Tanzania.* New York: NOK, 1978.

Okoko, K.A.B. *Socialism and Self-Reliance in Tanzania.* London: KPI, 1987.

Smith, William E. *We Must Run While They Walk: Portrait of Africa's Julius Nyerere.* New York: Random House, 1971.
———. "Transition," *New Yorker*, 2, no. 2 (March 3, 1986): 72–83.

Sheldon Avery

Juan Domingo Perón

1895–1974

President of Argentina, 1946–1955, 1973–1974

Juan Domingo Perón was the single most important political leader of Argentina in the twentieth century. He rose to power in the waning days of World War II, claiming that he would lead Argentina to greatness in the post-war era. He made good on many of his promises. Living standards rose for the working class, Perón's Third Position helped define the non-aligned nations in the early years of the Cold War, and women received the right to vote in Argentina. Perón was acclaimed as a great national leader, although opposition to his policies grew after 1950. Perón jailed many opponents, closed opposition newspapers, and as economic problems increased, a military uprising forced him from power in 1955. He fled but continued to influence Argentine politics from exile in Spain. In 1973, Perón returned to be elected president once again, but died within a year, bequeathing the Peronist Party as his enduring legacy.

BIOGRAPHICAL BACKGROUND

Perón was born in Lobos, a small town on the pampas, the grassy plains of central Argentina, on October 8, 1895. His father, the son of a medical doctor, was a tenant rancher in Lobos. Perón spent his formative years in the country, first in Lobos and, later in the Patagonia. Learning to ride, enjoying the active life, Perón would exhibit a life-long interest in physical fitness.

In 1904 Perón went to live with his grandparents in Buenos Aires, since his father believed he needed access to educational opportunities available in a large city. Perón found his life's vocation early, enrolling in military school in 1911 and receiving his commission as a second lieutenant in the infantry in 1913. He would become a model soldier, and was stationed in the Campo de Mayo garrison near Buenos Aires, where he taught noncommissioned officers.

This handsome bachelor enjoyed army life. He joined the army general staff in 1929 and played a minor role in the coup that overthrew the elected president, Hipólito Yrigoyen, the following year. He married Aurelia Tizón in 1929, and settled down to a successful career, serving as military attaché to the Argentine embassy in Santiago Chile from 1936 to 1938. At age forty-three Juan Perón could have been proud of his modest achievements, but with the death of his wife in 1938, he felt adrift. Sent to Italy to observe conditions in Europe at the outbreak of World War II, Perón came away impressed with Mussolini's Italian regime and with the accomplishments of Axis powers. Perón would later be accused of being a fascist, although his political doctrine was never as coherent or militant as the European fascists.

Perón exhibited a life-long skill of making people think he agreed with them while using them for his own purposes. In 1943, when a military coup toppled the government of Ramon Castillo, Perón was a member of the GOU, or Group of United Officers, which spearheaded the coup. Perón was appointed to oversee press and radio broadcasting, along with the seemingly insignificant post as head of the Department of Labor. In January 1944, at a benefit for victims of a powerful earthquake in the city of San Juan, Perón met a young radio actress, Eva Duarte, who would become his second wife. Her unwavering support and skill in mobilizing the masses would help propel Perón into the presidency.

Elected twice in open and honest elections, Perón sought to lead Argentina to greatness. His policies transferred wealth away from the landowning oligarchy that had dominated recent governments and toward the growing urban working class. After initial success, opposition mounted, and Perón was overthrown in a bloody military coup in 1955.

Perón's exile took him to Paraguay, Panama, Venezuela, and the Dominican Republic. While abroad he received visits from a variety of followers, and was wooed at a distance by Argentine presidential candidate Arturo Frondizi. Ever the master of evasiveness, Perón responded with pleasantries and support, but no firm commitment. Everyone who spoke with him came away firmly convinced that Perón shared his views. But no one could claim to be given full authority to act in his name. As a result, no individual within Argentina could replace the exiled leader, and the increasingly diverse branches of the movement remained loyal to their exiled chief.

Perón finally settled in Spain in 1960 and married María Estela Martínez, whom he had met in Panama. She had worked as a dancer under the name Isabel and, at age thirty, attached herself to the sixty-six-year-old Perón. She would often act as a go-between, returning to Argentina and meeting with groups of Peronists.

In 1971, Alejandro Lanusse replaced Roberto Levingston as the military president of Argentina and indicated that he would work for the return of a civilian government. However, the military was still not prepared for Perón's return to power. A provision was added to the election regulations, which stated that any candidate for president must be resident in Argentina before August of 1972. Perón had missed that target and supported Héctor Cámpora as his stand-in candidate for the 1973 elections.

Cámpora received nearly fifty percent of the vote in the March elections, stunning many political observers, who had hoped that Perón's absence for so many years would weaken his support. Perón was finally free to return to an Argentina with a Peronist government. His arrival on June 20, 1973, was marked by violence as various factions staged gun battles with each other and the police outside the airport. No accurate figures were ever reported, but it is estimated that hundreds were killed. This was evidence that Perón's coalition, which had hung together awaiting the return of its exiled leader, was beginning to fall apart.

Perón lost no time in taking back power. Cámpora quickly resigned, and new elections were scheduled. Nothing stood in the way of Perón's election to the presidency with his wife as vice-president. The Perón-Perón ticket triumphed, and on October 12, 1973, a seventy-eight-year-old Juan Perón began his third term in office. This term, however, was marked by increasing violence, and Perón's ability to maintain control over the various factions began to slip. He tried to discipline the youthful socialists and maintain his authority over the unions. But ill health and age made the job more difficult and, when he died in June 1974, his victorious coalition, the Justicialist Party, had no center. Isabel assumed the office of the president, but was incapable of governing a country increasingly racked by violence and economic crises. Although Isabel was overthrown by a military coup in 1976, Perón's legacy has survived in the Peronist Party whose nominee, Carlos Menem, was elected president of Argentina in 1989.

PERÓN AS A GREAT LEADER

Perón began his quest for the presidency shortly after the 1943 military coup. He maneuvered to have his post in the Department of Labor elevated to an independent secretariat of Labor and Social Welfare. In early 1944 Perón's mentor, General Farrell, replaced General Ramírez as president. Perón was given the Ministry of War and, in July, appointed vice-president in addition to his other posts. This gave Perón considerable power, and he used it to win the support of organized labor, which had not fared well under previous military regimes. He moved to end the restrictive Law of Professional Associations that had limited union activity. He set up arbitration tribunals, which often ruled in favor of the workers. Existing labor legislation was finally being enforced consistently, and the workers were pleased with their new champion.

Perón freed jailed Communist labor leader José Peter, gave workers a 40 percent wage increase, the right to organize and negotiate, and paid holidays. More than two hundred agreements between employers and unions were signed, extending benefits to two million workers. In early October 1945 a new Law of Professional Associations was promulgated, recognizing the rights labor had won under Perón.

Later in October, after President Farrell announced elections for the following year, opposition to Perón increased among some military groups. Many did not like his policies toward labor, and others were scandalized by his public alliance with actress Eva Duarte, twenty years his junior. After Perón was arrested and held on a small island in the Río de la Plata, labor leaders began to organize a massive march to demand his freedom. These working-class supporters took off their shirts and waved them like banners, leading middle-class observers to refer to them disdainfully as "shirtless ones." The magnitude of support for Perón overwhelmed security, and the government was forced to produce Perón, who waved and encouraged the crowd. Later, Perón would claim the "shirtless ones" as his special followers.

Perón resigned from his government offices and became a candidate for the presidency. On February 24, 1946, he won a majority in the first freely contested elections in Argentina since 1928, and began his first term in office in June. During this first term Perón's accomplishments were many. Real wages of industrial workers increased by 20 percent between 1945 and 1948. Women were given the vote in 1947. Hostels were built for young working women, and vacation resorts were constructed for workers. The Perón administration built nearly 160 new schools, twelve hospitals, and low-cost apartments.

Perón's administration was proudly nationalistic. On July 9, 1947, Argentina's Independence Day, Perón declared national economic independence. His Five Year Plan, he said, was aimed at giving Argentina control over its own economic development. Internationally, Perón championed Argentina as a world leader. Juan Bramuglia, a lawyer for the railroad union, became foreign minister, and later served in the United Nations, where he defended Argentina's claims to the Falkland (Malvinas) Islands against an imperialist England, and explained Perón's Third Position. The latter was an early attempt to create a nonaligned movement, defending the position of smaller nations seeking to remain neutral in the Cold War.

Perón's wife, Evita, added to his popularity, especially through her charitable works. Slighted by the fashionable ladies who ran the country's largest charitable organization, Sociedad de Beneficencia, Evita had the government take it over. She became its head and opened an office in the old Department of Labor building, where she oversaw the disbursement of millions of dollars. Her door was open to the poor who came to plead for help. Evita's popularity made her one of the keys to Perón's success in his first presidency.

In March 1949 a new constitution guaranteed social justice for workers. Perón's ideas were described as *justicialismo*, a form of social justice, which listed a Bill of Rights for Labor. All Argentines had the right to: (1) work, (2) fair wages, (3) training, (4) good conditions in the workplace, (5) preservation of health, (6) well-being, (7) social security, (8) protection for the family, (9) economic improvement, and (10) defense of professional interests. The new constitution also permitted the direct election of senators, recognized the government's right to intervene in the economy, and allowed a sitting president to succeed himself, permitting Perón's reelection in 1951.

PERÓN THE TYRANT

While Perón's second presidency, in 1952–1955, does not present a rigid shift in his policies, it does mark a period of increasing tyranny as opposition to his regime mounted. From the beginning, however, Perón exhibited tendencies to treat harshly opponents he could not co-opt. When José Peter, head of the important metallurgic union, would not support Perón, Cipriano Reyes was given permission to create a more pliant union. Favors and recognition only went to those who showed their loyalty to Perón. In 1948, trumped-up charges of a plot to assassinate Perón and Evita led to the arrest of many political enemies and two priests who had preached against his regime. When a judge refused to accept the government's patently fictitious evidence, he was removed from the bench.

There were a number of abuses of power. Shortly after becoming president over a compliant congress, Perón accepted reinstatement in the military and simultaneous promotion to the rank of general. Perón purged the police force of political opponents, and intervened in previously autonomous universities by appointing trustees loyal to him. A new Peronist student organization was started to rival the existing student group.

Perón's monopolization of power was effective. Labor unions were obedient; the congress was a rubber stamp for his policies; and the popularity of his second wife, Evita, ensured control of the masses. Yet there was opposition. The military was adamantly opposed to the nomination of Evita for the vice-presidency in 1952. When she withdrew, it was for reasons of health, as she had been recently diagnosed with uterine cancer. Elements in the military were still unhappy at Perón's growing power. Although an abortive military coup in 1951 did not effect the outcome of that year's elections, many middle-class and wealthy Argentines had come to regard Perón's policies of industrialization as damaging to the country's traditional agricultural wealth.

Evita's death shortly after the June inauguration marked one turning point in Perón's presidency. Certainly the public outpouring of grief over the loss of what some called an Argentine saint, showed how important she had been to the image of the regime. Perón's subsequent attentions to young female athletes, and his alliance with fourteen-year-old Nelly Rivas, would become topics of scandal. But more important, changing economic conditions, especially after the Korean War, meant reduced revenues for Argentine exports, and increasing opposition to Perón's policies that favored industrial workers.

The centerpiece of Peron's economic policies was the Argentine Institute for the Promotion of Exchange (IAPI). This agency established prices the government would pay farmers for cereals and other agricultural exports. These prices were invariably below the world market price. When the government sold these commodities abroad, it made a handsome profit, which was used to finance industrial policies and better living standards for many Argentine workers. However, the wealthy landowners who produced much of Argentina's export crop were unhappy with this system and began to cut back on production. The combination of bad weather, fewer acres in production, and a fall in world prices, hit Perón's government hard.

As opposition mounted, Perón responded by closing down unfriendly newspapers, jailing (perhaps torturing) rival politicians, and attacking the Roman Catholic Church when it criticized his policies. In June 1955 a bloody, unsuccessful coup left scores of civilians dead as the presidential offices at the Casa Rosada were bombed by military planes. A second attack followed in September. Called the Liberating Revolution by its military leaders, this coup was successful. Perón refused to call out and arm the workers, claiming he wanted to spare the country civil war, and he fled the country.

SUGGESTIONS FOR FURTHER READING

Alexander, Robert J. *Juan Domingo Perón: A History*. Boulder, Colo.: Westview Press, 1979.

———. *The Perón Era*. New York: Columbia University Press, 1951.

Barager, Joseph R., ed. *Why Perón Came to Power: The Background to Peronism in Argentina*. New York: Alfred A. Knopf, 1968.

Crowley, Eduardo. *Argentina: A Nation Divided 1890–1980*. London: C. Hurst and Company, 1984.

Hodges, Donald C. *Argentina, 1943–1976: The National Revolution and Resistance*. Albuquerque: University of New Mexico Press, 1976.

Page, Joseph A. *Perón, A Biography*. New York: Random House, 1983.

Rock, David. *Argentina, 1516–1982*. Berkeley: University of California Press, 1985.

James A. Baer

Peter the Great

1672–1725

Emperor of Russia, 1689–1725

Peter the Great came to power at the beginning of the Age of Reason, an era of profound impact on Western history which questioned old assumptions, the relationships between the rulers and the ruled, and the known physical laws of the universe, which subsequently led to breakthroughs in science, social relations, and politics. What attracted Peter to the views of the Enlightenment, however, were not so much its philosophical principles as its utilitarian application designed to strengthen the state. Peter accomplished this with resounding success, and in the process transformed his realm into an empire of great stature.

Peter's reforms, however, did little to embrace the principles of the Enlightenment. Instead, they only served to underscore the differences between Russia and the West, particularly on social and political issues such as the question of serfdom. In Europe, serfdom was on the decline while in Russia the state took steps to strengthen it from above.

The tragedy of Peter's reign lies in the fact that his "westernization" of Russia, superficial at best, was achieved almost exclusively from above and served primarily the interests of the state. The state's control of every facet of Russia's reforms hampered the independent growth of interest groups, such as a bourgeoisie jealously guarding its privileges against the powers of the state. Peter's reign served to consolidate serfdom as well as to strengthen every aspect of autocratic rule to such a degree that Russia has continued to feel the weight of his heavy hand even to this day.

BIOGRAPHICAL BACKGROUND

Peter the Great, born on June 9, 1672, was the youngest son of Tsar Alexia and his second wife, Natalia Naryshkina. In 1682 the patriarch of Moscow and leading *boyars* (hereditary nobles) named him the new tsar instead of his older, mentally disturbed, half-brother Ivan, the offspring of the tsar's first marriage to Maria Miloslavskaia. This decision produced a deadly conflict between the Miloslavskii and Naryshkin families. Peter's half-sister, Sofia, organized the *streltsy* (literally, "shooters") who staged a bloody palace coup in which many of the Naryshkin family were cut down before the very eyes of the ten-year-old Peter. Sofia then crowned Peter and Ivan as co-tsars, but it was she who wielded political power.

Sofia exiled Peter to the village of Preobrazhenskoe near Moscow, where he surrounded himself with individuals disenchanted with Sofia's rule, particularly after her disastrous campaign against the Crimean Tatars (1687–1689). In 1689, units trained by Western officers seized the throne of Muscovy for seventeen-year-old Peter. Sofia was sent to a convent and power fell into the hands of Peter's mother. Peter finally assumed political control upon his mother's death in 1694.

Peter came to power at a time of intense conflict between nativist Russian forces and those who looked for guidance to Western institutions. Peter's exile at Preobrazhenskoe, away from the cultural and political influence of Moscow, proved to be decisive. There his restless and curious mind fell under the influence of Western officers, shipbuilders, and craftsmen who symbolized the superiority of Western technology.

The first significant event, which set the stage for the remainder of his reign, came in 1695 when Peter resumed a traditional Russian land campaign against the Ottoman Turks at Azov. He found out, however, that he needed to build a navy to conquer it. This he accomplished the following year by creating the first Russian navy *ex nihilo* and, in doing so, began his reorganization of Russian society. Peter then took his celebrated journey (1697–1698) to the West, which took him as far as England in the hope of obtaining an alliance against Turkey. When that fell through, he spent the remainder of his time trying to learn Western technology and to recruit craftsmen.

The first of his two sojourns to the West was cut short by a rebellion by the *streltsy*, who had been mobilized again by Peter's opponents, this time against his embrace of heretical, Western ways. Among the conspirators was his first wife, Evdokiia, the mother of the tsarevich Alexis, who was forced to become a nun. Muscovite society was becoming irrevocably split into Westernizers and Slavophiles.

The crowning glory of Peter's reign came when his reorganized forces avenged an earlier defeat at the hands of Charles XII of Sweden by defeating his army at Poltava in 1709 and his fleet in 1714. Peter's victories made possible a Russian presence on the Baltic Sea, notably the creation of a new capital, St. Petersburg. Peter was unable to settle the Polish and Turkish questions, but he set the course of Russian western and southern expansion for subsequent Russian rulers, from Catherine the Great to Joseph Stalin.

Peter tore Muscovite Russia from its ancient moorings, which brought him into conflict with the *boyars*, *streltsy*, cossacks, peasants, national minorities, the Russian Orthodox Church, the Old Believers, and even his own family. They all had to yield to and pay for Peter's overriding quest for centralization and the transformation of his state into a European power of consequence. When Peter suddenly died, on February 8, 1725, he left his indelible imprint on a society that was alternately proud and resentful of the price of imperial glory.

PETER AS A GREAT LEADER

When Peter came to power, Western influences had already been introduced by his father, Alexis, and his half-sister, Sofia. Russia's position, however, was reflected in the uncertainty of Alexis who, in the words of the historian V. O. Kliuchevskii, "firmly rested one foot on the native Orthodox ground and lifted the other to cross the boundary—and permanently remained in this uncertain position." It fell to Peter to take that fateful step over the boundary.

Peter's embrace of Western ideas was in part an historical accident, his exile to Preobrazhenskoe, where he came under the influence of westerners who had settled in Russia, notably the Dutchman Franz Timmermann, who taught him the basics of mathematics and navigation, and the Scot Patrick Gordon, who introduced him to the art of war in the Western manner. It was there that he trained his famous guard regiments, personally loyal to him.

At first, Peter's infatuation with Western technology remained without practical application. During his first military campaign, however, against the Turks at the port of Azov, he realized the need of a navy after he was unable to dislodge the Turks by land and had to stand by helplessly as they kept the port supplied by sea. It was at this point that the broad outlines of his thirty-one-year reign became recognizable: to build the Russian navy—during the five months of the winter of 1695–1696—he had to reorganize Russia. Shipyards were built, timber and other materials assembled, and foreign shipwrights, Russian carpenters, and tens of thousands of unskilled Russian laborers were gathered at Preobrazhenskoe and at Voronezh on the upper Don River. The result was the first Russian fleet of twenty-five armed galleys and thirty sea-going boats, both modeled after the Dutch pattern, as well as 300 transport barges and rafts. The fleet sailed as soon as the ice broke on the Don and in July Peter conquered Azov. The success at Azov whetted Peter's appetite for additional Western technology, and he sent fifty young men to the west, primarily to study shipbuilding.

In 1697, Peter himself set out on an eighteen-month journey to the West to create an alliance against the Ottoman Turks. The journey marked the first instance of a ruler of Moscow venturing abroad. Nothing, however, came out of this diplomatic initiative; but his "Grand Embassy" then acquired a new mission, to learn as much as possible from Western navigators, scientists, and philosophers and to hire over 750 Western artisans, mostly Dutchmen, to work in Russia.

Shortly after his return to Moscow, Peter turned to another foreign threat, that of Sweden in the north. The year 1700 saw the beginning of the "Great Northern War" of twenty-one-years' duration against Sweden's warrior king, Charles XII. In November 1700, at Narva on the southern shores of the Gulf of Finland, Charles' 8,500 highly trained and disciplined troops routed 45,000 Russian soldiers and gunned them down, in Charles' words, "like wild geese." Peter himself barely escaped capture. He refused, however, to acknowledge defeat. In defiance of all logic, in the spring of 1703, after dislodging a small Swedish force at the mouth of the Neva River, he founded a fortification with the Dutch name of Sankt-Piterburkh (later Germanized into Sankt-Peterburg). Peter's foreign policy throughout most of the rest of his reign focused on securing the defense of his "window to the West."

After the Battle of Narva, Charles turned toward Poland and thus gave Peter the breathing space he needed to rebuild and train his army in the Swedish style. The showdown came deep inside Russia, at Poltava in June 1709, where Peter's numerically superior, and this time disciplined, forces defeated the overextended Swedes. Charles barely managed to flee into Turkey. Peter, who had personally taken part in the battle, thanked his captured "teachers" for the "lessons" they had taught him.

The "glory of Poltava" had several consequences. It marked the beginning of the end of Sweden's imperial ambitions south of the Baltic and gave notice to the rest of Europe that Russia's isolation had ended. Peter began to establish diplomatic posts in the West, and by the time of his death, Russia had a foreign service comparable with any in Europe. The enhanced status of the House of Romanov eliminated the old resistance to marriage alliances. In the year after Poltava, Peter's niece Anna married the Duke of Courland, the first Russian princess in two centuries to marry a foreigner. In 1711 Peter's son, the tsarevich Alexis was married off to Charlotte of Brunswick-Wolfenbuettel, and in 1725 his daughter Anna married the Duke of Holstein-Gottorp, ironically, a nephew of Charles XII of Sweden.

For Peter, Poltava was "the final stone in the foundation of St. Petersburg." It was then that construction began in earnest. In 1712, it became the nation's capital and by the time of Peter's death, the city had 40,000 inhabitants. Peter eliminated the Swedish naval threat to St. Petersburg when, in May 1714, he led his own numerically superior navy against the Swedes off Cape Hango, a victory he considered as important as Poltava.

Peter learned more from the Swedes than the art of war. To finance and build his navy and army, Peter needed a modern, rational administration, if only for the reason of efficiently collecting ever higher taxes. He replaced the boyars' *duma*, a council of hereditary nobles, with a Senate that answered to him and governed in his absence. The fifty-odd *prikazy* (departments) were merged into ten colleges, to oversee the affairs of state.

Peter's service state, in which he was the first servant, demanded an educated elite. To that end, he founded the Academy of Sciences and other educational institutions. In 1714, he demanded that noblemen show proof of competence in geometry and mathematics before they were permitted to marry. In Peter's scheme of things, everyone had an obligation and he determined an individual's status by a Table of Ranks based on talent rather than birth as before.

Peter's system drew upon individuals of ability irrespective of background. Among those who rose to preeminent positions were the son of a groom, Alexander Menshikov; the peasant Ivan Pososhkov; the Ethiopian slave Hannibal; the Swiss Francis Lefort; the Jew Peter Shafirov; the Ukrainian archbishop Feofan Prokopovich; and his lowly-born Lithuanian second wife, Catherine. Those at the top, however, jealously guarded their positions and resented the newcomers. In 1723, 93 percent in the highest four ranks came from families that had held equivalent positions in Muscovite Russia. The greatest changes came in the lower ranks.

At the time of his death, Peter's Russia had become a power to be reckoned with. Its industry, notably metallurgy, and its armed might ranked among the leaders of Europe. The Swedish problem had been solved, and for the first time Russia was stronger than its old enemy Poland. Peter's territorial acquisitions were relatively small but significant. After the death of Charles XII (1718), the Swedish government finally signed the Treaty of Nystad (1721) by which it ceded in perpetuity all territory from Riga northeast to the source of the Neva River as well as eastern Karelia to the city of Vyborg. In 1721 the Senate bestowed on Peter the titles of "the Great" and "imperator" in recognition of the transformation of the Grand Duchy of Muscovy into the Russian empire. Peter then turned against the Persian empire and during 1722–1724 seized from it much of the Caspian shore, including the cities of Derbent, Resht, and Baku.

Peter, by the force of his personality, had transformed Russia. He brought his country into the concert of Europe, transformed the outlook of the ruling elite, and established military supremacy over his immediate neighbors to the west and north. It was no wonder that historians from disparate backgrounds such as the tsarist S. M. Soloviev (1820–1879), the liberal P. N. Miliukov (1859–1944), and the contemporary Soviet diplomatic historian N. N. Molchanov have sung his praises. Soloviev called him "the greatest leader in Russian history," and Miliukov saw him as the "first Russian revolutionary" who had torn down the old order and reconstructed it in his image. Molchanov praised Peter's intensification of "the country's development" as a "truly heroic achievement for the greatness, glory, and might of our country."

PETER THE TYRANT

The preparations for Peter's second Azov campaign, in 1696, revealed not only his organizational talent, but also the extraordinary financial, social, and human cost he was prepared to pay. Approximately one million individuals, out of a population of 12–13 million, were ultimately conscripted to realize his projects that ranged from the construction of canals and factories to the creation of the new capital in a northern swamp on the sixtieth parallel. But Peter's calculations took into account only the goals, not the hundreds of thousands who perished.

Peter's projects demanded vast sums of money, approximately 80 percent of which went for military expenditures. By the time of his death, the army consisted of 210,000 regulars, 110,000 supplementary troops, and 24,000 sailors, the largest in Europe in both absolute numbers as well in percentages of the population. Peter decreed that the church and its monasteries finance one fully rigged and armed ship for every 8,000 serf households it owned and civil landowners, one ship for every 10,000 households. When the merchants petitioned for relief from this burden, Peter immediately increased their number of ships. Peter taxed everything, beehives, bath houses, "un-German" dress by the townspeople, beards, and more. The poll tax of 1719 merged all peasants, free or serf, into one category: they all had the same duty, to pay the tax. The landlord became the tsar's tax collector and conscription agent with enhanced authority over the population. But as one of Peter's admirers, Ivan Pososhkov the author of *The Book of Poverty and Wealth* (1724), pointed out, the "direct owner" of the peasant was not the landowner, but "the autocrat of Russia" because the "landlord's Possession is a temporary one" and "the wealth of the peasantry is the wealth of the tsar." Peter also fused the nobility into one class by doing away with the distinction between *boyars* and serving nobles: they all became instruments of the state.

In the end, Peter increased taxes more than threefold to about 20 percent of income in a relatively poor nation. Kliuchevskii compared Peter to "a coachman who whips on his emancipated horse while pulling constantly at the reins." Peter's actions spawned the rebellions of Cossacks in the Ukraine under Ivan Mazepa (1708) and that by Kondrati Bulavin (1707–1708) along the Don.

Peter ruled through a mixture of divine right absolutism and enlightened despotism by virtue of his service to the state. His reforms produced a bitter reaction, not only because of the financial burden but also because they tore Russia from its foundation. Peter unabashedly embraced Western symbols—dress, architecture, language, calendar, foreign advisers—and openly ridiculed Russian ways, such as church ceremonies, without much concern for public opinion. His actions served to widen the divisions between an oppressed people and those who ruled them, the service gentry who had thrown in their lot with Peter, learning foreign tongues and affecting foreign ways.

The resistance was centered around the Russian Orthodox Church, whose political power Peter broke. In 1721 he abolished the office of the patriarch and placed the church directly under state control governed by the "Most Holy Governing Synod," which suggested a gathering of church dignitaries but was in reality a ministry of the state reporting directly to the tsar. The Old Believers, who had rejected the church reforms of the seventeenth century, joined the widespread resistance. Peter became the Antichrist (or its servant), an iconoclast, imposter, heretic, tyrant, blasphemer, Latinizer, the Magog of Ezekiel's prophecy, a German, a Swede, a Muslim in disguise. A full treatment of the opposition to Peter has yet to be written. It went well beyond Pososhkov's famous image of Peter pulling the chariot of state uphill while millions pulled in the opposite direction.

To deal with the resistance, Peter institutionalized Russia's secret policy agencies. The first was the *Preobrazhenskii Prikaz*, initially an administrative office of the Preobrazhenskii guard regiment, which in the 1690s had been given the task of restoring order after disturbances in Moscow. In 1696 it was granted jurisdiction throughout all of Russia to deal with political offenses, the most serious of which were treason and rebellion punishable by death, flogging, mutilation, or perpetual exile to Siberia. The records of the *Preobrazhenskii Prikaz* showed that by 1708 Peter faced a national resistance from all segments of society, an opposition that became an obsession with him.

In 1718, Peter created the chancellery for Secret Inquisitorial Affairs to deal with the case of his son Alexis. In 1690 he had welcomed his newborn son as another recruit for his army. He gave Alexis a Western education and married him off to a German princess. But the son, revolted by his father's forceful personality and Western ways, began to conspire with his father's opponents. Alexis fled abroad, only to be forcefully returned, imprisoned, condemned, and tortured to death at the hands of interrogators who had sought to determine the extent of the conspiracy. Peter's treatment of his son was widely perceived as a great scandal. He executed numerous high-ranking clergymen and demanded that priests violate the sanctity of the confessional. The chancellery continued in one form or another into the nineteenth century, after which it was replaced by other such agencies.

Peter's crowning glory was his foreign policy, but even here his legacy had a darker side. The capture of Azov, achieved at great cost, was undone after Poltava, when Peter pursued Charles XII only to be routed by the Turks at the Prut River. It was Peter who drew upon the blueprint for Russia's ambitious foreign policy beyond its eastern Slavic borders, a policy that continued well into the twentieth century, but generally with unhappy military, economic, social, and political consequences because it embroiled Russia in numerous conflicts with its neighbors, who feared the military tradition he had created. Peter was the first tsar to strike against Moldavia and Wallachia, and in the seven Turkish wars up to 1878, Russian armies followed his example in the Balkans. He was the first to call on Balkan Christians to rise against the Muslim Turks and join hands with the Russian liberators. He was the first to demand that Orthodox Christians, not Catholics, control the holy places in Jerusalem. To defend St. Petersburg, Russian governments needed to control Finland, which led to additional wars. His German marriages for his family only heightened anti-foreign sentiment and eventually gave Russia an essentially German ruling house.

Peter's overriding concern was the state; yet he failed to give it lasting stability. In 1682, as a boy of ten, he had been traumatized by the massacre of members of his family at the hands of the *streltsy*, the lawless representatives of medieval Russia. When the *streltsy* rose again while he was abroad in 1698, he quickly returned and broke their power by executing more than a thousand of them, beheading some with his own hands. After the death of his son, he proclaimed in 1722 that the ruler had the right to name his successor, but on his deathbed the stricken tsar proved unable to finish his command to "give everything." The guard regiments, which had served him in his rise to power, stepped into the political vacuum and it was they who arbitrarily determined for the next generation who should rule Russia. The supremacy of the guards not only made it possible for the nobles to free themselves from state service but resulted also in the renewal of political instability—often characterized by political murder—rather than continuity. After Peter's death the political pendulum swung wildly: Moscow once again briefly became the nation's capital and his supporters were disgraced. Menshikov was sent to Siberia and Pososhkov died in prison, as feuding families resumed their fight for political power.

Peter's misfortune was that he had not involved a larger number of people in his reforms. As a result, these reforms never reached the heart of Russian society. In effect, he created two nations, in which a Europeanized nobility kept the lower stratum in check by force and intimidation.

The finance minister of Tsar Nicholas I, Egor Kankrin, once declared that "we must be called not *Russians*, but *Petrovians*" and that the country "should be called *Petrovia*." Kankrin's "Petrovia," with its reliance on force, military might, secret police, arbitrariness, and an antagonistic relationship with the outside world, continued to exist until the end of the twentieth century.

SUGGESTIONS FOR ADDITIONAL READING

Cracraft, James. *The Church Reform of Peter the Great.* Stanford, Calif.: Stanford University Press, 1971.

Kliuchevsky, V. O. *Peter the Great.* New York: Vintage, 1961 (reissued, Boston: Beacon Press, 1984).

Massie, Robert K. *Peter the Great: His Life and Work*. New York: Alfred A. Knopf, 1980.

Miliukov, Paul, et al. *History of Russia, I: From the Beginnings to the Empire of Peter the Great*. New York: Funk & Wagnalls, 1968.

Riasanovsky, Nicholas V. *The Image of Peter the Great in Russian History and Thought*. New York: Oxford University Press, 1985.

Schuyler, Eugene. *Peter the Great, Emperor of Russia: A Study of Historical Biography*. 2 vols. New York: Russell & Russell, 1884.

Sumner, B. H. *Peter the Great and the Emergence of Russia*. London: English Universities Press, 1951.

———. *Peter the Great and the Ottoman Empire*. London: Blackwell, 1949.

Waliszewski, K. *Peter the Great*. New York: D. Appleton, 1987.

Harry Piotrowski

Pheidon

c. 600 B.C.

King of Argos, First Half of the Seventh Century B.C.

So rapid and remarkable were the changes happening in Greece around 700 B.C. that the time is known as the Age of Revolution. For 450 years, conditions in the Aegean had been dismal enough to win the title "Dark Age" for those centuries. Beginning about 1200 B.C., a number of factors ranging from climatic change to collapse of international trade to random raids by wandering groups ended the flourishing civilizations of the eastern Mediterranean. The entire region suffered, but Greece suffered perhaps most of all. In place of citadels like Mycenae commanding the wealth of kingdoms containing 200 villages and 50,000 people, tiny hamlets of a few acres and a handful of inhabitants now defined life for most. One important Dark Age town was home to fifteen souls in the eleventh century B.C. Since population had plummeted downward by 90 percent as a result of the difficulties, these hamlets were largely isolated from one another. Each member of the tiny communities lived, worked, and struggled like every other member.

From midpoint in the eighth century B.C., population rose dramatically; tiny villages in the near vicinity of one another were drawing—or being drawn—together into a single larger community; contact with other villages and with more distant, non-Greek cultures was flooding Greek imagination with knowledge of new ideas, institutions, and people. The end product would be the Classical Greek polis, or city-state.

Archaeological evidence shows that these developments began sooner in Argos than in many parts of Greece. By the eighth century B.C. there was noticeable growth in population in the village of Argos while outlying towns sharing the plain with Argos did not expand; some even declined. Argos had the advantages of a good water supply, a rugged citadel, and a strategic position through which people and products were likely to pass when entering or leaving the southern Peloponnese. It was also blessed with an especially clever leader. Within the expanding village of Argos, divisions based on wealth and influence took shape; some land-wealthy aristocratic families enjoyed far greater prominence than most people who were poor or even poverty-stricken.

BIOGRAPHICAL BACKGROUND

Pheidon began his career as a legitimate king and ended it as a tyrant. He altered his position deliberately, seeing a new sort of leadership in the world outside Greece and transplanting it to his own Greek state. In implementing his tyranny, he transformed the future of Classical Greece.

That career was as hereditary leader of the northern Peloponnesian city-state of Argos during the seventh century B.C., probably its first half. Two events quite securely associated with Pheidon—defeat of the Spartan army and presidency of the Olympic games—occurred in 669 and 668 B.C. While it is arguable that these events came at the start of Pheidon's career, it seems more likely that they were its capstone.

Pheidon belonged to the upper stratum in Argos, holding a specially privileged rank through his inherited position. The Greek word for his post is *basileus*, usually translated "king" but denoting a role more akin to a chief, recognized as preeminent for his wealth and lineage but most especially for his own competent leadership in war and in peace. He was, in Homeric terms, a "man of account in battle and in counsel." Pheidon's family was a kingly line of long duration: the first of the line was Temenos, and from him, succession passed to twelve descendants before coming to an end about 480 B.C. Pheidon's tenancy of this traditional position coincided with an auspicious time for even greater growth of his young state.

PHEIDON AS A GREAT LEADER

> The best of all land is the Pelasgian plain: best are the horses of Thrace, the women of Sparta, and the men who drink the water of fair Arethusa.
>
> But better still than these are the dwellers between Tiryns and Arcadia of the many sheep, the linen-corsleted Argives, the goads (or cattle spurs) of war.
>
> But you, men of Megara, are neither third nor fourth nor twelfth, nor of any place or account at all.[1]

Such is a list of typically good things of an anonymous poet. The poem was preserved in a Byzantine collection, but it reflects conditions of the seventh century B.C. The reference to the Argives as goads of war reflects a brief period of glory for that state. This sudden display of Argive strength is regularly associated with Pheidon, particularly to a military innovation known as the hoplite revolution. First to employ the new tactics, Argos gained a strong advantage over other Greek states.

Suddenly there were more soldiers, their equipment was better (and better matched), and they behaved in new ways on the battlefield. In place of individual combats between champions of the states at war, less wealthy and less prominent adult males took their places in side-by-side formations several ranks deep. Equipped alike, each soldier was supposed to wear greaves, a corselet, and a helmet, to grasp a small, round shield (hoplon) in his left arm, and to carry both a long stabbing-spear and a short stabbing-sword. Battle doctrine required that formation stay tight and try to push back—to overpower and perhaps rupture—the opposing front line, not to kill the opponents but to cause them to break formation and run away. Looking rather like a porcupine, a formation of hoplites advanced steadily and in unison, each member attempting to thrust his spear above or below the shield of the enemy hoplite opposite him. As warriors in the front rank fell, those behind stepped forward to fill the space. These tactics became the basis of Greek warfare for the rest of antiquity, but when newly introduced, they brought unexpected repercussions.

Many of those repercussions were internal to each individual state. Hoplite warfare required greater numbers than individual combat, which had been the duty and privilege of the heads of wealthier, more prominent families. Nearly equals of the king, the aristocrats of most states were increasingly able to limit kingly power during the seventh century B.C. In Argos, however, Pheidon recognized the value of the support he could win for himself through the creation of a sizable, equipped force of non-elite members of the community. In his inherited position, Pheidon was able to undertake the innovation, strengthening his own station in the process. Other important Argive families were among the first to experience limitations to their established role.

The military revolution also points to economic change. While hoplite equipment was not extremely costly, it was beyond the means of most people living during the impoverished centuries of the Greek Dark Age. What specialization there was in the Dark Age was likely practiced by a few traveling craftsmen. Greater, permanent diversification required more than self-subsistence agriculture on small family plots. An early turn in Argos to production of simple goods like olive oil and textiles for trade may have provided the base for specialization required to provide equipment for the newly created hoplites. A hundred or more hoplites needing new or replacement arms could easily occupy the full attention of several metalsmiths.

Military and economic changes seem to come together in Argos early in the seventh century B.C. Beyond the poetic list of good things, archaeological evidence has provided a bronze breast plate of the hoplite sort, discovered in an Argive grave dated to the eighth century B.C., and although the hoplite shield is likely to have originated outside of Greece, it was later thought to be an Argive invention. The economic vitality suggested by the equipping of hoplites is apparent in yet another innovation: The ancients often granted the honor of minting the first Greek coins to the city of Argos, during the rule of Pheidon. A report deriving from the first century A.D. explained, "Pheidon of Argos was the first man of all to mint coin [and he did so] in Aegina. Distributing the coin and taking back the spits he dedicated them to Argive Hera."

We shall probably never know whether Pheidon was able to introduce such innovations because he had strengthened his inherited position or whether the innovations gave him greater power. What is clear is that Pheidon was clever and that he had the advantage of a model. In fact, recovery for the entire Greek world was quickened by contact with considerably more advanced cultures of the eastern Mediterranean. In the early decades of rejuvenation, much of the impetus came from the kingdom of Lydia just east of the Greek states along the coast of Asia Minor. A line of strong monarchs pushed that kingdom to new heights of prosperity and power in the seventh and early sixth centuries B.C. Herodotus stated in a matter-of-fact tone: "The Lydians were the first people we know of to use a gold and silver coinage and to introduce retail trade" (I.94). True coinage accelerated trade and commerce, but an early use by the Lydian kings was as a means of paying troops, for Lydia's power rested on military strength.

There are grounds for believing that Pheidon of Argos learned of the triad of Lydian strength—massed infantry force, a standard of wealth, and unbridled kingly power—through friendship with the Greek polis of Miletus on the other (eastern) side of the Aegean. Sensing their advantages for his own small mainland state, he implemented them. Pheidon and his Argive hoplites became the "goads of war" attempting to recover, first, the "heritage of Temenos," essentially the northern and eastern Peloponnese, and, then, the entire "inheritance of Herakles," or the full Peloponnese. In the process, the Argives seized Olympia from the Eleans and celebrated the games under Argive presidency; defeated the Spartans at Hysiae, south of Argos; intervened in civil disturbances in Corinth; may have aided Corinth's neighbor, Megara; and probably engaged in a struggle among Aegina, Athens, and Epidaurus. In every instance, Argive presence was decisive.

PHEIDON THE TYRANT

In making Argos a massive little power, Pheidon created a nontraditional image of his town and of himself. It was Aristotle who remarked that Pheidon began as a king and ended as a tyrant, Greece's first tyrant. The word for "king" (*basileus*) has roots that extend back to the Mycenaean Age; the word for "tyrant" (*tyrannos*), by contrast, was a recent borrowing, apparently imported from the wealthy Asia Minor kingdom, Lydia. Its earliest recorded use in a Greek source occurs in a lyric poem of the seventh-century warrior-poet Archilochus, who sang proudly that

For Gyges' gold I do not care
I do not envy him or dare
High heaven, nor lust for tyrannis
Far from my eyes are things like this.[2]

For Greek states in the seventh and early sixth centuries B.C. just emerging from five centuries of isolation and poverty, Lydia was the nearest representation of unimaginable wealth and power. The thin ribbon of Greek states stretching along the western coast of modern Turkey began to feel the pressure of Asian Lydia pressing its way toward the sea from the high country just at their backs. From the middle of the seventh century B.C., Lydian armies began marching on the territory of the Greek states. The person commanding the wealth and might of these armies was like nothing in Greece: he was no *basileus* but a kind of leader without Greek counterpart.

In later antiquity such powerful figures were more common, so that Greek philosophers sought to define the nature of their power. For Aristotle there were two forms of tyranny that rested on consent, and a third that was simply a rule of force exercised by a single person who is unlimited by anyone or anything. In Aristotle's view, Pheidon's possession of military superiority in the hoplite phalanx was the key to his new position of power. With this tool, he was freed from limitations by his aristocratic peers, and since he utilized this superiority to recover "ancestral domains," he aggressively directed Argive power against other states.

When the island state of Aegina (situated in the gulf between the Peloponnese and Attica) grew in naval strength, it became embroiled with the Athenians who sailed against Aegina. Argive aid to the Aeginetans brought defeat of the Athenians. Perhaps to the Aeginetans' dismay, Pheidon took control of their state, where, traditionally, he coined the first Greek silver coinage. There is a strong belief that Pheidon attempted to annex nearby Corinth, without success, and met his death when participating in civil strife in Corinth. Certainly the hostility between Argos and Sparta, further south in the Peloponnese, was real and persistent. The northern Peloponnesian state of Sicyon, too, probably felt the hand of Pheidon's Argives. Some modern scholars have even seen Pheidon's Argive hoplites as participants in a whole series of wars extending to Greek states of the eastern Aegean, particularly Samos and Miletus.

Indirect confirmation of Pheidon's far-reaching tyrannical power comes in political and military developments beginning about the middle of the seventh century B.C., when evidence points to the widespread adoption of hoplite tactics and the rise to power of individuals with unlimited power. Only by following the Argive military model were neighboring states able to hold their own against the "goads of war." And the adoption of hoplite tactics required a champion who could withstand the conservative aristocratic elements of his own state. Tyrants appeared in Corinth, Epidaurus, Megara, and Sicyon; there was an attempt at tyrannical control in Athens while the Spartans become avid tyrant-deposers. All these states had felt the might of Pheidon.

Pheidon's imitators were not slow to realize the advantage of massed infantry, even if the first effect was only to preserve the territorial integrity of their states against an aggressor like Argos. Also clear were the possibilities of extending boundaries. Pheidon's career provided both the pattern and the need for similar developments in neighboring states. By following his example, the younger generation of tyrants ended the advantage of the linen-corsleted Argives, the goads of war.

Pheidon met his death in the flurry of innovation that he initiated: it is thought that he died fighting in the civil war in Corinth that produced that state's first tyrant.

NOTES

1. *Palatine Anthology*, translated by W. R. Paton, vol. 5, Loeb Classical Library (New York: G. P. Putnam, 1918).
2. Translated by Colin Edmonson for this author.

SUGGESTIONS FOR ADDITIONAL READING

There is no full account of Pheidon and his career either ancient or modern. Several of the developments attributed to Pheidon are in a forthcoming book: Carol G. Thomas and D. P. Wick, "Croesus and Coinage," *Decoding Ancient History: A Toolkit for the Historian as Detective*. Englewood Cliffs, N.J.: Prentice-Hall, 1994. I am grateful to David Wick for his suggestions on this discussion. They have enlivened it and made it more intelligible.

Andrews, A. *The Greek Tyrants*. New York: Harper & Row, 1963.

Bradeen, D. W. "The Lelantine War and Pheidon of Argos." *Transactions of the American Philological Association* 78 (1947): 223–241.

Kagan, Donald. "Pheidon's Aeginetan Coinage." *Transactions of the American Philological Association* 91 (1960): 121–136.

Kelly, Thomas. *A History of Argos to 500 B.C.* Minneapolis: University of Minnesota Press, 1976.

Tomlinson, R. A. *Argos and the Argolid: From the End of the Bronze Age to the Roman Occupation*. Ithaca, N.Y.: Cornell University Press, 1972.

Carol G. Thomas

Philip II of Habsburg
1527–1598

King of Spain, 1556–1598

In the English-speaking countries, King Philip II has become the embodiment of the Black Legend of Spain. He is portrayed as a king dressed in funereal black, sleeping with a coffin in his bedroom to remind himself of inevitable death. This is the spectral monster who is described as sending the Spanish Armada to crush English and Dutch Protestantism in 1588.

Another facet of the same distorted history blames Philip for the 270 Protestants burned at the stake during his four-year marriage to Mary Tudor of England. That legend overlooks the fact that Philip actually tried to restrain that slaughter, and if the queen is called "Bloody Mary" the blame might be better assigned to Reginald, Cardinal de la Pole, Archbishop of Canterbury.

Philip is variously described as deliberately refusing to visit his wife and to give her the child she so desperately wanted, while offering his adulterous love to continental paramours. It is much closer to the truth to observe that he used Mary's insistence on his company as a means of forcing her to commit England to a bootless war against France, in which England lost Calais.

All of these half-truths might be better understood if Philip could be seen as a classic obsessive-compulsive personality, convinced that his will, the good of the state, and divine providence were one and the same.

BIOGRAPHICAL BACKGROUND

Philip was born on May 21, 1527, at Valladolid in Castile, the largest part of a Spain united by his maternal great-grandparents, Ferdinand of Aragon and Isabella of Castile. His parents were Princess Juana of Portugal and the Holy Roman Emperor, Charles V (1519–1556), who by inheritance through his mother and her parents had been king of Spain since 1516. From his father and paternal grandparents, Charles had become not only

Holy Roman emperor but lord of what are now approximately the Benelux countries, then called the Low Countries or the Netherlands, as well as the county of Franche-Comté (now in eastern France). As Spanish king, Charles also ruled large parts of southern Italy. During his reign he added the north Italian Duchy of Milan to his territories, while the conquests of Cortes and Pizarro enormously enlarged his American lands and Magellan's voyage added the Philippines to the world's first truly global empire. However, as a result of all this, Charles found himself in intermittent warfare with the French, thanks to mutually incompatible claims to some of these European territories, the German Lutherans of the empire, and the Ottoman (Turkish) Empire in the Mediterranean. With significant differences in detail, Philip II was to be similarly embroiled.

With Charles frequently away to visit his various domains and war with his enemies, Philip was raised by his mother and several governors and tutors; the latter came from the high aristocracy and educated clergy. He had two younger sisters and later an illegitimate half-brother, Don Juan. With his mother's death in 1539, Philip began attending meetings of royal councils. In 1543 he married his cousin, Maria Manuela of Portugal, who died two years later in giving birth to their son, Don Carlos. From the mid-1540s, Charles had Philip visit the Netherlands, recognized him as heir to some of his possessions besides Castile, and composed sets of written instructions for his son on kingship. During 1551–1554, Philip acted as Charles' regent for all Spain while the emperor conducted his final war with the French and Lutherans in the north. In that last year, as part of his father's diplomacy he married Mary Tudor, queen of England, thus surrounding France by an Anglo-Spanish-imperial alliance. That crumbled with Mary's death in 1558 and the Protestant Elizabeth's succession to the throne of her childless sister.

In the meantime, in 1556 Charles abdicated all his titles. His younger brother, Ferdinand, received the imperial throne and the Austrian Habsburg lands, derived from their father's legacy. Philip II as king of Spain was awarded not only the Spanish-based Italian and American domains, but the Netherlands and Franche-Comté. While most of the latter lands technically lay within the Holy Roman Empire, they had long been economically linked to Spain and they also gave Philip territory north and east of his hereditary French enemy. The fragmentation of the German states of the empire and the serious land-based Ottoman threat on Austria's southeast frontier explain Charles' decision to separate those states from Spain.

While Charles had wound down his struggle with the German Lutherans, he left Philip a continuing war with the French. For all Spain's wealth, bankruptcy was unavoidable by 1557. The continuing range of Philip's commitments and expenses, for all the American treasure and fiscal bleeding of Castile especially, is shown by his similar bankruptcies in 1575 and

1597. The first, noted above, contributed to the making of peace with France in 1559, celebrated by Philip's marriage to the French princess, Elizabeth of Valois. That treaty sealed the long-term domination of the Italian peninsula by Spain. The other reason to the end the war was to free Philip to respond to the growth of Protestantism in its Calvinist form in the Netherlands as well as a transient Protestant "scare" in several Castilian cities. Like his father, Philip was convinced that if religious unity ended, state and society would fall into chaos and violence.

The 1560s were difficult for Philip. He mandated religious reforms for the Netherlands to combat heresy and extend greater central control over those seventeen separate provinces. However, they inspired both Calvinist militancy and resistance from local, usually Catholic elites, setting the stage for the subsequent Dutch Revolt which began definitively in 1572. Turkish and North African Muslim piratical actions threatened the western Mediterranean, but in this area Spain was successful in checking the Ottomans and their North African satellites at Lepanto in 1571. France fell into religious and civil war until the century's end. While that neutralized her as Spain's traditional foe, French Calvinists' sympathy toward and occasional support of the Dutch Calvinist rebels was a dangerous prospect for Philip. Near the end of the period a Calvinist member of the royal family was the legitimate French king; that drove Philip to involve Spain directly in France's internal affairs with ultimately counterproductive consequences. In 1568 his wife Elizabeth, who had given him two daughters, died, as did his mentally impaired son from his first marriage. Now past forty, the king had to be anxious about the royal succession as Aragon did not allow female rule. In that same year, in the Spanish south, the Granada Moriscos, thinly Christianized Muslims, rose against new attempts to bring them to Christian order. Fortunately for Philip they received neither alliance nor support from their African coreligionists, but it took two years of hard fighting before Spanish armies, led by Philip's half-brother, Don Juan, subdued them. That triumph led to Don Juan commanding the allied Christian fleet at Lepanto the next year. Last but not least, all through the 1560s and 1570s relations with England steadily deteriorated. Some of Philip's envoys to London involved themselves in schemes to assassinate Elizabeth and replace her with her Catholic cousin, Mary Stuart. The English occasionally aided the Dutch rebels, covertly and later overtly (as well as the French Calvinists), raided Spanish Atlantic shipping, and from Philip's point of view, were unhappily reducing the numbers of English Catholics by various means.

In 1570 he married Anna of Austria, his niece, who in 1578 provided him at last with an heir, the future Philip III. From the 1570s until well past Philip's own death the Dutch Revolt raged on. By the end of his reign it was already clear that Spain could not reconquer the increasingly Calvinist northern provinces, which became the Dutch Republic (or United Provinces), any more than the "rebels" could dislodge Spain from an increasingly Catholic south, the Spanish Netherlands, the future Belgium. Given Dutch commercial, financial and maritime successes, that was to have grave economic consequences for Spain, which had been so closely connected to and reliant upon those lands partly in lieu of structural weaknesses in these areas at home.

The Portuguese royal family had died out in the direct line by 1580, and through his mother, Philip had the best claim to the country's throne. By 1581 he had consolidated his position, while promising considerable autonomy to his new subjects. This accession also made him ruler of Portugal's own global empire from Brazil to parts of Africa and southeast Asia. On one hand it appeared to many that Philip was threateningly poised to be a "universal monarch," and indeed, Portuguese ships were to be a significant component of the Armada. But in fact the acquisition added new responsibilities, commitments, and above all, expenses, to Spain's already formidable array of similar demands.

The "cold war" with England became a "hot" one during 1584–1585. Diplomatic relations were severed and England moved quickly to support the Dutch formally, especially after the murder of William of Orange, their leader, by a Spanish agent, while stepping up attacks on Spanish shipping. With Mary Stuart's execution in 1587 by Elizabeth's government, a Catholic succession was gone; Mary's Protestant son, the future James I, would succeed to the English throne later. Philip and his advisers were convinced that unless England was at least neutralized, the Dutch would never be subdued and the French and other continental Protestants would always have a Protestant power to look to. Thus the Armada was launched in 1588; its total defeat was a guarantee of Dutch independence and gave heart to European Protestants, while maintaining English freedom of action.

The 1590s saw Philip's twilight and in many ways failure. An expensive intervention in French affairs ended in a treaty in 1598 that withdrew Spain from France and recognized Henry IV as king; he had, however, converted to Catholicism in 1593, which began to undercut the rationale for Philip's actions, which included promoting a claim to the French throne for his older, half-French daughter. At home, in 1591–1592 he had to put down a revolt in Aragon, triggered by resentment at Castilian dominance. As he lay dying on September 13, 1598, he knew that he was leaving a Spain bankrupt and strained to its fiscal limits albeit still a great power by any contemporary criteria, but in the hands of an incompetent teen-ager, already dominated by his chief adviser.

PHILIP II AS A GREAT LEADER

There is no question that Philip II was the dominant ruler in Europe during the second half of the sixteenth century, the traditional Anglo-American view of Elizabeth I of England notwithstanding. Contemporaries certainly understood that, the English included. The vast extent of Philip's domains coupled with his seemingly inexhaustible resources dictated that even if he had lacked his intelligence, industry, and conscientiousness in carrying out his duties, anyone in his position had to be a major figure on the continent at that time.

Spaniards called him "the prudent king." That reflected not only the character traits mentioned above but Philip's extreme attention to all the details of government, large and small, and his high sense of justice. Following his revered father's advice, he never allowed a single individual or faction at court to dominate him personally, much less shape and control policies. Rather, he consulted with them, balanced them against one another in terms of royal favor, and made the key decisions himself. At the same time, as was customary then in Catholic countries, high-ranking members of the clergy bureaucratically served the king, as did many from the lesser nobility and bourgeoisie. So while Philip often deliberated at seemingly inordinate length, he consulted widely, and had an administration sufficiently representative of those who counted socially and politically, to retain the esteem in which his Spanish subjects held him. By controlling all this, he avoided the pitfalls of weak monarchy that had characterized much of the previous century in Spain and which marked France during Philip's own times.

Philip's sense of justice is perhaps best revealed by his handling of his first son, Don Carlos. As that young man grew, his mental instability increased; shortly before his death in 1568 the king confined him. Even if Carlos had not died, it seems certain Philip would have not allowed him to succeed to the throne. That he did pass away suddenly and mysteriously was a public scandal, to which the king responded with great reserve. It was clear, despite emerging myths about this sad event, that Philip acted from necessity and justice—toward his subjects—in handling what must have been an exceptionally painful matter.

Philip saw himself as the secular-military arm of Catholicism against the forces of Protestantism, a belief that resonated among many Spaniards. That his means of executing that goal usually coincided with Spanish national interest and not always with those of other Catholic leaders, such as the popes and lay Catholic rulers, seems to have been irrelevant to Philip. Thus the naval victory over the Turks at Lepanto, led by Spain, was seen in just that light in the struggle against Islam. National support for the sending of the Armada was enthusiastic. Clearly, Philip's subjects shared that view.

Despite the Inquisition's continuing efforts to mold Spain into a society marked by religious unity and social conformity, the age of Philip II was an integral part of the "Golden Age," culturally and artistically, as the name Cervantes shows. During the 1570s and 1580s particularly there was some easing of these pressures, which allowed for the great flowering of

Spanish Catholicism, exemplified by St. Teresa of Avila and St. John of the Cross, among others. There is no question that the king played a key role in this, with his appointments of sympathetic Inquisitors-General and his own understanding of the faith. Furthermore, the king was a sophisticated connoisseur of the arts, as the building of the Escorial and his artistic patronage indicate.

It is also worth mentioning that Philip's reign saw the increasing of royal administrative control over the Americas and some reduction of white settlers' freedom to abuse the Indians. Within certain "colonial" limits, Philip's notions about justice included protecting the natives from the worst excesses at the colonists' hands. He also demonstrated paternal care for their religious well-being, if on Spanish terms alone; thus the institutionalization of the church in the Americas and evangelization were consistently supported by him.

PHILIP II THE TYRANT

Although Philip inherited the Inquisition from his predecessors, he supported it warmly. Equally, the demographic collapse of the native American peoples was well under way when he ascended the throne in 1556. Nor did he initiate violent Catholic-Protestant confrontations. But to many contemporaries and until fairly recently outside Spain, Philip was viewed as an absolutist tyrant.

This is best shown in the *Apology* of William of Orange, the great Dutch leader, in 1581. In addition to presenting a powerful argument for rejecting Spanish sovereignty, William recounted the works of others who had assailed Spain—and Philip—for the treatment of the Indians, the persecution of Spain's Moriscos and the Inquisition's never-ending operations. This pamphlet, ghost-written by William's advisers, had a wide circulation throughout Protestant Europe; the rounding-up, trials, and executions of the minuscule number of native Spanish Protestants in Philip's early years did not go unnoticed either.

The *Apology* crystallized the collection of rumors that had floated about concerning the circumstances surrounding Philip's first son and his death in 1568. Now Don Carlos was depicted not only as fully competent to succeed his father, but sympathetic to Netherlanders' attitudes on political autonomy and religious pluralism, which Philip so resoundingly rejected. Furthermore, the son was in love with his youthful stepmother, Elizabeth of Valois, who reciprocated that emotion. Don Carlos was betrayed by a confidant in Philip's service and done away with as an act of state. This wildly erroneous view had a long history, as much later romantic drama (Schiller) and opera (Verdi) shows.

As a result of violence against Catholics and a challenge to Philip's regent in the Netherlands in 1566–1567, he sent a Spanish army under his best general, the duke of Alba, to restore order and religious uniformity. A so-called Council of Blood supervised the hunting-down of heretics and rebels; some of the highest-ranking nobles were executed as customary aristocratic status and privilege were overridden. Such measures, accompanied by efforts (with varying success) to increase the provincial taxes, led to the enduring and successful revolt beginning in 1572. In the mid-1570s the fighting was especially fierce. Towns resisting Alba's army were treated brutally if and when they finally surrendered. That not only stiffened the will of many other cities and regions but contributed to the blackening of both Philip and his country. By the 1580s the long-lasting "Black Legend" of Spain was well in place: a powerful land ruled by an austere fanatic, dedicated to dominating the continent, if not the globe, politically and religiously. The annexation of Portugal, interference in French internal and dynastic affairs, and sailing of the Armada were all seen in that light by many then and since.

SUGGESTIONS FOR ADDITIONAL READING

Elliott, John H. *Imperial Spain, 1469–1716*. Reprint. New York: Penguin, 1991.

Kamen, Henry. *Spain, 1469–1714*. London: Longman, 1983.

Grierson, Edward. *King of Two Worlds: Philip II of Spain*. New York: G. P. Putnam's Sons, 1974.

Lovett, A. W. *Early Habsburg Spain, 1517–1598*. New York: Oxford University Press, 1986.

Lynch, John. *Spain under the Habsburgs. Vol. 1, 1516–1598*. 2nd ed. New York: New York University Press, 1984.

Mattingly, Garrett, *The Armada*. Boston: Houghton Mifflin, 1959.

Merriman, Roger B. *Rise of the Spanish Empire in the Old World and the New. Vol. 4, Philip the Prudent*. New York: Macmillian, 1934.

Parker, Geoffrey N. *Philip II*. Boston: Little, Brown, 1979.

Pierson, Peter O. *Philip II of Spain*. London: Thames and Hudson, 1975.

Rule, John and John Te Paske, eds. *The Character of Philip II*. Boston: D. C. Heath, 1963.

Paul J. Hauben

Abd al-Karim Qassem

1914–1963

Ruler of Iraq, 1958–1963

In 1916, in the worst year of World War I, Britain had sent an agent to Cairo to open negotiations with the Sherif of Mecca, hereditary protector of the Moslem holy cities of Mecca and Medina. The British hoped that by supporting a Hashemite prince, descended from Mohammed, they could raise an Arab revolt against the Ottoman Turks, whose Sultan was styled *Caliph ul-Islam* or Commander of the Faithful. The Sherif was led to believe that he would be the sovereign of a great Arab kingdom after such a victorious struggle. The difficulty lay in the fact that Britain had secretly agreed to divide the Arabic-speaking lands with France under the terms of the Sykes-Picot Treaty. The British had also long been in negotiations with the World Zionist Organization and had ultimately offered public support for a Jewish homeland in Palestine, on November 2, 1917, under the terms of the Balfour Declaration.

In a twist of supreme irony, the Hashemites found themselves evicted from Mecca and Medina by an obscure Arab rival, Ibn Saud, and then thrust out of Syria by the French. The British therefore attempted a partial fulfillment of their wartime pledge. The Treaty of San Remo in 1920 had given France dominion in Syria and Lebanon. Britain had received Palestine and Iraq. None of these geographic expressions, in the past, had been legally defined terms. Therefore, boundaries were drawn without regard to such obvious considerations as the unity of river systems, or the effect of mountains on the natural boundaries of countries.

The British attempted to satisfy two of their old wartime pledges by dividing the lands that had fallen to their share at San Remo. Palestine west of the Jordan was opened to Jewish settlement. Palestine east of the Jordan became the Kingdom of Transjordan under the Hashemite Prince Abdallah. Iraq was awarded to Abdallah's brother Faisal, thereby enthroning two Hashemite kings under British protection.

In Iraq the British attempted to establish a British-style constitutional monarchy. From the beginning, however, there were rejectionist pressures against this entirely foreign institution.

At the advent of World War II, Iraqi nationalists attempted to lead the country into the German-Italian camp. Only decisive British military force prevented that triumph for Hitler. British victory in 1945 did not reconcile the Iraqis to London's domination.

In the decade after World War II, the bewildering array of parties arose to contest for leadership of the country. The *Ba'th* Arab nationalist socialists found themselves contesting the claims, or cooperating closely, by turns, with cliques of army officers, with Communists, or with religious or ethnic parties representing Sunni or Shi'ite Muslims, with Kurds, or even with clan or tribal groups.

BIOGRAPHICAL BACKGROUND

Abd al-Karim Qassem was born in Mahdiyya, a poor quarter of Baghdad, on December 21, 1914, the youngest of the three sons of Qassem bin Muhammed bin Bakr. His father was a Sunni Arab and his mother was descended from a clan of Shi'ite Kurds who had migrated from Iran to Iraq. Although the family was poor, subsisting on the father's income as a small grain and sheep dealer, Qassem attended a government elementary school and later received a scholarship for his secondary school education. He taught elementary school after he graduated, but decided upon a military career in 1932, when the newly independent government of Iraq began recruiting lower- and middle-class recruits for officer candidate school. Qassem graduated from the Iraqi Military College in 1934 as a second lieutenant, finished the Staff College course with high grades in 1941, and went on to pass a senior officers' course in Britain in 1950.

He saw action during the Iraqi tribal revolts of 1935, and seems to have been promoted after Bakr Sidqi, a Kurdish officer, seized control of the government the following year, initiating the first of a series of military coups that would plague Iraqi politics. He was not, however, involved in the pan-Arab revolt against the British in 1941, which resulted in the removal of pan-Arab nationalists from the Iraqi officer corps. Qasssem served against Israel in 1948–1949 and was stationed in Mafraki, Jordan, during the Suez crisis of 1956.

By then, a brigadier commander, Qassem had also become politically involved. Acknowledged as head of the Iraqi Free Officers movement, a small, clandestine group in existence perhaps as early as 1952, Qassem began plotting to overthrow the monarchy. He and his co-conspirators were dissatisfied with British influence in Iraqi politics. Although Iraq had become independent in 1932, the British, who had ruled the country as a mandate after 1921 and suppressed the pro-Axis revolt in 1941, remained the power behind the Iraqi throne. The Free Officers opposed Iraq's pro-

Western stance and its association with the Baghdad Pact. The latter had been created by the Western powers as a bulwark against the Soviet Union to the north, and Egypt's new president, Gamal Abd al-Nasser, to the south. Iraqis were impressed with Nasser, who not only proclaimed a policy of political nonalignment, but accepted arms from Communist Czechoslovakia, denounced the Baghdad Pact, nationalized the Suez Canal, and transformed his military defeat by Britain, France, and Israel at the Suez Canal into a propaganda victory, emotionally exciting to the Arab world.

Two years later, in 1958, during a distracting political crisis in Lebanon, the Free Officers seized their opportunity to topple the Iraqi government. Fearing for his throne if the violence spread to Jordan, King Hussein requested military assistance from his cousin, King Faisal II of Iraq. Ordered to proceed to Amman, Jordan, Qassem's troops headed for Baghdad instead. They took the radio station and the royal palace, killing the young king and his uncle, the Crown Prince. Prime Minister Nuri al-Sa'id, the mainstay of Iraq's pro-British policy, was murdered while escaping through the streets of Baghdad disguised as a woman.

Having achieved power, however, Qassem had no incisive plan for a government and the Free Officers were divided over their support of Nasser as the pan-Arab leader of the Arab world, or of an independent, nationalist Iraq. In the end, this political struggle was to dominate Qassem's rule and to prevent the implementation of the domestic reform that could have made him a truly great leader. Most of the dilemmas faced by Qassem still plague modern Iraq.

QASSEM AS A GREAT LEADER

Once in power, Qassem set an independent foreign policy for Iraq. No longer pro-West, Iraq was now to be neutral in the East-West struggle for the Middle East. He took Iraq out of the Baghdad Pact and sought military and economic aid from the Soviet Union.

He sought to unify the country through a program of social and economic reform. Considering the Bakr Sidqi coup as the formative event in his life, Qassem saw in the success of the Kurdish rebel, Bakr Sidqi, the possibility of including more of Iraq's diverse ethnic and religious groups in the political process than the Sunni Muslim Arabs that had dominated the monarchy. From 1921 until 1958, the Sunni military officers that had fought with King Faisal I in World War I, their relatives, and the Shi'ite and Sunni tribal landowners had controlled Iraqi politics and the economy. The poorer class of Shi'ites and Kurds, together, made a substantial majority of Iraq's population, after the virtual expulsion of Iraq's Jewish middle class, when the state of Israel came into being. That new majority supported the revolutionary regime. Now Qassem, an officer from the wrong side of Baghdad, had the opportunity not only to set Iraqi foreign policy right in nationalist terms, but to improve the lot of poor Iraqis.

Supported by the Iraqi Communist Party, which had been suppressed under the monarchy, Qassem moved to help the urban poor by lowering rents, permitting trade unions, reducing income taxes, shortening the work day to eight hours, and initiating new housing and slum clearance projects. Economic plans on the Soviet model were proposed, and after bitter negotiations, Qassem began the process of creating an independent Iraqi oil company by depriving the IPC (Iraq Petroleum Company) of its total control of that resource. The additional oil royalties were earmarked for expanded health services and education. The number of schools was increased dramatically, the University of Baghdad established, and women were encouraged to enter the professions of teaching and nursing. Disputes regarding family status and inheritance were treated in secular rather than religious courts. Women became equal to men in matters of inheritance.

In the countryside, peasants were to be subject to Iraqi law instead of the landlord's jurisdiction, and were not condemned to servitude because of debt. Water and rural electrification projects were begun, and an Agrarian Reform Law began the process of land redistribution. Because of the sheer enormity of the project, and the government's lack of the bureaucratic apparatus to implement it, the program only began to take effect by 1961.

It was too late. Three years after his accession to power, Qassem had already lost the ability to rule effectively. Increasingly, his goal became merely to remain in power, as the political support that had enabled him to take control in 1958 had not only evaporated, but had actively turned against him.

QASSEM THE TYRANT

Qassem's problems stemmed from his personality and his lack of political acumen. A loner, and not particularly charismatic, he had achieved leadership because of his military seniority and had never built a firm political base. Where Qassem could have rallied moderate political support, he failed. Parliament was dissolved, along with the monarchy, and as political crises ensued, Social Democrats, Kurds, and Communists turned against him, leaving Qassem as sole ruler, to rely increasingly on a demagogic foreign policy in an attempt to rally popular support for the regime.

From the beginning, Qassem's nemesis was Egyptian president Nasser, whom he saw as his competitor for leadership in the Arab world. Early on, Qassem faced a challenge from Abd al-Salem Aref, who was allied to the powerful Ba'th nationalist party, as well as the various pan-Arab parties, and including the supporters of Nasser. For the moment, Qassem was able to outmaneuver Aref and remove him from power, with the help of the Iraqi Communists. However, he faced repeated assassination attempts, as he offended the nationalists by his alliance with the left.

Then, fearful of emerging Communist power among the urban poor, the trade unions, and the newly emancipated peasants, Qassem turned on his Communist allies. Despite promises to license political parties, hold free elections, and draw up a constitution by 1961, Qassem jailed Communists and suppressed even moderate Social Democratic politicians.

Members of the old regime became targets of a televised show trial and were jailed or executed. This tribunal, the Mandawi Court, was also used as a propaganda platform against the British, the Americans, and Nasser. Relations with the Kurds soon soured when they demanded more autonomy than Qassem was prepared to allow. A costly, bitter rebellion followed that lasted intermittently until the 1980s.

Appealing more and more for popular backing, Qassem took to sensationalist foreign ventures in order to mobilize support for his regime as his domestic programs began to falter. He claimed Iranian Khuzistan for Iraq and denounced the border agreements over the Shatt al-Arab (Iraq's narrow stretch of seacoast) signed with Iran in 1935. When Kuwait became independent in 1961, he laid claim to Kuwait as an integral part of Iraq, asserting that Kuwait had once been part of the Ottoman province of Basra. Qassem took no military action because of strong British reaction and Kuwait's acceptance into the Arab League. He did, however, sever diplomatic relations with all countries that supported Kuwait, thus isolating Iraq within the Arab and international communities.

By the end of 1962, Qassem had alienated all potential allies in Iraq, as well, except for a much weakened Communist Party and a few army officers. The war with the Kurds began to take its toll, taxing the central government to the detriment of the domestic reform program. Qassem, spending most of his time in the Ministry of Defense building, was preoccupied with rooting out all opposition to his rule. Meantime, Aref, under house surveillance, plotted with the Ba'th to overthrow Qassem. Plans for a coup were set for 1962 but were delayed when Qassem's intelligence services discovered the conspiracy.

In 1963, Qassem's opponents were successful. The perpetrators who overthrew him were Arab nationalists, organized by the Ba'th, which because of its cell organization and secrecy, was best equipped for success. On February 8, 1963, the Ba'th and its allies, including Abd al-Salam Aref, took over major installations in Baghdad and the Rashid Military Camp, defeating Communist demonstrators. Qassem requested safe conduct out of the country, in return for surrender. He and three associates were shot to death on February 9, 1963.

SUGGESTIONS FOR ADDITIONAL READING

Dann, Uriel. *Iraq Under Qassem: A Political History*. New York: Praeger, 1969.

Khadduri, Majid. *Republican Iraq: A Study in Iraqi Politics Since the Revolution of 1958*. London: Oxford University Press, 1969.

Marr, Phoebe. *The Modern History of Iraq*. Boulder, Colo.: Westview Press, 1985.
Simon, Reeva S. *Iraq Between the Two World Wars: The Creation and Implementation of a Nationalist Ideology*. New York: Columbia University Press, 1986.

Reeva S. Simon

Qin Shih Huang Di (Ch'in Shih Huang Ti)

259–210 B.C.

First Emperor of All China, 221–210 B.C.

In all of its long history, China has never experienced free, democratic government. Tyranny has been the rule through twenty-three centuries. It would be unhistoric to assert that there is an element in Chinese culture that precludes the existence of checks against tyranny. However, with all of its creative genius, liberty has eluded China.

Nevertheless, the act of building an empire covering a vast area and encompassing peoples speaking many dialects and languages, and possessing disparate cultures, is certainly an aspect of creative greatness worth recording.

Qin Shih Huang Di was the first emperor of all China. His dynasty did not last, but the realm he created exists to this day.

BIOGRAPHICAL BACKGROUND

The man who would become China's first great unifier, the first emperor of China, was born in 259 B.C., the son of the ruler of the state of Qin and a concubine of that ruler's first minister. He was named Cheng and at the age of thirteen, in 246 B.C., he succeeded his father to the throne of Qin and was known as King Cheng. In the ninth year of his reign he came of age and took up direct rule. The state of Qin was already in ascendance when he came to the throne, its armies winning a string of victories against rival states and expanding its borders. Moreover, King Cheng was from the outset assisted by very able ministers, one of whom, Li Ssu, would remain by his side until the very end.

While entrusting military decisions to his able ministers and generals, he displayed decisiveness in governing, effectively meting out rewards and punishments. Qin overthrew the reigning Chou dynasty in 256 B.C. and then defeated the remaining states one by one. King Cheng of Qin brought the whole of China under his control. He then took himself a new title, declaring himself Huang Di, sovereign emperor. Indeed, he proclaimed himself the first emperor (*shih*) of a dynasty that would rule for 10,000 generations (Chinese forever).

His dynasty actually came far short of that, lasting only thirteen years, but Qin Shih Huang Di's place in history would nevertheless match his own grandiose vision. As first emperor of China he achieved extraordinary feats of empire building and territorial expansion, institutional development, and physical constructions. In order to unify the vast empire he centralized power and standardized administration, law, language, and even weights and measures. He built a magnificent new imperial capital, Hsienyang, near present-day Xian, immense palaces, the fabulous imperial mausoleum (with its thousands of life-size clay soldiers that were discovered and unearthed only a few decades ago), and one of man's largest construction projects: the Great Wall. He left a great legacy for China, but in accomplishing so much in a short eleven-year reign as emperor, he proved to be as destructive and brutal as he was constructive and wise. There is little doubt that the oppressiveness of his regime shortened its life. The Qin dynasty collapsed in 208 B.C., only two years after the death of its great founder, Qin Shih Huang Di.

QIN SHIH HUANG DI AS A GREAT LEADER

Beyond question, the remarkable achievements of Qin Shih Huang Di—the elimination of forces that kept China divided and at war, the unification of the nation, and the creation of a centralized state that would remain the model for imperial China for over two thousand years—mark him as an outstanding ruler, one of history's "great men." To fully appreciate his accomplishments as unifier and founder of the enduring imperial system of government, it is necessary to review briefly the historical context of his reign, the conditions of a divided China prior to the Qin unification.

The preceding dynasty, the Chou, had been established along feudal lines in the twelfth century B.C. The ruler of the Chou enfeoffed his sons and other loyal supporters, but as centuries passed the central power of the Chou waned to the point that it could not prevent endemic warfare between the contending feudal states. The final two centuries of the Chou dynasty, a period known in China as the Warring States period, was not only characterized by warfare but also by the erosion of feudalism. The authority of the heredity nobility was being undermined by a new breed of untitled administrators, many of whom had acquired wealth and land through commerce. Rulers of the surviving states, of which Qin was one of the largest and most powerful, greatly depended on these new men of means in developing the economic and military strength of the state.

Various reasons have been offered for the success of Qin in conquering the rival states, such as a favorable geographic location, but among the major factors are the superior organization of the Qin state and the leadership provided by King Cheng, the future Qin Shih Huang Di. When he came to the throne of Qin in 246 B.C., the military conquest was well under way, but it was during his reign that Qin armies defeated the remaining six rival states and thus brought all of China under its sway in 221 B.C. It is difficult to determine to what extent he was personally responsible for the military victory. He was served by excellent generals and political advisers, but it is to his credit that he used these able men wisely. In any case, there is no reason why he, as ruler of the victorious Qin, should not be given full credit for its conquest of China.

More important, however, and less disputable, is his role in consolidating power and creating the new imperial government. First he elevated his title to make it commensurate with his newly won position as solitary ruler over the expansive unified empire. He rejected the title *wang* (king), which had been used by rulers of the separate states, in favor of *huang di*, which may be rendered "sovereign emperor." He proclaimed that hereafter the emperor would rule the entire realm by edict. Nor would he reward relatives and supporters with fiefs, for that would only result eventually in the return of feudal separatism and warring states. Instead, Shih Huang Di was determined to centralize power and carry out a thorough unification program.

Shih Huang Di's unification policy was based squarely on the tenets of legalism, a political philosophy which had previously been adopted in the state of Qin. Legalism stressed the need for strong central government and thus called for the abolition of feudalism and the Confucian philosophy on which it was based. According to legalism, the state should be governed by the promulgation of universal laws and the strict enforcement of those laws. On a stone monument Shih Huang Di would later proudly inscribe the following words: "The Sovereign Emperor came to the throne, made decrees and laws which all his subjects heeded. . . . Beneath his wide sway all things find their place; all is decreed by law."

Rule by law and the universality of law are two concepts that characterize the modern world, but were not beyond the comprehension of this early great ruler of China. The emperor was no doubt guided in his unification program by his trusted adviser, Li Ssu, known to be a skillful practitioner of legalism. The unification program featured the creation of an efficient central government bureaucracy, the requirement that all leading families of the vanquished states live in the capital region, the collection of all weapons belonging to those states to be melted down into large bells and statues in the capital, and the establishment of a new territorial administration. In place of rule by hereditary feudal barons or kings, the realm was divided into commanderies and prefectures to be administered by imperial appointees.

Another important dimension of Shih Huang Di's unification program was standardization. Not only was the legal code to be made uniform and universal, but so also were the written language, coinage, and weights and measures. Shih Huang Di was especially far-sighted in adopting such eminently rational and functional measures. The long-range impact of the standardization of the written language cannot be overstated, for it made possible written communication over space and time and was thus instrumental in maintaining Chinese civilization and unity over the centuries. The standardization of coinage and weights and measures facilitated commercial as well as government affairs. Shih Huang Di went so far as to decree a standard length of vehicle axles so that all roads would be of the same width.

The first emperor of China is also noted for his foreign-policy accomplishments. In addition to subduing resistance within China, his armies greatly expanded the territory of the empire to the south, and in the north they drove the "barbarians" (the nomadic tribes) out of China. To protect China from the boundaries to the north, Shih Huang Di undertook the construction of the Great Wall as a defensive bulwark. It should be pointed out that large stretches of his 2,000-mile-long wall had already been built by several of the former states, and that the Qin emperor's accomplishment was to link these pieces together into one continuous wall. It was nonetheless a prodigious feat, especially considering the brevity of his reign. While the wall was not impregnable and had to be garrisoned with troops, it did contribute to the security of the Chinese people and the preservation of ancient Chinese civilization. Moreover, it became one of mankind's most spectacular man-made landmarks.

China's first emperor was a hard-working monarch who took great interest in affairs of state. He is said to have had the pile of documents weighed in the morning and would not retire in the evening until a certain weight of them had passed through his hands. Whatever his faults as a ruler, Shih Huang Di was a powerful ruler whose achievements were enormous and whose impact on Chinese history was immense.

QIN SHIH HUANG DI THE TYRANT

From the very beginning of his political career, Qin Shih Huang Di conformed to the pattern or style of rule deeply rooted in China's ancient past: despotism. His despotic tendencies were revealed in the cruelty of his punishments during his twenty-five-year reign over the state of Qin, prior to becoming emperor of all China. In the ninth year of his reign, for example, he crushed a plot against him by one of his chief ministers and ordered the culprit and twenty of his followers to be dismembered and their heads pilloried. He also ordered that some four thousand families who had been under the former minister's administration be removed to a remote area of China.

Among the factors which may have contributed to the brutality of Shih Huang Di were several assassination attempts. In 226 B.C., while still king of the state of Qin, he had one captured assassin dismembered and then sent his army to destroy the state of which the assailant was an agent. The legalist philosophy to which he adhered called for swift, sure, and severe punishments in order to enforce law more effectively.

As emperor, Shih Huang Di was also influenced by Taoism and superstitions related to this school of thought. He gave heed to the popular form of Taoism that promised extraordinary powers, including immortality, to its devout followers. Shih Huang Di, having developed a great fear of death, sent Taoist leaders out in search of the highly coveted elixir of immortality. His quest for the special powers that his Taoist mentors promised, as well as his own insecurity and dread of death, led him to adopt some rather peculiar measures. Acting on the Taoists' advice, he determined that in order to achieve a certain superhuman state of being and to make his power still more awesome, he should thereafter keep his whereabouts hidden. He ordered that hundreds of palace buildings be linked by covered roads and hidden passages and then decreed that, on the punishment of death, none of his attendants should ever reveal his presence. On at least one occasion the emperor invoked that penalty with a vengeance. The story goes that he noticed from a high mountain lookout that the grand councilor traveled with too many carriages and chariots, and when he noticed soon afterward that this official reduced the number, the emperor was enraged because it meant that someone in his company at the mountain lookout had revealed his words and thus his presence there. When none admitted to it, he had all who had been with him at that time arrested and executed. Thereafter his movements were kept secret.

As time went on the emperor's behavior became still more impetuous and erratic. Several of his scholar-advisers lamented that the emperor never listened to them, "that he loves to intimidate men with punishments and death," and that he never heard his faults condemned because those below "cringe in fear and try to please him with flattery and lies." So saying, they fled. When Shih Huang Di learned of this, he flew into a rage, denouncing them for their disloyalty and for having libeled him. He then had his chief councilors interrogate all court scholars who then incriminated one another to save their own necks. As a result, 460 of them were found guilty of breaking the law and were buried alive at the capital. Thus did Shih Huang Di serve warning to scholars throughout the land. When the emperor's eldest son dared question the severity of this action, he was banished to the northern frontier, supposedly to supervise the army there.

Perhaps the most heinous crime committed by this despotic ruler—albeit a cultural crime—was his ordering the "burning of the books." On the recommendation of Li Ssu, Shih Huang Di in 213 B.C. banned many books including such classics as the *Book of History* and the *Book of Poetry*, and the histories of the former states (excepting that of Qin)—works generally associated with Confucian teachings—and ordered that all copies of them be collected and burned. The purpose seems to have been to wipe out completely the memory of the past, especially the records and teachings regarded as supportive of feudalism and useful to those who desired a return to the Confucian-based feudal order. Persons retaining copies of the outlawed books were to be publicly executed along with their families, and officers who knew of violations and failed to report them were to be punished in the same way. Shih Huang Di's dictim was that "those who use the past to criticize the present should have their clans exterminated." Instead, he advocated the legalist position of "emphasizing the present while slighting the past." Although the loss caused by the book burning was mitigated somewhat by the fact that some copies of the banned books escaped the burning, this act did irreparable damage to China's centuries-old pursuit of knowledge.

Finally, we should not ignore the inhumanity involved in the corvée labor used by the emperor on his many massive building projects including, of course, the Great Wall. Ancient records tell us that a labor force of some 700,000 men was drafted to build the mammoth O-pang palace, which was but one—albeit the largest—of several thousand palaces in Hsienyang, the emperor's capital. No accurate figures are available on the work force assembled to build the Great Wall, but there are many references to the oppressive nature of this forced labor and the many thousands that perished in it. Shih Huang Di's colossal mausoleum, the construction of which began well before he became emperor, also represents both his vanity and his cruelty. He went to great lengths to ensure that this tomb, with its many sealed treasures, never be entered, even ordering the gates to be shut with its thousands of laborers left interred within, lest any live to tell of its location.

Here then was a despotic ruler whose great and enduring accomplishments were offset by his violence and abusive treatment of his people. On the one hand, his subjects and posterity benefited greatly from his major contributions, notably the unification of the Chinese empire and the establishment of a centralized, bureaucratic system of imperial rule that would endure until the twentieth century. On the other hand, his tyrannical rule may well be one of history's cruelest. Some historians have justified his violence as a necessary means to achieve his worthy ends. Others argue that there was no necessary connection between his great achievement and his cruelty; that he should be both praised for the former and condemned for the latter. Still another school of thought has it that the main credit for the great constructive work of the Qin dynasty should go to his able minister, Li Ssu, and that a man as uncultured, superstitious, vain, impetuous, and cruel as Qin Shih Huang Di could not have been capable of such monumental accomplishments. It is this writer's view that the despotic emperor and his able minister must share the credit, because both his despotism, though excessive, and his minister's abilities were necessary to erect the new imperial China.

SUGGESTIONS FOR FURTHER READING

Bodde, Derk. *China's First Unifier: A Study of the Ch'in Dynasty as Seen in the Life of Li Ssu*. Leiden, Holland: Brill, 1938.

Cotterrell, Arthur. *The First Emperor of China*. New York: Penguin, 1982.

Li Yu-ning, ed. *The First Emperor of China: The Politics of Historiography*. White Plains, N.Y.: International Arts and Sciences Press, 1975.

Ssu-ma Ch'ien. *Shih Chi (Records of the Grand Historian)*. Translated by Yang Hsien-i and Gladys Yang. Hong Kong: Commercial Press, 1974.

Wayne C. McWilliams

Stenka Razin

c. 1630–1671

Russian Cossack Rebel

Russian history, particularly since the establishment of the Romanov dynasty in 1613, has been characterized by extremes, by repeated attempts on the part of the authorities to solidify their power, and by rebellions against the center. Stenka Razin's rebellion (1667–1671) was not only the most dangerous challenge to the Romanovs' rule but left an indelible imprint on the political history of Russia.

Razin's rebellion took place at a time when serfdom was beginning to disappear in Western Europe and when the residents of the cities began to assert themselves against those in power—kings, nobles, and clergy. New political relationships were needed and eventually hammered out—frequently violently—by a series of compromises between the contending classes. In Russia, however, political developments took a different road. The sharing of power among contending classes never became a part of Russia's political experience. By the mid-seventeenth century, the relationships between the rulers and the powerless were frozen into immobility, first by the autocracy's role in mandating serfdom from above on behalf of its supporters, and then by the violent peasant reactions to it. In the end, those in power were gripped by a constant fear of the "dark people" they controlled. The dispossessed, in turn, dreamed of liberation, vengeance, and control of the land they worked for the benefit of their oppressors. The autocracy and its defenders sought to teach the peasants the "charm of the knout," in Alexander Pushkin's words, but the peasants responded with their traditional weapons—axe, pitchfork, and torch. Under such conditions a social contract between contending classes could not be created.

BIOGRAPHICAL BACKGROUND

Stepan Timofeevich Razin was born circa 1630 of a well-to-do Cossack family in Zimofeiskaia Stanitsa near the Don River Cossacks' main settlement of Cherkassk. His godfather was the elected leader of Cherkassk, Kornilo Iakovlev, who accepted from the tsar the customary annual military salary in exchange for guarding the frontier against the Tatars and Kalmyks. At the same time, Iakovlev sought to maintain the Cossacks' traditional independence from the encroaching heavy hand of Moscow. The events during the years when Stenka (the diminutive of Stepan) Razin was growing to manhood made this precarious balancing act all but impossible. These years saw the beginning of the transformation of the Grand Duchy of Muscovy into the Russian empire.

There was nothing in Razin's early life to suggest he would turn against Moscow. His first recorded act consisted of a pilgrimmage in 1652, at about the age of twenty-two, via Moscow to the Solovetskii monastery on the White Sea. Six years later he returned to Moscow as a member of a Cossack delegation to negotiate the military salary. In 1661 the elders in Cherkassk entrusted him with the important task of negotiating an alliance with the Kalmyks against the Nogai Tatars, a task he successfully completed and one that served the interests of both the Don Cossacks and Moscow. At the end of that year, he reported in Moscow on the success of his diplomatic mission and from there made a second pilgrimmage to Solovetskii. In 1663 he commanded a Cossack regiment in a successful expedition against the Crimean Tatars.

A number of factors produced Razin's peasant rebellion, the greatest in Russian history. Russian serfdom had come out of the chaos of the latter years of the reign of Ivan the Terrible (1533–1584) and the Times of Troubles of the early seventeenth century when peasants lost their previous right to move. In 1649 the national assembly passed the fateful Law Code of 1649, which sought to end the perpetual wandering of Russia's peasants and codified state serfdom from above. The law divided Russia into fixed hereditary classes subordinated to the needs of a modernizing—that is, increasingly centralizing—state. The main beneficiaries were the serving gentry who gained control of their serfs and tied them to the land. The Code of 1649 was meant to halt the flight of peasants, particularly to the south where they could expect a safe haven. Thus the state's new principle of "once a serf, always a serf" clashed with the Cossacks' axiom that "from the Don, no one is handed over."

In 1653 the assembly also declared Russia's suzerainty over the eastern parts of the Polish empire, thus setting the stage for a fateful war (1654–1667) that produced a wave of peasant migrations eastward, swelling the suburbs of the towns with bandits, peasants, and paupers, who sought to avoid taxation and military recruitment, potential rebels all. In 1658, Tsar Alexis (1645–1689) made the retrieval of serfs a state function and sent search parties that netted thousands of runaways in the middle Volga River and Tambov regions, both of which later became Razin strongholds. All this was accompanied by heavy taxation and ruinous inflation and contributed to a widening gap between rich and poor. These developments coincided with a continent-wide millenarian religious movement from which the Russians were not immune. In the eyes of many, Patriarch Nikon became the Anti-Christ and Tsar Alexis the prophesied Beast of the Apocalypse. Simple common folk and even the lower clergy of the church resented the translation of the liturgy into modern Russian as well as other reforms of church practice. Out of that conflict came the Raskolniki or "Old Believers," a mass religious revolt that acquired political overtones for the successive tsars of Russia. Most significantly, the war brought death to approximately one-fifth of the Russian population through hunger, disease, and destruction.

When Razin launched his rebellion against Moscow in 1670, Muscovy had become depopulated, but the Don region had swelled to 25,000 inhabitants, three times the number at the outset of Alexis' reign twenty-five years earlier. Among them were the remnants of the army of the Cossack Vaska Us, Razin's immediate forerunner, who in 1666 had suffered defeat at Tula, a scant one hundred miles south of Moscow.

Along the Don, Cossack society had become split along class lines. The hungry and "naked" upstream residents deeply resented the "house owners" downstream around Cherkassk, who refused to accept all refugees as equals. This division, contrary to the old basic law of Cossack equality, was exacerbated by the Cossack prohibition against the cultivation of land lest it lead to serfdom. The established settlers monopolized the traditional occupations of Cossacks, hunting and fishing, and in the process forced the "naked" to either work for them or turn to the Volga to engage in another Cossack occupation, piracy. The refugees were thus twice victimized, first by Moscow's codification of serfdom and then by the class structure along the Don. The region had become a political tinder box.

In 1667, motivated by the lure of piracy, Razin launched a series of successful attacks against merchant ships along the lower Volga. He then plundered Persian, Turkmen, and Russian settlements along the shores of the Caspian Sea. During this ostensibly nonpolitical stage in Razin's career, the first signs of a potential social rebellion already began to appear. In the spring of 1668 he contacted the now discredited Patriarch Nikon, exiled over the age-old question of establishing a political alliance against Moscow. By the end of 1669, he became the avowed champion of the "naked," the dispossessed.

As early as 1667, the tsar called on Iakovlev to restrain the defiant Razin. At that time Iakovlev was reluctant to go against his godson, in part because he was determined to preserve the autonomy of the Cossack Host. But, during the winter of 1669–1670, when Razin burned his bridges behind him, particularly after murdering the tsar's envoy Gerasim Evdokimov, he became also a threat to the loyal Cherkassk oligarchy.

In March 1670, Razin gathered an army of six thousand Cossacks and crossed over to the Volga and launched his bloody political revolution. He announced in his manifestos that he had come to free Russia from those who oppressed its people, from *boyars* (hereditary nobles), greedy merchants, provincial governors, and foreigners. City after city fell to Razin: Tsaritsyn and Astrakhan, then Saratov and Samara. By September 1670, he was in control of an eight-hundred-mile stretch of the Volga and stood before the gates of Simbirsk, a city the tsar himself had founded in 1648, threatening to take his rebellion into the land between the Volga and Oka rivers, the very heart of Muscovy.

It was at Simbirsk that the fate of Razin's rebellion was decided. In October 1670, his forces were defeated and upon his retreat to Cherkassk, his own godfather took him prisoner. He was taken in chains to Moscow, tortured at length, and publicly quartered on Red Square in June 1671, at the age of forty-one.

STENKA RAZIN AS A GREAT LEADER

Razin's uprising was not the first manifestation of class warfare in Russian history. In 1606, during the Times of Troubles (1598–1613), Ivan Bolotnikov led his army of peasants, serfs, slaves, and serving gentry to the very gates of Moscow, ostensibly to rid Russia of the boyars. Bolotnikov did not declare himself a rebel against the monarchy. He promised, instead, the rejuvenation of a Russia under a just tsar without the oppressive and treasonous nobility. Razin's rebellion started from the same premise.

When Razin began his rebellion, he issued manifestos assuring the "naked" that he intended to rid Russia of the tsar's betrayers, "the boyars, the governors and officials in the towns . . . and to give freedom to the common people." Another target was the increasing presence of foreigners in Russia—Germans, Scots, and Dutch—who were generally lumped under the heading of "Germans." Razin followed another of Bolotnikov's examples, "thievish letters" smuggled into Moscow urging slaves to kill their masters. Razin's seditious letters eventually made their way into every corner of the land, including Karelia in the north, Siberia, and Moscow itself.

Razin's rebellion differed from that of Bolotnikov in that it focused more clearly on Russia's class division. Bolotnikov's support came largely from the peasantry, but a large number of serving gentry, who nursed their grievances against the boyars, also joined him. By the time of Razin's rebellion, however, the serving gentry and the boyars had been fused into one class. This time it was along more sharply delineated lines: serfs, Volga boatmen, the urban and rural poor, Old Believers—against the nobles.

Razin drew on the class divisions within the religious establishment. The lower clergy, mostly from peasant stock, played an essential part in the rebellion as they joined ranks against the hierarchy of the Russian Orthodox Church. It was they who brought the element of religious, millenarian fanaticism to the uprising. Razin's appeals, however, were directed against any and all disaffected individuals irrespective of religious beliefs. In his manifestos to Muslim Tatars, the battle for justice was in the name of Mohammed. He stood for the Blessed Virgin and the official Orthodox faith, but he also welcomed Old Believers who had rejected the changes recently mandated by Patriarch Nikon. The Old Believers, however, did not play a major role—unlike during the rebellion of Emelian Pugachev during the 1770s—because the schism within the church had not yet become a major political force of social protest along the borders of the empire. After Razin's death, the myth circulated that he had been an Old Believer who had been blessed by the Old Believers' spiritual leader, the martyr Avvakum. But Razin could not have been an Old Believer because he also sought to enlist Nikon, the Old Believers' arch enemy. Razin thought Nikon might prove to be a willing ally as he had come from a humble peasant background on the Volga, an upstart very much resented by the healous boyars. But Nikon, who had insisted on being addressed as "Grand Sovereign" by the tsar, wanted no part of a rebellion by the "naked."

Until suffering injury and defeat at Simbirsk in September 1670, Razin enjoyed an aura of courage and invincibility of nearly mythical proportion. After his conquest of Astrakhan in August 1669, residents hailed him as a *bogatyr*, a valiant knight. His imposing physical presence and his character—magnanimous, sociable, cruel and bold—won him many followers and before long they began to see him, instead of Alexis, as their real sovereign. They called him *batiushka*, Little Father, a term of respect and endearment reserved for the tsar. Razin became a man of more than human qualities, a savior sent by providence. The government responded with its own manifestos denouncing him as a "traitor and desecrator of the holy cross."

Razin's manifestos proclaimed his loyalty to the tsar, but his actions spoke a different message. Borrowing another leaf from Bolotnikov, Razin produced a *tsarevich*, an heir to the throne, an imposter who claimed to be Alexis' son who had not died in 1669 as reported, but who had escaped "the violent hands of the boyars." Razin's entourage also contained a second imposter who claimed to be Nikon.

Razin's significance lies in the fact that he presented a permanent challenge to the state's final decree, which consigned large masses to hereditary poverty and exploitation. From the time he rose in rebellion in 1670 until the abolition of serfdom in 1861, the legacy of Razin loomed large in the consciousness of nobles and peasants alike. The former feared his return, the latter prayed for it. No other historic figure captured the imagination of the downtrodden as did Razin. Razin became a Christ-like martyr who had laid down his life for the people, who remembered his courage, his appeals to elementary social justice, his treacherous betrayal to the authorities, and his stoic demeanor in the face of his brutal execution. Like Christ, he had died a martyr's death, yet was immortal. He was still alive, preparing for the proper moment to come to the aid of the oppressed and to give them the wealth he had seized from the rich.

Razin's execution produced only a temporary quiet and when the next large peasant rebellion broke out, that of Kondrati Bulavin in 1707, Cossacks claimed to have remembered Razin. In the Soviet novel by Aleksei Chapygin, a young man loyal to the tsar, upon being told that the executed Razin was his father, vows that "from now on I shall think upon freedom and speak of it to others and work for it." Folk songs referred to this or that "son of Razin," and songs about Razin were reworked into songs about other rebels, such as Pugachev. The authorities remained well aware of the danger of Razin's legacy. When Alexander Pushkin, who called Razin "the only poetic figure in Russian history," sought to publish his collection of *The Songs of Stenka Razin* (1826), the censors prevented the publication of songs justifying Razin's destructive fury as righteous wrath.

Even Lenin identified his cause with that of Razin. On May Day 1919, he unveiled a statute in honor of Razin on the very spot where he had given his life to the cause of social justice and freedom. Lenin, however, had also learned from Razin's errors—the lack of a constructive program and discipline.

STENKA RAZIN THE TYRANT

There is no reason to doubt that Razin was genuinely motivated by a desire for justice, to redress the misery that serfdom, arbitrary justice, cruel punishment, and heavy taxation had brought. In an age when torture and gruesome murder of political opponents was established practice, Razin frequently showed a considerable measure of restraint. In one such instance, after the murder of officials and wealthy merchants in Astrakhan in the summer of 1670, Razin intervened to limit the carnage.

Yet his rebellion on behalf of social justice always had a darker side to it. Looting—justified as political act—was central in Razin's campaigns. That was the reason he twice attacked Astrakhan at the mouth of the Volga, Russia's wealthy "window to the East." The second attack on Astrakhan proved to be a major, perhaps even fatal, strategic blunder. Razin, having taken Tsaritsyn (today's Volgograd), instead of taking his army up the Volga into the heart of Muscovy, decided to conquer Astrakhan. The diversion of Razin's forces gave Alexis sufficient time to organize an effective resistance. Razin's rebellion frequently took a back seat to the primordial desire for vengeance which instilled an indelible horror among those in power.

Although Razin enlisted Orthodox believers and professed to be fighting for the Holy Virgin, his rebellion became also an assault on the church, its hierarchy and central beliefs. The death sentence read to him at the time of his execution charged him with blasphemy, the prohibition against the building of churches, the expulsion of priests, and interference in church services, particularly the rejection of the church's wedding ceremony by reviving a pagan ritual where bridal couples danced around a tree. In his private life, Razin leaned toward the religion practiced by the ancients before the official conversion of Kiev Rus in 988. During his initial presence in Astrakhan in August 1669, he drowned his young captive Persian mistress in the Volga to calm the waters of the raging river in accordance with the heathen belief in human sacrifice. Similarly, the murder of the tsar's representative, Evdokimov, by the traditional Cossack method of drowning also served the purpose of pacifying the Don.

Razin's was an uncompromising rebellion. He would either root out the nobility or they would crush him. He saw no place for them in his scheme of things. Bolotnikov at least had distinguished between the boyars and the serving gentry. Razin introduced an elementary and immediate form of people's justice. Governors who had oppressed the local population would be tried and executed on the spot in brutal fashion; those with whom the people were on good terms were often acquitted. The cruelty of the rebellion alienated many, particularly those in the cities, who nursed their own grievances against Moscow. The only servants of the tsar who came over to the side of Razin were musket-carrying soldiers whose standard of living frequently resembled that of the dispossessed in the suburbs. The church's hierarchy, although alienated from the tsar's increasing power at the expense of the church, could not find a good reason to join the rebellion. Nikon, instead, denounced it as an act of sacrilege.

Razin was unable to put to effective use the ethnic divisions within Russia. He had little success in enlisting the support of the Cossacks' traditional enemies, the Tatars and Kalmyks. Tatar princes on the Volga who had been baptized and granted estates remained loyal to the crown. The non-Russian tribesmen along the Volga—the Mordva, Mari, and Churvash—who had their lands confiscated by Russians, however, did join the rebellion.

The rebellion came at a time of increased political centralization. Razin looked backward, to a time when free men lived unencumbered by the heavy hand of government. But he was swimming against a tide he could not overcome. The Cossacks, as an independent Host, were irrevocably becoming a relic of the past. The Zaporozhian Cossacks along the Dnieper River under Bohdan Khmel'nyts'kyi had already lost their independence, and nothing came of Razin's dream of a unified Cossack Host between the Dnieper and Yaik (now Ural) rivers because of deep-seated rivalries. The rebellion managed only to underscore what set Russian society apart, without offering solutions to overcome the divisions. The conquest of cities, their reorganization along Cossack custom, punishment of the guilty, and the equal division of loot did not constitute a viable political program.

Razin's rebellion was doomed to defeat, as is generally the case when disciplined troops face disorganized forces. Razin enjoyed the support of a seasoned, disciplined, and courageous core of Cossacks, but the majority of his army always consisted of a badly equipped rabble of questionable fighting qualities. The crucial test came at Simbirsk, where the governor, Prince Ivan Miloslavskii, a relative of the tsar's first wife, organized the first effective resistance. Members of the gentry, many of them veterans of the Polish war, trained by foreign officers and equipped with the latest muskets and artillery, fought back until the loyal Tatar chief Iurii Bariatinskii arrived. Razin's force of six thousand were no match for Bariatinskii's elite troops, trained by German and Scottish officers, whose artillery tore huge holes in Razin's line. In defeat, Razin discovered that the citizens of Samara and Saratov—who had once opened the gates of their cities to him—would not receive him, and he continued to the Don, where the downstream Cossacks turned against him. The battle of Simbirsk marked the victory of the boyars and their "German friends" over those who had sought to rid Russia of the oppressive hereditary nobility and foreign influences. The westernization of Russia was well under way before Peter the Great appeared on the stage.

Razin's rebellion represented the culmination of the conflict between the centralizing state and men who claimed to be free but who in the case of the Cossacks also represented the spirit of lawlessness and anarchy. Razin's rebellion was another chapter in the old conflict between the *veche*, the ancient local assembly, and triumphant autocratic tradition.

SUGGESTIONS FOR ADDITIONAL READING

Avrich, Paul. *Russian Rebels: 1600–1800.* New York: Shocken Books, 1972.

Chapygin, A. *Stepan Razin: A Novel.* London: Hutchinson International Authors, 1946; Hyperion reprint, 1973.

Sokolov, Y. M. *Russian Folklore.* New York: Macmillan, 1950.

Vernadsky, George. *A History of Russia: The Tsardom of Moscow, 1547–1682.* New Haven, Conn.: Yale University Press, vol. 5, pt. 2, 1969. Chapter 6, pt. 1, "The Razin Uprising, 1667–71," pp. 609–626.

Harry Piotrowski

Richard II

1367–1400

King of England, 1377–1399

Richard II was the second king of England whose forced abdication was followed by his murder. The murdered Edward II, though, was followed by his son in 1327, so there was no debate about inheritance by primogeniture. Richard II lost his throne to his first cousin, Henry IV, who bypassed the claims of Philippa, daughter of his uncle Lionel of Clarence. This meant that for the first time in English history, Parliament served as an arbiter for the rights of a king. When, sixty-one years later, the heir to the House of York began the War of the Roses by attempting to dethrone Henry IV's grandson, he was partially strengthened by his having married Anne Mortimer, the heiress of the line of Clarence.

The events that led to Richard II's tyrannical last years began following the premature death of his beloved wife, Anne of Bohemia. Few historic figures have careers marked by such a contrast between their creative, happy years and the self-destructive tyrannical phase at the end of their life. Certainly, few tyrannies have had such tragic results.

BIOGRAPHICAL BACKGROUND

Richard II was born at Bordeaux on January 6, 1367. His father, Edward the Black Prince, eldest son of King Edward III, was a distinguished warrior and commander of English forces during the Hundred Years' War. Richard's mother, Joan, the "Fair Maid of Kent," had earned the reputation of being gentle and peace-loving, and it was under her influence that Richard was raised. Richard's education was entrusted to two Garter knights, Sir Guichard D'Angle and Sir Simon Burley; the latter, a lover of books, has been credited with filling the young prince's mind with high-handed notions of regal power. Although the son of a war hero, Richard soon developed into a sensitive and rather high-strung boy, who exhibited a distaste for war and feats of arms, preferring instead more refined and cultured pursuits, including art and literature and fine dress. When his father died unexpectedly in 1376, Richard became heir to the throne; and with the death of Edward III in 1377 Richard was crowned king at the tender age of ten.

Since he was only a boy in 1377, the early years of Richard's reign were directed by a council of twelve magnates. Several critical issues, many inherited from the previous reign, proved troublesome in this period, especially the continual problem of French raids along the English coast. In a Parliament at Nottingham in 1380 it was decided to impose a poll tax in order to combat the French. This tax fell especially hard on the poor, and protests against its imposition, along with other grievances, erupted into violent protests, the most well-known of which was the Peasants' Revolt of 1381. After committing widespread havoc and murder in London, the rebels demanded a meeting with King Richard. During the meeting at Smithfield outside London the rebels suddenly threatened the royal party with arrows drawn. Only Richard had the presence of mind to calm this dangerous situation, and he persuaded most of the rebels to leave the scene after promising them several concessions. Richard was then only a boy of fourteen. Of course the hardcore of the rebels led by Wat Tyler, who did not leave, were butchered.

His brave performance at Smithfield marks a turning point in Richard's minority, after which he began to assert more influence. His marriage to Anne of Bohemia in 1382 was followed by the building up of a circle of royal favorites. Perhaps overly influenced by the likes of Burley, the young Robert de Vere, and others, Richard began to spend lavishly and to exhibit other signs of royal extravagance, all the while ignoring mounting criticism of his policies. Especially irksome to many of the nobility was Richard's pursuit of peaceful relations with France. All of this came to a head in 1386 when Parliament impeached Richard's chancellor, Michael de la Pole, and then saddled Richard with a commission of government for a one-year period. Through various means Richard attempted to subvert the commission's authority, resulting in an armed confrontation between parliamentary and royalist forces. In the Battle of Radcot Bridge in December 1387, Richard's forces were defeated, de Vere fled abroad, and Richard had to yield. The outcome was the so-called Merciless Parliament of 1388. Several lords appellant, led by Richard's uncle the Duke of Gloucester and by the Earls of Arundel and Warwick, "appealed" several of Richard's "evil councilors" with treason and then executed many of them, including Richard's old tutor, Sir Simon Burley. The appellants then took over the reins of government. Their rule was suddenly and dramatically interrupted May 3, 1389, when Richard announced that, since he had attained his majority, he was fit to rule on his own once again.

The years 1389 to 1397, often referred to as a period of "appeasement," saw little outward rancor between Richard and his enemies. Nevertheless, several incidents in these years suggested that harmony was more apparent than real, and that Richard was merely biding his time until he could avenge the wrongs done him in 1388.

Richard struck suddenly in 1397, beginning what many historians feel was a "second tyranny." In July of 1397 three of the appellant ringleaders (Gloucester, Arundel, and Warwick) were suddenly seized and "appealed" of treason in a Parliament summoned for September 1397 and referred to as the Revenge Parliament. Gloucester had by that date already been murdered in a Calais prison, but Arundel was executed and Warwick was banished for life.

Richard then began to tighten his hold on the government, pursuing a policy of increasingly despotic rule. This would eventually prove his ruin. Early in 1398 there arose a dispute between the two remaining Appellants, Richard's cousin Henry Bolingbroke (duke of Hereford) and the Duke of Norfolk. In September of that year Hereford and Norfolk were prepared to settle their differences in a judicial combat at Coventry. At the appointed hour, however, Richard suddenly and unexpectedly aborted the combat, and ordered both combatants into exile, thus ridding himself of the last Appellants. But when Richard's uncle, John of Gaunt, the Duke of Lancaster, died in February 1399, Hereford (Gaunt's son) was in line to inherit the vast Lancastrian estate, thereby posing a potential threat to the king's power. In order to prevent this, Richard seized the entire Lancastrian estate. Serious questions regarding the legality of Richard's action were immediately raised in the minds of all men of property, and the seizure of the Lancastrian inheritance was the real beginning of the Lancastrian revolution. Richard's biggest mistake, however, was to embark on a second expedition to Ireland in July 1399, either ignoring or overlooking mounting baronial hostility to his increasing autocracy. Using the excuse of laying claim to his wrongfully seized inheritance, Bolingbroke took advantage of Richard's absence in Ireland to return to England and to lead a baronial revolution against Richard's rule. Landing in the north, Bolingbroke was soon joined by a host of other discontented nobles and together they set out for the west of England. When Richard returned from Ireland in August 1399, he discovered that his forces had deserted him. Seeking refuge in Conway castle in Chester, where he could have remained safely, Richard was tricked into surrendering and was then returned to London a prisoner of Bolingbroke's forces. A Parliament was summoned in Richard's name to meet in September 1399, and it was here that thirty-three articles of deposition were read out and Richard was then forced to abdicate. Bolingbroke then ascended the throne as Henry IV. Richard was subsequently taken under guard to the Lancastrian stronghold of Pontrefact in Yorkshire, where he was either starved to death or died of beatings in February 1400.

It has often been argued that Richard II was himself responsible for his tragic fate. But despite numerous attempts to fatham his character and personality—from Shakespeare to the present—no consensus has been reached regarding the "real" Richard. Indeed, Richard II has been portrayed in widely divergent ways, ranging from a brave man of courage and action to a pitiful weakling and neurotic, perhaps insane. As depicted by his contemporaries, however, Richard's was a character combining these traits.

RICHARD II AS A GREAT LEADER

Despite his tragic downfall, the reign of Richard II is generally considered a high-water mark in later medieval England in the areas of foreign policy, religion, and the arts. Most of the developments in these affairs were the direct result of Richard's personal interest and involvement.

Richard's foreign policy attempted to reverse centuries of English attitudes toward Ireland and France. In the case of the former, Richard was the first English king to visit Ireland since 1210; Richard twice led expeditions there in order to provide for greater stability, and to arrange for some sort of diplomatic—rather than military—solution to the island's problems. Regarding the latter, Richard's pursuit of peace as a way of ending centuries of Anglo-French hostilities not only represented a departure from previous practice, but also aroused among many magnate warhawks suspicion and hatred of his plans. In the Treaty of Calais (1361) peace between England and France had been reached; but renewed hostilities broke out in 1369 and continued intermittently into Richard's reign. Richard's conclusion of a twenty-eight-year truce in 1396, cemented by his marriage to the seven-year-old Isabella, daughter of Charles VI, held out the promise of an extended period of peaceful relations with the French.

Richard was also instrumental in leading an assault against the recent outbreak of the Lollard heresy. Followers of the radical Oxford theologian John Wycliffe, the Lollards have often been called "proto-Protestants" in that many of their criticisms of existing church practices wound up being adopted first by John Huss and then ultimately by Martin Luther. Among others, these criticisms centered on perceived abuses among the clergy, the rejection of many of the sacraments, and the Lollards' adoption of Wycliffe's English Bible. Driven by his staunch orthodoxy, Richard II was determined to stamp out the Lollard heresy. According to a contemporary chronicler, when the Lollards learned of Richard's imminent return from Ireland in 1395, they "drew into their shells like tortoises." Also in that year Richard forced the chancellor of Oxford University to condemn Wycliffite teachings, and to banish many Lollards.

Richard's most important contributions lay in his patronage of cultural and artistic endeavors, leading many scholars to label Richard as a forerunner of Renaissance ideals of kingship. Important to Richard's plans for royal absolutism was the establishment of a brilliant court culture. As a means to this end Richard encouraged and supported many poets, artists, and artisans, and he commissioned several artistic projects. For this Richard was often criticized by contemporaries, one of whom made the snide comment that Richard's courtiers "were knights of Venus rather than of Bellona . . . armed with words rather than weapons." Geoffrey Chaucer was a member of the Richardian court circle; and it has been argued that many of his *Canterbury Tales* may have been written with the court audience in mind. John Gower, too, was associated with Richard II. Gower tells us in his own words that Richard requested of him "some newe thing," resulting in Gower's dedication of *Confessio Amantis* to his royal patron. Several additional literary figures were attached to Richard's court, among them Sir John Clanvowe and Thomas Hoccleve. Moreover, Richard's interest in the architectural and plastic arts resulted in several works and commissions. Richard was responsible for the rebuilding of Westminster Hall, and it has been observed that the hammer-beam roof design was Richard's own. Under Richard a whole host of craftsmen was maintained at court, including Henry Yevele and Hugh Herland. Above all else, it should be remembered that Richard II was the first English king to commission a portrait panel of his own likeness for iconographic purposes—this was the famous Westminster portrait. And the magnificent Wilton Diptych was in all likelihood commissioned by Richard for similar purposes of glorifying his royal magnificence.

RICHARD II THE TYRANT

Notwithstanding his positive achievements Richard II has received round condemnation for many of his less favorable actions. Whether Richard's policies during the later years of his reign amounted to tyranny, there is no escaping the fact that, after 1397, he turned his reign into some sort of personal autocracy.

There is little question that these actions provoked widespread criticism of Richard and his allies and that, in turn, there arose a nearly universal, desire to deprive him of power.

Although Richard took the first open steps toward tyranny in 1397, several untoward developments in the earlier 1390s hinted at future trouble between king and Parliament. At the Smithfield tournament of 1390 Richard distributed badges decorated with the livery of the white hart to his newly recruited royal archers; and after 1397 these were joined by an expanded force of Cheshire archers. Also, Richard's quarrel with London in 1392 ended when the Londoners were required to buy back their lost privileges at a staggering cost. As expenses from the household reveal, Richard began gradually to rebuild a new courtier party during the 1390s. Richard also seems to have even prepared the groundwork for freeing himself from parliamentary fetters by connecting the Commons speaker, Sir John Bushy, to the royal household. It seems equally clear that Richard even "packed" Parliament; thirty-three of the new members sent to Parliament in 1397 were associated with Richard's household.

For all of these reasons Richard had little difficulty in achieving his ends in the Revenge Parliament of 1397. That Richard meant to even the score with the former appellant lords was made crystal clear when Gloucester, Arundel, and Warwick were seized without warning and charged with treason. Arundel was the first to meet the executioner's axe, Gloucester was smothered to death in Calais, and Warwick, after confessing "like a wretched old woman," had his sentence of death commuted to permanent exile on the Isle of Man. Having dealt with his enemies, Richard then rewarded his friends by creating a series of new lordships, and he even rewarded himself by transferring several lucrative estates to the crown. Finally, several high-ranking members of Parliament were forced to swear before the shrine of Edward the Confessor to uphold all of the enactments of this session.

His appetite having been whetted in the Revenge Parliament of 1397, Richard then embarked on a two-year period of open tyranny. Two aspects of Richardian reforms warrant the use of the term "tyranny"; in addition to their comprehensiveness, his enactments were invasions of subjects' rights of property; and many of Richard's actions were viciously vindictive. For example, forfeitures for treason attending the Parliaments of 1397–1398 were extended to include the estates of the victims' families and retainers. Again, in the summer of 1397 Richard demanded—and received—a number of "forced" loans from men of the realm, most of which he failed to repay.

Richard really got down to brass tacks in the Shrewsbury Parliament in 1398. Here he rammed through a wide array of far-reaching measures, some of which were not enacted until the summer of 1398, the combined effect of which was to make clear Richard's program of absolutism. It is noteworthy, for instance, that one of this Parliament's most significant acts was to grant Richard the wool subsidy for life, thus effectively liberating him from financial dependence on parliamentary grants. One of this session's first acts was the annulment of all the enactments of the Merciless Parliament, since these were "done without authority and against the will and liberty of the king and the right of his crown." As if to add insult to injury, Richard then demanded that all those suspected of having sided with his enemies in 1387–1388 make cash payments for royal pardons. Nor were individuals his only targets; it has been estimated that upwards of seventeen counties, each paying one thousand marks per shire, were similarly forced to buy their way back into Richard's good graces. In addition, many individuals in these counties were forced to sign their names to "blank charters," the net effect of which was to extract large sums of money from his subjects. On top of all this, Richard demanded from many segments of society forced oaths and pledges guaranteeing their acquiescence in royal absolutism.

SUGGESTIONS FOR ADDITIONAL READING

Barron, Caroline M. "The Tyranny of Richard II," *Bulletin of the Institute of Historical Research* 41 (1968): 1–18.

Du Boulay, F.R.H., and Caroline M. Barron, eds. *The Reign of Richard II*. London: The Athlone Press, 1971.

Eberle, Patricia J. "The Politics of Courtly Style at the Court of Richard II," in Glyn S. Burgess and Robert A. Taylor, eds., *The Spirit of the Court*. Cambridge: Cambridge University Press, 1985, pp. 168–78.

Goodman, Anthony. *The Loyal Conspiracy: The Lords Appellant under Richard II*. Coral Gables, Fla.: University of Miami Press, 1971.

Jones, Richard H. *The Royal Policy of Richard II: Absolutism in the Later Middle Ages*. Oxford: Basil Blackwell, 1968.

Mathew, Gervase. *The Court of Richard II*. London: John Murray, 1968.

Steel, Anthony. *Richard II*. Cambridge: Cambridge University Press, 1941.

Stow, George B. "Richard II as Insane: The Course of an English Historiographical Myth," in James. L. Gillespie and Anthony Goodman, eds., *Richard II: Power and Prerogative*. Oxford: Oxford University Press, 1993.

Tuck, Anthony. *Richard II and the English Nobility*. London: Edward Arnold, 1973.

George B. Stow

Richard III

1452–1485

King of England, 1483–1485

Richard III is known to most as Shakespeare's archetypal villain, the scheming hunchback who usurped the English throne in 1483 and murdered his nephews, Edward V and Richard. He has defenders, however, including novelists, historian Paul Kendall, and members of the Richard III Society in England and the Friends of Richard III in America—who regard him as a hero unfairly maligned by Tudor propaganda. While most historians recognize that the Tudor depiction, though exaggerated, contains a significant element of truth, Richard differed from his contemporaries only in degree. As Charles Ross notes, "the later fifteenth century in England is now seen as a ruthless and violent age as concerns the upper ranks of society, full of private feuds, intimidation, land-hunger, and litigiousness, and consideration of Richard's life and career against this background has tended to remove him from the lonely pinnacle of Villainy Incarnate on which Shakespeare had placed him." He was twice exiled as a child, his father was killed in battle, his brother Edmund murdered, his brother George executed, and many of his acquaintances died violently. If Richard was brutal, it was because he learned well the lessons his society taught him. If his method of becoming king is hardly laudable, he was a competent monarch nonetheless.

BIOGRAPHICAL BACKGROUND

Richard was born on October 2, 1452, at Fotheringhay Castle in Northamptonshire, the eleventh and last child of Richard, duke of York and his wife Cicely, daughter of Ralph Neville, earl of Westmorland. Early in the Wars of the Roses, York sought to control Henry VI, but in 1459 was forced into Irish exile, while his eldest son, Edward, fled to Calais. Henry placed the duchess of York and her sons, George and Richard, in the duchess of Buckingham's custody, but after Edward and the earls of Salisbury and Warwick invaded England in June 1460 and captured Henry at Northampton in July, they moved to London. Following York's death at Wakefield in December and the Lancastrian victory at St. Albans in February 1461, the boys' mother sent them to Duke Philip the Good of Burgundy. However, their brother took the throne as Edward IV after his victory at Towton in March and summoned them home. At his coronation in June, Edward made them Knights of the Bath and granted them lands, naming George duke of Clarence and Richard duke of Gloucester.

The next few years of Richard's life are obscure, but by late 1465 he entered the household of the "kingmaker"—Richard Neville, earl of Warwick—where he remained until 1468 or 1469. Edward endowed Clarence with vast estates and responsibilities in the 1460s, but was less generous with Richard, who became a Knight of the Garter in 1466, constable of England and chief justiciar of South Wales in 1469, and warden of the west marches against Scotland in 1470. Unlike Clarence, however, Richard opposed Warwick's treason in 1469–1471, fought with Edward against Robin of Redesdale's rebellion, and joined him in exile in Holland during Henry VI's brief return to the throne (October 1470–April 1471). Upon Edward's return, Richard helped reconcile him with Clarence and fought in April at Barnet, where Warwick died, and in May at Tewkesbury, where Henry was captured. Edward made him steward of the duchy of Lancaster, justiciar of North Wales, and great chamberlain of England (briefly) in 1471 and warden of the royal forests north of Trent in 1472. Richard received lands formerly belonging to Warwick and various Lancastrians and built a powerful northern affinity, inheriting much of the Kingmaker's influence. He married Warwick's daughter Ann, despite opposition from Clarence, who had married her older sister, Isabel, and wished to monopolize the inheritance. Relations between the brothers were strained until Clarence's execution for treason in 1478.

Richard accompanied Edward on his lackluster French campaign in 1475 and became great chamberlain (again) and lord admiral in 1478. Virtually northern viceroy, he became lieutenant-general in 1480, raising troops to counter an expected Scots invasion. In 1482 Edward attempted to oust James III of Scotland in favor of his brother, Alexander, duke of Albany. Though this failed, Richard—commanding the English forces—captured the town and (later) the castle of Berwick and, advancing to Edinburgh, obtained pardon for Albany and favorable terms from James. A grateful Parliament made his wardenship of the west marches hereditary and granted him additional Scottish lands which he might conquer.

Edward IV died on April 9, 1483. His heir, Edward V, was thirteen, too young to assume full responsibilities as king. A power struggle ensued between Richard and the Woodvilles, family of the dead king's wife and the new king's mother, Elizabeth. Edward IV may have made Richard his nephew's protector, though Rosemary Horrox questions this. The Woodvilles planned an early coronation for young Edward and attempted to have him escorted to London by a large army under his uncle, the Earl of Rivers. But Richard and the duke of Buckingham arrested Rivers and Lord Richard Grey at Northampton, sent for Edward V at Stony Stratford, told him the Woodvilles planned to seize the government, and escorted him to London, arriving on May 4. Elizabeth fled to sanctuary at Westminster with her daughters and younger son, the duke of York.

Richard rescheduled the coronation for June 22, summoned a Parliament for June 25, moved Edward to the Tower of London, replaced Archbishop Rotherham with Bishop Russell of Lincoln as lord chancellor, and confiscated the property of Elizabeth's older son, the marquis of Dorset. By June 10 Richard claimed that a Woodville conspiracy against him was afoot and summoned forces from the city of York. On June 13 he arrested his former ally, William Lord Hastings, who was immediately executed without trial, and Lord Stanley, Bishop Morton, and Rotherham. He also arrested Elizabeth Shore (sometimes inaccurately called "Jane") for attacking him through sorcery. Despite mounting tension in London, Archbishop Bourchier—at Richard's behest—persuaded Elizabeth to send the duke of York from sanctuary to the Tower.

Richard again postponed the coronation, but by June 20 decided to assume the throne. On June 22, Dr. Ralph Shaw preached at St. Paul's Cross and on June 24 Buckingham spoke at the Guildhall, arguing that the crown belonged to Richard. Though Parliament was cancelled, an assembly of lords recognized Richard as king on June 25, and he began his reign on the 26th. The previous day, his ally, the earl of Northumberland had executed Rivers, Lord Grey, and Sir Thomas Vaughan at Pontrefact without trial. Richard was crowned on July 6 at Westminster. Thereafter he embarked upon a lengthy progress through his realm.

Richard's usurpation and the belief that he had murdered his nephews led to rebellion in October. The plot was initiated by southern magnates, some former members of Edward IV's household. For reasons that remain obscure, however, Buckingham also became involved. The plotters contacted Henry Tudor, who planned to invade England, in conjunction with an insurrection in southern England and Wales on October 18, and take the throne. However, Richard discovered the plot, the southeastern rebels moved prematurely, Buckingham's rising failed, and storms prevented Tudor's landing. Richard executed Buckingham and other leaders, placed numerous members of his northern affinity on the commissions of the peace and in other offices in the southern shires, where many received substantial land grants, and summoned a Parliament for January 1484, which passed an act of attainder against about 100 rebels.

Richard remained alert to a renewed assault. In March he persuaded his nieces to leave sanctuary and, following his queen's death on March 16, apparently considered marrying the eldest, Elizabeth, whom Tudor had promised to wed if he gained the throne. Richard's exhortations to the bishops in March to attack immorality were probably an attempt to bolster his image. His insecurity was exacerbated by the death of his heir, Edward of Middleham, in April (he had two illegitimate children, John and Katherine). Richard established new commissions of array in the spring and undertook a lengthy progress, traveling to Yorkshire and Durham, returning to London in August, spending the fall at Nottingham and Christmas at Westminster. Meanwhile he persuaded the duke of Brittany to withdraw protection from Richmond, but the latter fled to France, where he obtained Charles VIII's support. There were continued rumblings of discontent in England and in October new uprisings in Calais and East Anglia, which smoldered until year's end. Richard exhorted the southern shires to vigilance and in December issued a proclamation against Tudor.

Early in 1485 he learned that Tudor was planning an invasion and incurred further unpopularity by levying a forced loan to strengthen his defenses. Richard had recognized Clarence's son, Edward, earl of Warwick as royal heir, but now replaced him with his sister's son, John de la Pole, earl of Lincoln. In June Richard returned to Nottingham. He issued new commissions of array and placed Lord Lovell in command of the English fleet at Southampton. Tudor landed near Milford Haven on August 7, marched to Shrewsbury, and thence to Bosworth. Wearing his crown into battle, a demoralized Richard met Tudor on August 23. Hampered by the terrain, Lord Stanley's desertion, and Northumberland's inability or unwillingness to join the fray, Richard attempted to engage Tudor in personal combat, but was killed before reaching him. His naked body was thrown over a horse, taken to Leicester, and displayed for two days before he was buried at Grey Friars. Though Henry VII built a tomb for him, it was destroyed during the Reformation, and Richard remains the only English monarch since the Norman Conquest without a suitable burial place.

RICHARD III AS A GREAT LEADER

One of the strongest points in Richard's favor is his loyalty to Edward IV, in spite of the fact that he received substantially less reward than Clarence prior to the latter's execution in 1478. Richard built his affinity in Edward IV's interests and associated membership therein with service to the crown. More generally Richard was devoted to the Yorkist cause, and even his usurpation of the throne and arbitrary use of power can be seen as an attempt to maintain Yorkist control of the realm and continuity with Edward's regime. Prior to the October 1483 rising he employed many members of Edward's household and many of the same local officials.

As duke and king, Richard demonstrated the good lordship expected of medieval magnates. He skillfully built influence in the north, where he assumed leadership of the Kingmaker's affinity and won the loyalty of other noblemen, including the powerful Northumberland. He established lesser affinities in East Anglia, Wales, and elsewhere. Richard displayed considerable ability as a soldier. It is often overlooked that he deserves credit for suppressing "Buckingham's rebellion" and that he came near to winning the Battle of Bosworth. Had he done so, Henry Tudor would merit small attention in history books and Richard—given more time—might have erased his negative image. After all, Edward IV and Henry VII were usurpers, too.

Richard worked hard at governing. His one Parliament is best known for attainting rebels, but it also ratified his title and passed legislation regulating landholding, uses, and the cloth trade, increasing protection for defendants in felony cases, and outlawing benevolences, arbitrary taxes levied by Edward IV. He also created the Council of the North as a counterpart to Edward's council for Wales. Richard was genuinely pious, patronized religious institutions, founded numerous chantries and collegiate establishments, and planned a college at York. He showed real interest in scholarship, the new humanism, and music. Certainly he deserves approbation for giving Henry VI a decent tomb. His success in foreign policy was limited by lack of money and the use of Tudor as a diplomatic pawn by Brittany and France.

RICHARD III THE TYRANT

Many crimes imputed to Richard by Polydore Vergil, Thomas More, William Shakespeare, and others are unproven. Reportedly he suggested killing the recorder of York when that city obstructed Edward IV's return in 1471. It is alleged that he and Clarence murdered Edward, the prince of Wales, at Tewkesbury and that Richard murdered Henry VI in the Tower. Though neither is impossible, it is unlikely that Richard would have acted without orders from Edward IV. The charge that Richard murdered Thomas, the bastard of Fauconberg, in 1471 is false and so almost certainly is the rumor that he murdered his wife in 1484. His alleged role in Clarence's death is discounted even by his implacable critic More. However, it says something that contemporaries believed such stories, and there is an element of poetic justice in Richard's treatment by Tudor propagandists, since he was, as Ross notes, "the first English king to use character-assassination as a deliberate instrument of policy."

Many allegations against Richard are real enough. He shared responsibility for executing the duke of Somerset and other Lancastrians in 1471, though this must be viewed in the context of war. In 1474 he and Clarence deprived their mother-in-law of any right in the Warwick inheritance. Particularly difficult to excuse are the summary executions without trial of Hastings, Rivers, and others and his mistreatment of Mistress Shore, whose patient endurance of punishment won her considerable sympathy. His legislation against benevolences was compromised by his resort to a forced loan.

Most damning is that Richard usurped the throne and murdered his nephews. He claimed the crown on dubious grounds, first alleging that Edward IV was a bastard, then charging that his marriage to Elizabeth Woodville was invalid and his children illegitimate. There is little reason to doubt that he had his nephews murdered. This created a vicious circle that ultimately led to Bosworth. It cost Richard the loyalty of Edward IV's servants. Following the 1483 rebellion, he had to rely on his own affinity, and the intrusion of his northern followers into southern shires created further disaffection, including the risings in the fall of 1484. As Richard gave more authority and rewards to a shrinking group of dependable servants, other magnates concluded that they had no future under him and threw their support to Henry Tudor.

SUGGESTIONS FOR ADDITIONAL READING

Bennett, Michael. *The Battle of Bosworth.* New York: St. Martin's Press, 1985.

Hanham, Alison. *Richard III and His Early Historians, 1483–1535.* Oxford: Oxford University Press, 1985.

Horrox, Rosemary E. *Richard III: A Study in Service.* Cambridge: Cambridge University Press, 1989.

Kendall, Paul Murray. *Richard the Third.* New York: W. W. Norton & Company, 1955.

Kendall, Paul Murray, ed. *Richard III: The Great Debate. Sir Thomas More's History of King Richard III. Horace Walpole's Historic Doubts on the Life and Reign of King Richard III.* New York: W. W. Norton & Company, 1965.

Pollard, A. J. *Richard III and the Princess Tower.* New York: St. Martin's Press, 1991.

Potter, Jeremy. *Good King Richard? An Account of Richard III and His Reputation, 1483–1983.* Rprt. London: Dorset Press, 1989.

Ross, Charles. *Richard III.* Berkeley: University of California Press, 1981.

Saccio, Peter. *Shakespeare's English Kings: History, Chronicle, and Drama.* Oxford: Oxford University Press, 1977.

Seward, Desmond. *Richard III: England's Black Legend.* New York: Franklin Watts, 1984.

William B. Robison

Maximilien Robespierre
1758–1794

Revolutionary Leader in France
Dominant Leader of the Committee of Public Safety, 1793–1794

Maximilien Robespierre is the most controversial leader of the French Revolution. For conservatives, Robespierre represents the "excesses" of the Revolution, the very embodiment of the Reign of Terror, the guillotine, and mass executions of innocent people. For liberals, he was a necessary evil, a dictator necessitated by foreign war and domestic factionalism. For Marxists, Robespierre was a positive leader, who not only organized the war economy and fought the enemies of France, but also offered a social program to the artisans and shopkeepers of Paris that was a prelude to a proletarian revolution. Finally, there are those who interpret Robespierre as a flawed utopian who attempted to impose his ideal of a Republic of Virtue by force.

Few political leaders cry out for psychological probing as this man does. Maximilien Robespierre was a complex personality and his evolution into a dictator, even a paranoid one, was not predictable or inevitable. Had he continued to live the quiet life as a small-town lawyer, Robespierre would have remained a local champion of progress and tolerance, a convert to the Enlightenment in a respectable provincial setting. But the outbreak of the French Revolution changed his life radically as it had for so many other young men in his generation. At thirty, Robespierre was elected to the 1789 meeting of the Estates-General.

BIOGRAPHICAL BACKGROUND

Maximilien Robespierre was born in the provincial town of Arras in 1758. He was a serious, earnest young man with a touch of self-righteousness about him. Brought up by his two aunts, he lived a very private, even "bookish" childhood. It seems he had no close friends and never fell in love. There was a strong ascetic strain in Robespierre, a character trait that earned him a reputation for self-control and also for aloofness. He won a scholarship to the University of Paris and learned his Latin authors, rhetoric, and the law. Returning to Arras, he became a lawyer, apparently an idealistic one who fought for victims of religious intolerance.

As a member of a literary society in Arras, Robespierre imbibed the political thought and social criticism of his time with a special attraction to Jean-Jacques Rousseau's quest for sincerity and "virtue" in a corrupt urban world. In 1789, Robespierre emerges as a respected provincial lawyer who knew how to speak in public, was aware of national problems, and had an idealistic bent.

During the first two years of the French Revolution (1789–1791), French laws and institutions were thoroughly reformed. At this stage of his career Robespierre was still a modest young deputy who was learning about parliamentary politics. He observed the shifting alliances and factions in the National Assembly, the explosion of a political press, pamphlets, and clubs, and the growing power of the Paris municipal government and its forty-eight wards, all maneuvering for influence and power. In these years Robespierre earned a reputation for integrity and developed an eloquence in his speeches that drew increasing attention from the Assembly. It was Robespierre who proposed the self-denying law which made all the delegates to the first Assembly of 1789 ineligible for the second in 1791. Six months later as war clouds gathered, he cautioned the "crusaders" in the Assembly by arguing that liberty could not be spread abroad by force. Ironically in the light of his later behavior, Robespierre opposed capital punishment.

After the attempted flight of the king in June 1791 and the discrediting of the constitutional monarchists, Robespierre followed the Jacobin Club in its move toward republicanism. He called for universal male suffrage and the end of property qualifications for voting and office holding. He was rapidly becoming a "democrat," a new word on the political landscape anywhere in the Western world. During the momentous year 1792, Robespierre and his allies, the popular street leaders Georges Danton and Jean-Paul Marat, led the republican faction inside and outside the National Assembly. After the outbreak of the war and the establishment of the first French Republic, the Jacobin Party pushed for a policy of administrative centralization, mobilization for total war, and the arrest of "counterrevolutionaries," an elastic term that embraced all those who emigrated, clergy who refused to take an oath to the new religious settlement, and anyone "suspected" of supporting foreign enemies.

ROBESPIERRE AS A GREAT LEADER

Instead of a person whose ideas and behavior developed gradually over the years, Robespierre almost suddenly emerged as the one politician who might be able to control the French Revolution and bring it to a successful conclusion. He had a keen political sense, judged events and personalities acutely, and knew how to manipulate the institutions of power around him. A blend of political acumen and a high idealism made him very successful for a time and in the end very dangerous. Yet Robespierre's bid for power cannot be understood apart from the extraordinary circumstances in France in 1793.

March 1793 was a disastrous month for the French revolutionaries. Already plagued by inflation, food shortages, desertions, a disloyal nobility and clergy, a rebellious peasantry, and a war with England, Austria, Prussia, Holland, Spain, and Savoy, the new government of France now witnessed the outbreak of a guerrilla war in its western provinces and the desertion of one of its generals at the front. The revolutionaries had executed their king two months before and were regarded by all of Europe's governments as "regicides" and outcasts of civilized society. All of these circumstances created a psychology of hope and fear among the French revolutionaries. Hope that the great revolution would fulfill their ideals of Liberty, Equality, and Fraternity. Fear that all their efforts would be in vain and that they would pay with their lives for having killed their king. The new French Republic was beleaguered indeed.

Robespierre was a part of this psychology of hope and fear. He reacted with determination and a clear program. The nation had to mobilize all its resources for the struggle, draft every available man, ration food, fix prices and wages, weed out opposition at home, punish slackers, speculators, and food hoarders, and "suspend" due process of law to expedite arrests of "counterrevolutionaries." The Jacobin Party did not rely on votes alone. They put pressure on their opponents in the parliament (the Convention) by using their national network of clubs, their allies in the Paris municipal government, and above all by mobilizing the wards of Paris, flooding the streets with an armed populace to threaten their opponents in the Convention. By June 1793 Robespierre and his party had gained control of the Paris government and launched their program. The new Jacobin government now established the Committee of Public Safety, a twelve-man executive committee, confirmed monthly by the vote of the Convention, but with unlimited powers to administer the country in wartime. Robespierre was the spokesman of this committee.

The symbol of this war dictatorship was the guillotine. The purpose of this formidable blade was to frighten as much as to execute the "enemies of the Republic." Guillotines were set up in every town in France, symbols of a policy called the Terror. The policy was further implemented by the creation of a special Revolutionary Tribunal, a law court that progressively dispensed with the rules of judicial due process—jury trial, defense lawyers, cross-examination of witnesses, and validation of evidence. In May 1794, Robespierre and the committee pushed through the "Law of Suspects" which made it possible to condemn people "suspected" of treasonous acts on the basis of accusations that were often unverified.

The Committee of Public Safety could not have enforced its program without a national network of support. The main basis of its power was in the two thousand Jacobin clubs throughout the towns of France which received and implemented the policies from Paris. Many of their members were local professional men not unlike Robespierre before the Revolution. For the most part, they supported Robespierre's policies as necessary until the war was won. In addition, the committee sent special agents called "Representatives on Mission" to the provinces to accelerate execution of the new laws, especially those pertaining to the draft and requisition of supplies for the army. These agents were also sent to the army to enforce discipline and report any signs of disaffection or treason.

These harsh methods were successful in accomplishing the aims of the French Republic. By the spring of 1794 the French armies had decisively beaten their enemies on the continent; there was no longer a danger of invasion. In addition, the armed insurrections within France had also been defeated, though not without executions of at least twenty thousand "traitors." The country was organized into a military state with the largest army of its time (almost one million men), well equipped, and supported by a war economy that fixed prices and wages, pursued hoarders, and condemned speculators who made large profits from war supplies. There was little room for amnesty in this crisis year. Altogether about forty thousand people died in this year, half with guns in their hands fighting against the Republic. Yet the war both abroad and at home had been won.

Robespierre and his colleagues on the committee were also dependent on the people of the wards of Paris—shopkeepers, artisans, and day laborers. These people were intensely patriotic, believing rightly that they had the most to gain from a revolution of equality. They were therefore very active, meeting nightly in their wards and bombarding the committee with petitions and demands. Robespierre and his eleven colleagues, almost all middle-class professional men, were uneasy with this support, but they could not afford to ignore it, at least until the war had been won. Hence, like good politicians they provided a program to satisfy these unruly allies.

Some historians believe that this program represented the beginnings of the welfare state, even the vanguard of a preproletarian revolution. The program included a guarantee of food for everyone at low prices, the distribution of land to the poor, public education, social security for the aged, ill, and injured, and a progressive income tax. Comprehensive as this program was, most of it was only a promise for the future. When Robespierre fell from power in July 1794, the program was abandoned entirely. Still, this evidence makes Robespierre something of a social reformer as well as a war dictator.

ROBESPIERRE THE TYRANT

The year of the Terror was also the year when the Revolution evolved its own political culture, promoted by Robespierre and the Jacobins, but also having a life of its own. It was a political culture that affected every corner of daily existence. First there was the new revolutionary calendar that replaced the Christian calendar and dated the Year I from the establishment of the Republic. The names of places and even persons were changed to erase memories of the royalist and aristocratic past. Hundreds of squares once called Place Royale became Place de la Liberté. Nobles were called "the former" count or marquis and everyone was addressed as "Citizen" in the new egalitarian society. Paintings, sculpture, public monuments, even playing cards and dishes evoked public virtues, philosophers of the Enlightenment, or classical heroes like Hercules and Brutus. Babies were often named Gracchus or Spartacus instead of Pierre or Henri. The schools taught all children to recite the Declaration of the Rights of Man and to be vigilant against foreign enemies. It was patriotic to wear the small tricolor flag at all times. One should sing the new militant national anthem, "La Marseillaise," loudly, especially during patriotic ceremonies and on Republican holidays.

For the Jacobins, patriotic festivals were essential to inculcate a sense of civic duty. They were elaborately prepared, employed huge floats decorated with symbols of the Republic, and were orchestrated by leaders in classical Roman garb, appealing to a mass audience. Robespierre delivered long orations at these patriotic festivals, stressing civic sacrifice for the Fatherland and warning all citizens to be ever vigilant against the enemies of the Republic. Robespierre tried to channel popular religious feelings into a civic religion that emphasized a continued Christian belief in a Supreme Being and the immortality of the soul, but also stressed civic discipline. Robespierre believed that all education should be aimed at making virtuous citizens, not unlike the Spartans of ancient Greece. Hence we return again to the visionary strain in Robespierre that went back to his youth, perhaps to his reading of Rousseau.

Unfortunately for the success of Robespierre's civic religion, even revolutionaries fighting for Liberty and Equality were no more virtuous than any other human beings. Robespierre's self-righteousness now combined with his utopian Republican vision. He became incapable of tolerating people who, while not actively anti-Republican, were not sufficiently committed to his Republic of Virtue. There was a touch of John Calvin's "God's Elect" in this vision of the "Citizen," but with Robespierre it was unchecked by any mercy for the sinful or tolerance for the self-indulgent. Robespierre promoted an atmosphere of fear.

This passion for civic virtue, perhaps always latent in Robespierre, now emerged in full force. By June 1794 it was clear that the foreign and domestic enemies of France had been defeated and the counterrevolutionaries were no longer a menace. Yet Robespierre continued the Reign of Terror and the suspension of civil liberties, claiming without evidence that there were still traitors to be found and executed. His old revolutionary comrade, Georges Danton, was condemned officially for "treason," but the real reason for Danton's execution was his desire to end the Terror. Before his death Danton warned even sincere republicans: "The Revolution is devouring its own children." Robespierre lived only four months after Danton. His own Jacobin Party did not support him when the deputies shouted him down as a "tyrant." He was executed in July 1794. With Robespierre's death, the Terror came to a sudden end.

SUGGESTIONS FOR ADDITIONAL READING

Blum, Carol. *Rousseau and the Republic of Virtue; the Language of Politics in the French Revolution.* Ithaca, N.Y.: Cornell University Press, 1986.

Connelly, Owen. *French Revolution, Napoleonic Era.* New York: Holt, Rinehart, and Winston, 1979.

Hampson, Norman. *Will and Circumstance: Montesquieu, Rousseau and the French Revolution.* Norman: University of Oklahoma, 1983.

Jordan, David P. *The Revolutionary Career of Maximilien Robespierre.* New York: The Free Press, 1985.

Korngold, Ralph. *Robespierre: First Modern Dictator.* London: MacMillan, 1937.

Marat, Jean. *Robespierre.* New York: Scribner's, 1974.

Palmer, Robert. *Twelve Who Ruled: The Committee of Public Safety During the Terror.* Princeton, N.J.: Princeton University Press, 1973.

Parker, Harold T. *The Cult of Antiquity and the French Revolutionaries: A Study in the Development of the Revolutionary Spirit.* New York: Octagon, 1965.

Rude, George. *Robespierre: Portrait of a Revolutionary Democrat.* New York: Viking, 1975.

Thompson, James. *Robespierre.* 2 vols. New York: Howard Fertig, 1968.

Robert Forster

Joseph Stalin (Josif Vissarionovich Dzhugashvili)

1879–1953

General Secretary of the Soviet Communist Party and Dictator of the Soviet Union, 1924–1953

Akaki Bakradze, a noted literary critic and politician from Joseph Stalin's native Georgia, noted that "Stalin was born to be two legends." During his lifetime he was deified by the Soviet media for his accomplishments in creating and safeguarding a strong Soviet state. Only three years after Stalin's death he was condemned as the personification of evil. Although Bakradze concluded that Stalin was neither a god nor a devil but merely an extraordinarily strong political leader, historians have continued to debate the true meaning of Stalin's career.

Following Lenin's death in January 1924, Stalin gradually established his complete control over the Bolshevik party. Stalin was a dedicated Marxist-Leninist who also craved absolute personal power. He dramatically changed the lives of the majority of the inhabitants of the Soviet Union by establishing communism in the countryside and modernizing the country's industry. He literally transformed the Soviet Union into a military and industrial world power. Relying on this industrial power, Stalin was able to defeat Hitler and, after 1945, to extend his influence over much of Eastern and Central Europe.

All of this was accomplished by enormous human sacrifice. Millions of Russians and other ethnic groups in the Soviet empire starved to death or were murdered in Stalin's concentration camps. With the exception of Adolf Hitler, Stalin had no equal as a mass murderer in modern times. Surprisingly, contemporaries often misinterpreted his policies. In September 1935, for example, on the eve of Stalin's show trials, the correspondent Louis Fischer informed Americans that police terror was being curtailed and the "framework of a democracy" could clearly be seen in the Soviet Union. Even two of Stalin's official critics, Nikita Khrushchev and Mikhail Gorbachev, praised him for protecting socialism during a period of crisis. History has shown both of these Soviet leaders wrong. Stalin's strong military and industrial power in the end proved to be a house of cards that crumbled and disintegrated as soon as police and party repression were abolished.

BIOGRAPHICAL BACKGROUND

Josif Vissarionovich Dzhugashvili, who adopted the pseudonym Joseph Stalin in 1912, was born on December 21, 1879, in Gori, Georgia, a town in the Russian Caucasus. His father, Vissarion, was a poor cobbler. His mother, Yekaterina, was a deeply religious, illiterate washerwoman who wanted Stalin to become a priest. The couple had already buried three of their children before Stalin was born. As a child, Joseph Stalin suffered smallpox and an accident that left him with facial scars and a withered left arm. When young Stalin was only eleven years old, his brutal father died.

In 1888, Stalin enrolled in an ecclesiastical elementary school in Gori. An excellent pupil, he gained entry into the Tiflis Theological Seminary in 1894. Like many fellow seminarians in Georgia, Stalin soon joined a secret revolutionary organization in Tiflis. He was expelled from the seminary in 1899 and subsequently devoted himself completely to the underground Social Democratic (Marxist) movement in the Caucasus and in the oil fields of Baku.

Between 1902 and 1917, Stalin was arrested eight times and spent half of his time in prison or in exile. Before his last pre-war arrest and exile to Siberia in 1913, he had joined Lenin's Bolshevik faction of the Social Democratic movement and produced an essay on "Marxism and the National Question."

In 1902 he married a peasant girl, Yekaterina Svanidze, who bore him a son before she died in 1908. Although in 1919 he married Nadezhda Alliluyeva, a young daughter of a Bolshevik comrade, Stalin noted that the death of his first wife killed his "last warm feelings for people." His second wife committed suicide in 1932 during the height of the collectivization and industrialization drive.

After the February 1917 revolution, which overthrew the tsarist government in Russia, Stalin returned to Petrograd (Leningrad). Although legend during the Stalin era exaggerated his role in 1917, Stalin played an important part in Bolshevik activities. Between 1917 and 1920 he was a member of both the Central Committee and the Political Bureau of the Bolshevik party. In addition, Stalin was commissar for nationalities. By 1922 Stalin was secretary-general of the Communist Party of the Soviet Union and a member of the three other major party organs—the Organizational Bureau, the Central Committee, and the Politburo.

Lenin died in January 1924, leaving a testimony that warned the party leadership of Stalin's ambitions. Cleverly allying himself with various wings of the Bolshevik party, Stalin eliminated all of this major opponents between 1924 and 1928. In the latter year, Stalin not only established his personal dictatorship but also adopted the party's left-wing economic program by abolishing the neo-capitalism of the New Economic Policy and introducing massive industrialization and collectivization. To ensure his complete triumph over any potential opposition, Stalin initiated a series of Purge Trials between 1936 and 1939, which eliminated the majority of old party leaders.

Between 1941 and 1945, Stalin was engaged in a struggle for survival with Nazi Germany. Stalin unwittingly helped Hitler by purging some of his best military leaders in 1937. After initial German victories, Stalin's military stopped Hitler's forces, first in front of Moscow in December 1941, and then again at Stalingrad in late 1942. The postponement of the second front by the Western Allies fed Stalin's paranoia, though it had been his accommodation with Hitler in 1939 that had forced Britain to fight alone for so long. Stalin was sufficiently aware of reality that he returned to the exploitation of Russian religious feeling, after having pursued a devoutly atheist policy throughout his official career. Once again Russians were called upon by a suddenly revivified church hierarchy to fight for "Holy Mother Russia."

Following the retreat and eventual defeat of the Germans, Stalin decided to establish his own puppet regimes in much of Eastern Europe. This guaranteed Soviet security and opened up new areas for exploitation. Stalin's policy in Eastern Europe, particularly in Poland, after 1945 was a major factor in the emergence of the Cold War. Stalin met this challenge from the West by continuing his old emphasis on heavy industry at the expense of consumer goods.

During the last years of Stalin's life (1945–1953), he introduced new cultural and political purges. Milovan Djilas, a Yugoslav communist who was invited to dinner parties in the Kremlin after 1945, remembered the bizarre atmosphere in which Stalin encouraged heavy drinking bouts similar to Peter the Great's notorious debaucheries. Stalin died on March 5, 1953, several days after suffering a stroke. He was buried next to Lenin in Moscow's Red Square. In 1961, after Khrushchev's de-Stalinization, his body was removed from the mausoleum and placed in a tomb behind Lenin's celebrated resting place.

STALIN AS A GREAT LEADER

The Soviet historian and former dissident, Roy Medvedev, argued that Stalin was "fanatically dedicated" to power. Indeed, Stalin held power longer than any other Soviet leader and as long as most nineteenth-century tsars. Isaac Deutscher, a Marxist historian, argued, however, that Stalin was not merely power hungry but was truly dedicated to the Bolshevik revolution. During the 1930s an official personality cult, disseminated in literature, pictures, and statues, depicted the Soviet ruler as the wise and unerring interpreter of Marxist-Leninism.

Stalin used his dictatorial powers to transform Russia into a leading economic and military power. Stalin liked to call the massive industrialization drive between 1928 and 1932 a "revolution from above." Historians have explained it as the second Bolshevik revolution. Stalin had a greater impact on the overwhelming majority of the Soviet population than Lenin. As late as 1928, 75 percent of the 147 million Soviet citizens lived in rural, agricultural communities. By 1940, 97 percent of the peasant households had been herded into collectives. The surplus rural population was absorbed by new urban industries. Between 1926 and 1939, 20 million people moved from rural to urban centers. In addition, industrialization came to vast rural Asian regions of Russia, hitherto untouched.

On February 4, 1931, Stalin informed a gathering of industrial managers that Russia had always suffered "beatings" from foreign powers because of her backwardness. He reminded his audience of Lenin's remark that Russia would have to overtake the capitalistic powers or perish. The Soviet leader launched his massive First Five-Year Industrialization Plan in 1928. The results were impressive. Between 1928 and 1938 iron and steel production increased by 400 percent, and coal output expanded threefold. By 1940 the Soviet Union was the world's second-largest oil producer and the third-largest steel producer. Particularly impressive was the fact that in 1938 Soviet metal industries produced ten times as much in value as they had in 1929.

Relying on intensive labor efforts by workers like Alexei Stakhanov and schools to educate illiterate peasants, production was increased. Foreign observers like John Scott were enthusiastic about the accomplishments of Soviet industrialization at a time when much of the Western world suffered mass unemployment. The British left-wing intellectuals, Sidney and Beatrice Webb, described Stalin's accomplishments in the early 1930s as "a new civilization," while the journalist William Henry Chamberlin concluded in 1934 that Stalin's Russia was experiencing a "new iron age."

Stalin also made a major contribution to the Soviet Union's international and military position, eventually raising her to the rank of world power. Stalin's foreign policy during the 1930s sought to establish a collective security system that would contain the danger of Fascism and Nazism. After the Western powers appeased Hitler in Munich in September 1938, Stalin decided to protect the narrow interests of the Soviet Union. In August 1939 he signed a nonaggression pact with Hitler that enabled the German dictator to launch his attack on Poland a month later.

Stalin had hoped for a long war that would deplete the strength of both Hitler and the Western powers. Disregarding warnings from his agents, he continued to supply Hitler with vital raw materials between 1939 and 1941. On June 22, 1941, Hitler's armies shocked Stalin by launching a massive assault on the Soviet Union. Several weeks passed before the Soviet dictator regained his composure. Eventually, Stalin emerged as a competent leader who stopped Hitler's advance on Moscow in December 1941, a real turning point of the war. Stalin's armies pushed Hitler's legions back and forced the surrender of Berlin on May 2, 1945. Stalin's role during World War II endeared him to many of his countrymen as the savior of "Mother Russia."

At the end of World War II, Stalin's armies had gained control over much of Eastern Europe. After the defeat of Germany, Stalin also expanded his influence in Asia by entering the war against Japan and acquiring the southern half of Sakhalin and the Kurile Islands. In 1949, Soviet scientists tested the first Soviet atomic bomb, propelling the Soviet Union into the role of a world superpower. Stalin challenged the will of Western democracies during the Berlin crisis of 1948–1949 and the Korean War of 1950–1953. The resulting arms race after 1950, ironically, would eventually bankrupt the economy of the Soviet Union. Stalin had created a world power, but at the expense of consumerism and the future viability of the first Communist state in history.

STALIN THE TYRANT

One contemporary German communist compared Stalin to "Hitler plus Asia." Terror and political persecution had been part of Bolshevik rule since late 1917. But Stalin, who liked to compare himself with the sixteenth-century Russian tsar Ivan the Terrible, ordered the murder of thousands of suspected and imagined political enemies. Like another Russian tsar, Peter the Great, Stalin used brutal methods to modernize the country, regardless of the toll paid by the population. Finally, after 1945, Stalin extended his terror to Eastern and Central Europe, eliminating former political, economic, and cultural elites, while simultaneously exploiting the resources of these client states for the benefit of the Soviet Union.

Beginning in late 1929, when Stalin accelerated the collectivization drive, he directed his first massive terror against the rural population of the Soviet Union. Millions of peasants were forced to give up their farms and join collectives. Agriculture was so badly disrupted, in part because of peasant resistance, that the countryside faced massive famines. At the same time Stalin continued to export grain in order to earn foreign currency for his industrialization. Perhaps as many as ten million peasants died between 1929 and 1934 as a result of forced collectivization and famine.

In addition, Stalin's rapid industrialization also relied on the use of slave labor organized and controlled by the police in gulags, or concentration camps. By 1941 the complex Soviet police organization supervised 17 percent of production in the construction industry, employing over one million prisoners and slave laborers in that industry alone. Furthermore, millions of Soviet citizens were forced to do manual labor, particularly in Siberia where millions died.

Stalin also unleashed his terror against old Bolsheviks and other population groups suspected of defiance. On December 1, 1934, he initiated his purge of the party by ordering the murder of Serge Kirov, the party boss in Leningrad. Subsequently a series of purge trials in 1936–1938 eliminated party and military leaders who might present a challenge to Stalin's total power. Old Bolsheviks were imprisoned, tortured, and executed. Stalin himself took a personal interest in the interrogations. The terror transformed the ruling elite between 1934 and 1939 and purged the party of over one million members. Even wives of suspects and children as young as twelve were arrested. Mass graves containing over 100,000 victims of Stalin's terror have been unearthed in the vicinity of Minsk, Belarus. Robert Conquest, the most knowledgeable scholar on Stalin's terror, concluded that at least twenty million men, women, and children died because of Stalin's economic and police measures. The fictitious "Jewish doctors' plot" was merely one of the more flamboyant aspects of his paranoia.

Stalin told one of his associates that in a generation no one would remember "all this riff-raff" which he had ordered executed. Considering the brutality of Stalin's rule, it was not surprising that Harrison Salisbury, an American journalist in Moscow during Stalin's funeral, was amazed to see women crying in the streets. An even more intriguing tribute to Stalin came from Lev Kopselev, a former labor camp inmate whose brother had died in a gulag. He remembered that he cried when he heard of Stalin's death. For the moment, at least, Stalin's achievements still seemed to outweigh his terror.

SUGGESTIONS FOR ADDITIONAL READING

Conquest, Robert. *The Great Terror: Stalin's Purge of the Thirties.* New York: Macmillan, 1968.

Daniels, Robert V., ed. *The Stalin Revolution.* Lexington, Mass.: D. C. Heath, 1990.

Deutscher, Isaac. *Stalin. A Political Biography.* New York: Oxford University Press, 1967.

Lewis, Jonathan, and Phillip Whitehead. *Stalin: A Time for Judgement.* New York: Pantheon, 1990.

McNeal, Robert H. *Stalin: Man and Ruler.* New York: New York University Press, 1988.

Medvedev, Roy A. *On Stalin and Stalinism.* Translated by Ellen de Kadt. Oxford: Oxford University Press, 1979.

Seaton, Albert. *Stalin as Military Commander.* New York: Praeger, 1976.

Tucker, Robert, C. *Stalin as Revolutionary, 1879–1929.* New York: Norton, 1973.

———. *Stalin in Power: The Revolution from Above, 1928–1941.* New York: Norton, 1990.

Volkogonov, Dmitri. *Stalin Triumph and Tragedy.* Translated by Harold Shukman. New York: Grove Weidenfeld, 1991.

Johnpeter H. Grill

Pyotr Arkad'evich Stolypin
1862–1911

Prime Minister of Russia, 1906–1911

Alexander Zenkovsky has called Pyotr Arkad'evich Stolypin "Russia's last great reformer." Stolypin rose to power in Russia during the period between the two great revolutions: that of 1905, which shook the autocratic system, and that of 1917, which swept it away. The 1905 revolution had caused Tsar Nicholas II to issue the October Manifesto, which established a Duma, or parliament, with the power to pass legislation. To some, it seemed that this partially democratic body spelled the end of the autocracy and the beginning of a Western-style constitutional monarchy. The tsar, however, retained many prerogatives, including the right to prorogue the Duma and to legislate in its absence, under Article 87 of the October Manifesto. Stolypin came to power in 1906, just as the First Duma was being dismissed. The Second Duma, which also opposed the policies of Nicholas, was dismissed in 1907 and a new electoral law was promulgated. Stolypin could work with the Third Duma, which was allowed to last for a full five-year term, continuing after Stolypin's assassination.

Pyotr Stolypin's most important policy was a series of land reforms designed to do away with the traditional peasant commune and to create an independent farmer in Russia. The Second Duma opposed these reforms for a variety of reasons. Many Slavophiles looked upon the land commune as a part of the Russian soul, a traditional organ that dated back to early Russian history. The Socialists looked upon it as an organ that trained the peasants in socialism and one which some thought would allow them to pass from feudalism to socialism, skipping the phase of capitalism. The government, on the other hand, had become alarmed with peasant institutions when many peasants participated in the revolts of 1905 and voted for opposition parties in 1906 and 1907. The commune did retard agriculture. Stolypin sought to transform the Russian countryside into a force of order that supported the government by abolishing the commune.

BIOGRAPHICAL BACKGROUND

Pyotr Arkad'evich Stolypin was born on April 12, 1862, in Dresden, Germany. He was the son of Arkadii Dmitr'evich Stolypin, descendent of a great noble family, a general in the Russian artillery and later Commandant of the Kremlin Palace. His mother, Natalia Mikhailovna Gorchakova, was the daughter of a Russian foreign minister. In 1884, Stolypin married Olga Borisovna Niedhardt, the daughter of a prominent Muscovite family, by whom he had six children (five girls and a boy). In 1885, he graduated from St. Petersburg University. He entered the Ministry of Internal Affairs but soon moved to provincial service, an unusual line of advancement for a future important statesman. In 1887 he became a marshal of the nobility in Kovno, first on the county (*uezd*) then on the district (*gubernia*) level. In 1902 he was appointed governor of Grodno and in 1903 he became governor of Saratov on the Volga, one of the most tumultuous cities of the empire. Here he came to the attention of the authorities in St. Petersburg during the revolution of 1905. Saratov was the place of exile for many revolutionaries. Stolypin's courage in putting down local disorders marked him as a coming man.

Stolypin was appointed Minister of Internal Affairs by Nicholas II in the spring of 1906. He is reported to have protested the appointment on account of his youth (he was the youngest member of the cabinet) and to have asked instead for the post of deputy minister. Nicholas II refused this request and indeed in July 1906 promoted him to chairman of the Council of Ministers (in effect, prime minister) while he retained his old post. Meanwhile, the First Duma was dismissed and new Duma elections were called.

Shortly after the dissolution of the Duma in August 1906, an attempt was made on Stolypin's life. Two revolutionaries disguised as gendarmes entered the home where he was vacationing on Aptekarskii Island. When they were prevented from approaching Stolypin's office, they exploded their bombs, killing some thirty people. A balcony on which Stolypin's son and one of his daughters were standing was hurled to the ground, leaving the girl permanently maimed. Stolypin was uninjured.

The wave of revolution that had begun in 1905 had not ceased, and Stolypin saw his first job as restoring order to the state. According to government figures, 1,126 officials were killed in 1906 and 3,000 in 1907. A similar number were wounded. In order to stop this violence, Stolypin resorted to field courts-martial which had the power to execute revolutionaries who committed acts of terrorism. Between August 1906 and April 1907, 1,102 people were executed by these military courts and another 127 were sentenced to hard labor. Only 21 were acquitted.

Stolypin also sought to win the peasantry back for the regime. In 1906 he introduced the first of his agrarian reforms, which were designed to make the peasants into landholders and ease the agricultural crisis in Russia. These reforms were introduced by ukase, since they did not have the support of the Duma. Many Duma members wanted to seize the nobles' estates and distribute them to the peasant communes, a solution to the problem of peasant land hunger that Stolypin opposed. The Second Duma, elected in 1907, proved to be as hostile to the monarch as the first. More avowed revolutionaries had been elected, since many Constitutional Democrats (Kadets) where barred from running because they had signed the anti-government Vyborg Manifesto after the dissolution of the First Duma. Stolypin could not work with this Duma, and as a result it was dissolved on June 16, 1907. Then, using Article 87 of the October Manifesto, Stolypin revised the electoral laws, cutting the representation of the peasants and the workers and greatly increasing the power of the Octoberist Party, which supported the government and the Stolypin reforms. The Third Duma, more cooperative, passed his agrarian reforms in 1911.

There were a number of other matters upon which Stolypin worked between 1907 and 1911. He wished to expand the relationship between Russia and Finland, which was an independent grand duchy ruled by the tsar. Stolypin sought to coordinate Finnish and Russian legislation in such matters as defense, currency, and postage. After 1908, Finnish laws would have to pass through the Council of Ministers before becoming effective. In 1910 the Duma was also given the right to agree to Finnish legislation, with the proviso that Finnish members would be included in both houses: the State Duma and the State Council.

Stolypin's most important crisis in 1911 concerned the plan to establish *zemstvos* (*uezd* and *gubernia* organs of local self-government) in the western provinces of Russia. This issue provoked a storm of protest in Russia nationalistic circles. When the issue was first brought up in 1910, the conservatives in the upper house of the Duma, the State Council, opposed the policy because Stolypin would be limiting the voting rights of the local Polish nobility in order to ensure a Russian majority. After a ten-month delay, the Western Zemstvo Bill was rejected by the State Council. Stolypin was furious and threatened to resign. To placate him, Nicholas II agreed to prorogue the Duma for one day, pass the Western Zemstvo Bill under Article 87, and also to exile two conservative state counselors from St. Petersburg. Stolypin won on the issue of the passage of the Western Zemstvo Bill, but his methods seemed a betrayal of the principles of the October Manifesto. It was widely rumored that he had lost the confidence of the tsar as well. His fall seemed to be only a matter of time when he was wounded by an assassin, Dmitrii Bogrov, at the Kiev Opera House in the presence of the tsar on September 14, 1911. He died of his wounds in Kiev on September 18.

STOLYPIN AS A GREAT LEADER

Pyotr Arkad'evich Stolypin is often described as the last man who had a chance to save the Russian empire after the revolution of 1905. His clear vision and forceful personality were tied to a program designed to bring immediate benefits to the peasants who constituted the overwhelming majority of the population. His reforms were designed to ease the problem of land hunger and arrears in taxes that had kept the peasant population in poverty since the Emancipation Statute of 1861. There is no question that the Russian peasantry was not prosperous in 1900. The Russian peasant in fact held more land than many of his Western European counterparts, but the communal form of agriculture held down productivity. The commune (*mir, obshchina*), not the peasant, held title to the land. The land was repartitioned periodically among the peasants of the *mir*. All peasants must hold equal land and equally good land. To assure a fair distribution of both the best land and the worst, the land was divided into strips, often so narrow that the peasant could barely run a plow through his holdings. The commune had to meet to decide what crops to plant in each area, since the strips could not be planted individually. The traditional nature of the commune meant that Russia had not participated in the agricultural revolution of the seventeenth and eighteenth centuries. The tradition-bound peasants used a three-field system with one fallow field rather than a nine-field system using root and grass crops. Nor could the peasant improve his land. The repartitional tenure meant that he would lose his improvements within a short time after they had been completed. The result was that in a good year the peasant often only reaped five grains for every grain sown. In a poor year peasant yields fell below three to one, the point at which agriculture became impossible.

The Russian government had supported the commune until the 1905 revolution, which proved that the peasants were not happy, satisfied residents of the state. Doubts had, however, already been expressed about the traditional form of agriculture. Before 1905, Sergei Witte, Vladimir Gurko, and Appolon Krivoshein had all expressed the feeling that the commune should be abolished. Stolypin had a predisposition toward that point of view. In the 1870s, an uncle had abolished the commune on his estates with good results. Stolypin's early career was in the western provinces, where private peasant landholding was more common than in the rest of European Russia. In addition, his experiences at Saratov, where some peasants held land privately, helped to convince him of the correctness of this course.

In a speech before the Duma, Stolypin described his policy as "a wager on the sober and the strong." By making the most energetic of the peasants prosperous, he would create a cadre in the countryside that would permanently support the tsar. Stolypin proposed to the First Duma that peasants be allowed to claim their strips of land as hereditary, and he later proposed that they be allowed to consolidate them into a single farm. He lowered the rate of interest at the Peasant Land Bank and allowed peasants who were trying to buy land for themselves to borrow one hundred percent of the value of that land. The peasant who held private land might work on the *otrub* or *hutor* system. In an *otrub*, the central village, with its peasant huts, remained, but the peasants owned their own fields and went out to work them each day. Under the *hutor* system, which Stolypin favored, the village disappeared, and the peasant built a new house amidst his fields. In most areas that adopted the Stolypin reforms the *otrub* was more common.

Stolypin's reform was passed by imperial ukase in 1906. In 1910 the Third Duma adopted a statute that was more radical than Stolypin's proposal. It allowed for the simple majority of a commune to decree redistribution rather than the two-thirds majority for which Stolypin had called. In 1911 the final form of the bill was adopted and signed by Nicholas II. Stolypin felt that if he had twenty years of peace, he could transform the Russian countryside. Indeed, in the years between 1906 and 1914, approximately a million families privatized and consolidated ten million *desiatinas* (27 million acres). In addition, 9.5 million *desiatinas* of noble land were acquired by the peasants. The privatized land proved extremely productive, with some estimates ranging as high as an astonishing 42 percent increase in productivity. It seems clear that the Stolypin reforms were transforming rural Russia. But Stolypin did not have his twenty years of peace. Three years after his assassination, Russia blundered into World War I. The war spawned a revolution that swept away his reforms along with the Russian empire.

STOLYPIN THE TYRANT

While Stolypin as a reforming benefactor of the peasantry may seem attractive, there were many elements to his regime that were far less benign. Stolypin came to the prime ministry at a time when the Russian empire was still suffering from the disorder associated with the revolution of 1905. He saw his first function as creating order within the state and was perfectly willing to use brutal remedies to destroy the revolutionary movement. His institution of field courts-martial for those involved in disorder squared badly with early twentieth-century concepts of justice. The fact that these courts-martial could impose the death penalty without appeal made them doubly sinister. The revolutionaries justly hated Stolypin and soon dubbed the nooses used to hang prisoners tried by these courts as "Stolypin neckties."

Stolypin was not a democrat. His relationship with the Duma proved that he was not unwilling to submit to the popular will. Although he accepted the existence of the Duma and was willing to work with it as long as it would cooperate with him, he nonetheless used extra-constitutional means whenever he found it expedient. His dismissal of the Second Duma and revision of the electoral laws was nothing short of a coup d'état against the Kadets and Socialist revolutionaries who had won the elections of 1906 and 1907. Even when he had a relatively pliant Third Duma, Stolypin did not scruple about using Article 87 to govern. The land reforms, Stolypin's greatest achievement, were in effect for four years by imperial ukase before they were adopted by democratic means, and were accepted only by a Duma that had been manipulated so that it did not reflect the views of the majority of the Russian people. Stolypin's high-handed methods could also be used against conservatives as in the case of the Western Zemstvo Bill. Stolypin's violation of the constitutional rights of the State Council and his exile of two leading members as punishment for thwarting his will proved the minister's power, but alienated important segments of society and resulted in a decline in Stolypin's prestige.

Stolypin also catered to the forces of Russian nationalism. The legislation on the Finnish diet was unpopular in Finland, reminding Finns of the dark days early in the reign when Nicholas II had tried to Russianize Finland. The Western Zemstvo Bill was manipulated to assure that a great Russian majority would dominate in these areas. In all, Stolypin did little to solve one of the most intractable problems facing Imperial Russia.

SUGGESTIONS FOR ADDITIONAL READING

Atkinson, Dorothy. *The End of the Russian Land Commune, 1905–1930.* Stanford, Calif.: Stanford University Press, 1983.

von Brok, Maria Petrovna. *Reminiscences of my Father, Peter A. Stolypin.* Translated by Margaret Patoski. Metuchen, N.J.: Scarecrow Press, 1970.

Conroy, Mary Schaeffer. *Peter Arkad'evich Stolypin: Practical Politics in Late Imperial Russia.* Boulder, Colo.: Westview Press, 1976.

Ferro, Marc. *Nicholas II: The Last of the Tsars.* Translated by Brian Pearce. New York: Oxford University Press, 1993.

Gurko, V. I. *Figures and Features of the Past.* Stanford, Calif.: Stanford University Press, 1939.

Hennessy, Richard. *The Agrarian Question in Russia, 1905–1907: The Inception of the Stolypin Reforms.* Giessen, Germany: Wilhelm Schmitz Verlag, 1977.

Lieven, Dominic. *Russia's Rulers Under the Old Regime.* New Haven, Conn.: Yale University Press, 1989.

Massie, Robert. *Nicholas and Alexandra.* New York: Atheneum, 1966.

Pavlovsky, George. *Agricultural Russia on the Eve of the Revolution.* 1930. Reprint. New York: Howard Fertig, 1968.

Robinson, Geroid Tanquary. *Rural Russia Under the Old Regime.* Berkeley: University of California Press, 1962.

Tokmakoff, George, *P. A. Stolypin and the Third Duma: A Study of Three Issues.* Lanham, Md.: University Press of America, 1981.

Zenkovsky, Alexander V. *Stolypin: Russia's Last Great Reformer.* Translated by Margaret Patoski. Princeton, N.J.: The Kingston Press, 1980.

Jackson Taylor, Jr.

Tito
(Josip Broz Tito)
1892–1980

Prime Minister of Yugoslavia, 1945–1953
President of Yugoslavia, 1953–1980

Considering the fate of Yugoslavia since 1991, the life of Marshal Tito assumes special significance. In retrospect, his tyrannical rule seems benign. The hatreds between Slovenes, Serbs, Croats, Bosnian Moslems, Albanians, and Macedonians are utterly incomprehensible to anyone unfamiliar with the historic circumstances that gave birth to that new term, "ethnic cleansing." It would be necessary to study the history of the South Slav peoples, linguistically so similar, who are torn today between Greek Orthodoxy, Roman Catholicism, and Islam. Certainly, all of them remember ancient slights and mutual injuries. The Serbian monarchy, which ruled the country between the two world wars, and Tito, who ruled it during 1945–1980, shared a common ability to create a sense of nationhood, transcending the linguistic, religious, ethic, and historic memories that might pull it apart. Now that Yugoslavia no longer exists, the career of Marshal Tito offers special interest because he accomplished the unification of a people who seem beyond reconciliation today.

BIOGRAPHICAL BACKGROUND

Josip Broz, known in history by his adopted name Tito, was born at the village of Kumrovec, near Zagreb, Croatia (then part of Austria-Hungary), on May 7, 1892. He was the seventh of the fifteen children of Franjo Broz, a poor Croat farmer. His mother, Marija-Micika Javorsak, was a Slovene peasant. At the age of thirteen he became a locksmith apprentice, and later a metalworker. He became involved in the Social Democratic Party of Croatia, with its radical socialist program. When World War I erupted in 1914, he was already a conscript in the Austrian military. He was wounded and taken a prisoner of war by the Russians in 1915. In Russia, he witnessed the Russian Revolution and the civil war, becoming a dedicated Communist. He finally returned to his native Croatia, now part of the newly created Yugoslavia, in 1920.

In Zagreb, where he settled with his Russian wife, he became a Communist activist. In the ensuing years he was imprisoned several times for his subversive activities. The Yugoslav party executive rewarded him by sending him to Moscow for additional "training" at the height of Stalin's notorious Purge Trials of the 1930s. In 1939 he was formally elected General-Secretary of the Communist Party of Yugoslavia, surrounding himself with a coterie of dedicated revolutionaries, including Edvard Kardjeli, Milovan Djilas, Alexander Rankovic, and Ivo Ribar. As an avowed Stalinist in monarchist Yugoslavia, he adopted the name of Tito.

In 1941 the Germans invaded Yugoslavia. Tito made a call for general resistance and organized the Partisans, a Communist resistance guerrilla force. The Partisans established an uneasy relationship with the Chetniks, royalist guerrillas led by Draza Mihailovic. They had a common cause but held to incompatible ideologies: bitter conflicts between them proved inevitable. By 1942, Tito's army was some 150,000 strong, a significant force to combat the Germans. In 1943 the Germans surrounded the Partisans of Naretva, but the Partisans brilliantly broke through the trap. Tito himself was wounded in a subsequent encounter. In late 1943 he formed an Anti-Fascist Council and established a provisional government, naming himself president, secretary of defense, and marshal of the armed forces. His subsequent successes against the Germans made him a significant player in the region. Indeed, both Winston Churchill and Stalin courted him with private meetings. Significantly, the Partisans liberated their country without direct assistance from the Soviet Red Army, thus giving Stalin no pretext to establish a puppet Soviet regime in Yugoslavia.

With the collapse of the Nazi invasion and the crushing of the Chetnik forces by the Partisans, Tito, now completely in control over Yugoslavia, established a Soviet-type regime. He ruthlessly and systematically eliminated all possible opposition—his Chetnik arch-rival, Mihailovic, was captured, publicly tried, and summarily executed in 1946. Since his country was devastated by the war and internecine conflict, Tito launched an ambitious five-year economic plan, which included the collectivization of agriculture. The Soviets provided some help, but Stalin began to resent the Yugoslav determination to maintain political independence from Moscow.

The fundamental problem was Tito's unwillingness to play the expected role of obedient disciple to the Kremlin boss. Stalin grew apprehensive of "Titoism," namely a nationalist version of Communism. Thus, when Tito politely inquired about the cause of Soviet displeasure, he received an abusive letter. Stalin apparently believed that he could bring Tito down promptly: "I will shake my little finger—and there will be no more Tito," he boasted. Tito, on the other hand, did not grasp, at first, the reasons for Stalin's wrath, particularly since Yugoslavia was generally emulating the Soviet political and socio-economic model, even adopting a plan for the collectivization of the farms (subsequently abandoned in 1953 because of stiff peasant resistance). In 1948, Stalin broke with Tito and expelled the Yugoslav Communist Party from the Cominform. For a while it even appeared as if the Soviets might invade Yugoslavia.

But Tito did not budge under the intense Soviet pressure. After an eight-hour speech at the Fifth Party Congress, he rallied his supporters to defy Stalin's isolation of Yugoslavia. In this endeavor he received major support from the West, which saw Tito now as a natural ally against Stalin's expansionist policies. Tito also launched a program of administrative and economic decentralization, giving the component Yugoslav republics greater autonomy. Yugoslavia, however, retained a one-party system of government.

When Stalin died in 1953, the Soviet policy changed from outright confrontation to reconciliation. Soviet premier Nikita Khrushchev came to pay homage to Tito in Belgrade twice (in 1955 and 1968)—a humiliating recognition of Tito's triumph over Stalin. In 1955 a constitution establishing a new Socialist Federative Republic of Yugoslavia was promulgated and Tito was formally elected its first president.

For the remainder of his life Tito advocated a policy of "nonalignment" in regard to both the Soviet Union and the United States. He emerged as the leader of the "Third World," involving diverse nonaligned member-states. He also promoted the concept of "separate roads to socialism," an alternative to the rigidly doctrinaire Soviet or Maoist Chinese models. He became a vigorous and highly visible elder statesman in the world community, traveled extensively, and was honored to the end by his people. He had a penchant for fine clothes, loved hunting and fishing, and was an accomplished pianist. His personal life was complicated—he was married three times and, at the end of his life, was estranged from his wife Jovanka—but under his ruthless yet charismatic leadership Yugoslavia seemed an island of stability even at the height of the Cold War.

Tito died, after various complications, on May 4, 1980, and was buried with full military and state honors on his private estate at Dedinje. Ironically, even the most pessimistic prognosticators at that time failed to predict how central Tito was to the unity of what was still known then as "Yugoslavia."

TITO AS A GREAT LEADER

Tito distinguished himself as an extraordinary war leader, an astute and original statesman, and the father of post-war Yugoslavia. He originated what has become known as Titoism—a curious blend of national communism, self-determination and federalism, independence from great-power influence, and a quasi-capitalistic economy.

Tito made significant contributions both to the theory and practice of modern guerrilla warfare. His natural affinity for strategy and tactics served well not only during the war, when his partisans frustrated the formidable German military machine, but in the ensuing Yugoslav internal struggle. Tito successfully dealt with the Serbian Chetniks led by Draza Mihailovic, the Croat Ustashi (fascists) of Ante Pavelic, the Serbian nationalists of Milan Nedic, and diverse other groups. His affinity for machiavellian politics also helped to deal both with the Soviets and the Western Allies.

During the post-war period Tito's most important accomplishments were the creation of a Yugoslav national Communist state and successful defiance of Soviet domination. In light of recent developments, the preservation of Yugoslav unity, albeit by means of rigid Communist controls, must be considered a spectacular achievement. Created in 1918, the country was composed of six republics (Serbia, Croatia, Slovenia, Bosnia-Herzegovina, Macedonia, and Montenegro) and two autonomous districts (Vijvodina and Kossovo-Metohija), home to five nations (Serbs, Croats, Slovenes, Montenegrins, Macedonians) and several nationalities (Magyars, Albanians), three main languages (Serbo-Croatian, Slovene, and Macedonian), two alphabets (Cyrillic and Latin), three major religions (Orthodox Christian, Roman Catholic, and Moslem), and a centuries-old legacy of unremitting hatred and violence. Tito, by the sheer weight of his ability and willful personality, was able to neutralize the powerful centrifugal forces now so much in evidence.

Tito's bold defiance of Stalin has become legend. The Soviet bullying actually served to unite the disparate factions in Yugoslavia, keeping the Partisan spirit vibrantly alive. Clearly, in the event of a Soviet invasion Tito was ready to go into the mountains to fight the Soviets with his customary tenacity—a fact that could not go unnoticed in Moscow. Indeed, the official Yugoslav military doctrine called for a defensive strategy based on self-sufficient regional guerrilla warfare, which could be carried on for a long time. Tito not only steered Yugoslavia through the crisis and preserved its independence, he also became a vocal advocate of the seemingly heretical concept of "separate roads to socialism."

The confrontation with the Soviet colossus no doubt led him to develop the Third World principle, to counterbalance the geo-political ambitions of the two superpowers. The central premise for this was a policy of proclaimed neutrality and nonalignment. In practical terms, this idea had great appeal to many countries formerly controlled by colonial powers. Tito actually became the official spokesman of the Third World bloc of nations and presided over some of their official gatherings. One such event was the 1961 Belgrade Conference of Nonaligned Nations, which was attended by such notables as India's Nehru, Ethiopia's Haile Selassie, and Egypt's Nasser.

In his domestic policies, Tito proved far more flexible and enlightened than his doctrinaire Soviet counterparts. He was not a democrat, but Yugoslavia never became a prototype of the Soviet police state. Tito permitted a modicum of private enterprises, decentralization of the economy, and ethnic diversity. Under his tutelage, Yugoslavia developed something of a communist civil society (Djilas' notorious "new class"), whereby some criticism of the regime was tolerated. Moreover, the Yugoslav system under Tito's tutelage resembled a continuous political experiment. Tito's Yugoslavia had several constitutions, reflecting the gradual decentralization of the country. The constitution of 1974 also called for a rotating presidency on the basis of ethnic lines. Tito was particularly sensitive to the age-old conflict between the two foes, the Serbs and the Croats. Although a Croat by birth, he never allowed his ethnic ancestry to cloud his impartiality.

Tito was one of the last "great men" of the twentieth century, something of an anachronism in the post–World War II world of power blocs, globalization, and techno-monoliths. His own worldview had been shaped by concerns of a bygone era, by Balkan complexities, tragedy, and wartime travails. He was driven by the impossible dream, Yugoslavia—united, proud, prosperous, and triumphant—and dedicated his life's energies to it. Himself an irrepressible rebel and a visionary, he nevertheless convinced his fellow Yugoslavs that the dream had materialized. Yet, to his credit, he was also a pragmatic statesman, adroitly adjusting to the changing realities of his time.

TITO THE TYRANT

For all of his remarkable qualities (trumpeted endlessly by a state-controlled media), Tito remained to the end an avowed Communist believer, with distinct autocratic, perhaps even megalomaniac impulses. He had certain Stalinist qualities, without, of course, Stalin's pathological psychopathic manifestations. Tito indeed was a firm believer in the Stalinist model until his Kremlin hero broke with him. Under him Yugoslavia remained a one-party, Communist regime that did not permit any direct opposition. Although he later permitted a measure of private enterprise, this proved secondary to the socialist principle of control of key economic sectors by the government. Tito remained blind to the fact that his vision of socialism, driven by the customary Marxist "class-struggle" ideals and proletarian orientations, was at odds with the realities of his relatively poor and predominantly agrarian Balkan country. Thus, despite the Stalinist legacy of failure, Tito actually wished to collectivize Yugoslav agriculture; this failed to occur, not because of a change of ideology on his part but mostly because the farmers resisted. Moreover, that Yugoslavia did not evolve into a monolithic, Brezhnev-type technocratic dinosaur was not so much the result of Tito's democratic instincts as of the inherent ethnic stubbornness and defiance of the various peoples he ruled. For all of his pragmatic instinct, Tito was mesmerized into immobility by a defunct ideology, whose historical basis dated back to the mid-nineteenth century. Like all of its major practitioners—from Lenin and Stalin in the Soviet Union to Mao in China and Castro in Cuba—he assumed that the end justified the means and that the presumed veracity of his political philosophy gave him the right to impose it upon others. This was arrogant abuse of power.

Believing that he represented the force of history, Tito saw himself beyond such "weaknesses" as friendship, loyalty, and tolerance, characteristics of ordinary mortals. Thus, political considerations and ideological orthodoxies, practiced to absurdity by his rival Stalin, evoked some appeal in Tito as well. At the end of World War II, when partisan victory was well in hand, Tito permitted the systematic butchery of his ideological antagonists, particularly the hated Chetniks. Their leader, Draza Mihailovic, was humiliated by means of an orchestrated public trial before his execution by a firing squad. Tito proved intolerant of some of his moderate critics: he personally ordered the incarceration of Archbishop Stepanic and even his good friend and wartime companion, Milovan Djilas. Hundreds, if not thousands, of people were sent to jail at various times for no other reason than that they seemed to threaten his grip on power.

Even in the waning years of his life he was susceptible to ideological miasma, although his ideological affinities concerned the practical rather than the abstract. In his dogged pursuit of Yugoslav's "neutrality" he came to depend on disparate allies whose agenda was often different from his. The powerful "neutral bloc" that Tito envisioned as a powerful counterbalance to Soviet and American "expansionism" proved, in the end, chimerical: from the outset it remained stridently anti-Western and therefore largely inconsequential in the global balance of power. Moreover, he lived to see Fidel Castro snatch from him the mantle of leadership of the Third World. Similarly, Tito's characteristic finessing of ethnic conflicts of Yugoslavia, consisting of bullying tempered by piecemeal concessions, pitting one group against another, and evoking anti-Soviet paranoia, merely postponed the inevitable. Like Stalin and his successors, who envisioned a new "Soviet Man" as an alternative to bourgeois ethnicity, Tito was driven by the "Yugoslav" concept—a supra-national stereotype to replace the mundane petty nationalism of his people. In his presumption, he overlooked Balkan history. Rather than finding a legitimate formula to overcome the inherent ethnic contradictions, he resorted to political machinations. He also failed to groom a competent and legitimate successor, perhaps jealous of his own self-made role as Yugoslavia's greatest leader. This proved his greatest folly.

Finally, Tito did not escape from the customary "cult of personality" and other megalomaniacal tendencies that seem to afflict all Communist dictators, from Stalin to Romania's Ceausescu. To the end of this days he proved a conscious mythmaker. The Yugoslav media, firmly controlled by the Tito political machine, daily reminded the people about the great historical figure in their midst. Ironically, even the outside world came to subscribe to the mythology. It is reputed that Tito had seventeen castles and hunting lodges maintained just for him, along with a private island with a private zoo and then the famous presidential compound on Uzicka Street, in the Dedinje district, combining four luxurious villas and a huge garden. An egotist, he was partial to extravagant flattery and other such venalities. He spent the rest of his days in luxurious surroundings, pomp, every whim being promptly satisfied by a coterie of devoted admirers and paid sycophants.

SUGGESTIONS FOR FURTHER READING

Adamic, Louis. *The Eagle and the Roots*. New York: Doubleday, 1952.

Auty, Phyllis. *Tito. A Biography*. New York: McGraw-Hill, 1970.

Chrisman, Henry M., ed. *The Essential Tito*. New York: St. Martin's Press, 1970.

Clissold, Stephen. *Whirlwind: An Account of Marshal Tito's Rise to Power*. New York: Philosophical Library, 1949.

Dedijer, Vladimir. *Tito*. New York: Simon and Schuster, 1953.

Djilas, Milovan. *Tito. The Story from Inside*. New York: Harcourt Brace Jovanovich, 1980.

Doder, Dusko. *The Yugoslavs*. New York: Random House, 1978.

MacLean, Fitzroy. *The Heretic. The Life and Times of Josip Broz-Tito*. New York: Harper & Bros., 1957.

Roberts, Walter R. *Tito, Mihailovic and the Allies, 1941–1945*. New Brunswick, N.J.: Rutgers University Press, 1973.

Ulam, Adam B. *Titoism the Cominform*. Cambridge, Mass.: Harvard University Press, 1951.

Alexander Sydorenko

Trajan (Marcus Ulpius Traianus)

53–117

Roman Emperor, 98–117

No Roman emperor has a higher reputation than Trajan. Dante's *Divine Comedy* preserves the legend that the pagan emperor even won entry into the Christian heaven (*Purgatory* 10 and *Paradise* 20). Historians today go at it differently, but in spite of some modern efforts to tarnish his luster, notably and properly for excessive militarism, and to improve the standing of his predecessor Domitian, there is no reason to doubt that Trajan was a good ruler.

While emperor, Trajan received the appellation "*optimus princeps*," and the label is still used. The English "best emperor" fails to catch the implications of the Latin. *Princeps* put him in the line of "good" emperors, those who modeled their reigns on Augustus, the *princeps* and the first *princeps*, so Trajan is in select company, rather as an American president might hope to be paired with but not excel Washington. As a good emperor was posthumously declared a god, so a great president may now acquire a mundane immortality by appearing on a postage stamp. Second, *optimus* ought not to be taken as meaning "without equal," but rather that none could be better. The word was also widely used of Jupiter and thus associates the mortal emperor with the immortal ruler of the heavens and protector of Rome's empire.

Archaeological and epigraphic data are steadily enhancing our evaluation of Trajan's reign, particularly in the provinces. Britain and North Africa are proving rich. Literary sources are inadequate. In Rome stands Trajan's column, whose spiral bands present an illustrated but textless account of the conquest of Dacia. Trajan's ashes once rested in a chamber at its base but are long gone, and his statue once topped the column: one of St. Peter replaced it centuries ago.

Like Vespasian, Trajan was primarily a military man. Also like Vespasian, he was careful to follow the precedent of Augustus and to avoid tyrannical conduct. The late fourth-century chronicler Eutropius says that the Senate hoped emperors would be "happier than Augustus, better than Trajan." His contemporary Theodosius I (379–395) claimed to be descended from Trajan's family; both were from Spain, but there is no known tie. A century later, the Ostrogoth Theodoric (493–526) took Trajan as his model.

BIOGRAPHICAL BACKGROUND

Trajan is frequently but misleadingly designated the first provincial emperor, because the Ulpii were from Baetica (southern Spain). The family, resident in Spain for some time, originated in Italian Tuder, not far from the Flavian home of Reate (see Vespasian). The emperor's father, M. Ulpius Traianus, was an early adherent of Vespasian and perhaps the old family friend. This Trajan evidently married a Marcia—her name is inferred from that of their daughter Marciana—whose family owned brickyards in the vicinity of Ameria, near both Reate and Tuder. She was possibly an older sister of Marcia Furnilla, second wife of Vespasian's son Titus. Further, Ulpia, sister of the senior Trajan, was a grandmother of Hadrian. In other words, the emperor Trajan was succeeded in 117 by his cousin, member of another Italian family resident in Baetica.

Trajan *pater* was one of Vespasian's chief colleagues. The emperor appointed him consul for part of 70 or 72, raised him to the patriciate in 73, chose him to govern the vital military provinces of Cappadocia-Galatia and then Syria in 72//3–77/8. His final known assignment was the proconsulship of Asia in 79–80. His son was consul in 91. To be consul was quite different from being emperor, however, and it is uncertain when the younger Trajan became a candidate for the purple. The murder of Domitian in September 96 ended the Flavian dynasty and moved the problem of imperial succession to center stage.

The Senate promptly chose M. Cocceius Nerva as the next emperor. With no son, elderly, and facing widespread discontent in the military where Domitian had been popular, Nerva could neither found a dynasty nor establish firm control. After about a year he adopted Trajan, whom he had made legate of Upper Germany in the fall of 96. "Father" and son were consular colleagues from January 1, 98. The adoption obviously signified designation to succeed. It was common practice in Roman society for a childless person to adopt a grown man in order to continue a family line. Adoption to ensure imperial succession was not new either: both Augustus and Claudius had adopted their wives' sons by previous husbands—Livia's son Tiberius and Agrippina's son Nero; Galba had adopted the blue-blooded but otherwise unqualified and unrelated L. Piso in 69 in a doomed effort to gain support.

Nerva's choice was a good one, though some think it was not freely made: high-ranking officers, Trajan among them, may—there is no certainty—have quietly issued an ultimatum. A competent commander, career military man, Flavian loyalist and son of Vespasian's marshal, Trajan gained immediate acceptance. Nerva obligingly died in late January 98, and Trajan became *princeps.*

The succession was untroubled and the new emperor spent 98 and part of 99 with the Rhineland and Danubian armies. He thus received the imperial powers in absentia. We need not see these events as a military coup. Trajan was widely and genuinely popular: the people (especially in Rome), soldiers, and senators (among whom were the senior army commanders) all accepted him. Nerva may have intended all along to select him. There is only the slightest hint of a rival and no influence of wicked women, freedmen, or urban mob.

Trajan was of simple life style and habits, and his court continued the decorous respectability of the Flavians. If less well educated than Vespasian, the new emperor was without serious vices. If over-fond of the bottle, he was never dissolute. Homosexual predilections did, however, imply that he would not have a son or son-in-law to follow him. His wife. Plotina, and widowed sister, Marciana, were matrons of the best sort. Through her daughter, Marciana was grandmother of Sabina, unloved wife of Hadrian. This tie provides another reason for Hadrian's eventual accession. In the event, Trajan did not arrange as smooth a transition as had Nerva. On August 8, 117, Trajan died suddenly at Selinus on the south coast of Asian Minor without having formally designated Hadrian, who was himself at Antioch in Syria. Worse, Hadrian was not unanimously acceptable to the high command. Plotina may have kept Trajan's death a secret for a few days until an official statement could be released that the ailing Trajan had indeed adopted Hadrian and named him next emperor just before dying. The sequel is another story.

TRAJAN AS A GREAT LEADER

First, an observation about vocabulary and sources. Rulers who manifest political tact enjoy a higher reputation than those who govern with scant regard for others' sensibilities. In the Middle Ages most historians were clerics, so ecclesiastical concerns dominated their outlook. Kings who violated the church's interests and teachings suffered condemnation in the chronicles; and pious rulers, generous to the church, fared well. In Rome most historians were senators and judged the emperors by senatorial standards: they wrote favorably of those who respected the Senate's and individual senators' *dignitas*, or sense of worth, and damned those whom they perceived to be hostile to senatorial interests. Modern historians have to make allowances for the writers' biases.

K. H. Waters has argued that Domitian the tyrant and Trajan the model emperor "were in fact committed to an almost identical policy . . . of increasing autocracy," and the latter was "every whit as autocratic" as the former. Neither all senators nor society outside the Senate had such a dim view of Domitian. Trajan seems to have governed with an eye on how posterity would regard him, and it is difficult to tone down the brilliance of official imagery (on coins and buildings) and the adulation of a writer like Pliny. We do well to distinguish between autocrat and tyrant. Trajan *was* an autocrat, as absolute as conditions of the time allowed. He was *not* a tyrant as that technical term was understood in Greece and Rome: an arbitrary, illegal ruler. Trajan was as "constitutional" as an emperor could be: Nerva, ostensibly of his own free will, had adopted and designated him his successor and the Senate had invested him with the imperial powers. Trajan did not repress the Senate or senators, seize unlimited powers and wield them irresponsibly, or rely on the army. He was *civilis* and *optimus princeps*. Under him freedom and Principate coexisted (see also Tacitus, *Agricola* 3).

Of Vespasian it was noted that his claim to fame is to have restored the Principate of Augustus after the tyranny of Nero and the horrors of civil war. Trajan's claim can fairly be stated as having restored the Principate of Vespasian after the (alleged) tyranny of Domitian and the threat of another civil war. The brief reign of Titus (79–81) left little mark in history. The fifteen years of Domitian (81–96) were not the pure evil that senatorial writers would have us believe. Nerva's sixteen months (in 76–78) have been dismissed as "nothing but . . . a mere hiccup in the digestive process by which the monarchy absorbed into itself all power." Nonliterary evidence (epigraphy, archaeology) shows few sharp breaks from the 70s onward. Seen from this perspective, the reign of Trajan is in many respects a continuation of the Flavians and feeds smoothly into the era of Hadrian and the Antonine emperors who endured until the 190s.

Trajan appears almost perfect in the sources. Without a doubt he was respectful of the Senate and senators. Unlike Vespasian, he acceded without civil war, and since he had neither children nor brother he could not found a dynasty. Also unlike the first Flavian, he declined to hold serial consulships and abstained from the censorship altogether. Domitian had made him consul in 91, Nerva in 98; after that Trajan was consul in 100 and only three times (all briefly) by 117. It was easy to forego the censorship, for Domitian had discredited the office by holding it permanently. No emperor was censor after Domitian.

Finally, Trajan did not have to face philosophical opposition in the Senate. There was simply no viable alternative to an emperor. Tacitus' *Agricola* can be read as a plea for senators to serve the state capably and not to engage in showy but futile opposition, which only invited imperial retaliation and damaged the Senate as a body. Most senators and equestrians would have agreed.

On death Trajan received swift promotion to the ranks of the deified emperors. Declarations of deification were a senatorial prerogative, posthumous seals of approval. Trajan thus resides eternally with Augustus, Vespasian, and the many other gods of Rome.

TRAJAN THE TYRANT

Trajan was too astute to appear unequivocally tyrannical. One can regard the Parthian War of 115–117 as military megalomania and unwise, but no more. Otherwise one can point to trends that almost imperceptibly led through the "military monarchy" to the point wherein armed soldiers chose the emperor in the days of the late Empire. Certain themes stand out; all can be traced in specialized studies.

One is clearly the increasing absolutism of the emperor, though students must realize that a Roman emperor could not be a twentieth-century dictator without twentieth-century technology such as monopoly of the media; he could not even be as absolute as Louis XIV. The Roman Empire was a pre-industrial society, with only primitive means of communication, a small governing class and minimal bureaucracy, and a scattered, overwhelmingly rural population.

By virtue of their proconsular *imperium* ever since Augustus, all emperors were commanders in chief of the armed forces. Regional commanders might have armies of perhaps 40,000 men, but they held office usually for only three years. More importantly, their titles specified their subordinate standing: as legates their *imperium* was secondary, delegated to them by their superior, and as proconsuls they were inferior to the emperors as proconsuls. Proconsular *imperium* also permitted emperors to intervene in the relatively peaceful (hence largely unarmed) and prosperous provinces ostensibly under the administration of the Senate. A number of studies discuss the abundant evidence for imperial orders going to imperial and senatorial governors, or conversely for those officials consulting the emperors on their own. The most famous example is Pliny, whom Trajan sent in to govern the normally senatorial province of Bithynia-Pontus, along the south coast of the Black Sea.

Emperors became the source of more and more legislation. In part this was because they controlled the agenda of the Senate and could sponsor laws during its sessions, even by messages rather than in person. In part it was because their instructions (*edicta* and *mandata*) and replies (*responsa*) to governors and other officials were cited as precedents by lawyers and applied throughout the empire. In part it was because they were a court of final appeals for disputed cases. Emperors also came to control imperial finances, once divided into imperial and senatorial treasuries but amalgamated over the first century.

Emperors controlled all military promotions, so both equestrians and senators stood as clients: emperors were patrons in a way inconceivable before Julius Caesar. Trajan used this power to continue the Vespasianic policy of bringing talented provincials into public—that is, imperial—service. Senators owed their status to imperial favor, so it is no wonder that the Senate was loyal to Trajan.

Creeping imperial paternalism and autocracy were balanced by creeping senatorial abdication of responsibility and reluctance to show initiative. Pliny's obsequious and boring "Panegyric oration" is worth reading as witness to the growth of flattery. It is ominous to find the consul telling Trajan, "You bid us be free, and we are; you bid us speak freely, and we do" (sec. 66). Senators may have excused such servility as recognition of reality, and it partly was. Historians see it as a sign of a disturbing trend. The dangers became reality long after Trajan.

SUGGESTIONS FOR FURTHER READING

There is no recent biography of Trajan in English. The ancient sources are available in "The Loeb Classical Library" and the "Penguin Classics" series.

Campbell, B. *The Emperor and the Roman Army*. Oxford: Oxford University Press, 1984.

Hammond, M. *The Antonine Monarchy*. Rome: Papers and Monographs of the American Academy in Rome, vol. 19, 1959.

Jones, B. W. *The Emperor Domitian*. New York: Routledge, 1992.

Luttwak, E. *The Grand Strategy of the Roman Empire*. Baltimore: Johns Hopkins University Press, 1976.

Miller, F. *The Emperor in the Roman World*. London: Duckworth, 1977.

McDermott, W., and A. E. Orentzel. *Roman Portraits: The Flavian-Trajanic Age*. Columbia: University of Missouri Press, 1979.

Sherwin-White, A. N. *The Letters of Pliny: A Historical Commentary*. Oxford: Oxford University Press, 1966.

Syme, R. *Tacitus*. 2 vols. Oxford: Clarendon Press, 1958.

Waters, K. H. "Traianus, Domitiani continuator," *American Journal of Philology* 90 (1969): 395–405.

———. "Trajan's character in the literary sources," in J.A.S. Evans, ed., *Polis and Imperium: Studies in Honour of E. T. Salmon*. Toronto: University Press, 1974, pp. 233–249.

Thomas H. Watkins

Vespasian (Titus Flavius Vespasianus)

9–79

Roman Emperor, 69–79

Vespasian has generally been regarded as one of Rome's better emperors. Writing around 120, Tacitus remarked that unlike his predecessors, Vespasian alone changed for the better on becoming emperor (*Histories* 1.50). Had the full text of Tacitus' work survived, we would be well informed for the period 69–96. Instead, however, we have only the narrative of the civil war of 69 and the initial stages of recovery in 70. The manuscript breaks off after Vespasian had been granted the imperial powers but before he arrived in Rome: his actual reign is not on record. For narrative there is the Byzantine abridgment of Book 65 of Cassius Dio's *Roman History*, written in the early third century. Suetonius' biographies of Vespasian and the other two Flavian emperors, his sons Titus (79–81) and Domitian (81–96), provide much information about the reign and Vespasian's distinctive personality, but they tend to be anecdotal rather than systematic. Indeed, Vespasian is one of the few emperors to stand out as an individual. His family was of equestrian (roughly "middle-class") central Italian background, though Vespasian—preceded by his brother Flavius Sabinus—became a senator and rose to the consulship in 51 and command in the Jewish War in 67.

Vespasian was thus not only unrelated to the Julio-Claudian emperors but not even a member of the senatorial aristocracy by birth. There is a reasonable parallel with Gaius Marius, who lived a century and a half earlier and is now well known as the leading character in C. McCollough's excellent novel *The First Man in Rome*. Also of equestrian, small-town stock, when campaigning for the consulship of 107 B.C., Marius portrayed himself as a plain military man and outsider, not one of the corrupt senators of the ruling elite. A string of military victories and consulships permitted Marius to become a *princeps*, the Latin word lying behind the novel's title and from Augustus' time a designation for emperor. Only in retrospect does Augustus seem the first emperor. He was careful to avoid the apparent monarchism of Julius Caesar and strove to mask his supremacy in acceptably "Republican" forms—such as *princeps*, a term long applied to a leading senator but now taking on a new meaning. His conservatism and political tact were major factors in his success. Later emperors were largely judged by the extent to which they adhered to the standards Augustus established. Like Marius, Vespasian shrewdly cultivated the public image of the rugged Roman of the old days and masked considerable education and sophistication. Like Augustus, his chief precedent, Vespasian sought to respect "Republican" traditions and masked his enormous powers behind civilian forms.

BIOGRAPHICAL BACKGROUND

We owe to Suetonius most of our knowledge of Vespasian's family background and life to his mid-fifties. The Flavii were from Reate in the upper Tiber valley, Sabine country, and he retained something of the outlook and values of the rural Italian to his dying day. His blocky physique, permanently strained facial expression, blunt speech and wit, frequently off-color and even crude, were famous. Suetonius transmits a number of his remarks, including his deathbed "Alas, I think I'm becoming a god." His father, T. Flavius Sabinus, was a tax collector, wealthy enough to provide his sons with a high-quality education and to finance their political careers. The Flavii were wealthy, for the life style of a politically active senator required a great deal of money. It is, however, possible that the brothers had received gifts and legacies, common practice in the upper classes.

The older son, named for his father, reached the consulship in 45 under Claudius, who made him governor of the lower Danubian frontier in 50. He remained in this post, imperial legate (*legatus Augusti*) of Moesia with pro-praetorian *imperium*, until 56. Nero, emperor from 54, held Sabinus in high regard and appointed him to the important job of prefect of the city. Sabinus held this position through the remainder of Nero's reign. It made him responsible for the policing of Rome, as he had command of the Urban Cohorts, a force of perhaps six thousand men (not to be confused with the more prestigious, tougher, and larger Praetorian Guards). Galba, who succeeded Nero in the opening round of the vicious civil war of 68–69, removed Sabinus as prefect in 68. In January 69, Otho assassinated Galba, took over as emperor, and reappointed Sabinus urban prefect. Vitellius, proclaimed emperor by the eight legions along the Rhine, defeated Otho in north Italy in April; Otho committed suicide, but the new emperor retained Sabinus in office. Sabinus was killed in the confused fighting of December between troops supporting his brother (see below) and those loyal to Vitellius. In brief, Sabinus was likely a smoother operator than Vespasian, and he undoubtedly had good connections with the power brokers under Claudius and Nero. Down to 66 and perhaps 69 Sabinus was the more important of the brothers. He blazed the trail; Vespasian followed along a cleared, if perhaps unpaved, roadway.

Vespasian, junior by some six years, was likewise a T. Flavius, but took his *cognomen* from his mother, Vespasia Polla. In 43 as propraetor, he was legate of Legion II Augusta, one of the four legions in the invasion of Britain; Sabinus probably commanded one of the others. After the initial victory over the Britons at the Medway River, Vespasian methodically campaigned across the south, storming the hillfort of Maiden Castle near Dorchester and perhaps establishing the fortress at Exeter. He held the consulship for part of 51 and was proconsul (governor) of Africa about 63. Falling asleep during one of Nero's theatrical performances netted him banishment from the court and an apparent end to his career.

The Jewish revolt of 66 proved his big break, for he was brought out of retirement and given command of the large Roman army in 67. This was a special assignment, as the regular imperial legate (governor) of Syria stayed in office: Nero evidently regarded Vespasian as "safe," unlikely to prove disloyal. Even though his brother was an imperial councilor, Vespasian's resurrection must have come as a surprise, for he had ties to the anti-Neronian faction that had been purged following suppression of a conspiracy in 65. His older son, Titus, had deftly divorced Marcia Furnilla, daughter and niece of conspirators; and his younger son may already have been engaged to the daughter of the prominent general Domitius Corbulo, whom Nero had ordered to commit suicide in the winter of 66–67 because of suspected involvement in the conspiracy.

As in Britain, Vespasian campaigned methodically, unspectacularly, and thoroughly. By the spring of 68 he had pretty well crushed the revolt outside Jerusalem. When reports of the rebellion against Nero arrived, he ceased operations. The civil and Jewish wars are too complex a tale to be told here. The eastern legions proclaimed Vespasian emperor on July 1, 69: the two in Egypt took the initiative, those in Syria and Judaea soon followed, and those along the Danube joined a bit later. Flavian troops invaded Italy and took Rome in December. During the fighting both Flavius Sabinus and Vitellius were killed. The Senate conferred the imperial powers on Vespasian, who remained in Alexandria and came to Rome about ten months later.

VESPASIAN AS A GREAT LEADER

As emperor Vespasian pursued policies in much the same way he had campaigned as general: methodically and unspectacularly. His sober, commonsense approach to the many problems besetting Rome ushered in a new era. One practical achievement was to increase government revenues by imposing new taxes and doubling or tripling old ones. As best he could, he made Augustus his model, a wise move and welcome after the flamboyant extravagance of Nero. Like Augustus he came to power through civil war; like Augustus he strove to restore peace, stability, and a civil tone to government; like Augustus he emphasized Roman traditions (the contrast with Nero is striking) and downplayed his military superiority; like Augustus he lived simply, socialized widely, and was readily accessible. On the whole, historians agree, he was successful, and this establishes his place as a great leader. He died at Reate and swiftly joined Augustus and the rest of the Olympian host.

In two aspects, one broad and the other narrow, he was unlike Augustus. The consolidation of powers in the years since the first emperor's death in 14 made Vespasian far more imperial. And Vespasian had a grown son, Titus. Only two emperors had had sons at all: Drusus had died suspiciously in 23, fourteen years before his father, Tiberius; and Nero had dispatched Claudius' son Britannicus, a boy of about eleven, in 55. Vespasian determined to establish a dynasty and made Titus, born in 39 and an experienced commander, his colleague from the start of the reign. This monarchical position and open dynasticism lie behind the judgment that Vespasian was a tyrant.

Vespasian's good reputation, like his deification in 79, stems largely from his success in restoring peace after the civil war, in removing the army from politics (it stayed out until 193), and in bringing back an ordered, civilian, stable government. In sum, he recreated the Principate of Augustus as much as was possible: one cannot set back the clock, but Vespasian ruled as *princeps* more than as *imperator*, as first citizen more than as general. Consequently, an understanding of the nature of the Principate of Augustus must precede assessment of Vespasian or any other emperor. Considerations of space permit only a summary.

Over the years from 36 to 2 B.C., Augustus won a batch of different powers and honors and titles, themselves mostly rooted in centuries of tradition and therefore eminently respectable. The most important "settlements" were in 27 and 23 B.C., when he received first, the name Augustus ("Revered") and second, the "greater proconsular *imperium*" and tribunician power; the latter two gave him command of the imperial military forces, the right to intervene in all provinces of the empire, and to conduct much governmental business such as to introduce and veto legislation. All powers gradually coalesced into a single undifferentiated imperial power conferred by a law originating as a resolution of the Senate. The earliest known block grant occurred at the opening of Vespasian's reign (it survives in part), and this effectively created the office of emperor. Insofar as he was Augustan, Vespasian was republican and by definition not tyrannical.

Vespasian exhibited leadership in several areas, sometimes continuing policies of the much-maligned Claudius. He brought a number of new men, some of them from the provinces, into the Senate and advanced their careers. Thereby he created an empire-wide senatorial aristocracy, many of its members men of real talent and by no means sycophants or courtiers. Three good examples are M. Ulpius Trajan, father of the later emperor (see the entry on him); Sextus Julius Frontinus, who eventually held three consulships and governed Britain (73/4–77/8); and Gnaeus Julius Agricola, nowadays chiefly known for this governship of Britain (77/8–83/4), commemorated by his son-in-law, Tacitus. Inscriptions preserve the careers of many Vespasianic senators.

Emperor Vespasian recognized the rapid advance of Roman culture throughout the Iberian peninsula by extending Latin rights there. The grant allowed local town officials to become full citizens and permitted all Latins to marry Romans and utilize Roman law and business transactions. Many other individuals acquired Roman citizenship through service in the auxiliary forces of the Roman army, a policy Vespasian continued. He thus accelerated the creation of a truly imperial citizenship. His armies pushed the frontiers outward in Britain, Africa (Tunisia and Algeria), and across the upper Danube and Rhine rivers (now the Black Forest region). The government promoted economic development and urbanization in the former military districts now brought under civilian control. As noted elsewhere, Trajan continued many Flavian policies.

VESPASIAN THE TYRANT

A rigid categorization of almost any emperor as "leader" and "tyrant," as though he wore two different uniforms, is highly artificial. Centralization of governmental powers in the person of the emperor and an imperial bureaucracy under his control was a process spread across several centuries, not an event. Before 200 there were only three truly tyrannical rulers in the modern sense of the word: Gaius "Caligula" (37–41), Nero (54–68), and Commodus (180–192). It is more profitable to concentrate on "political correctness," the extent to which emperors patterned themselves after Augustus and how they treated the Senate and senators. In Greece and Rome a tyrant was an illegal ruler, someone who seized and stayed in power by illegal and arbitrary means, usually military force and a network of cronies, someone who ignored customary propriety and accepted forms.

Rome never officially created the office of emperor with clear powers, determined means of selection of emperors, or devised ways to limit or depose unsuitable rulers. Frustrated senators might conspire or, more safely, take revenge after an emperor's death by refusing deification and condemning his memory. Such was the (undeserved) fate of Tiberius and Vespasian's younger son, Domitian. Trajan was the beneficiary, as Vespasian profited from revulsion against Nero and the horrors of civil war. A related point here is that Roman politics never had either parties, platforms, or a real cabinet of ministers. Emperors consulted an informal group of "friends" (*amici principis*), but this body had no formal composition or duties. Rome thus lacked a vehicle through which persons could build up a permanent basis for organized support or constitute a "loyal opposition." It was difficult to disagree with an emperor in any meaningful way without seeming disloyal or subversive. Suspicious or insecure emperors made the problem worse.

A balanced assessment ought to incorporate emperors' provincial and frontier policies: the spread of Roman culture through spoken and written Latin, urbanization, architecture, technology and public works, a monetary economy, Roman citizenship, and widespread security. Ancient writers were never much interested in these topics, though we today regard them as essential.

Vespasian was never "tyrannical" in the sense of resembling, say, Nero. He was, however, authoritative in a few regards. He may have begun to plot for supreme power well before his troops proclaimed him, at which time he (tactfully) professed reluctance. He dated his reign from this proclamation, July 1, 69, not from recognition by the Senate some months later. In theory, the Senate not the troops should make the emperor. As emperor he held the consulship almost every year and was censor annually from 73. Possibly Vespasian was trying to show respect for these ancient offices by holding them, but more likely he was amassing powers and perhaps indulging his vanity. Whichever the case, this monopolizing of offices caused considerable offense to senators. Further, he used *imperator* as his title, as did all successors: this military title emphasized the nature of his rise to power.

Exasperated by the ostentatious boorishness and plain bad manners of some philosophically minded senators, he expelled a few obstinate opponents and ordered the execution of one, Helvidius Priscus. The victims probably elicited scant sympathy, as many felt they had brought troubles on their own heads and everybody knew Vespasian was no tyrant. Nevertheless, senators disapproved of arbitrary, imperatorial actions against their own, and all remembered the vindictiveness and cruelties of Nero. Finally, one can regard his dynasticism as tyrannical. Rather than choosing the best-qualified for successor or consult with the Senate, Vespasian was determined to be followed by his son Titus, whom he made almost a full partner.

SUGGESTIONS FOR ADDITIONAL READING

There is no full-scale biography of Vespasian in English. The ancient sources are in "The Loeb Classical Library"; the "Penguin Classics" series has translations of Tacitus and Suetonius.

Grant, M. *The Twelve Caesars*. New York: Charles Scribner's Sons, 1975.
Hammond, M. *The Antonine Monarchy*. Rome: Papers and Monographs of the American Academy in Rome, vol. 19, 1959.

Henderson, B. W. *Five Roman Emperors: Vespasian, Titus, Domitian, Nerva and Trajan, A.D. 69–117*. New York: Barnes and Noble, 1969.
MacMullen, R. *Enemies of the Roman Order: Treason, Unrest and Alienation in the Roman Empire*. Cambridge, Mass.: Harvard University Press, 1966.
Millar, F. *The Emperor in the Roman World*. London: Duckworth, 1977.
Nicols, J. *Vespasian and the Partes Vespasianae*. Wiesbaden, Germany: Historia Einzelschriften 28, 1984.
Talbert, R.J.A. *The Senate of Imperial Rome*. Princeton, N.J.: Princeton University Press, 1984.
Wacher, J. *The Roman World*. 2 vols. London and New York: Routledge and Kegan Paul, 1987.
Wellesley, K. *The Long Year: A.D. 69*. Boulder, Colo.: Westview Press, 1975.

Thomas H. Watkins

Wilhelm II (Frederick Wilhelm Albert Victor von Hohenzollern)

1859–1941

German Emperor, 1888–1918

This extremely complex man has fascinated psychoanalysts as well as historians. He loved his British grandmother, Queen Victoria, but detested his mother, Victoria. He overcompensated for the physical disability of a useless hand, by mastering horsemanship and all sorts of weaponry. He did not hesitate to leap into an area to assist the staff at a circus in subduing an unruly animal. While asserting his masculinity, he associated closely with overt homosexuals, though German law was extremely homophobic. In foreign policy, he asserted Germany's right to be first in all things, even when he risked his country's alliances by doing so. He frequently made public statements that were embarrassing to his government and which had to be "explained away" afterward.

At the same time, this very bright man fully understood the mechanics of a capitalist society. He made conscious efforts to befriend businessmen who could advance Germany's economy. In a country where social anti-Semitism was common, the emperor cultivated the friendship of the Jewish shipping magnate Albert Ballin. At the same time, he chose as court chaplain Adolf Stöcker, whose Christian Socialist doctrines were racially hostile to Jews in the same sense that the Nazis were to be, forty years later.

He favored a program of social welfare that made the German working class more secure than any other in the world. At the same time, he made public statements that gave the impression that he regarded the sons of that working class, the common soldiers of his army, as expendable pawns.

The emperor was immature and reckless. He totally failed to understand the genius of Bismarck's policy. It is entirely possible that World War I might have taken place even if Bismarck's policy could have been continued. Nevertheless, it is evident that Wilhelm II bears a great part of the blame for the war, though today no one attempts to put all of the guilt on his shoulders.

BIOGRAPHICAL BACKGROUND

The heir to the Hohenzollern dynasty of Prussia was born on January 27, 1859, the first of eight children born to Prince Frederick Wilhelm and his English wife, Victoria. His German grandfather, Wilhelm I, was regent in Prussia. His mother was the oldest child of Queen Victoria of England and Prince Albert. In their honor, the infant was christened Frederick Wilhelm Albert Victor, but his family called him Willy.

He began life with the struggle of a breech birth. In the process, his left shoulder and arm were damaged, and other injuries occurred that became apparent as he grew older: paralysis of the left arm, deafness in his left ear, and a disturbance in his balance. There may also have been brain damage. The variety of painful physical therapies he endured did not help. His paralyzed left arm grew slowly and remained approximately three inches shorter than the right. Throughout his life he had to have special eating utensils made for his right hand, combining knife, fork, and spoon, and his clothes specially tailored. The love of uniform, ceremony, and bold behavior characteristic of his later life were undoubtedly compensations for these embarrassing disabilities.

Wilhelm was never close to his parents. High-strung, restless, and quick tempered, he was in the hands of governesses until age six. He had difficulty managing paper and pen, but a phenomenal memory for poetry and recitation. He loved being praised for his achievements. In 1866, Dr. George Hinzpeter, a serious, deeply religious man, became Wilhelm's tutor. Isolated from his family, Wilhelm had twelve-hour days of study and exercise. In 1873, Hinzpeter stayed with Wilhelm at preparatory school in Kassel until he completed his studies in 1877, and indoctrinated Wilhelm with a deep sense of duty to God and country.

Wilhelm was equally impressed by the excitement, honor, and glory earned by the Prussian army during the wars of the 1860s, which led to the unification of the German Empire in 1871. His grandfather, by then Prussian King and Emperor Wilhelm I, ordered him to Potsdam to serve as a lieutenant in the First Foot Guards. He went eagerly, exhilarated by military life. Although his parents insisted he enroll at the University of Bonn, he was an indifferent student. He asserted his independence by ignoring classes, partying, and traveling with friends. He was a charming, impulsive, and headstrong young man, quick-witted yet lacking in common sense and sensitivity. He was most susceptible to flattery.

Wilhelm rejoined his regiment in 1879 without completing a degree. There he fell increasingly under the influence of conservative army officers, which estranged him even farther from his parents. In February 1881 he married Princess Augusta Victoria, who was related to the Danish royal house. They moved directly to Potsdam, foregoing a honeymoon, so Wilhelm could be with his regiment. Their family grew rapidly: six sons and a daughter were born between 1882 and 1892.

The year 1888 was the "three-emperor year." In March, Wilhelm I died and Crown Prince Frederick ascended to the dual thrones of Prussia and the German Empire as Frederick III. He was the hope of liberals in Germany, who dreamed that he would establish an English-style parliamentary government. But the nation learned, with horror, that Frederick III was terminally ill of throat cancer. He reigned only ninety-nine days and was succeeded by his twenty-nine-year-old son, Wilhelm II, on June 15, 1888.

Unprepared though he was, Wilhelm II wanted to rule in his own right. He forced Prince Otto von Bismarck, the engineer of German unification, into retirement in 1890. Throughout his thirty-year reign, Wilhelm II took an active interest in politics and diplomacy, in sharp contrast to his grandfather, who left most state affairs to the direction of Bismarck. Accordingly, historians refer to the portion of the German Empire from 1871 to 1888 as the Bismarckian period, and the period from 1888 to 1918 as the Wilhelmian.

During the Wilhelmian period the parties of the left persistently demanded constitutional reform to make the government more responsible to the people. The agrarian and conservative upper classes struggled to preserve their prerogatives, represented by the aristocrats in the army and bureaucracy who most influenced Wilhelm.

And whereas Bismarck had worked to demonstrate that Germany was a peaceful, satisfied nation after unification, Wilhelm II strove to find Germany's "place in the sun" as a great power. The construction of a new navy, and its employment in Asia and Africa as an arm of German diplomacy, alarmed Britain, France, and Russia. Wilhelm II's staunch, Germanic support of Austria-Hungary inevitably embroiled Germany in the rivalry over the Balkans between Austria and Russia. Although Wilhelm did not want war, his unbending support of Austria triggered World War I and led Germany to launch its forces against France on August 4, 1914.

As the war dragged on, the German General Staff gained almost total political control in Germany, eclipsing both emperor and government. German political opinion turned against the war, and in 1917 called for peace. In 1918, following the failure of a major German offensive, demands were heard for peace and for the abdication of the emperor. On November 9, two days before the cease-fire and armistice, Wilhelm abdicated and fled to Doorn, Holland. His wife joined him, but died in the spring of 1921. He later married the much younger Princess Hermine of Schönaich-Carolath.

During his exile he published three works heavy with self-justification: *My Memoirs 1878–1918* (1922), *My Early Life* (1926), and *My Ancestors* (1929). When Adolf Hitler first came to power in 1933, Wilhelm hoped that the reestablishment of a strong central government might mean restoration of the monarchy. Hitler, however, did not oblige. Once World War II broke out, England invited him to safety, but he declined. He sent Adolf Hitler a congratulatory telegram on the fall of Paris to the German army in 1940. A year later, in June 1941, after twenty-two years in exile, he died at Doorn.

WILHELM II AS A GREAT LEADER

Wilhelm II came to power in a nation surging with new industrial and commercial growth. By fostering a climate supporting investment and industrial development, Wilhelm's reign helped make Germany Europe's greatest industrial power by 1900. German population grew to 67.8 million by 1914, in part because of slowing of emigration after the late 1880s. By 1910, Germany was producing almost twice as much steel as Britain and 50 percent more pig iron. By 1913, Germany produced one-third of the world's potatoes and led all other nations in the production of dyestuffs and pharmaceuticals, while producing 50 percent of the world's electrical equipment.

Wilhelm also promoted the development of the German navy and merchant marine, bringing Germany into second place behind Britain in shipping tonnage. New commercial treaties helped German foreign trade double between 1900 and 1913, almost approaching that of Britain. More than ten thousand miles of railroad track were added during his reign. Average annual personal income more than doubled between 1871–1875 and 1911–1913. The German banking industry supported this burgeoning economy through the development of branch banks. Social legislation restricted working hours for women and children, and extended mandatory accident, old-age, and invalids' insurance for workers.

There was also a revitalization of cultural life during the reign of Wilhelm II. The ponderous monumental architecture of the early days of the empire gave way to the whimsy and line of *Jugenstil*, the German variety of *art nouveau*. The sciences flourished, with the development of x-ray techniques by Roentgen in 1895, Max Planck's quantum theory of physics in 1900, and Einstein's theory of relativity in 1905. German universities were international centers for research and scholarship; publication of books, periodicals, and the daily press flourished. The public enjoyed the poetry of Rainer Maria Rilke and the musical creativity of Anton Bruckner, Gustav Mahler, and Richard Strauss. The novelist brothers Thomas and Heinrich Mann, historian Theodor Mommsen, and sociologists Wilhelm Dilthey and Max Weber reflected the vitality of intellectual life across a broad spectrum of the population.

WILHELM II THE TYRANT

The vibrant economy and cultural life of the German Empire could not conceal deep strains originating in Bismarck's 1871 imperial constitution. Like Prussia, the other member states retained their monarchs. The bicameral national legislature consisted of an upper house (*Bundesrat*) whose appointed delegates acted only on instructions from their state's executive. That was the core of national government. The lower house (*Reichstag*), elected by universal manhood suffrage, could only vote against government bills. There was no executive cabinet, just a single minister, the chancellor, appointed by and responsible only to the emperor. Notably missing from the federal constitution were any guarantees of individual rights or civil liberties.

With his political skill and the support of Wilhelm I, Bismarck dominated this system as federal chancellor and Prussian minister president. But whereas Wilhelm I and Bismarck had worked together harmoniously for almost twenty years, Wilhelm II had eight Chancellors in his thirty-year reign. His immaturity and exaggerated self-importance magnified the sense of political crisis.

His policies were often contradictory. Striving for his grandfather's image of nonpartisan rule, he would not abandon his conservative associates. Initially he proclaimed himself the "people's emperor" and sought to win support from the working classes by ending, in 1890, the ban that outlawed the Social Democratic Party. But in 1894 he began demanding laws to restrict all political parties and labor unions. He asserted his "personal regime," believing that he ruled by grace of God. But critical public opinion infuriated him and often resulted in the dismissal of government ministers, whom he blamed for his bad press. His interview with the British *Daily Telegraph*, published in 1908, outraged German public opinion by implying that the German populace was hostile to Britain. Some even called for his abdication, leaving Wilhelm obviously shaken and subdued. Domestic political affairs thus had an aura of constant tension and instability.

Wilhelm II always identified with the military more than the civilian government. He loved uniforms, sometimes changing his own many times a day. The military cabinet was independent from the civilian government, reporting to him alone. Without consulting the diplomats, it developed the Schlieffen Plan to attack France through Belgium in the event of war, a violation of existing treaties.

Wilhelm appointed Admiral Alfred von Tirpitz to build a German fighting fleet and inaugurated the Kiel Canal to help it cross from the Baltic to the North Sea. Germany's fleet employed new construction materials and techniques, initiating an arms race with Britain, which had a larger but older fleet. Determined to show the German flag, Wilhelm provoked France and Britain with confrontations in Morocco in 1905 and 1911. In 1913 he sided with the army in the notorious Zabern Affair, when a German officer ordered force used against French demonstrators.

To safeguard the new German empire, Bismarck had created a framework of defensive alliances. Its cornerstone was the Dual Alliance of 1879, promising military aid to Austria if it were attacked by Russia; Austria, similarly, would aid Germany if France attacked it. The alliance was purely defensive: neither state would support the aggression of the other. As rivalry between Russia and Austria increased over the Balkans, Bismarck signed the secret Reinsurance Treaty with Russia in 1887, promising German neutrality if Russia moved to gain access through the Turkish straits to the Mediterranean. In return, Russia promised neutrality in case of an unprovoked French attack on Germany. When Wilhelm II learned of the latter treaty, he refused to extend it in 1890, believing it betrayed the Austrian alliance. This rebuff inclined Russia to seek support from France and was a prelude to the Dual Entente. When Italy joined the Dual Alliance in 1881, and England the Dual Entente in 1907, Europe was divided into two increasingly hostile camps.

As the navy and diplomats asserted German trade and colonial interests around the globe, Wilhelm proclaimed Germany's "world policy." He sometimes embarrassed his diplomats by failing to consult them before speaking out on world events. In 1896, during negotiations over an alliance with Britain, he sent the "Krueger Telegram" to the president of the Transvaal in South Africa, congratulating him on defeating a raid by British forces. In 1914, after the assassination of the heir to the Austrian throne, Austria wanted Germany's support for punitive action against Serbia, believed to have backed the assassin. Without consulting his foreign secretary, Wilhelm personally assured Austria that Germany would stand by it. That "blank check" is said to have initiated the aggressive Austrian policy that sparked World War I.

Once war was inevitable, the German General Staff implemented the Schlieffen Plan to launch a preemptive strike against France through Belgium. The rapid maneuver carried the German armies almost to Paris. But the war on the western front stagnated into trench warfare. German victories on the eastern front against the Russians could not turn the tide.

During World War I the German General Staff gained practical control over the civilian government. Over civilian objections they declared unlimited submarine warfare in 1917, which brought the United States into the war on the side of the Entente. This made defeat inevitable, and the *Reichstag* passed a peace resolution in July, 1917. But the war dragged on until the fall of 1918, when some members of the *Reichstag* also began to call for Wilhelm's abdication. The emperor sought refuge with the General Staff, but shortly thereafter sailors mutinied in Kiel, and popular rebellions broke out in Munich. On November 9, 1918, at the urging of his last chancellor, Wilhelm II abdicated and the Social Democrats proclaimed the German Republic.

Wilhelm II had not created any of the complex constitutional and diplomatic structures that so burdened the German Empire. His headstrong meddling in politics and diplomacy nevertheless contributed to its military defeat and political overthrow in 1918.

SUGGESTIONS FOR ADDITIONAL READING

Balfour, Michael. *The Kaiser and His Times*. New York: Norton Library, 1972.

Cecil, Lamar. *Wilhelm II, Prince and Emperor, 1859–1900*. Chapel Hill and London: University of North Carolina Press, 1989.

Cowles, Virginia. *The Kaiser*. New York: Harper & Row, 1963.

Evans, Richard J., ed. *Society and Politics in Wilhelmine Germany*. London: Croom Helm Ltd., 1978.

Fischer, Fritz. *Germany's Aims in the First World War*. New York: W. W. Norton & Co., 1967.

Hull, Isabel V. *The Entourage of Kaiser Wilhelm II 1888–1918*. Cambridge: Cambridge University Press, 1982.

Kohut, Thomas A. *Wilhelm II and the Germans: A Study in Leadership*. New York: Oxford University Press, 1991.

Nichols, J. Alden. *The Year of the Three Kaisers: Bismarck and the German Succession, 1887–88*. Urbana and Chicago: University of Illinois Press, 1987.

Orlow, Dietrich. *A History of Modern Germany, 1870 to Present*. Englewood Cliffs, N.J.: Prentice-Hall, Inc., 1987.

Palmer, Alan. *The Kaiser: Warlord of the Second Reich*. New York: Charles Scribner's Sons, 1978.

Eleanor L. Turk

Thomas Wolsey

c. 1472–1530

Archbishop of York, Cardinal, Papal Legate,
Lord Chancellor of England

Thomas Wolsey was Henry VIII's leading minister from 1513 until 1529. By 1515, when he was made cardinal (by Pope Leo X) and lord chancellor, he was the most powerful man in England next to the king. This power ultimately depended on the good will of his sovereign, perhaps his only real friend, and this he knew; so great was his influence, however, that he was accused of forgetting who was king and who the minister. While his role in determining royal policy is debated, clearly he ran the government for his pleasure-loving master, who was not quite eighteen when he came to the throne in 1509 and almost twenty years younger than Wolsey. Condemned by contemporaries as tyrannical and corrupt, Wolsey is characterized by modern historians as vain and self-aggrandizing, but able, sincere, and responsible for genuine reforms, even if he did not always complete what he began. Scholars still debate whether his ascendancy was a continuation of the medieval tradition in church and state of the beginning of modernization accelerated by the English Reformation of the 1530s.

BIOGRAPHICAL BACKGROUND

Wolsey was born about 1472 in Ipswich, Suffolk county, England to Robert Wolsey, a butcher, and his wife, Joan Daundy Wolsey. He probably attended grammar school in Ipswich and in 1484 entered Magdalen College, Oxford, where he received the Bachelor of Arts (at age fifteen, he claimed) and Master of Arts. In 1497 he was elected a fellow of Magdalen, the next year was ordained and made junior bursar of the college, and in 1499 became senior bursar. In 1500 the marquess of Dorset appointed Wolsey rector of Limington, Somerset, and in 1501 he received a papal dispensation to hold multiple church offices. He was chaplain to Henry Deane, Archbishop of Canterbury and keeper of the Great Seal, from 1501 to 1503, residing at Lambeth Palace, and from 1503 to 1507 to Sir Richard

Nanfan, governor of Calais, where he gained experience in government and foreign affairs.

Wolsey entered royal service in 1507 as Henry VII's chaplain. He also became secretary to Richard Foxe, who was Bishop of Winchester, lord privy seal, and director of foreign policy. In 1508 Henry sent Wolsey to Scotland to mollify James IV following the Earl of Arran's arrest in England and to the imperial court to arrange a royal marriage with Maximilian's daughter Margaret—both missions failed. Henry VIII appointed Wolsey as his almoner in 1509, a privy councilor in 1510, and registrar of the Order of the Garter in 1511. He organized Henry's invasion of France in 1513 and negotiated a treaty with Louis XII in 1514. The same year he became Bishop of Lincoln and then Archbishop of York. Wolsey successfully managed two parliamentary sessions in 1515, though he faced sharply anticlerical sentiment in the House of Commons, and in 1516 he launched a sporadic campaign of domestic reform. In 1518 he persuaded Leo X to make him the papal legate *a latere*, and in 1524 Clement VII took the unprecedented step of granting this to him for life. In 1519 he banished several rivals from court and in 1521 arranged the treason trial of the powerful Duke of Buckingham.

Meanwhile, Francis I's victory at Marignano in 1515 compelled Wolsey to renew the old Habsburg alliance, but in 1516 Ferdinand of Spain died, and in 1517 Maximilian was reconciled to Francis by the Treaty of Noyon. However, in 1518 Wolsey achieved a diplomatic triumph with the Treaty of London, which brought peace in Europe and the (unfulfilled) promise of a crusade against the Turks. This was undone in 1519 by Maximilian's death, Charles V's election as emperor, and the beginnings of the Reformation. In 1520, Wolsey organized the spectacular meeting of Henry and Francis at the Field of the Cloth of Gold at Calais, but also began secret negotiations with the emperor that led in 1521 to the Treaty of Bruges, providing for a "Great Enterprise" against France by 1523. However, the Earl of Surrey's invasion of France in 1522 failed, the Treaty of Windsor postponed Anglo-imperial action, and Suffolk's invasion in 1523 lacked Habsburg support. After Charles defeated Francis at Pavia in 1525, Wolsey allied with France in the Treaty of the More and in 1526 joined the anti-Habsburg League of Cognac, though England avoided participation in the Italian war. The fiscal demands of Wolsey's policies caused serious problems at home, where he antagonized taxpayers by demanding "loans" in 1522 and 1523, seeking to "anticipate" payment of a parliamentary subsidy in 1523, and attempting to levy a nonparliamentary tax called the Amicable Grant in 1525.

In 1527, Wolsey took up the "King's Great Matter"—Henry's quest for divorce from Catherine of Aragon. At a secret court Wolsey and the Archbishop of Canterbury, William Warham, found Henry's marriage invalid. In 1528, Clement VII granted a decretal commission to Wolsey and Cardinal Compeggio, and in 1529 Wolsey opened the legatine court at Blackfriars to hear the case. However, his efforts were frustrated by the failure of his foreign policy. Though he sought peace with Charles in 1527, the emperor (Catherine's nephew) opposed the divorce and by virtue of his capture of Rome was able to prevent papal cooperation with Wolsey's efforts. Clement revoked the case to Rome in 1529, and England was isolated when Charles and Clement made peace and France and Spain agreed to the Treaty of Cambrai.

Wolsey's failure led to his disgrace. He was convicted of *praemunire* (appeals to the pope over the king's head), surrendered his offices and possessions, and retired to Esher. In 1530 the king pardoned Wolsey, restored him to the see of York, and made him bishop of Winchester. But he began building support in his archdiocese and secretly negotiated with France and the empire, which led to his arrest for treason. He died of an intestinal ailment on November 29 at Leicester Abbey while on his way to trial in London.

CARDINAL WOLSEY AS A GREAT LEADER

Wolsey has always been controversial. Though George Cavendish—his gentleman usher and first biographer—portrayed him favorably, others did not. At least some modern scholars credit him with an occasionally brilliant foreign policy and with beginning many of the reforms associated with the Henrician Reformation and Thomas Cromwell. Recently additional emphasis has been given to his patronage of the arts and education.

His foreign policy produced spectacular results, but these were often ephemeral and there were no lasting successes. For example, the capture of Therouanne and Tournai in 1513 gratified the king's desire for military glory but was of little strategic value, and the peace that Wolsey negotiated thereafter with France evaporated upon Louis XII's death. On the other hand, the fact that the Treaty of London in 1518 was short-lived does not detract from Wolsey's skill in arranging it (though the idea initially was Leo X's). As so often, his work was undone by circumstances beyond his control. And if England was isolated at Wolsey's fall, it is still true that his diplomacy gave Henry VIII an equal role on the international stage with Charles and Francis, though they commanded resources greater than England's.

At home Wolsey's Lord Chancellorship allowed him to promote justice, a sincere object even if not fully realized. There was a modest increase in the Court of Chancery's business, though how active a personal role he played is uncertain. His main interest lay in the court of Star Chamber, which he determined to use to enforce the law (and his will) upon overmighty subjects and to make justice available to all Englishmen. In 1516 he announced his intention to reform various "enormities in the realm" (threats to law and order) in an oration before king and council, and he repeated this in 1517 and 1519. He regularly sat as a judge, prosecuted corrupt officials, and provided a popular alternative to the Common Law courts. Though his pursuit of lawbreakers was inconsistent and the organization of the court was not complete at his fall, Wolsey's enhancement of Star Chamber's role genuinely benefited the English people.

Wolsey also attacked illegal enclosures of land. After a national inquiry in 1517, he proceeded against over 250 individuals, though it is not known how many of those convicted actually removed their enclosures. Here again, though, he failed to follow through completely, for in the Parliament of 1523 he retreated from enforcing his policies and declared amnesty for the landowners involved. His later proclamations against enclosures in 1526, 1528, and 1529 were largely ignored. A similar fate characterized other initially vigorous campaigns with regard to justice, finance, defense, marketplace abuses, sumptuary laws, unemployment and vagabondage, ecclesiastical sanctuary, and Ireland.

However, Wolsey produced real innovations in government. One was the introduction of the subsidy, a more effective form of parliamentary taxation than the old system of fifteenths and tenths. But while it raised substantial revenue in 1513, 1515, and 1523, it was not enough—even combined with other taxes—to support the king's wars, and in the 1520s Wolsey resorted to more controversial measures. Wolsey also attempted unsuccessfully to rejuvenate the Council of the Marches in Wales under Princess Mary and the Council in the North under the Duke of Richmond (the king's illegitimate son) in 1525 and proposed reform of the royal household. In 1524 he dissolved several small monasteries with the intent of building colleges at Ipswich and Oxford, contemplated reforming Cambridge and Oxford, and eventually did establish Cardinal (later King's) College, Oxford, in 1527 and Ipswich School (which did not survive) in 1529. Though his patronage of the arts is often ascribed to ostentation, he was a generous and sensitive patron.

CARDINAL WOLSEY THE TYRANT

Among his contemporaries Wolsey inspired the resentment of the nobility—notably Buckingham and the successive dukes of Norfolk—and the condemnation of the devout, both Catholic and Protestant. The poet John Skelton savaged Wolsey in *Why Came Ye Not to Court?*; men as different as clergyman Nicholas Harpsfield, royal tutor John Palsgrave, and Protestant Biblical scholar William Tynedale added their criticisms; and Catholic historians Polydore Vergil and Nicholas Sander and Protestant chroniclers Edward Hall and John Foxe blamed Wolsey for the English Reformation.

Wolsey's reforms and judicial activism were real enough, but frequently gained him political advantage. In 1517 he took undue credit for suppressing the Evil May Day riots in London and used the occasion to embarrass his enemies there. The magnates he prosecuted in Star Chamber appear to have been guilty as charged, but not coincidentally they were also his enemies, and convictions did not always end their abuses. Buckingham's imprudent behavior made his destruction in 1521 virtually inevitable, but he also posed a threat to Wolsey. Reform of the royal household in 1519 and the Eltham Ordinances of 1526 allowed Wolsey to remove rivals from the Privy Chamber, replace them with loyal followers, and prevent the groom of the stool from becoming independent of his control. His efforts at raising extra-parliamentary revenue between 1522 and 1525 were extremely unpopular, and the Amicable Grant provoked a full-blown rebellion in Suffolk. Certainly he aroused hostility by indulging in such grandiose ceremonies as that which accompanied his receipt of the cardinal's hat and by the conspicuous consumption evidenced in his building the sumptuous palace at Hampton Court.

To both Catholic and Protestant reformers, Wolsey exemplified clerical corruption. Rumors about him abounded—he allegedly had to resign as senior bursar of Magdalen after misappropriating funds, and in 1500 Sir Amyas Paulet purportedly put him in the stocks in Limington for either drunkenness or fornication (both stories are dubious). However, other abuses attributed to him were real enough. He was one of the most notorious pluralists of the Reformation era, becoming vicar of Redgrave in Suffolk in 1506, vicar of Lydd in Kent in 1508, dean of Lincoln in 1509, canon of Hereford Cathedral and vicar of Torrington in Devon (resigning at Limington) in 1510, canon of Windsor in 1511, dean of Hereford in 1512, canon and then dean of York (resigning Hereford) in 1513, Bishop of Tournai in 1513, Bishop of Lincoln and then Archbishop of York (resigning Lincoln) in 1514, a cardinal in 1515, Bishop of Bath and Wells (resigning Tournai) in 1518, abbot of St. Albans (in violation of canon law) in 1521, and Bishop of Durham (resigning Bath and Wells) in 1523. All that prevented his acquiring the Archbishopric of Canterbury was that Warham outlived him, but this did not deter Wolsey from interfering in the see's affairs and extorting money from subordinates.

While Wolsey attended religious services regularly, he was not celibate (fathering an illegitimate son, Thomas Winter), conducted himself with great pomposity, and hardly set an ideal example for his flock. He also aroused opposition by attempting to protect the church from governmental interference. In 1515, Parliament attacked clerical immunity from secular courts after the apparent murder of accused heretic Richard Hunne in the Bishop of London's prison and the subsequent harassment by conservative churchmen of friar Henry Standish for defending the government's right to prosecute criminous clerks. The king firmly asserted his own rights in the case and refused Wolsey's request that it be referred to the pope. Wolsey's attempt to reform the orders of monks and friars came to little, and he paid almost no attention to problems among the secular clergy. Most historians no longer believe that Wolsey subordinated English foreign-policy interests to the papacy or his desire to be pope (he sought election in 1522 and 1523). However, as papal legate he concentrated in his own hands an unprecedented amount of power, comparable to that later exercised over the English church by Henry VIII following the break with Rome and passage of the Act of Supremacy.

SUGGESTIONS FOR ADDITIONAL READING

Bernard, G. W. *War, Taxation, and Rebellion in Early Tudor England: Henry VIII, Wolsey, and the Amicable Grant of 1525*. New York: St. Martin's, 1986.

Cavendish, George. *The Life and Death of Cardinal Wolsey, 1641*. In Richard S. Sylvester and Davis P. Harding, eds. *Two Early Tudor Lives*. New Haven, Conn.: Yale University Press, 1962. Reprint, 1969.

Coleman, Christopher, and David R. Starkey, eds. *Revolution Reassessed: Revisions in the History of Tudor Government and Administration*. Oxford: Clarendon Press, 1986.

Elton, Sir Geoffrey. *Reform and Reformation: England 1509–1558*. Cambridge, Mass.: Harvard University Press, 1977.

Gunn, S. J., and P. G. Lindley, eds. *Cardinal Wolsey: Church, State, and Art*. Cambridge: Cambridge University Press, 1991.

Guy, John A. *The Cardinal's Court: The Impact of Thomas Wolsey in Star Chamber*. Hassocks, England: Harvester, 1977.

Gwyn, Peter. *The King's Cardinal: The Rise and Fall of Thomas Wolsey*. London: Barrie and Jenkins, 1990.

Pollard, A. F. *Wolsey*. London: Longmans, Green, 1929. 2nd ed. 1953. Reprint with introduction by A. G. Dickens. Westport, Conn.: Greenwood, 1978.

Ridley, Jasper. *Statesman and Saint: Cardinal Wolsey, Sir Thomas More, and the Politics of Henry VIII*. New York: Viking, 1983.

Williams, Neville. *The Cardinal and the Secretary: Thomas Wolsey and Thomas Cromwell*. New York: Macmillan, 1975.

William B. Robison

Index

Note: Page numbers in **bold** indicate main entries in the text.

About the Editor and Contributors

LAWRENCE P. ADAMCZYK is Assistant Professor of History at Western Montana College at Dillon. His research and publications emphasize diplomatic, Italian, and British history.

SHELDON AVERY is Professor of History and Chairman of the Social Science Department at Harford Community College, Maryland. He taught African History in Uganda and has published two books and numerous articles involving that area.

JAMES A. BAER is Associate Professor of History at Northern Virginia Community College in Alexandria. He has published studies of urban social history, and specializes in Argentina.

H. W. BASSER is Professor of Judaic Studies at Queen's University, Ontario, Canada, and has served as visiting professor at Hebrew University in Jerusalem. He has edited and published six volumes treating classical Hebrew texts.

PETER W. BECKER is Chairman of the Department of History at the University of South Carolina at Columbia. He has translated books and published many articles in his field. He is editor of *The Proceedings of the South Carolina Historical Association.*

ERIC A. BELGRAD is Chairman of the Political Science Department at Towson State University in Maryland. He has published numerous articles on International Law, and has served as faculty co-advisor for the *Towson State Journal of International Affairs* since 1965.

ARNOLD BLUMBERG is Professor of History at Towson State University, Maryland. He is the author of four books and numerous articles on diplomatic history.

DAVID M. CROWE is Professor and Chairman of the History Department at Elon College, North Carolina. His books include *A History of the Gyp-*

sies of Eastern Europe and Russia and *The Great Powers & the Baltic States: Foreign Relations, 1938–1994.*

ROBERT FORSTER is Professor of History at Johns Hopkins University. He is author of three books in French social history and co-editor of seven volumes of translations of *Sections from the Annales*, the French historical journal.

BERTRAM M. GORDON is Professor of European History at Mills College, Oakland, California. He is the author of *Collaboration in France During the Second World War* along with articles on the twentieth-century French Right.

JOHNPETER H. GRILL is Professor of History at Mississippi State University. His books deal with the *Nazi Party in Southwestern Germany* and *Hitler and the American South*. He has also published essays on the U.S.S.R.

PAUL J. HAUBEN is Professor Emeritus of History at the University of the Pacific, Stockton, California. He has published two books on imperial Spanish history, as well as eleven essays in related fields.

KARL G. LAREW is Professor of History at Towson State University, Maryland. He has published studies dealing with European, diplomatic, and American military history, including two relating to early-twentieth-century Turkey.

MARILYNN M. LAREW, adjunct Professor of History at Towson State University, has published a history of Bel Air, Maryland. She has produced numerous studies of modern terrorism. Her current research concerns traditional Asian elements in the Vietnamese wars.

AARON LICHTENSTEIN teaches English at the City University of New York. His book, *The Seven Laws of Noah*, a study in Near Eastern and Talmudic religious law, is now being published in French by Editions Osiris.

WAYNE C. McWILLIAMS, Professor of History at Towson State University, specializes in Japanese history and has taught in Japan. He also teaches Chinese History. He is co-author of *The World since 1945: A History of International Relations.*

LUCILE MARTINEAU is Professor of French at Smith College. She is the author of numerous articles on the historical theater of France and Quebec. She has also published some work on French politics after 1945.

PETER MERANI is Professor of Political Science and Co-Director, Center for the Study of International Relations and Public Policy at Towson State

University. His publications principally concern Indian and Near Eastern diplomacy.

GERALD W. MORTON is Professor of English at Auburn University, Montgomery, Alabama. He has published several studies on sixteenth- and seventeenth-century English literature including two books on the Cavalier poet and playwright, Mildmay Fane.

ARMIN MRUCK, Professor Emeritus of History at Towson State University teaches at Carl von Ossietzky Universitaet in Oldenburg, Germany. Beside his interest in Renaissance studies, he publishes work concerning the anti-Nazi Resistance.

GERSHAM A. NELSON is Chairman of the History Department at Frostburg State University, Maryland. He has published studies on Liberation Theology, the Rastafarians, and the Jamaican peasantry.

HARRY PIOTROWSKI, Professor of History at Towson State University, specializes in Russian and Soviet history. He has taught at Germany's Oldenburg University. He is co-author of *The World since 1945: A History of International Relations.*

CLIFTON W. POTTER, JR., is Professor and Chairman of the History Department at Lynchburg College, Virginia. He has published a number of essays on the use of medallic art as propaganda in Elizabethan England.

WILLIAM B. ROBISON is Professor of History at Southeastern Louisiana University at Hammond. He is co-editor of *The Historical Dictionary of Stuart England* and author of several articles on the Reformation and politics in Tudor England.

J. MARTIN RYLE is Professor of History at the University of Richmond. His area of research specialization and publication is the Soviet Union.

REEVA S. SIMON is Assistant Director of the Middle East Institute, Columbia University. She has published *Iraq Between the Two World Wars* and *The Middle East in Crime Fiction* and is co-editor of *The Encyclopedia of the Modern Middle East.*

LAWRENCE SONDHAUS is Associate Professor of History at the University of Indianapolis. His publications involve topics in the political, diplomatic, and military history of Central Europe from the Napoleonic Era through World War I.

W. M. SPELLMAN is Assistant Professor of History at the University of North Carolina, Asheville. He has published *John Locke and the Problem of Depravity* and *The Latitudinarians and the Church of England, 1660–1700.*

GEORGE B. STOW is Professor of History at La Salle University, Philadelphia. His edition of the *Vita Ricardi Secundi* was published by the University of Pennsylvania. He has also produced numerous essays on King Richard II.

ALEXANDER SYDORENKO is Professor of History at Arkansas State University at Jonesboro. He has published a book and numerous essays on Russian and Ukrainian cultural and intellectual history.

JACKSON TAYLOR, JR., is Associate Professor of History at the University of Mississippi. He has published several essays on Russian history in the late nineteenth and early twentieth centuries.

CAROL G. THOMAS is Professor of Ancient Greek History at the University of Washington. She is the author of forty essays and author/editor of eight books. She has served as president of *The Association of Ancient Historians.*

ANDREW TROUT is Professor of History at Indiana University Southeast, New Albany, and is the author or co-author of two books and various essays on the history of Old Regime France, Paris, and public finance.

ELEANOR L. TURK is Professor of History at Indiana University East, at Richmond. Her primary area of research and publication is Wilhelmian Germany, though she has a strong secondary interest in Renaissance Germany.

THOMAS H. WATKINS is Professor of History at Western Illinois University, in Macomb. He is the author of several essays in Roman history as well as of a forthcoming biography of L. Munatius Plancus.

ROBERT H. WHEALEY is Associate Professor of History at Ohio University at Athens. He is the author of *Hitler and Spain: The Nazi Role in the Spanish Civil War 1936–1939* and sixteen journal essays.